Southern Living®

2017 Annual Recipes

Oxmoor House®

DOUBLE-CRUST CHICKEN
POT PIES (PAGE 26)

CLOCKWISE FROM TOP LEFT:
- CHICKEN AND HERBED CORNMEAL DUMPLINGS (PAGE 25)
- SWEET-AND-SPICY SHORT RIBS WITH EGG NOODLES (PAGE 28)
- MINI MEATLOAVES WITH POTATOES, LEEKS, AND BRUSSELS SPROUTS (PAGE 31)
- BRUSSELS SPROUT SLAW WITH APPLES AND PECANS (PAGE 40)

ROASTED PORK CHOPS
WITH BEETS AND KALE
(PAGE 31)

CORNBREAD WITH LEMON-
THYME BUTTER (PAGE 55)

YOGURT POUND CAKE WITH
POMEGRANATE SYRUP
(PAGE 56)

CLOCKWISE FROM TOP LEFT:

- HAM AND LIMA BEAN FRIED RICE (PAGE 66)
- TORTELLINI, WHITE BEAN, AND TURNIP GREENS SOUP (PAGE 66)
- QUICK AND EASY SPAGHETTI BOLOGNESE (PAGE 64)
- SAUSAGE CALZONES (PAGE 59)

NASHVILLE HOT
CHICKEN DIP (PAGE 51)

SUCCOTASH
SALSA (PAGE 51)

BACON-PIMIENTO
GUACAMOLE (PAGE 51)

SMOKY BLACK-EYED
PEA HUMMUS (PAGE 51)

COLLARD
DIP (PAGE 51)

CREAMY CRAB
DIP (PAGE 51)

CREAMY CHICKEN AND BACON
WITH HERBED PUFF PASTRY (PAGE 85)

BUTTER TOFFEE-PECAN
LAYER CAKE (PAGE 74)

NEW POTATO AND FENNEL
SALAD (PAGE 99)

RADISHES IN WARM HERB
BUTTER (PAGE 99)

TARRAGON ASPARAGUS
WITH EGGS (PAGE 99)

"CARROT CAKE" BISCUITS AND PINEAPPLE-CINNAMON BUTTER (PAGE 97)

HONEY-PORT LACQUERED HAM WITH WHIPPED DIJON CREAM (PAGE 97)

13

CLOCKWISE FROM TOP LEFT:
- CHEESE PUFFS WITH HAM SALAD (PAGE 121)
- BITE-SIZE POTATOES O'BRIEN (PAGE 118)
- SHRIMP AND BACON SALAD SLIDERS (PAGE 118)
- SNICKERDOODLE DOUGHNUT HOLE MUFFINS (PAGE 117)

BLUEBERRY-CORN-
MEAL CAKE (PAGE 135)

15

GRILLED SIRLOIN
TACOS (PAGE 124)

QUESO FUNDIDO
WITH MUSHROOMS
AND CHILES
(PAGE 123)

GUACAMOLE WITH
JICAMA (PAGE 123)

GRILLED CHICKEN
TACOS (PAGE 124)

16

Our Year at Southern Living

Dear Friends,

The 2017 edition of *Southern Living Annual Recipes* brings you each and
every one of the hundreds of amazing recipes that have graced the pages
of the magazine throughout the year. Our Test Kitchen is passionate about
inspiring and guiding readers to cook together, eat together, and make lasting
memories around the table. As we've done for over 50 years, each staff recipe
is methodically developed and meticulously tested so that you can cook any
recipe with confidence.

Like our magazine, food in the South is dynamic and ever changing. While we
remain rooted in Southern tradition and celebrate mouthwatering mainstays
like Squash Casserole (August, page 237) or Classic Southern Pound Cake
(May, page 137) that you'll find in our "Southern Classic" column, we also
strive to bring you the latest and greatest recipes from the region's culinary
trailblazers, popular restaurants, and up-and-coming tastemakers. We tap
into new trends, explore heritage foodways, and share a rich array of dishes
that highlight Southern food that is as relevant today as ever.

We believe that everyone has time to make and enjoy a home cooked dinner,
and our "Quick-Fix" recipes each month show you easy shortcuts that never
skimp on flavor. "One and Done" is the minimalist cook's resource for inspired
one-dish meals, while "Healthy in a Hurry" puts good-for-you into fast food.
Set party-going intimidation aside and never again ask "What Can I Bring?"
with our handy feature that highlights perfectly portable, crowd-pleasing
dishes that are sure to get you invited back soon. And, as always, "Save Room"
for the decadent desserts for which *Southern Living* is famous.

Happy cooking and eating, y'all!

Katherine Cobbs

Katherine Cobbs
Executive Editor

Contents

Top-Rated Recipes

We cook, we taste, we refine, we rate, and at the end of each year, our Test Kitchen shares the highest-rated recipes from each issue exclusively with *Southern Living Annual Recipes* readers.

JANUARY

- Chicken and Herbed Cornmeal Dumplings (page 25) Flavoring the dumplings with fresh tarragon and parsley gives this classic Southern dish an herbal twist.
- Double-Crust Chicken Pot Pies (page 26) Two layers of golden, crispy crust envelops a hearty vegetable filling for a perfect cold-weather meal.
- Pam Lolley's Crispy Chicken with Rice and Pan Gravy (page 28) Making the pan gravy ups the down-home comfort food quality of this quick and easy fried chicken and rice meal.
- Robby Melvin's Turnip Greens with Hot Water Cornbread (page 30) Pair these zesty turnip greens with a fluffy slice (or two) of hot water cornbread for a standout weeknight meal.
- Emily Nabors Hall's Cheeseburger Pizza (page 29) What's better than cheeseburgers and pizza? A cheeseburger pizza! Top this "Americana" pizza with all of your family's favorite toppings.
- Skillet Shrimp Chilaquiles (page 36) Homemade tortilla chips and seasoned shrimp combine in this zesty version of the traditional Mexican dish.
- Butterscotch Pie with Whiskey Caramel Sauce (page 41) This pie features the best aspects of any dessert: a light and crunchy crust, a boozy filling, and caramel and whipped cream drizzled on top.

FEBRUARY

- Dreamy Lemon Cheesecake (page 45) This vibrant citrus cheesecake, filled with lemon sandwich cookies, cream cheese, and lemon curd, is as refreshing as it is delicious.
- Grapefruit Tart (page 48) A surprising saltine cracker crust perfectly

complements this seasonal tart's tangy grapefruit filling.
- Emily's Red Beans and Rice (page 55) This New Orleans-inspired hearty side dish combines enough tender beans and buttery rice to feed the whole family.
- Greek Meatballs with Cucumber-Yogurt Sauce and Rice (page 58) A no-cook cucumber-yogurt sauce enhances the distinctive Mediterranean flavors of the meatballs.
- Winter Vegetables and Gnocchi (page 59) Trade dumplings for potato gnocchi, add wintertime vegetables, and enjoy an easy-to-prepare comfort meal.
- Steak, Sweet Potato, and Blue Cheese Salad (page 66) Sweet potatoes, savory steak, and blue cheese collide in a filling and flavorful salad.
- Molten Red Velvet Cakes (page 69) This showstopper combines moist red velvet cake, a gooey chocolate center, and cream cheese whipped topping. What more could you ask for in a Valentine's Day dessert?

MARCH

- Triple-Layer Chocolate-Caramel Cake (page 75) The addition of a bit of bourbon and coffee yields a rich, heavenly cake that will leave guests begging for the recipe on their way out the door.
- Banana Pudding Poke Cake (page 77) Whether the vanilla pudding is homemade or instant, it lends light texture and pleasing flavor to this banana-flavored cake.
- Cream Soda Confetti Sheet Cake with Strawberry-Sour Cream Buttercream (page 78) Topped with pastel sprinkles, jimmies, and confetti,

the star ingredients of this whimsical cake are cream soda and homemade Strawberry-Sour Cream Buttercream.
- One-Pan Chicken with Lemon, Olives, and Artichokes (page 82) Don't worry about a sink full of dishes; every step of this recipe can be completed in one cast-iron skillet.
- Oven-Fried Chicken with Spring Salad (page 84) Simple yet delicious, our crispy oven-fried chicken and vinaigrette-dressed salad are a match made in weekday dinner heaven.
- Shrimp and Sausage Gumbo (page 87) For our favorite go-to gumbo recipe, serve smoked spicy sausage, fresh shrimp, and a mix of vegetables and spices over a bed of steamed white rice.
- Golden Beet-and-Potato Breakfast Bake (page 89) Combine traditional breakfast foods like eggs, bacon, and hash browns with golden beets for a healthy and satisfying start to your day.

APRIL

- Spring Lettuce and Leek Soup (page 95) We're in love with the verdant color and garden-fresh flavor of this soup. Process it in a blender before serving to achieve a smooth, creamy texture.
- "Carrot Cake" Biscuits and Pineapple-Cinnamon Butter (page 97) Say goodbye to rolling biscuits out of a can and say hello to this tasty upgrade. Our favorite savory biscuit recipe is simply wonderful, especially when paired with pineapple-cinnamon butter.
- Coconut Meringues with Elderflower Strawberries (page 100) With its light and airy consistency and boozy

strawberry topping, this dessert will become a new Easter dinner tradition.

MAY

JUNE

JULY

AUGUST

- Slow-Cooker Corn Chowder (page 235) After simmering in a slow cooker for a few hours, serve this creamy and indulgent chowder with fresh corn on top for an extra dose of flavor.
- Old-School Squash Casserole (page 237) This recipe is the end all and be all of squash casseroles. Our secret? Healthy helpings of Swiss cheese, mayonnaise, freshly cracked black pepper, and crushed crackers.

SEPTEMBER
- Double-Chocolate Pecan Pie (page 257) Every bite of this pie is indulgent, rich, and chock-full of pecans. The cocoa-infused crust adds even more chocolate to satisfy your sweet tooth.
- Pumpkin-Spice Bundt with Brown Sugar Icing and Candied Pecans (page 257) This rich, decadent cake includes a few of our favorite fall ingredients: candied pecans, pumpkin spice cake, and sweet Brown Sugar Icing.
- Skillet Caramel Apple Pie (page 252) Scoop a slice of this caramel and bourbon-infused pie straight from the skillet. Or, if it looks too good to wait, grab a fork and dive in. We won't judge!
- Potato-Bacon Hash (page 248) Start your day off right with this hearty, filling breakfast hash. Our recipe includes thick slices of bacon, browned-to-perfection potatoes, and a heaping helping of vegetables.
- Baked Shells and Greens (page 268) This quick-fix meal is a great weeknight main that can be altered to fit your family's tastes. Ready in 30 minutes, it's loaded with many of the same ingredients as lasagna without the involved preparation.

OCTOBER
- Bacon-and-Chive Grit Fries with Smoky Hot Ketchup (page 283) This is not your mama's grits recipe. Cheese and bacon-filled grits are rolled into fries and fried until they're golden brown and ready to be smothered in our Smoky Hot Ketchup.
- Braised Cola-and-Bourbon Brisket (page 287) We pair tender cuts of braised brisket with carrots, parsnips, and a drizzling of thick gravy to make a comforting cold-weather dish.
- Country Ham and Shrimp Grits (page 282) Our take on this traditional Lowcountry favorite includes chopped country ham, piles of Creole-seasoned shrimp, and, of course, warm grits.
- Chicken, Sweet Potato, and Corn Slow-Cooker Chowder (page 291) Let your slow cooker do all of the work to make this creamy chowder. The chicken, sweet potatoes, and vegetables slowly simmer to perfection, giving you time to run errands or prepare the rest of the meal.
- Southern Wedding Soup (page 294) For a fun twist on a classic Italian soup, we use pork-and-beef meatballs and fresh greens to add Southern flavors and flair by the spoonful.

NOVEMBER
- Angel Biscuits (page 308) These heavenly buttermilk biscuits can be made up to one week in advance and stored in the refrigerator until the day of your holiday dinner.
- Best-Ever Macaroni and Cheese (page 305) Rich, creamy, and oozing with two types of Cheddar cheese, this elevated version of everyone's favorite comfort food makes a standout side dish.
- Cornbread Dressing with Smoked Sausage and Apples (page 304) Adding sausage and crisp apples to our Cornbread Dressing recipe brings hearty, smoky flavors to a classic comforting side dish.
- Double-Decker Pecan Cheesecake Pie (page 326) This double-the-fun dessert combines the best elements of two crowd favorites: cheesecake and pie. Creamy layers of cheesecake meld with a brown sugar pie filling that gets sprinkled with pecans for a dessert that's out of this world.
- Over the Moon Chocolate Pie (page 325) From the graham cracker crust and rich, whiskey-splashed chocolate filling to the fluffy marshmallow topping, this dessert is inspired by the Moon Pie dessert snack.

DECEMBER
- Snowy Vanilla Cake with Cake Ball Ornaments (page 358) Recreate our gorgeous cover cake recipe by adorning this smooth vanilla cake with cream cheese buttercream frosting and adorable cake ball ornaments.
- Sausage-and-Cheese Grits Quiche (page 355) Spend more time opening presents on Christmas morning by preparing the cheese grits and sausage for this warm, hearty breakfast casserole up to two days in advance.
- Herbed Potato Stacks (page 348) Tired of serving mashed potatoes to your holiday guests year after year? These little stacks of thinly sliced and herbal-spiced potatoes will be a much-celebrated substitution.
- Cranberry Sangria Punch (page 344) Our spin on Christmas-party punch really does pack a punch. Add a few spiked cranberries and apple and orange slices to your glass to complete the sangria recipe.
- Stuffed Beef Tenderloin with Burgundy-Mushroom Sauce (page 347) For this decadent centerpiece of a main course, roll and stuff pieces of beef tenderloin with creamy greens and top with a light mushroom sauce.
- Fudgy Pecan Bourbon Balls (page 336) With only four ingredients, create dozens of bite-sized, bourbon-infused chocolates that work great as hostess gifts or after-dinner treats.

22

January

THE SOUTHERN LIVING COMFORT FOOD COOKBOOK

Cold winter months make us long for warm, soul-satisfying home-cooked meals. Dig in to our collection of COMFORT CLASSICS, SLOW-COOKER SUPPERS, ONE-POT MEALS, FAMILY FAVORITES, and SHEET PAN DINNERS from our very own Test Kitchen pros.

SKILLET MAC AND CHEESE WITH CRISPY BREADCRUMBS

Comfort Classics

New sensational twists on signature Southern dishes that will feed and please a crowd

CHICKEN AND HERBED CORNMEAL DUMPLINGS

Skillet Mac and Cheese with Crispy Breadcrumbs

ACTIVE 15 MIN. - TOTAL 55 MIN.
SERVES 6

- 12   oz. uncooked large elbow macaroni
- ¼   cup salted butter
- ¾   cup chopped yellow onion (from 1 onion)
- 3   Tbsp. all-purpose flour
- 1   Tbsp. finely chopped garlic (2 to 3 garlic cloves)
- 2   cups whole milk
- 8   oz. sharp Cheddar cheese, shredded (about 2 cups)
- 6   oz. processed cheese (such as Velveeta), cubed (about 1 ½ cups)
- 1   cup mayonnaise (such as Duke's)
- ½   tsp. kosher salt
- 6   Tbsp. coarsely chopped fresh flat-leaf parsley, divided
- ¾   cup whole-milk ricotta cheese
- 1   large egg
- 1 ½   cups panko (Japanese-style breadcrumbs)
- 2   Tbsp. salted butter, melted

1. Prepare pasta according to package directions; set aside. Preheat oven to 350°F.
2. Melt butter in a 12-inch cast-iron skillet over medium-high. Add onion, and cook, stirring, until just beginning to brown, 4 to 5 minutes. Add flour and garlic to skillet; cook, stirring, until fragrant, 1 to 2 minutes. Add milk; bring to a boil. Reduce heat to low. Gradually add Cheddar and processed cheese, whisking until melted. Remove from heat. Stir in cooked pasta, mayonnaise, salt, and ½ cup of the parsley.
3. Stir together ricotta and egg in a small bowl. Gently stir ricotta mixture into pasta mixture, leaving large swirls. Bake in preheated oven 10 minutes.
4. Meanwhile, stir together panko, melted butter, and remaining 2 tablespoons parsley until blended. Top pasta with panko mixture, and bake until top is lightly browned, about 10 minutes.

Chicken and Herbed Cornmeal Dumplings

ACTIVE 20 MIN. - TOTAL 40 MIN.
SERVES 6

- ¼   cup salted butter, divided
- 2   cups sliced carrots (about 3 small carrots)
- 1   cup diagonally sliced celery (about 2 stalks)
- 1   cup chopped yellow onion (about 1 onion)
- ½   cup plus 2 Tbsp. all-purpose flour, divided
- 3 ¼   cups chicken broth
- 1   bay leaf
- ¾   tsp. kosher salt, divided
- 3   cups coarsely shredded rotisserie chicken (from 1 chicken)
- ½   cup coarse plain yellow cornmeal
- 1   tsp. baking powder
- ¼   tsp. baking soda
- ½   cup whole buttermilk
- 2   Tbsp. chopped fresh flat-leaf parsley
- 1   Tbsp. chopped fresh tarragon

1. Melt 2 tablespoons of the butter in a Dutch oven over medium-high. Add carrots, celery, and onion; cook, stirring occasionally, until onions are tender, 5 to 6 minutes. Add 2 tablespoons of the flour; cook, stirring occasionally, 1 to 2 minutes. Add broth, bay leaf, and ½ teaspoon of the salt; bring to a boil. Cook, stirring occasionally, until thickened, 4 to 5 minutes. Stir in chicken. Remove Dutch oven from heat.
2. Whisk together cornmeal, baking powder, baking soda, and remaining ½ cup flour and ¼ teaspoon salt in a medium bowl. Cut remaining 2 tablespoons butter into flour mixture with a pastry blender or fork until mixture resembles coarse meal. Add buttermilk, parsley, and tarragon, stirring just until dough is moistened.
3. Heat Dutch oven over medium. Drop dumpling dough by tablespoonfuls ½ to 1 inch apart into chicken mixture. Cover and cook until dumplings are done and dry to the touch, 15 to 20 minutes. Serve immediately.

DOUBLE-CRUST
CHICKEN POT PIES

Double-Crust Chicken Pot Pies

ACTIVE 45 MIN. - TOTAL 1 HOUR, 15 MIN.
SERVES 6

- 2 (14.1-oz.) pkg. refrigerated piecrusts
- ½ cup (4 oz.) unsalted butter, divided
- 2 (6-oz.) boneless, skinless chicken breasts
- 8 oz. cremini mushrooms, quartered
- 1½ cups diced russet potato (about 1 small)
- ½ cup chopped yellow onion (from 1 onion)
- ½ cup diced carrot (about 1 small)
- 1 Tbsp. chopped fresh thyme
- 2 tsp. finely chopped garlic (about 3 garlic cloves)
- 2 tsp. chopped fresh oregano
- ¼ cup all-purpose flour
- 2½ cups chicken stock, divided
- 1 tsp. kosher salt
- 1 tsp. black pepper
- ¼ tsp. crushed red pepper
- ¾ cup frozen green peas
- ½ cup heavy cream
- 1 large egg yolk
- ½ tsp. water

1. Preheat oven to 400°F. Let piecrusts stand at room temperature 15 minutes. Unroll 2 piecrusts onto a lightly floured surface. Cut 3 (5-inch) circles from each crust. Gently roll each circle into an 8-inch round. Coat 6 (12-ounce) ramekins with cooking spray. Gently fit 1 piecrust round into each ramekin, lining the bottom and sides. Gently crimp dough over the top edge of ramekin to secure it. Prick dough with a fork along bottom and sides. Place ramekins on a rimmed baking sheet, and bake in preheated oven until lightly browned, 13 to 16 minutes.

2. Melt 2 tablespoons of the butter in a large skillet over medium-high. Add chicken; cook until done, 5 to 6 minutes per side. Remove from pan; let stand 10 minutes. Shred the chicken.

3. Add remaining 6 tablespoons butter to skillet. Add mushrooms; cook, stirring occasionally, 5 minutes. Add potato, onion, carrot, thyme, garlic, and oregano to skillet; cook, stirring occasionally, until onions are tender and lightly browned, 7 to 8 minutes.

4. Whisk together flour and ½ cup of the stock in a small bowl, and add to skillet. Stir in salt, black pepper, crushed red pepper, and remaining 2 cups stock; bring to a boil. Reduce heat to medium, and simmer 5 minutes, stirring occasionally. Stir in peas, cream, and shredded chicken. Transfer mixture to a bowl, and cool 10 minutes.

5. Stir together egg yolk and water in a small bowl. Unroll remaining 2 piecrusts onto lightly floured surface. Cut 3 (5-inch) circles from each piecrust. Gently roll each circle into a 5½-inch round. Fill each ramekin with about ¾ cup chicken mixture, pressing down to level mixture. Top each ramekin with 1 (5½-inch) dough round, pressing to seal to bottom crust. Brush tops with egg mixture, and, if desired, top with leaf cutouts or rounds from extra dough. Cut small slits in tops of dough to vent steam. Bake at 400°F until golden brown, 22 to 25 minutes.

STEAK AND PEPPERS
WITH RICE

Slow-Cooker Suppers

No time to cook? No need for it. Here, meals that taste like you spent hours over the stove-top.

Steak and Peppers with Rice

ACTIVE 20 MIN. - TOTAL 7 HOURS, 20 MIN.
SERVES 4

- 2½ lb. chuck roast, trimmed and cut into ¼-inch slices
- 1 tsp. kosher salt, divided
- ¾ tsp. black pepper, divided
- 2 Tbsp. canola oil
- 1 cup unsalted beef stock
- 3 Tbsp. soy sauce
- 2 Tbsp. tomato paste
- 3 red bell peppers, sliced
- 1 large yellow onion, sliced
- 1 (5-oz.) pkg. uncooked yellow rice, cooked according to package directions
- 2 Tbsp. chopped fresh cilantro

1. Sprinkle beef with ½ teaspoon each of the salt and black pepper. Heat oil in a large heavy skillet over medium-high. Cook beef, in batches, turning to brown on all sides, about 1 minute per side. Whisk together stock, soy sauce, and tomato paste in a small bowl.

2. Place bell peppers and onion in a 5½- to 6-quart slow cooker, and sprinkle with remaining ½ teaspoon salt and ¼ teaspoon black pepper. Place beef on vegetables, and pour stock mixture over beef and vegetables. Cover and cook on LOW until beef is tender and vegetables are softened and beginning to caramelize, about 7 hours.

3. Divide hot cooked yellow rice among 4 bowls. Using a slotted spoon, spoon bell peppers and onions over rice. Top with beef, sauce from slow cooker, and cilantro.

Sausage-and-Collard Greens Stew

ACTIVE 10 MIN. - TOTAL 4 HOURS, 21 MIN.
SERVES 6

- 1 lb. mild sausage links, casings removed
- 1 cup chopped leek (from 1 leek)
- 4 cups unsalted chicken stock
- 8 oz. chopped fresh collard greens
- 1 Tbsp. chopped garlic (2 to 3 garlic cloves)
- 1 tsp. kosher salt
- ¾ tsp. black pepper

- 3 cups cooked ditalini pasta (about 1 ½ cups uncooked)
- ¼ cup heavy cream

1. Cook sausage in a large skillet over medium, stirring to break apart with a wooden spoon, until just beginning to brown, about 6 minutes. Add leek, and cook until sausage is browned and leek begins to soften, about 5 minutes.

2. Add sausage, chopped leek, and pan drippings to a 6-quart slow cooker. Add stock, collards, garlic, salt, and pepper. Cover and cook on LOW until vegetables are softened and sausage is cooked through, about 4 hours. Stir in cooked pasta and heavy cream just before serving.

Creamy Turnip Soup

ACTIVE 15 MIN. - TOTAL 6 HOURS, 15 MIN.
SERVES 6

- 4 cups unsalted chicken stock
- 1 ¼ lb. medium turnips, chopped
- 1 ¼ lb. Yukon Gold potatoes, peeled and chopped
- 1 medium-size yellow onion, chopped (about 1 ½ cups)
- 2 garlic cloves, smashed
- 4 thyme sprigs
- 1 tsp. kosher salt
- ¾ tsp. black pepper
- ¼ cup heavy cream
- 6 thick-cut bacon slices
- 6 cups chopped turnip greens (about 1 lb.)

1. Combine stock, turnips, potatoes, onion, garlic, thyme sprigs, salt, and pepper in a 6-quart slow cooker. Cover and cook on LOW until vegetables are very soft, about 6 hours. Remove and discard thyme sprigs. Add cream, and process soup using an immersion blender until smooth. (Or transfer to a blender, and remove center piece of blender lid to allow steam to escape. Secure lid on blender, and place a clean towel over opening in lid. Process until smooth.)

2. Just before serving, cook bacon in a nonstick skillet over medium until crisp, 6 to 8 minutes. Drain bacon on paper towels, reserving drippings in pan. Add turnip greens to skillet; increase heat to medium-high, and cook, stirring occasionally, until wilted and beginning to brown just around edges, about 3 minutes. Crumble bacon. Serve soup topped with crumbled bacon and wilted greens.

One-Pot Meals

Weeknights are tough, but making these two bright and flavorful dinners is not

Braised Chicken Thighs with Carrots and Lemons

ACTIVE 20 MIN. - TOTAL 45 MIN.
SERVES 4

- 8 bone-in, skin-on chicken thighs, trimmed (about 3 lb.)
- 2 tsp. paprika
- 1 tsp. kosher salt, divided
- 1 tsp. black pepper, divided
- 2 Tbsp. salted butter
- 1 lb. large carrots, halved lengthwise and cut into 1 ½-inch-long pieces
- 2 ½ Tbsp. all-purpose flour
- 2 cups chicken broth
- 4 thyme sprigs
- 1 lemon, sliced
- 3 cups hot cooked mashed potatoes (optional)

CREAMY TURNIP SOUP

SAUSAGE-AND-COLLARD GREENS STEW

BRAISED CHICKEN THIGHS WITH CARROTS AND LEMONS

SWEET-AND-SPICY SHORT RIBS WITH EGG NOODLES

1. Pat chicken dry with paper towels. Sprinkle chicken with paprika and ¾ teaspoon each of the salt and pepper. Melt butter in a large enamel-coated cast-iron skillet with lid over medium-high. Place half of chicken, skin side down, in skillet; cook until skin is golden brown, about 6 minutes. Remove chicken from skillet; repeat process with remaining chicken.
2. Add carrots to pan, and cook, stirring occasionally, until browned, about 7 minutes. Add flour to skillet; cook, stirring often, 1 minute. Add broth, thyme, and remaining ¼ teaspoon salt and pepper; bring to a boil. Place chicken, skin side up, on carrots. Partially cover with lid; reduce heat to medium-low, and cook until chicken is done, about 20 minutes. Remove thyme sprigs. Stir in lemons, and, if desired, serve over mashed potatoes.

Sweet-and-Spicy Short Ribs with Egg Noodles

ACTIVE 20 MIN. - TOTAL 2 HOURS, 50 MIN.
SERVES 4

2 Tbsp. chili powder
1 tsp. paprika
½ tsp. cayenne pepper
1½ tsp. kosher salt, divided
1 tsp. black pepper, divided
4 (9-oz.) beef short ribs, trimmed
2 Tbsp. canola oil, divided
3 cups frozen pearl onions, thawed
1 Tbsp. all-purpose flour
1 (12-oz.) bottle lager beer

3 cups chopped plum tomatoes (about 6 medium tomatoes)
2 cups beef broth
2 Tbsp. light brown sugar
2 bay leaves
8 oz. uncooked wide egg noodles
3 Tbsp. salted butter
3 Tbsp. chopped fresh flat-leaf parsley
1 Tbsp. chopped fresh thyme

1. Preheat oven to 325°F. Stir together chili powder, paprika, cayenne pepper, and ½ teaspoon each of the salt and black pepper; sprinkle over ribs. Heat 1 tablespoon of the oil in a Dutch oven over medium-high. Add ribs, and cook until browned on all sides, about 5 minutes. Remove ribs from Dutch oven; wipe Dutch oven clean.
2. Add remaining 1 tablespoon oil to Dutch oven. Add pearl onions; cook until lightly browned, about 4 minutes. Stir in flour, and cook, stirring constantly, 1 minute. Add beer, and bring to a boil, stirring and scraping to loosen browned bits from bottom of Dutch oven. Boil until liquid is reduced to about ½ cup, 3 to 4 minutes. Stir in tomatoes, broth, brown sugar, bay leaves, and ¾ teaspoon of the salt. Add ribs, bone side up; bring to a boil. Cover and transfer to preheated oven. Bake until ribs are very tender, about 2½ hours.
3. Prepare noodles according to package directions, and place in a medium bowl. Add butter, parsley, and remaining ¼ teaspoon salt and

½ teaspoon black pepper, stirring until butter is melted.
4. Remove and discard bay leaves from Dutch oven. Serve ribs and onion mixture over noodles. Sprinkle with thyme.

Our Family Favorites

The *SL* Test Kitchen pros develop new recipes every day, but it's their go-to classics that we had to share.

Pam Lolley's Crispy Chicken with Rice and Pan Gravy

ACTIVE 30 MIN. - TOTAL 40 MIN.
SERVES 6

CHICKEN
6 (6-oz.) boneless, skinless chicken breasts
2 tsp. kosher salt, divided
1½ tsp. black pepper, divided
2 large eggs
½ cup whole milk
2 cups panko (Japanese-style breadcrumbs)
1½ tsp. Italian seasoning
½ tsp. smoked paprika
3 Tbsp. salted butter
3 Tbsp. olive oil
HERBED RICE
4 cups hot, cooked long-grain white rice
2 Tbsp. salted butter
2 Tbsp. chopped fresh flat-leaf parsley
2 Tbsp. chopped fresh chives
2 tsp. chopped fresh thyme leaves
1 tsp. kosher salt
½ tsp. black pepper
ADDITIONAL INGREDIENT
Pan Gravy (recipe follows)

1. Prepare the Chicken: Preheat oven to 350°F. Place chicken breasts between 2 sheets of plastic wrap, and flatten to about ¾-inch thickness, using a rolling

PAM LOLLEY'S CRISPY CHICKEN WITH RICE AND PAN GRAVY

DEB WISE'S TAMALE PIE MIX-UP

pin or flat side of a meat mallet. Sprinkle chicken with 1 teaspoon each of the salt and pepper.

2. Whisk together eggs and milk in a shallow dish. Stir together panko, Italian seasoning, smoked paprika, and remaining 1 teaspoon salt and ½ teaspoon pepper in another shallow dish. Dip chicken, 1 piece at a time, in egg mixture, shaking off excess; dredge in panko mixture, coating well and pressing to adhere.

3. Melt 1½ tablespoons of the butter with 1½ tablespoons of the olive oil in a large skillet over medium. Cook 3 chicken breasts in skillet until golden, 3 to 5 minutes per side. Remove chicken from pan, and place on a rimmed baking sheet. Repeat with remaining butter, oil, and chicken. Bake in preheated oven until chicken is cooked through, about 10 minutes.

4. Prepare the Herbed Rice: Combine all ingredients in a bowl, and stir until butter is melted. Serve with chicken and Pan Gravy.

Pan Gravy

ACTIVE 10 MIN. - TOTAL 10 MIN.
MAKES ABOUT 2 CUPS

Whisk together ¼ cup melted **salted butter** and ¼ cup **all-purpose flour** in a large skillet. Cook over medium, whisking constantly, until bubbly, about 2 minutes. Gradually whisk in 2 cups **chicken broth**, ½ teaspoon **kosher salt**, and ¼ teaspoon **black pepper**. Cook, whisking often, just until mixture comes to a boil and is smooth and

thick, 2 to 5 minutes. (If mixture is too thick, stir in up to ½ cup more broth, ¼ cup at a time, until desired consistency is reached.)

Deb Wise's Tamale Pie Mix-Up

ACTIVE 35 MIN. - TOTAL 1 HOUR, 40 MIN.
SERVES 8

2 cups whole milk
1 cup plain yellow cornmeal
2 Tbsp. vegetable oil
2 cups chopped yellow onion (about 2 medium onions)
1 Tbsp. minced garlic (about 3 garlic cloves)
1 large green bell pepper, chopped (about 1 cup)
1 lb. ground beef
2 cups tomato sauce
1 cup frozen or drained canned corn
1 cup drained canned sliced black olives
2 Tbsp. plus 1 tsp. chili powder
2 tsp. kosher salt
½ tsp. black pepper
6 oz. extra-sharp Cheddar cheese, shredded (about 1½ cups)
Sour cream (optional)
Chopped fresh cilantro (optional)

1. Preheat oven to 350°F. Stir together milk and cornmeal; set aside.
2. Heat oil in a large skillet over medium-high. Add onion, garlic, and

bell pepper; cook, stirring occasionally, until the vegetables begin to soften, about 8 to 9 minutes. Add beef; cook, stirring often, until meat crumbles and is no longer pink, about 7 minutes.
3. Stir beef mixture into cornmeal mixture. Stir in tomato sauce, corn, olives, chili powder, salt, and black pepper. Transfer to a lightly greased 13- x 9-inch glass or ceramic baking dish.
4. Bake in preheated oven until set and well browned around edges, 55 minutes to 1 hour. Remove from oven; sprinkle with cheese. Return to oven, and bake until cheese melts, 3 to 4 minutes. If desired, top servings with a dollop of sour cream and sprinkle with cilantro.

Emily Nabors Hall's Cheeseburger Pizza

ACTIVE 30 MIN. - TOTAL 1 HOUR, 15 MIN.
SERVES 6

1 lb. fresh deli pizza dough
12 oz. ground beef
½ tsp. kosher salt
½ tsp. black pepper
8 oz. sliced fresh mushrooms
1 cup chopped yellow onion (about 1 onion)
¾ cup jarred pizza sauce
8 oz. Cheddar cheese, shredded (about 2 cups)
1½ cups preshredded low-moisture part-skim mozzarella cheese
1 cup pimiento-stuffed green olives
¼ cup ketchup

1. Place a large, rimmed baking sheet (at least 17 x 11 inches) in oven; preheat to 425°F. (Do not remove while oven preheats.) Unwrap pizza dough, and cover with a kitchen towel. Let dough stand while oven preheats.
2. Meanwhile, cook ground beef in a large nonstick skillet over medium-high, stirring often, until meat crumbles and is no longer pink, about 7 minutes. Sprinkle with salt and pepper. Remove from skillet with a slotted spoon, and drain on a plate lined with paper towels.
3. Add mushrooms to hot drippings, and cook, stirring occasionally, until light golden, about 5 minutes. Add onions, and cook, stirring occasionally, until softened and beginning to brown,

EMILY NABORS HALL'S
CHEESEBURGER PIZZA

ROBBY MELVIN'S
TURNIP GREENS WITH
HOT WATER CORNBREAD

about 4 minutes. Remove mushrooms and onions with a slotted spoon, and drain on paper towels.

4. Roll dough into a 17- x 11-inch rectangle. Remove preheated pan from oven, and carefully place the dough onto the pan.

5. Bake in preheated oven just until dough is set, about 5 minutes. Remove from oven, and top with pizza sauce, beef, mushroom-onion mixture, shredded cheeses, and olives. Drizzle with ketchup.

6. Return to oven, and bake until crust is golden and cheeses melt and begin to brown in places, about 15 minutes. Let stand 5 minutes before slicing.

Robby Melvin's Turnip Greens with Hot Water Cornbread

ACTIVE 45 MIN. - TOTAL 2 HOURS, 45 MIN.
SERVES 8

   8 bacon slices, chopped
1 ½ cups chopped yellow onion
        (1 medium onion)
   3 garlic cloves, minced
   3 cups reduced-sodium
        chicken broth
   1 (12- to 16-oz.) smoked ham hock
   1 lb. fresh turnip greens, stems
        removed, leaves chopped
   ¼ cup apple cider vinegar
1 ½ tsp. kosher salt
   1 tsp. black pepper
        Hot sauce (optional)
        Hot Water Cornbread
        (recipe follows)

1. Cook bacon in a large Dutch oven over medium, stirring occasionally, until almost crisp, about 14 minutes. Add onion, and cook, stirring occasionally, until onion is tender, about 8 minutes. Add garlic, and cook, stirring constantly, 1 minute. Stir in chicken broth; add ham hock.

2. Increase heat to high, and bring to a boil. Stir in turnip greens and vinegar. Reduce heat to medium-low to maintain a simmer; cover and cook to desired tenderness, about 2 hours. Remove meat from ham hock; chop meat, and discard bone. Stir chopped meat into turnip greens. Stir in salt and pepper. Serve with hot sauce, if desired, and Hot Water Cornbread.

Hot Water Cornbread

ACTIVE 15 MIN. - TOTAL 15 MIN.
SERVES 8

1 ½ cups self-rising cornmeal mix
   3 Tbsp. finely chopped scallions
        (about 2 medium scallions)
   1 tsp. fresh thyme leaves
   1 tsp. granulated sugar
   1 tsp. kosher salt
   1 cup boiling water
1 ½ cups canola oil

1. Stir together cornmeal, scallions, thyme, sugar, and salt in a medium bowl. Add boiling water, and stir until incorporated.

2. Heat oil in 10-inch cast-iron skillet over medium-high. Shape tablespoon-fuls of batter into slightly flattened patties, and fry, in batches, until

golden brown, about 2 minutes per side. Drain on paper towels. Serve with Turnip Greens.

Sheet Pan Dinners

Making your entire meal in one pan means cooking—and cleanup—are a breeze.

Chicken Sausage with Fennel and Apples

ACTIVE 10 MIN. - TOTAL 50 MIN.
SERVES 4

   6 Tbsp. olive oil
   ¼ cup apple cider vinegar
   1 tsp. kosher salt
   ¾ tsp. black pepper
   1 lb. Italian chicken sausage links
   2 small fennel bulbs, sliced,
        fronds reserved
   2 medium-size Honeycrisp
        apples, cut into 1-inch wedges
   2 (8.8-oz.) pouches microwavable
        ready-to-serve rice (such as
        Uncle Ben's Ready Rice)

1. Preheat oven to 375°F. Whisk together oil, vinegar, salt, and pepper in a small bowl. Toss together sausages, fennel, apples, and 6 tablespoons of the vinegar mixture in a large bowl. Reserve remaining vinegar mixture.

2. Place rice in a mound in the center of a lightly greased large rimmed baking sheet. Place sausages, fennel, and apples over rice, covering it completely, and drizzle with any remaining vinegar mixture from bowl. Bake in preheated oven until sausages are cooked through and fennel and apples are golden, about 40 minutes.

3. Chop reserved fennel fronds to equal 1 tablespoon. Divide vegetables, rice, and sausages evenly among 4 plates. Drizzle with reserved vinegar mixture, and sprinkle evenly with chopped fennel fronds.

CHICKEN SAUSAGE WITH FENNEL AND APPLES

ROASTED PORK CHOPS WITH BEETS AND KALE

MINI MEATLOAVES WITH POTATOES, LEEKS, AND BRUSSELS SPROUTS

Roasted Pork Chops with Beets and Kale

ACTIVE 10 MIN. - TOTAL 40 MIN.
SERVES 4

- 1 lb. baby beets, peeled and halved
- 2 tsp. grated garlic (about 3 garlic cloves)
- 3 Tbsp. olive oil, divided
- 1 tsp. kosher salt, divided
- ¾ tsp. black pepper, divided
- 4 (12-oz.) bone-in pork loin chops
- ¼ cup sour cream
- 1 Tbsp. Dijon mustard
- 1 Tbsp. honey
- 1 Tbsp. chopped fresh thyme, divided
- 3 cups finely shredded curly kale (stems removed)

1. Preheat broiler with oven rack about 10 inches from heat. Toss together beets, grated garlic, 1 tablespoon of the oil, and ¼ teaspoon each of the salt and pepper. Place on a large, lightly greased, aluminum foil-lined rimmed baking sheet. Broil in preheated oven 10 minutes.
2. Meanwhile, rub pork chops with 1 tablespoon of the olive oil, and sprinkle with ½ teaspoon of the salt and ¼ teaspoon of the pepper. Remove beets from oven, and nestle pork chops into beets. Return pan to oven. Bake until pork is just cooked through and beets are tender, about 15 minutes.
3. Whisk together sour cream, mustard, honey, 1 teaspoon of the thyme, ¼ teaspoon each of the salt and pepper,

and remaining 1 tablespoon oil in a small bowl. Transfer cooked beets to a large bowl; add shredded kale and 2 tablespoons of the sour cream mixture, and toss to coat. Cover with plastic wrap, and let stand 5 minutes. Serve pork chops over vegetable mixture. Sprinkle with remaining 2 teaspoons thyme, and serve with remaining sour cream mixture.

Mini Meatloaves with Potatoes, Leeks, and Brussels Sprouts

ACTIVE 15 MIN. - TOTAL 1 HOUR
SERVES 4

- 5 Tbsp. olive oil
- 2 tsp. chopped garlic (about 2 garlic cloves)
- 1 tsp. lemon zest plus 2 Tbsp. fresh juice (from 1 lemon)
- 1 tsp. kosher salt, divided
- ¾ tsp. black pepper, divided
- 12 oz. Brussels sprouts, halved
- 1 leek, chopped (about 1 ½ cups)
- 8 oz. red potatoes, cut into wedges
- 8 oz. lean ground beef
- 8 oz. mild ground pork sausage
- ¼ cup grated carrot (from 1 carrot)
- ¼ cup grated yellow onion (from 1 onion)
- ¼ cup fine, dry breadcrumbs
- 1 large egg, lightly beaten
- ¼ cup ketchup
- 1 tsp. soy sauce
- 1 Tbsp. chopped fresh flat-leaf parsley

1. Preheat oven to 400°F. Whisk together oil, garlic, lemon zest, lemon juice, and ½ teaspoon of the kosher salt and ¼ teaspoon of the pepper in a large bowl. Add Brussels sprouts, leek, and red potatoes, and toss to coat. Spread the vegetables on a lightly greased, aluminum foil-lined rimmed baking sheet. Bake vegetables in preheated oven 10 minutes.
2. Meanwhile combine beef, sausage, carrot, onion, breadcrumbs, egg, and remaining ½ teaspoon each salt and pepper in a large bowl. Mix gently just until combined. Shape into 4 (2- x 3-inch) loaves. Remove pan from oven, push vegetables to 1 side, and carefully place meatloaves on pan. Return pan to oven, and bake until meat is cooked through and vegetables are tender, about 35 minutes.
3. Whisk together ketchup and soy sauce in a small bowl. Spread over meatloaves. Increase oven temperature to broil, and broil until sauce begins to brown, about 2 minutes. Divide meatloaves and vegetables evenly among 4 plates. Sprinkle with parsley.

HAUTE CHOCOLATE

Come on—we know you're better than just-add-hot-water mixes.
Whip up one of these decadent drinks that can easily step in as dessert.

Boozy Buttermint White Hot Chocolate

Whisk together 4 cups **whole milk,** 1 cup **heavy cream,** and ½ cup white **buttermints** in a medium saucepan. Bring to a simmer over medium, stirring constantly, until mints are dissolved and mixture is hot, about 13 minutes. Remove from heat and whisk in 6 ounces chopped **white chocolate** and 2 teaspoons **vanilla** extract until smooth. Stir in ⅓ cup **Irish cream liqueur** (such as Baileys Irish Cream). Pour into 4 serving cups, and top each with ¼ cup **marshmallows.** Garnish with **mint** sprigs and crushed buttermints, if desired. **SERVES 4**

3-D Hot Chocolate

Whisk together 4 cups **half-and-half** and ½ cup canned or jarred **dulce de leche** in a medium saucepan. Simmer over medium, stirring constantly, until heated through, about 10 minutes. Remove from heat, and whisk in 8 ounces chopped **dark chocolate,** ⅓ cup of **Drambuie,** 2 teaspoons **vanilla** extract, and ¼ teaspoon **kosher salt** until the mixture is smooth. Next, beat 1 cup of cold **heavy cream** in a cold bowl with an electric mixer on high until stiff peaks form, about 1 minute. Pour hot chocolate mixture into 4 serving cups. Top each with whipped cream, a drizzle of dulce de leche, and chopped or shaved dark chocolate. Serve with **chocolate rolled wafer cookies** (such as Pirouette). **SERVES 4**

Toasted Coconut Hot Chocolate

Without shaking or tilting the can, carefully open 1 (13.66-oz.) can chilled **coconut milk.** Remove solidified cream from top, reserving liquid, and place in a bowl. Add 2 tablespoons **powdered sugar** and 1 teaspoon **vanilla** extract, and beat with an electric mixer until medium peaks form, about 3 minutes. Chill until ready to use. Whisk together remaining coconut milk liquid, 1 quart **unsweetened coconut milk** (such as So Delicious), ¾ cup granulated **sugar,** and ¼ cup unsweetened **cocoa** in a medium saucepan. Bring to a simmer over medium, stirring constantly. Cook, stirring constantly, until sugar is dissolved and mixture is hot, about 10 minutes. Remove from heat, and whisk in 6 ounces 60% cacao **bittersweet chocolate,** ¾ teaspoon **cinnamon,** ¼ teaspoon **kosher salt,** and 2 teaspoons vanilla extract. Pour into 4 serving cups, and top with whipped coconut cream, a sprinkle of ground cinnamon, **toasted coconut,** and **shaved chocolate. SERVES 4**

Frozen Pecan Pie Hot Chocolate

Unroll half of a 14.1-oz. package refrigerated **piecrust** onto a parchment paper-lined baking sheet; prick piecrust all over with a fork. Spray with **cooking spray.** Bake in 400°F oven until crisp, about 15 minutes. Let cool, and then break into large pieces; set aside. Beat 1 cup cold **heavy cream** and 2 tablespoons granulated **sugar** in a cold bowl with an electric mixer until stiff peaks form, about 1 minute; set aside. Process 1 pint **butter pecan ice cream,** 1 ½ cups **whole milk,** ⅓ cup **instant cocoa mix,** ⅓ cup **toasted pecans,** 3 tablespoons **cane syrup,** and ¼ teaspoon **kosher salt** in a blender until smooth. Drizzle the insides of 4 glasses with ⅓ cup **chocolate sauce.** Pour frozen hot chocolate mixture into prepared glasses. Top with whipped cream, piecrust pieces, and toasted pecans. **SERVES 4**

TORTILLAS TONIGHT

THINK BEYOND THE BURRITO AND SPICE UP DINNERTIME WITH THESE FAST, FRESH, FLAT-OUT DELICIOUS IDEAS

PICO DE GALLO PIZZAS, PAGE 35

BEEF FLAUTAS WITH BUTTER-MILK-AVOCADO CREMA, PAGE 35

MINI BLACK BEAN AND CHEESE ENCHILADAS, PAGE 35

SOUTHWESTERN CHOPPED CHICKEN SALAD, PAGE 36

Beef Flautas with Buttermilk-Avocado Crema

This restaurant favorite is easy to make at home, even on a weeknight. While the oil heats, set up an assembly line with the cooked meat, tortillas, and egg wash, and get rolling!

ACTIVE 30 MIN. - TOTAL 40 MIN.
SERVES 4

- 1 lb. fresh Mexican chorizo, casings removed (3 links)
- ½ cup chopped white onion
- 2 garlic cloves, minced
- 1 lb. ground chuck
- ½ tsp. chili powder
- 1 tsp. kosher salt, divided
- ¼ cup chopped fresh cilantro
- 12 (6-inch) flour tortillas
- 1 large egg, lightly beaten
- ⅓ cup canola oil
- 1 ripe avocado, chopped
- 1 cup sour cream
- ½ cup buttermilk
- 1 Tbsp. fresh lime juice

1. Crumble chorizo in a large skillet, and cook over medium-high, stirring occasionally, 5 minutes. Stir in onion and garlic, and cook, stirring occasionally, until onion is tender, about 5 minutes. Add ground chuck, chili powder, and ½ teaspoon of the salt; cook, stirring often, until beef is browned and done, about 10 minutes. Remove from heat, and stir in cilantro.
2. Using a slotted spoon, divide chorizo-beef mixture evenly among tortillas (about ¼ cup per tortilla), placing mixture just below center of each tortilla. Roll tortilla over filling, leaving about 1 inch of tortilla exposed. Brush exposed edge with a small amount of beaten egg; press gently to seal roll.
3. Heat oil in a large skillet over medium; fry flautas, in batches, until crispy, 3 to 4 minutes per side. Drain on paper towels.
4. Process avocado, sour cream, buttermilk, lime juice, and remaining ½ teaspoon salt in a food processor until smooth. Serve flautas with crema.

Mini Black Bean and Cheese Enchiladas

A real crowd-pleaser: These fun 4-inch flour tortillas (available at supermarkets) are just the right size for baking in muffin tins. Plus, they take only 30 minutes to pull together.

ACTIVE 30 MIN. - TOTAL 30 MIN.
SERVES 6

- 2 (10-ct.) pkg. miniature (4-inch) flour tortillas (such as Old El Paso)
- 1 (15-oz.) can black beans, drained and rinsed
- 1 (15-oz.) can refried black beans
- 1 (8-oz.) can red enchilada sauce (such as Frontera)
- 1 (4-oz.) can chopped green chiles
- 4 oz. Monterey Jack cheese, shredded (about 1 cup)
- 1 cup shredded iceberg lettuce (from 1 [8-oz] pkg.)
- ½ cup prepared pico de gallo
- ½ cup sour cream
- 3 Tbsp. thinly sliced scallions

1. Preheat oven to 350°F. Gently tuck tortillas into lightly greased (with cooking spray) cups of 2 (12-cup) muffin pans. Bake in preheated oven until tortillas have hardened and browned slightly on the sides, 12 to 15 minutes.
2. Stir together black beans, refried black beans, enchilada sauce, and green chiles in a medium bowl. Divide mixture evenly among baked tortilla cups. Sprinkle with cheese, and bake at 350°F until cheese melts, about 15 minutes.
3. Transfer mini enchiladas from muffin cups to a serving platter. Top evenly with lettuce and pico de gallo. Drizzle with sour cream, and sprinkle with scallions.

Pico de Gallo Pizzas

Large flour tortillas can be turned into personal pizzas—no dough rolling required! We topped ours with a mild and creamy Mexican melting cheese, but shredded mozzarella would also work.

ACTIVE 15 MIN. - TOTAL 45 MIN.
SERVES 4

- 2 (8-oz.) tomatoes, seeded and cut into 1½-inch pieces (about 3 cups)
- 1 small red onion, cut into ½-inch pieces (about ½ cup)
- 2 jalapeño chiles, seeded and cut into ½-inch pieces (about ½ cup)
- 3 Tbsp. fresh lime juice (from 2 limes)
- 1½ tsp. kosher salt
- ½ cup plus 2 Tbsp. roughly chopped cilantro, divided
- 1 Tbsp. plus 1 tsp. extra-virgin olive oil, divided
- 4 (10-inch) flour tortillas
- 4 oz. queso Chihuahua or other Mexican melting cheese, shredded (about 1 cup)

1. Stir together tomatoes, onion, jalapeños, lime juice, salt, ½ cup of the cilantro, and 1 tablespoon of the oil in a medium bowl. Let stand 30 minutes, stirring occasionally.
2. Preheat oven to 450°F. Place tortillas in a single layer on 2 rimmed baking sheets, and brush with remaining 1 teaspoon oil. Using a slotted spoon, divide tomato mixture evenly among tortillas, leaving a ½-inch border. Sprinkle evenly with cheese. Bake in preheated oven until tortillas are crisp and browned, 13 to 15 minutes, switching baking sheets top rack to bottom rack halfway through baking time. Sprinkle with remaining 2 tablespoons cilantro, and serve immediately.

SKILLET SHRIMP
CHILAQUILES

Southwestern Chopped Chicken Salad

Every bite of this salad is a delightful mix of flavors and textures, but the home-made baked tortilla chips on top steal the show.

ACTIVE 45 MIN. - TOTAL 1 HOUR, 30 MIN.
SERVES 4

- 2 (10-inch) flour tortillas
- 1 tsp. ground cumin
- ⅓ cup plus 1 Tbsp. olive oil, divided
- 1 tsp. kosher salt, divided
- 2 tsp. lime zest plus ½ cup fresh juice (from 6 limes)
- 1 shallot, minced (about 2 ½ Tbsp.)
- 1 Tbsp. apple cider vinegar
- 1 tsp. Dijon mustard
- 1 tsp. honey
- ¼ tsp. black pepper
- 4 cups chopped chicken (from 1 rotisserie chicken)
- 2 cups chopped ripe avocado (about 2 avocados)
- 2 romaine lettuce hearts, chopped
- ½ cup thinly sliced radishes (about 3 large radishes)
- ½ cup Pickled Red Onions (recipe follows)

1. Preheat oven to 425°F. Stack tortillas; cut in half, and cut crosswise into ½-inch strips. Place tortilla strips on a rimmed baking sheet. Toss with cumin, 1 tablespoon of the olive oil, and ¼ teaspoon of the salt. Spread strips in a single layer; bake in preheated oven until golden brown and crisp, 10 to 12 minutes, turning halfway through baking. Cool strips to room temperature.
2. Meanwhile, whisk together lime zest, lime juice, shallot, apple cider vinegar, Dijon mustard, honey, pepper, and remaining ⅓ cup oil and ¾ teaspoon salt until well combined. Set aside.
3. Toss together chopped chicken, avocado, romaine, sliced radishes, and Pickled Red Onions in a large bowl. Add 6 to 7 tablespoons vinaigrette; toss to coat. Place 2 cups salad on each of 4 plates; top each with 3 baked tortilla strips. Serve with remaining vinaigrette.

Skillet Shrimp Chilaquiles

Chilaquiles, fried tortillas simmered in salsa, is a classic Mexican breakfast. It also makes a fast and filling supper when topped with spiced shrimp.

ACTIVE 20 MIN. - TOTAL 30 MIN.
SERVES 4

- Vegetable or canola oil
- 12 (6 ½-inch) corn tortillas
- 1 ½ tsp. kosher salt, divided
- 2 ½ cups green chile salsa (such as Herdez)
- 1 lb. peeled and deveined raw medium shrimp
- ½ tsp. ancho chile powder
- 2 oz. queso fresco (fresh Mexican cheese), crumbled (about ½ cup)
- 1 ripe avocado, diced
- ¼ cup packed fresh cilantro leaves

1. Preheat oven to 400°F. Pour oil to a depth of 2 inches in a Dutch oven; heat oil over medium-high to 350°F. Stack tortillas; cut stack into quarters to create 48 tortilla wedges. Fry wedges, 12 at a time, in hot oil until lightly browned, about 1 ½ minutes per side. Quickly remove tortilla chips from oil, and drain on paper towels. Sprinkle chips evenly with ¾ teaspoon of the salt. Cool to room temperature, about 10 minutes.
2. Arrange half of chips in a 10-inch cast-iron skillet, and pour ½ cup salsa over chips. Top with remaining chips and 2 cups salsa. Cover skillet with heavy-duty aluminum foil, and bake in preheated oven 15 minutes.
3. Meanwhile, toss shrimp with ancho chile powder and remaining ¾ teaspoon salt.
4. Remove skillet from oven, and increase oven temperature to broil. Remove and discard foil. Arrange shrimp on top of tortilla mixture. Return to oven, and broil just until shrimp turn pink, 3 to 5 minutes.
5. Top with queso fresco, avocado, and cilantro. Serve immediately.

Pickled Red Onions

ACTIVE 5 MIN. - TOTAL 1 HOUR, 5 MIN.
MAKES 2 CUPS

- 1 cup hot water
- ½ cup red wine vinegar
- 1 Tbsp. granulated sugar
- 1½ tsp. kosher salt
- 1 red onion, thinly sliced

Stir together hot water, red wine vinegar, sugar, and salt until sugar is completely dissolved. Place sliced onion in a medium bowl. Pour vinegar mixture over onion; let stand 1 hour. Store in an airtight container in refrigerator up to 1 month.

Tortilla-Crusted Tilapia with Citrus Slaw and Chipotle Tartar Sauce

Crushed tortilla chips make a crispy breading for tilapia fillets. Use store-bought chips or make your own. (See how in Step 1 of Skillet Shrimp Chilaquiles—recipe opposite page.)

ACTIVE 30 MIN. - TOTAL 40 MIN.
SERVES 4

TILAPIA
- 4 (6-oz.) tilapia fillets
- ½ tsp. kosher salt
- ¼ tsp. black pepper
- 1 cup all-purpose flour
- 2 tsp. ground cumin
- 2 tsp. ground coriander
- 2 large eggs, lightly beaten
- 2 cups crushed corn tortilla chips
- ¼ cup canola oil, divided

SLAW
- 2 Tbsp. extra-virgin olive oil
- 1½ Tbsp. apple cider vinegar
- 1 Tbsp. orange zest plus 2 Tbsp. fresh juice (from 1 orange)
- 1 tsp. granulated sugar
- ½ tsp. kosher salt
- 4 cups thinly sliced purple cabbage (1 head cabbage)
- ½ cup thinly sliced scallions (about 4 scallions)
- ¼ cup finely chopped fresh flat-leaf parsley

SAUCE
- 1 cup mayonnaise
- ¼ cup drained dill pickle relish
- 2 Tbsp. chopped canned chipotle pepper in adobo sauce
- 1 tsp. fresh lime juice
- ½ tsp. onion powder

1. Prepare the Tilapia: Sprinkle both sides of tilapia fillets with salt and black pepper. Combine flour, cumin, and coriander in a shallow dish. Place beaten eggs in a second shallow dish; place crushed tortilla chips in a third shallow dish. Dredge fillets in flour mixture, dip in eggs, and dredge in tortilla chips, pressing to adhere.
2. Heat 1 tablespoon of the canola oil in a large nonstick skillet over medium-high. Place 2 fillets in hot oil; cook until golden brown on bottom, about 4 minutes. Turn fillets, add 1 tablespoon of the oil, and cook until fish flakes easily with a fork, about 4 minutes. Transfer fillets to a wire rack over a baking sheet. Keep warm in a 200°F oven. Repeat process with remaining 2 tablespoons canola oil and 2 fillets.
3. Prepare the Slaw: Stir together olive oil, vinegar, orange zest, orange juice, sugar, and salt in a large bowl. Add cabbage, scallions, and parsley; toss to coat. Let stand 10 minutes.
4. Prepare the Sauce: Stir together all Sauce ingredients.
5. Serve tilapia with Citrus Slaw and Chipotle Tartar Sauce.

WHAT'S THE DIFFERENCE? WHITE VS. YELLOW CORN TORTILLAS

Corn tortillas are made with fine corn flour called *masa harina,* which is typically white or yellow, depending on the dried corn used. While yellow and white corn tortillas can be swapped interchangeably in recipes, there are subtle differences between the two. Yellow corn tortillas have a stronger flavor and can stand up to spicy salsas and sauces. They also make great fried chips. White corn tortillas have a more delicate taste and softer texture that allows them to roll up easily without cracking. Blue corn tortillas, made with blue *masa harina,* are worth buying if you see them; they have a nutty, toasty flavor.

Light Pasta with a Kick

Got 30 minutes? That's all you'll need to make this satisfying one-pan penne

HEALTHY OPTIONS
You can sub kale, turnip greens, spinach, or other leafy greens for the collards.

One-Pan Pasta with Chicken Sausage, Mushrooms, and Collards

Rather than boiling the noodles in a separate pot, we cooked them with the chicken stock and other ingredients. The starch from the pasta thickens the broth, making a surprisingly rich sauce without butter or cream.

ACTIVE 23 MIN. - TOTAL 28 MIN.
SERVES 4

2 tsp. olive oil

12 oz. fully cooked sweet Italian-style chicken sausage (such as Al Fresco), cut into ¼-inch-thick slices
1 lb. cremini mushrooms, sliced
4 cups unsalted chicken stock
½ tsp. kosher salt
4 cups chopped, stemmed collard greens (about 3 oz.)
10 oz. uncooked penne pasta
1 cup thinly sliced red onion
1 Tbsp. thinly sliced garlic
1 Tbsp. red wine vinegar
½ tsp. crushed red pepper

Heat oil in a large, high-sided skillet over medium-high. Add sausage and mushrooms; cook, stirring often, until browned, about 8 minutes. Add stock and next 5 ingredients; bring to a boil. Cook, stirring constantly, until pasta is al dente and liquid is mostly absorbed, about 15 minutes. Stir in vinegar, and sprinkle with crushed red pepper.

Nutritional information (per serving):
Calories: 487 - Fat 13.2g (Saturated fat: 0.66g) - Protein: 29g - Fiber 4.96g - Carbohydrates: 64.19g - Sodium: 935mg

BRUSSELS SPROUT
SLAW WITH APPLES
AND PECANS,
PAGE 40

A Taste for Sprouts

Virginia Willis cooks
up three new ways with
this once-misunderstood
vegetable

FOR MANY YEARS Brussels sprouts were considered the dregs of the vegetable bin. Usually there's a grim story involving childhood and not being allowed to leave the dinner table until every smelly sprout was consumed. But even as a kid, I liked their mildly bitter flavor and never understood why they were so despised.

Fortunately, Brussels sprouts have enjoyed a culinary renaissance of sorts. Restaurant chefs searching for seasonal vegetables in the middle of winter sought to elevate the sprout. Banished are the days of bland and boiled. Chefs know that cruciferous vegetables like Brussels sprouts are high in an organic compound that contains sulfur—hence their stinky reputation. To minimize strong odors, it's necessary to reduce the cooking time, so chefs began roasting them quickly at high heat, bringing out the sprouts' natural sugars. Pairing them with smoky, salty bacon undeniably gave them a boost, as did deep-frying. The results are otherworldly good—crisp edges, tender inner layers, and lots of nooks and crannies for various sauces and spices. This is how dining trends work their way into home kitchens. Restaurant chefs do crazy-delicious things with an ingredient and the next thing you know, it turns up in recipes from "the South's Most Trusted Kitchen."

Traditional Quick-Pickled Brussels Sprouts

Chefs all across the South are putting up jars of local produce, lining their larders and dining room shelves with interesting twists on pickles. You too can have a little jar of big Brussels sprout flavor for snacking, sandwiches, or skewered to garnish a spicy Bloody Mary.

ACTIVE 15 MIN. - TOTAL 4 DAYS, 15 MIN., INCLUDING 4 DAYS CHILLING
SERVES 4

Cook 10 trimmed and halved **Brussels sprouts** in a large stockpot of boiling water until bright green, about 5 minutes. Drain and rinse under cold running water. Bring ¾ cup **water,** ¼ cup white **vinegar,** and 1 tsp. coarse **kosher salt** to a simmer in stockpot over medium; simmer until salt dissolves. Combine 10 black **peppercorns,** ¼ tsp. yellow **mustard seeds,** 1 sliced **garlic** clove, a pinch of **crushed red pepper,** and 1 fresh **bay leaf** in a sterilized pint jar. Place Brussels sprouts in jar; add hot vinegar mixture. (You may have some leftover liquid.) Cool to room temperature. Cover with lid, and chill 4 days or up to 2 weeks before serving. Store covered in refrigerator up to 1 month.

Fried Brussels Sprout Tacos

Even folks who aren't fans of Brussels sprouts will like them fried. Houston's popular Eight Row Flint takes fried Brussels sprouts one step further by transforming them into vegetarian tacos, providing the inspiration for this recipe. A splatter guard is helpful when frying the sprouts.

ACTIVE 30 MIN. - TOTAL 30 MIN.
SERVES 4

- 16 Brussels sprouts (about 12 oz.), trimmed and outer leaves removed
-     Canola oil
- 1 shallot, thinly sliced
- 1 jalapeño chile, very thinly sliced
- ½ tsp. kosher salt
- ½ cup crema Mexicana or sour cream
- 8 (6-inch) corn tortillas, warmed
- 1 cup very thinly sliced or grated carrots (2 large carrots)
- 4 radishes, thinly sliced
- ¼ cup cilantro leaves
-     Hot sauce
-     Lime wedges

1. Preheat oven to 200°F. Line a rimmed baking sheet with paper towels. Cut Brussels sprouts into quarters.
2. Pour oil to a depth of at least ¾ inch in a Dutch oven. (Oil should be just deep enough to submerge Brussels sprouts.) Heat oil over high to 325°F. Add about half each of the Brussels sprouts, shallot slices, and jalapeño slices to hot oil. (Do not overcrowd Dutch oven.) Fry, stirring occasionally, until golden brown and crispy, 2 to 3 minutes. Using a slotted spoon, transfer fried Brussels sprouts, shallots, and jalapeños to prepared baking sheet. Sprinkle with ¼ teaspoon of the salt. Transfer baking sheet to preheated oven to keep warm. Repeat process with remaining Brussels sprouts, shallots, jalapeños, and salt.
3. Place 1 tablespoon crema on each warmed tortilla; spread to edges of tortilla. Top tortillas evenly with Brussels sprouts mixture, carrots, radishes, and cilantro. Serve with hot sauce and lime wedges.

Brussels Sprout Slaw with Apples and Pecans

ACTIVE 20 MIN. - TOTAL 25 MIN.
SERVES 4

Thinly slice 1 lb. trimmed **Brussels sprouts** using a mandoline or food processor fitted with the slicer attachment. Transfer sliced Brussels sprouts to a large bowl. Add 6 Tbsp. extra-virgin **olive oil,** 1 Tbsp. lemon **zest,** ¼ cup fresh **lemon juice,** and ½ tsp. **crushed red pepper;** toss to coat. Add 1 diced Granny Smith or Honeycrisp **apple,** 2 oz. shredded **Parmesan** cheese, ⅓ cup toasted and chopped **pecans,** 1 Tbsp. **honey,** 1 tsp. **kosher salt,** and ½ tsp. **black pepper;** toss to coat. Let stand 5 minutes to allow the Brussels sprouts to wilt slightly and the flavors to marry.

To-Die-For Pie

We topped this classic butterscotch pie with spirited caramel you can make ahead

Butterscotch Pie with Whiskey Caramel Sauce

ACTIVE 55 MIN. - TOTAL 6 HOURS, 55 MIN., INCLUDING 5 HOURS CHILLING

SERVES 8

PIECRUST

- 1 ½ cups all-purpose flour
- 2 tsp. granulated sugar
- ½ tsp. sea salt
- ½ cup cold salted butter, cut into small pieces
- 2 to 3 Tbsp. ice water

WHISKEY CARAMEL SAUCE

- 1 ½ cups granulated sugar
- ½ cup water
- 1 cup heavy cream
- 1 Tbsp. rye whiskey
- ¼ tsp. sea salt

FILLING

- 3 large egg yolks
- 6 Tbsp. cornstarch
- 1 ¾ cups half-and-half, divided
- 1 ½ cups packed light brown sugar
- ¾ tsp. sea salt
- ¼ cup salted butter, cut into small pieces

- 1 Tbsp. rye whiskey
- 1 tsp. vanilla extract

TOPPING

- 3 cups heavy cream
- ¼ cup powdered sugar

1. Prepare the Piecrust: Pulse flour, granulated sugar, salt, and butter pieces in a food processor until mixture resembles coarse sand. While pulsing, add ice water, 1 tablespoon at a time, through food chute, just until mixture can be pressed together with fingertips. Form dough into a disk, and wrap with plastic wrap. Chill 1 hour.

2. Preheat oven to 400°F. Unwrap dough, and roll into a 12-inch circle on a lightly floured surface. Fit piecrust into a 9-inch pie pan, and trim, allowing ½ inch to extend over edge. Fold edge under, and crimp. Freeze 15 minutes.

3. Line piecrust with parchment paper, and fill completely with pie weights or dried beans. Bake in preheated oven until the crust is set and edge is light brown, about 15 minutes. Remove from oven; remove weights and parchment. Return to oven, and bake until golden brown, about 15 minutes. (If necessary,

shield edges with aluminum foil after 10 minutes to prevent excessive browning.) Remove piecrust from oven, and cool completely on a wire rack, about 1 hour.

4. Prepare the Caramel Sauce: Bring granulated sugar and water to a boil in a medium saucepan over high. Cook, without stirring, until mixture is a deep amber color, about 9 minutes. Remove from heat. Using a long-handled whisk and shielding hands from the steam, gradually whisk in cream until smooth. Whisk in whiskey and salt, and cool 30 minutes. (Mixture will thicken as it cools.) Store cooled Whiskey Caramel Sauce in an airtight container in the refrigerator for up to 1 month.

5. Prepare the Filling: Whisk together egg yolks, cornstarch, and ¼ cup of the half-and-half in a medium bowl. Set aside.

6. Stir together brown sugar, salt, and remaining 1 ½ cups half-and-half in a large saucepan. Bring to a boil over medium-high, and remove from heat. Slowly whisk hot brown sugar mixture into egg yolk mixture; return mixture to saucepan. Cook over medium-high, whisking constantly and making sure to reach all points in the bottom of the saucepan, until mixture comes to a boil. Boil, whisking constantly, 1 minute. (Mixture will be very thick and smooth.) Remove from heat, and whisk in butter pieces, whiskey, and vanilla. Cool 30 minutes. Spoon filling into cooled piecrust. Chill until filling is firm and cold, about 4 hours.

7. Prepare the Topping: About 1 hour before serving, beat heavy cream and powdered sugar with an electric mixer on high speed until stiff peaks form, 3 to 5 minutes. (Do not overbeat.) Spread whipped cream over pie filling; chill 1 hour. Drizzle Whiskey Caramel Sauce over pie.

BRAISING BASICS

This hands-off method of slow simmering is a lazy cook's dream. Follow these four steps for yielding flavorful, fall-off-the-bone meat.

1. SEAR Season the meat with salt and pepper. Add oil to a deep pot (with a tight lid), and heat over medium-high. Using tongs, brown the meat on all sides. Once it's browned, remove the meat from the pot and set aside.

2. SAUTÉ Toss and cook diced vegetables such as chopped carrots, onions, and celery into the leftover drippings from searing. Stir frequently over medium-high heat until all of the vegetables are tender and caramelized.

3. STIR AND SCRAPE Add braising liquid, such as wine, stock, or water, stirring with a wooden turner to loosen browned bits from the bottom of the pot. (This is called deglazing.) The browned bits dissolve in the liquid to make a rich sauce.

4. BRAISE Return the meat to the pot. Cover the pot with a layer of parchment paper, and press down, which will help seal in moisture. Bring the liquid to a simmer, and cover with the lid. Cook over low heat until the meat is fork-tender.

WHY BRAISING IS BETTER

1 Budget Friendly
Turn tougher, inexpensive cuts like chicken thighs, short ribs, and pork shoulder into melt-in-your-mouth meat.

2 Minimal Effort
Cook it in a heavy Dutch oven with a tight-fitting lid, or pull out your trusty slow cooker. (Just be sure to brown the meat beforehand.)

3 Liquid Leftovers
Cooking meat "low and slow" in a liquid yields a thick, flavor-packed sauce that shouldn't be wasted—freeze and reuse it in another meal!

HOW TO

WARM TORTILLAS

MICROWAVE Stack five or fewer on a microwave-safe plate, cover with a damp paper towel, and heat in 10-second increments.

STOVE-TOP Toast a few at a time in a cast-iron skillet. Flip occasionally until soft or slightly charred.

OVEN Wrap a stack of tortillas in aluminum foil, and place in a preheated 350°F oven for about 15 minutes.

PAM LOLLEY
SL Test Kitchen Professional

"For crisp, golden, pan-fried chicken, cook over medium heat so the bread-crumbs won't burn before the chicken is done inside."

THE BEST WAY TO CLEAN MUSHROOMS

Mushrooms are mini sponges: Soaking makes them soggy and slimy and keeps them from browning when cooked. Instead, gently wipe off any muddy bits with damp paper towels.

February

SUNNY DELIGHTS

Radiant **oranges,** vibrant **grapefruits,** luminous **lemons** and **limes**—in the South, sunshine grows on trees right in our own backyards. It's the height of citrus season now, and we squeezed these sweet-tart fruits into delicious desserts that are a refreshing remedy for the midwinter blues.

DREAMY LEMON CHEESECAKE PAGE 45

A water bath cooks the cheesecake gently, making it extra creamy with a smooth, crack-free top. You can make the lemon curd up to two weeks in advance; just be sure to store it in the refrigerator.

Clementine Upside-Down Cake

ACTIVE 30 MIN. - TOTAL 2 HOURS, 55 MIN.
SERVES 10

- ½ cup lightly packed light brown sugar
- ¼ cup honey
- 1 cup salted butter, softened, divided
- 4 clementines or mandarin oranges, thinly sliced (about ¼ inch)
- 1⅓ cups granulated sugar
- 1 Tbsp. orange zest
- 1 tsp. vanilla extract
- 1¾ cups all-purpose flour
- ¼ cup plain white cornmeal
- 1 tsp. baking powder
- 1 tsp. salt
- ½ tsp. baking soda
- ⅔ cup buttermilk
- 3 large eggs

1. Preheat oven to 350°F. Lightly grease the inside of a 9-inch springform pan. Snugly line pan with a 12-inch circle of heavy-duty aluminum foil, pressing any pleats flat.
2. Bring brown sugar, honey, and ¼ cup of the butter to a boil in a small saucepan over medium, stirring constantly. Remove from heat, and spread evenly in prepared pan.
3. Remove seeds from orange slices. Arrange in a single layer over sugar mixture.
4. Beat remaining ¾ cup softened butter with a heavy-duty stand mixer at medium speed until creamy; gradually add granulated sugar, and beat until light and fluffy, about 3 minutes. Stir in zest and vanilla. Whisk together flour, cornmeal, baking powder, salt, and baking soda in a small bowl. Whisk together buttermilk and eggs in another small bowl. Add flour mixture to sugar mixture alternately with buttermilk mixture, beginning and ending with flour mixture. Beat just until blended after each addition. Spread batter evenly over oranges.
5. Bake in preheated oven until a wooden pick inserted in center comes out clean, about 1 hour, 10 minutes to 1 hour, 15 minutes, covering with foil after 1 hour if cake has browned on top but not cooked through completely. Cool in pan on a wire rack 15 minutes.

CLEMENTINE UPSIDE-DOWN CAKE

This time of year, wooden crates of clementines line the produce department. Here's another way to eat those juicy little oranges other than out of hand: Slice them as thinly as you can with a very sharp knife or mandoline. Once the rinds bake on the cake, they'll be soft enough to eat.

6. Transfer springform pan to a rimmed baking sheet (to catch any drips). Remove sides of pan and invert cake onto a serving platter. Cool 1 hour before serving.

Dreamy Lemon Cheesecake

ACTIVE 20 MIN. - TOTAL 10 HOURS, 40 MIN.
SERVES 12

- 2½ cups crushed cream-filled lemon sandwich cookies (such as Lemon Oreo Sandwich Cookies) (about 25 cookies)
- 2½ Tbsp. salted butter, melted
- 5 (8-oz.) pkg. cream cheese, softened
- 1½ cups granulated sugar
- 2 Tbsp. all-purpose flour
- 4 large eggs
- 2 large egg yolks
- 1 Tbsp. lemon zest plus 5 Tbsp. fresh juice (about 2 lemons)
- 2 Tbsp. heavy cream
  Yellow food coloring gel paste (such as Spectrum Lemon Yellow Soft Gel Paste Food Coloring)
- 1 cup Lemon Curd (recipe follows)

1. Preheat oven to 350°F. Wrap outside of a lightly greased 9-inch shiny springform pan in a double layer of heavy-duty aluminum foil. Stir together crushed cookies and melted butter in a bowl. Press onto bottom of prepared pan.
2. Bake in preheated oven until lightly browned, 7 to 8 minutes. Cool on a wire rack until ready to use. Reduce oven temperature to 325°F.

3. Beat cream cheese with a heavy-duty mixer on medium speed until creamy, about 5 minutes. Gradually add sugar and flour, beating until smooth. Add eggs, 1 at a time, beating just until yellow disappears after each addition. Add egg yolks, 1 at a time, beating just until yellow disappears after each addition. Stir in lemon zest, lemon juice, and heavy cream.

4. Remove 3 cups of batter, and place in a medium bowl. Using a wooden pick, add a small amount of food coloring gel paste to the 3 cups of batter. Stir until batter is pale yellow, adding more gel paste if necessary.

5. Dollop half of untinted batter into prepared crust. Dollop half of pale yellow tinted batter on top of untinted batter dollops. Swirl together using a small knife, creating a marbled look. Repeat procedure with remaining halves of untinted and pale yellow tinted batters. Place springform pan in a roasting pan. Add boiling water to reach halfway up sides of springform pan.

6. Bake at 325°F until center is almost set but still slightly wobbly, 1 hour and 10 minutes to 1 hour and 20 minutes. Turn off oven, and let cheesecake stand in oven, with door partially open, 1 hour.

7. Remove cheesecake from roasting pan and water bath, and place on wire rack. Cool completely, about 2 hours. Cover with plastic wrap, using wooden picks to prevent plastic wrap from touching top of cheesecake. Chill 8 to 24 hours.

8. Gently run a knife around outer edge of cheesecake to loosen from sides of pan. Remove sides of pan. Spread top with 1 cup Lemon Curd.

Lemon Curd

ACTIVE 25 MIN. - TOTAL 4 HOURS, 25 MIN.
SERVES 8

- ½ cup salted butter, softened
- 2 cups granulated sugar
- 4 large eggs
- 2 large egg yolks
- 1 Tbsp. lemon zest plus 1 cup fresh juice (about 4 large lemons)

1. Beat butter and sugar with an electric mixer on medium speed until blended, about 45 seconds. Add eggs and egg yolks, 1 at a time, beating just until blended after each addition. Gradually add lemon juice to butter mixture, beating at low speed just until blended. Stir in zest. (Mixture will look curdled.)

2. Transfer mixture to a heavy 4-quart saucepan, and cook, whisking constantly, over medium-low until mixture thickens and coats the back of a spoon, 14 to 16 minutes.

3. Transfer curd to a bowl, and place plastic wrap directly on warm curd (to prevent a film from forming). Chill until firm, about 4 hours. Refrigerate in an airtight container up to 2 weeks.

Mixed Citrus Bars

ACTIVE 15 MIN. - TOTAL 1 HOUR, 25 MIN.
MAKES ABOUT 2 DOZEN BARS

- ½ cup toasted slivered almonds
- 2 ⅓ cups all-purpose flour, divided
- ½ cup powdered sugar plus additional for garnish
- 1 Tbsp. plus 1 tsp. lemon zest, divided
- 1 cup cold salted butter, cut into small cubes
- 6 large eggs
- 2 ¼ cups granulated sugar
- ¾ cup fresh lemon juice
- 1 ½ tsp. baking powder
- ¼ tsp. salt

1. Preheat oven to 350°F. Line bottom and sides of a 13- x 9-inch pan with heavy-duty aluminum foil, allowing 2 to 3 inches to extend over sides; lightly grease foil with cooking spray.

2. Pulse almonds, 2 cups of the flour, ½ cup powdered sugar, and 1 teaspoon of the lemon zest in a food processor until almonds are finely chopped and mixture is combined, about 5 pulses. Add butter, and pulse until mixture is crumbly, about 10 pulses. Press mixture evenly onto bottom of prepared pan.

3. Bake in preheated oven until lightly browned, 18 to 22 minutes.

4. Meanwhile, whisk eggs in a large bowl until smooth; whisk in granulated sugar, lemon juice, and remaining 1 tablespoon lemon zest. Stir together baking powder, salt, and the remaining ⅓ cup flour in a small bowl; whisk into egg mixture. Pour mixture over hot baked crust. Return to oven, and bake until filling is set, 24 to 26 minutes. Cool in pan on a wire rack 30 minutes.

5. Remove from pan, using foil sides as handles. Cool completely on a wire rack, about 30 minutes. Transfer to a serving dish. Remove foil; cut into bars, and garnish with powdered sugar.

The Best Way To Zest

Fresh citrus zest, or finely grated rind, adds a vibrant layer of flavor to sweet and savory recipes. If you've ever added lemon zest to cookies or lime zest to tacos, you know what we're saying. The best tool to unlock all that zing is a rasp grater (such as a Microplane), but how you use it can make all the difference. Instead of holding the citrus over the grater and letting the ribbons fall, try grating with the U-shape of the tool facing up—this will not only keep the shreds collected but also make it easier to avoid grating the bitter white pith.

MIXED CITRUS BARS

Why should lemons have all the fun? These classic cookie bars show off a rainbow of citrus flavors, from temptingly tart lemon and lime to delicately bright grapefruit and orange.

Lime Bars

Prepare recipe as directed, substituting **lime zest** for lemon zest and fresh **lime juice** for lemon juice. Using a small wooden pick, stir a small amount of **mint green food coloring gel** into filling mixture before pouring into crust in Step 4. Proceed with recipe as directed.

Orange Bars

Prepare recipe as directed, substituting **orange zest** for lemon zest and ½ cup fresh **orange juice** and ¼ cup fresh **lemon juice** for the ¾ cup lemon juice. Using a small wooden pick, stir a small amount of **red food coloring gel** into filling mixture before pouring into crust in Step 4. Proceed with recipe as directed.

Grapefruit Bars

Prepare recipe as directed, substituting **grapefruit zest** for lemon zest in the crust and ½ cup fresh **grapefruit juice** and ¼ cup fresh **lemon juice** for the ¾ cup lemon juice. Using a small wooden pick, stir a small amount of deep **pink food coloring gel** into filling mixture before pouring into crust in Step 4. Proceed with recipe as directed.
MAKES ABOUT 2 DOZEN BARS

Lemon-Vanilla Pound Cake with Lavender Glaze

ACTIVE 20 MIN. - TOTAL 3 HOURS, 45 MIN.
SERVES 16

- 1 cup salted butter, softened
- 3 cups granulated sugar
- 6 large eggs
- 2 Tbsp. lemon zest plus additional for garnish
- ⅓ cup fresh lemon juice
- 2 tsp. vanilla bean paste
- 3 cups all-purpose flour
- ½ tsp. salt
- ¼ tsp. baking soda
- 1 (8-oz.) container sour cream
  Vegetable shortening
  Lavender Glaze (recipe follows)

1. Preheat oven to 325°F. Beat butter with a heavy-duty electric stand mixer at medium speed until creamy, about 1 minute. Gradually add sugar, beating until light and fluffy, 3 to 5 minutes. Add eggs, 1 at a time, beating just until blended after each addition. Stir in lemon zest, fresh lemon juice, and vanilla bean paste.
2. Stir together flour, salt, and baking soda in a medium bowl. Add flour mixture to butter mixture alternately with sour cream, beginning and ending with flour mixture. Beat at low speed just until blended after each addition. Pour batter

into a greased (with shortening) and floured 10-inch tube pan.
3. Bake in preheated oven until a long wooden pick inserted in center comes out clean, 1 hour, 15 minutes to 1 hour, 30 minutes. Cool in pan on a wire rack 10 minutes; remove cake from pan to wire rack, and cool completely, about 2 hours.
4. Spoon Lavender Glaze over cake. Sprinkle with lemon zest.

Lavender Glaze

ACTIVE 5 MIN. - TOTAL 35 MIN.
MAKES ABOUT 1 CUP

- ½ cup whole milk
- 1 Tbsp. dried lavender buds
- 2½ cups powdered sugar
  Pinch of salt
- 1 Tbsp. plus 1 to 2 tsp. fresh lemon juice, divided

Bring ½ cup milk just to a simmer in a small saucepan over medium. Remove from heat, and stir in 1 Tbsp. dried lavender; let stand 10 minutes. Pour lavender milk through a fine wire-mesh strainer into a bowl, and cool completely, about 20 minutes. Whisk together powdered sugar, salt, 2 Tbsp. lavender milk, and 1 Tbsp. fresh lemon juice. Whisk in up to 2 teaspoons lemon juice, 1 teaspoon at a time, until desired consistency is reached.

LEMON-VANILLA POUND CAKE WITH LAVENDER GLAZE

Grapefruit Tart

ACTIVE 40 MIN. - TOTAL 4 HOURS, 52 MIN.
SERVES 8

- 1 ½ cups finely crushed saltine crackers (about 1 sleeve)
- 1 ½ cups granulated sugar, divided
- 7 Tbsp. salted butter, melted
- ¼ cup cornstarch
- ⅛ tsp. salt
- 1 ¾ cups fresh red grapefruit juice
- ¼ cup fresh lemon juice
- 4 large egg yolks
  Deep pink food color gel
- ⅓ cup salted butter, cut into 4 pieces
- 1 cup heavy whipping cream
- 3 Tbsp. powdered sugar
  Grapefruit slices

1. Preheat oven to 325°F. Stir together cracker crumbs, ¼ cup of the granulated sugar, and melted butter in a small bowl. Press mixture into a lightly greased 9-inch fluted tart pan with removable rim, pressing evenly up sides and on bottom.
2. Bake in preheated oven until crust is lightly browned, 12 to 14 minutes.
3. Meanwhile, combine cornstarch, salt, and remaining 1 ¼ cups granulated sugar in a medium-size heavy saucepan. Whisk in juices and egg yolks. Using a small wooden pick, stir in a small amount of deep pink food coloring gel. Cook over medium, whisking constantly, until mixture comes to a boil. Boil, whisking constantly, 1 minute. Remove from heat; whisk in ⅓ cup butter pieces.
4. Pour filling into prepared tart shell. Chill uncovered 4 to 24 hours.
5. Beat cream with an electric mixer at medium-high speed until foamy; gradually add powdered sugar, beating until soft peaks form. Dollop over tart. Top with quartered grapefruit slices.

Note: For a pretty garnish, cut thin grapefruit half-moon slices; then make one incision from the center to the rind. Gently twist the center until it creates a helix-like shape. The slices will keep their shape once nestled into the whipped cream.

GRAPEFRUIT TART

This tart's crunchy, slightly salty crust (made with saltine crackers) pairs beautifully with the tangy grapefruit filling and sweetened whipped cream.

Meyer Lemon Sponge Pudding

ACTIVE 20 MIN. - TOTAL 1 HOUR, 45 MIN.
SERVES 8

- 1 ½ cups whole milk
- 2 Tbsp. salted butter
- 3 large eggs, separated
- ½ cup all-purpose flour
- 1 cup granulated sugar, divided
- 1 Tbsp. finely grated Meyer lemon zest
- ⅓ cup fresh Meyer lemon juice
-   Pinch of salt

1. Preheat oven to 325°F. Combine milk and butter in a small saucepan, and cook over medium-low, stirring occasionally, until butter is melted and small bubbles appear around edge of milk, 3 to 5 minutes. Remove pan from heat.

2. Whisk together egg yolks in a large bowl until thick and pale; gradually whisk in about one-fourth hot milk mixture. Add remaining hot milk mixture to yolk mixture, whisking constantly. Stir together flour and ¾ cup of the sugar in a small bowl. Whisk sugar mixture into yolk mixture. Whisk in lemon zest and juice.

3. Beat egg whites and salt with an electric mixer at medium speed until foamy, about 30 seconds. With mixer running, gradually add remaining ¼ cup sugar, beating until stiff peaks form, 5 to 6 minutes. Stir one-third of egg white mixture into milk mixture until smooth. Gently fold in remaining egg white mixture until just combined.

4. Spoon pudding into 8 (6-ounce) ramekins or custard cups (about ¾ cup pudding per ramekin). Arrange ramekins in a baking pan or roasting pan. Add enough hot tap water to reach halfway up sides of ramekins (about 6 cups water for a 13- x 9-inch pan).

5. Bake in preheated oven until puddings are very lightly browned on top, about 30 minutes. Remove ramekins from water bath to a wire rack, and cool 15 minutes. Invert puddings onto individual serving plates. Serve immediately or at room temperature.

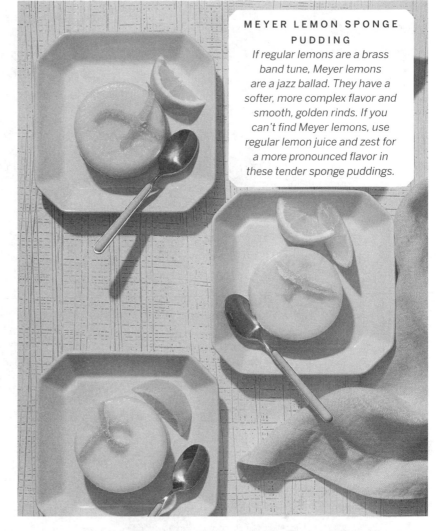

MEYER LEMON SPONGE PUDDING

If regular lemons are a brass band tune, Meyer lemons are a jazz ballad. They have a softer, more complex flavor and smooth, golden rinds. If you can't find Meyer lemons, use regular lemon juice and zest for a more pronounced flavor in these tender sponge puddings.

Southern Citrus

While the West may be known as America's salad bowl, the South is America's fruit basket. Florida alone accounts for over half of the country's citrus, with Texas being the third biggest producer. Just like tomatoes in the summer, between December and April, the South grows dozens of different varieties from flamingo pink-fleshed grapefruits to golden lemons and coral-colored oranges. Pick up these drops of sunshine at the grocery store or the farmers' market any chance you get.

KEY LIMES
Tiny and tart; bake them into the popular pie.

CARA CARA ORANGES
Sweet, bright red flesh; add wedges to salads.

SATSUMAS
Honey-like taste; juice it, or enjoy as is—it's Louisiana's clementine.

RIO STAR GRAPEFRUITS
Hot pink inside; squeeze into a Paloma cocktail.

KUMQUATS
Tangy with an edible peel; slice into fruit salad.

MINNEOLA TANGELO
Slightly pear-shaped tangerine hybrid; use for marmalade.

POMELO
Like an oversize grapefruit with less acidity; mix a margarita with the juice.

Super Dips

Score party points with these six winning combinations

❶ Succotash Salsa

Stir together 1 pt. **grape tomatoes,** diced; 1 (15.25-oz.) can **baby lima beans,** drained; 1 (15.25-oz.) can whole-kernel yellow **corn,** drained; ½ cup finely chopped sweet **onion;** ¼ cup extra-virgin **olive oil;** 3 Tbsp. chopped fresh flat-leaf **parsley;** 3 Tbsp. **white wine vinegar;** 1 tsp. **kosher salt;** and ¾ tsp. black **pepper** in a medium bowl. Serve with scoop-style **corn chips. SERVES 8**

❷ Nashville Hot Chicken Dip

Microwave 3 softened 8-oz. packages **cream cheese** on HIGH until melted, 1 to 2 minutes, stirring after 1 minute. Stir in ¾ cup **buttermilk,** 6 Tbsp. **hot sauce,** 1 Tbsp. **honey,** 1½ tsp. **cayenne** pepper, and ¾ tsp. **garlic powder.** Microwave on HIGH until hot, 2 to 3 minutes. Top with 1 Tbsp. sliced **scallions.** Serve with **cooked chicken wings. SERVES 8**

❸ Bacon-Pimiento Guacamole

Coarsely mash 3 peeled and pitted ripe **avocados** with 2½ Tbsp. fresh **lime juice** and ¾ tsp. **kosher salt.** Fold in 1 drained 4-oz. jar diced **pimientos,** ¼ cup finely chopped **red onion,** 6 cooked and crumbled **bacon** slices, and 2 Tbsp. chopped fresh **cilantro.** Serve with blue corn **tortilla chips. SERVES 8**

❹ Collard Dip

Stir together 1 softened 8-oz. package **cream cheese,** ¾ cup shredded **Swiss cheese,** ½ cup **mayonnaise,** ¼ cup grated **Parmesan** cheese, 2 Tbsp. minced **shallot,** ¾ tsp. black **pepper,** and ½ tsp. **kosher salt.** Fold in 1 thawed, drained 15-oz. package frozen chopped **collard greens.** Spread in a 3- to 4-cup baking dish; top with ¼ cup each shredded Swiss and grated Parmesan. Bake at 375°F until bubbly, 30 to 35 minutes. Serve with **baguette slices. SERVES 8**

❺ Smoky Black-Eyed Pea Hummus

Process 2 **garlic** cloves in a food processor until finely chopped. Add 2 (16-oz.) cans **black-eyed peas,** drained and rinsed; 6 Tbsp. extra-virgin **olive oil;** 3 Tbsp. **tahini;** 2 Tbsp. fresh **lemon juice;** 1 tsp. **smoked paprika;** ¾ tsp. **kosher salt;** and ½ tsp. black **pepper.** Process until smooth. Spoon into a bowl; top with 2 Tbsp. extra-virgin olive oil and ¼ tsp. smoked paprika. Serve with **pita chips.** Top with **lemon zest,** if desired. **SERVES 8**

❻ Creamy Crab Dip

Stir together 12 oz. fresh lump **crabmeat,** drained and picked clean of shells; ½ cup **sour cream;** ½ cup **mayonnaise;** ⅓ cup chopped **scallions;** 2 Tbsp. fresh **lemon juice;** 1 Tbsp. chopped fresh flat-leaf **parsley;** and 1 Tbsp. **Old Bay** seasoning. Top with fresh **chives.** Serve with **celery sticks. SERVES 6**

SIMMER
ALL DAY
PARTY
ALL NIGHT

Alon Shaya and his wife, Emily, celebrate a
New Orleans tradition by creating one of their own

WHEN CHEF ALON SHAYA moved to New Orleans from St. Louis, he had no idea that he'd play a leading role in reshaping the city's food scene. Fourteen years later, he now has multiple James Beard Awards and helms three of the busiest restaurants in the Crescent City: Domenica, a casual Italian restaurant just a stone's throw from the French Quarter; Pizza Domenica; and Shaya, a modern Israeli restaurant inspired by his birthplace. And while he may have gotten the city hooked on his ultra-smooth hummus and whole roasted cauliflower, New Orleans has also transformed the way he eats at home.

On Monday nights, the most coveted seat in town is not at one of his restaurants—it's in Shaya's home kitchen, where, like in many of his neighbors' homes, a pot of red beans is on the stove. Serving this dish to a constant rotation of friends is a weekly ritual for Alon and his wife, Emily. "I wanted to have a set time where we could catch up with everyone, get ready for the week, and drink some wine," says Emily.

Like beignets and po'boys, red beans and rice is a tradition that has been firmly ingrained in the New Orleans food culture. In the days before washing machines, Monday was considered "wash day" and called for a dinner that wouldn't require much attention, like red beans, which could simmer slowly all day and then be served over rice. Though Mondays may no longer be devoted to household laundry, the weekly tradition beats on throughout the city in homes, at restaurants offering special red beans and rice menus, and at bars, where patrons balance $2 plates of beans on their laps and dig in with plastic forks.

On Monday nights, Shaya ducks out early from his restaurant kitchens and heads home to be sous-chef, whipping up sides and washing dishes. He takes direction from Emily, who creates the night's signature dish and runs their kitchen with a smile and a dose of Southern charm honed from her days growing up in Calhoun, Georgia. "I know when I open the door it's going to smell like red beans in the house, and I love the comfort and familiarity of it," says Shaya. "I'll come home from work and she'll have a bunch of ingredients on the counter and I'll figure out the salad and some kind of appetizer." As if on cue, Emily shouts from another room, "Alon, you should probably make another skillet of cornbread." He replies, "Yes, chef!"

The Shayas commemorate each red beans night with a name. There was Candle Beans for the night the power went out. Small Beans for the rare nights when the crowd is less than five. Pop-Up Beans for the occasions when they moved the dinner to various friends' kitchens while their own was being renovated. Tonight is Big Beans, though it's not quite as large as the night they hosted 35 people in their cozy clapboard home in New Orleans' mid-city neighborhood. "There's a sense of responsibility," Shaya says. "You can't be fickle because it's now your friends' tradition to come eat red beans at your house."

Friends start arriving at dusk, shrugging off the heaviness of the start of the work week. They crowd in the kitchen, offering a hand with the last few preparations and sharing fresh news since the previous Monday. When dinner is ready, everyone digs in, reserving most of their plates for buttery rice topped with ladles of spicy, silky red beans, anchored by thick slices of sweet cornbread. Some gather at a weathered farm table that Emily kept from her childhood home. Others sit on stools around the kitchen island, a slightly more casual spot, but with the advantage of being closer to the food.

As the sweet sounds of Doc Watson's guitar play in the background, third and fourth servings are devoured, and no one wants to break the spell by being first to leave. In a time when traditions are losing their foothold, Emily and Alon have found a way to suspend time with each other and their closest friends.

The Shayas and their dog Henry on the front porch of their New Orleans home.

CORNBREAD
WITH
LEMON-THYME
BUTTER,
PAGE 55

CHARRED
ROOT
VEGETABLES
WITH BAGNA
CAUDA,
PAGE 55

APPLE AND
GOAT CHEESE
SALAD WITH
CANDIED
PECANS,
PAGE 56

YOGURT POUND
CAKE WITH
POMEGRANATE
SYRUP,
PAGE 56

Aperol and Blood Orange–Mint Spritz

This bubbly cocktail showcases blood oranges, which have a tart-sweet flavor. You can also use navel oranges.

Stir together ½ cup (4 oz.) **Prosecco** and ¼ cup (2 oz.) **Aperol.** Pour over ice with ½ cup fresh **blood orange juice** (about 3 oranges) in a tall glass. Garnish with **mint sprig,** if desired. **SERVES 1**

Emily's Red Beans and Rice

Alon might be the chef in the family, but he can't take credit for this meal's main event: wife Emily's red beans and rice. Her spicy, tender beans feed a large crowd, especially when served over fluffy, buttery rice.

ACTIVE 25 MIN. - TOTAL 3 HOURS, 30 MIN., PLUS OVERNIGHT SOAKING
SERVES 12

- ¼ lb. bacon, roughly chopped
- ¼ cup extra-virgin olive oil
- 1 medium-size yellow onion, diced
- 1 medium-size green bell pepper, diced
- 2 celery stalks, diced
- 1 bay leaf
- 1 Tbsp. sweet paprika
- 1 Tbsp. hot sauce (such as Tabasco), plus more for serving
- 1 ½ lb. dried red kidney beans (soaked overnight)
- 1 large smoked ham hock (about 12 ½ oz.)
- 2 qt. chicken stock
- 1 Tbsp. plus 1 tsp. kosher salt
- 2 tsp. granulated sugar Emily's Rice (recipe follows)
- 1 bunch scallions, green parts only, sliced

1. Place a heavy-bottomed Dutch oven over medium. Add bacon and olive oil, and cook, stirring often, until fat drippings are rendered, 3 to 5 minutes. Add onion, bell pepper, and celery, and cook, stirring often, until onion is translucent but not too broken down, 3 to 5 minutes. Add bay leaf, paprika, and hot sauce.
2. Drain, rinse, and sort soaked red beans; add beans and ham hock to pot. Pour in chicken stock, covering beans. Increase heat to high, and bring mixture to a boil, skimming off and discarding foam from surface. Reduce heat to low; cover and simmer until beans are tender, 3 to 4 hours. Remove ham hock about the last hour of cooking, and cut meat from bone. Chop ham meat, and add to beans, stirring to further break beans apart. (Check beans periodically to ensure they aren't boiling and sticking to the bottom of the pot.)
3. Remove and discard bay leaf. Stir in salt, sugar, and, if desired, more hot sauce just before serving. Serve beans over Emily's Rice. Garnish with scallions, if desired.

Emily's Rice

ACTIVE 5 MIN. - TOTAL 20 MIN.
MAKES 6 CUPS

- ½ cup canola oil
- 1 large yellow onion, diced
- ¼ cup unsalted butter, softened
- 1 bay leaf
- 2 tsp. kosher salt
- 2 cups uncooked jasmine rice
- 3 cups chicken broth or water

1. Heat oil in a saucepan over medium-high. Add onion, butter, bay leaf, and salt, and cook, stirring often, until onions are soft and translucent, about 6 minutes.
2. Add rice, and stir well. Stir in chicken broth, and bring mixture to a boil. Reduce heat to low; cover and cook 15 minutes.
3. Remove pan from heat, and let stand 5 minutes covered. Fluff rice with a fork.

Cornbread with Lemon–Thyme Butter

Classic Southern cornbread is even better with a bright citrus-herb compound butter.

ACTIVE 15 MIN. - TOTAL 1 HOUR
SERVES 8

- 3 Tbsp. canola oil
- 1 cup stone-ground cornmeal
- 1 cup all-purpose flour
- 2 Tbsp. granulated sugar
- 2 Tbsp. baking powder
- 1 tsp. kosher salt
- 2 large eggs
- 1 ¼ cups whole milk
- 2 Tbsp. unsalted butter, melted Lemon-Thyme Butter (recipe follows)

1. Preheat oven to 425°F. Grease a 10-inch cast-iron skillet with oil. Place skillet in preheated oven until hot, about 5 minutes.
2. Combine cornmeal, flour, sugar, baking powder, and salt in a large bowl. Whisk together eggs, milk, and butter in a separate bowl, and add to cornmeal mixture, stirring just until combined. Carefully pour batter into hot skillet.
3. Bake in preheated oven until golden brown, 15 to 20 minutes. Cool to room temperature in skillet, about 30 minutes. Serve with Lemon-Thyme Butter.

Lemon-Thyme Butter

ACTIVE 5 MIN. - TOTAL 5 MIN.
MAKES ABOUT 1 CUP

Stir together 1 cup unsalted softened **butter,** 1 ½ tsp. **lemon zest** plus 1 Tbsp. fresh **juice** (from 1 lemon), 1 tsp. fresh **thyme** leaves, and 1 tsp. **kosher salt.**

Charred Root Vegetables with Bagna Cauda

This Italian appetizer usually involves raw vegetables dipped into a pungent warm sauce. (Bagna cauda means "hot bath" in Italian.) Shaya substitutes roasted root vegetables for their caramelized sweetness.

ACTIVE 10 MIN. - TOTAL 35 MIN.
SERVES 10

- 1 lb. small carrots with tops, trimmed and halved lengthwise
- 1 lb. baby turnips, trimmed and halved
- 1 lb. small golden potatoes, halved
- 1 lb. red onions, cut into eighths
- ⅓ cup extra-virgin olive oil
- 4 tsp. kosher salt Bagna Cauda (recipe follows)

Preheat oven to 475°F. Toss together carrots, turnips, potatoes, onions, oil, and salt in a large bowl. Divide mixture evenly between 2 baking sheets, spreading in a single layer on each. Bake in preheated oven until vegetables are lightly charred and tender, 25 to 30 minutes, switching pans top rack to bottom rack halfway through baking. Serve vegetables with warm Bagna Cauda for dipping.

Bagna Cauda

ACTIVE 10 MIN. - TOTAL 15 MIN.
MAKES ABOUT ¾ CUP

Stir together 5 chopped **garlic** cloves, 5 chopped **anchovy fillets,** ½ cup extra-virgin **olive oil,** 1 **oregano** sprig, and 1 tsp. **kosher salt** in a saucepan over medium-low; cook, stirring occasionally, 5 minutes. Remove oregano sprig; whisk in 6 Tbsp. unsalted **butter.** Serve sauce warm.

Apple and Goat Cheese Salad with Candied Pecans

Whip up a salad full of delicious surprises like smoky candied pecans and a bit of orange zest and allspice in the vinaigrette.

ACTIVE 20 MIN. - TOTAL 30 MIN.
SERVES 8

CANDIED PECANS
- 1 large egg white
- 1 Tbsp. granulated sugar
- ½ lb. pecan halves (about 2 cups)
- ¼ tsp. smoked paprika
- ¼ tsp. kosher salt

VINAIGRETTE
- 3 Tbsp. extra-virgin olive oil
- 1½ Tbsp. fresh lemon juice
- ½ tsp. kosher salt
- ¼ tsp. orange zest
- ⅛ tsp. ground allspice

SALAD
- 3 Granny Smith apples, cored and thinly sliced
- 10 oz. winter greens (such as arugula or kale)
- ½ red onion, thinly sliced
- ¼ tsp. kosher salt
- ¼ tsp. cracked black pepper
- ½ lb. goat cheese, crumbled (about 2 cups)
- 2 Tbsp. good-quality aged balsamic vinegar

1. Prepare the Candied Pecans: Preheat oven to 350°F. Whisk together egg white and sugar in a bowl until light and frothy. Add pecans, paprika, and salt, and stir until pecans are completely coated. Spread in a single layer on a baking sheet. Bake in preheated oven until pecans are slightly toasted but still moist, 15 to 20 minutes. Remove pecans from baking sheet, and cool to room temperature, about 30 minutes.

2. Prepare the Vinaigrette: Whisk together olive oil, lemon juice, salt, orange zest, and allspice until combined.
3. Prepare the Salad: Toss together apples, greens, and onion in a large serving bowl; sprinkle with salt and pepper. Drizzle salad with Vinaigrette, and gently toss. Top with crumbled goat cheese and Candied Pecans. Drizzle with aged balsamic vinegar just before serving.

Yogurt Pound Cake with Pomegranate Syrup

Shaya adds Greek yogurt to the batter for a slight tang, then soaks the cake in a fragrant lemon-cardamom liquid and serves it with spiced Pomegranate Syrup.

ACTIVE 30 MIN. - TOTAL 2 HOURS, 30 MIN.
SERVES 12

- 3½ cups cake flour plus more for the pan
- 1½ tsp. baking powder
- ½ tsp. salt
- 3 cups granulated sugar, divided
- 1½ tsp. lemon zest
- 1 cup unsalted butter, softened, plus more for the pan
- 1 cup plain whole-milk Greek yogurt, at room temperature
- 6 large egg yolks
- 4 large eggs
- 1 tsp. vanilla extract
- ½ cup water
- ½ lemon (seeds removed)
- 6 cardamom pods
- 1 cup heavy cream
  Pomegranate Syrup (recipe follows)

1. Preheat oven to 350°F. Generously butter and flour a 14-cup Bundt or 10-inch tube pan. Sift together cake flour, baking powder, and salt.
2. Place 2½ cups of the sugar in a large mixing bowl or the bowl of a stand mixer. Sprinkle with lemon zest, and, using your fingers, rub into sugar. Add butter and yogurt, and beat with an electric mixer on high speed until light and fluffy, 5 to 8 minutes. (It will look broken and curdled at first, but that's okay.)
3. Add egg yolks and whole eggs, 1 at a time, beating well after each addition. Stir in vanilla. Gradually add flour mixture, beating on low just until incorporated. Pour batter into prepared pan. (Lift the pan a couple inches off the counter, and

let it drop. Do this a few times to get rid of any air bubbles in the batter.)
4. Bake in preheated oven on center rack until a long wooden pick inserted in center comes out clean, 50 to 60 minutes, rotating pan after 40 minutes. Cool cake in pan on a wire rack 15 minutes.
5. While the cake bakes, bring water, lemon half, cardamom pods, and remaining ½ cup sugar to a simmer in a saucepan over medium-high. Simmer, stirring occasionally, until sugar dissolves, about 8 minutes. Remove from heat; cover pan until ready to use.
6. After cake cools 15 minutes, invert onto a rimmed baking sheet, and remove pan. (Cake will be upside down.) Using a thin knife or wooden skewer, make about 16 slits or holes all over bottom of cake. Remove lemon half and cardamom pods from lemon-cardamom liquid, and discard. Gradually pour lemon-cardamom liquid over bottom of cake, ¼ cup at a time, allowing it to soak into cake after each addition. Cool cake completely before inverting onto a serving platter, about 2 hours.
7. Whip cream until light and airy. Serve cake with Pomegranate Syrup and whipped cream.

Pomegranate Syrup

ACTIVE 15 MIN. - TOTAL 15 MIN.
MAKES ABOUT ¾ CUP

Stir together ¾ cup granulated **sugar,** ½ cup **water,** ½ cup refrigerated **pomegranate juice,** 2 (3-inch) **orange peel strips,** and 1 (3-inch) **cinnamon stick** in a small saucepan over medium-high; bring to simmer. Reduce heat to medium-low, and cook, stirring occasionally, until syrupy, about 15 minutes. Remove pan from heat, and cool completely, about 30 minutes. Discard orange peel strips and cinnamon stick.

BUTTERMILK
CHICKEN TENDERS
WITH ROASTED
POTATOES AND
GREEN BEANS,
PAGE 67

A Month of Simple Suppers

We're taking weeknight meal planning
off your plate with a menu filled with
20 fast, fresh, mix-and-match recipes

WEEK 1

Creamy Chicken Alfredo Casserole

The whole family will enjoy this cheesy baked pasta, and you'll appreciate how quickly it comes together. We combined a few store-bought staples (rotisserie chicken, jarred Alfredo and pesto sauces) with fresh ingredients (baby spinach and basil) to make a one-dish dinner that will earn a spot in your regular weeknight dinner rotation.

ACTIVE 15 MIN. - TOTAL 50 MIN.
SERVES 4

- 1 (6-oz.) pkg. fresh baby spinach, chopped
- ⅓ cup refrigerated pesto sauce
- 1 (15-oz.) jar Alfredo sauce
- ¼ cup chicken broth
- 12 oz. uncooked penne pasta, cooked according to pkg. directions
- 2 ½ cups chopped rotisserie chicken
- 4 oz. preshredded low-moisture part-skim mozzarella cheese (about 1 cup)
- 2 Tbsp. thinly sliced fresh basil
- ¼ tsp. paprika

1. Preheat oven to 375°F. Toss together spinach and pesto in a medium bowl.
2. Stir together Alfredo sauce and chicken broth in another bowl. Spread one-third of Alfredo mixture (about ½ cup) into a lightly greased 11- x 7-inch baking dish. Top with half of spinach mixture.
3. Stir together cooked pasta, chicken, and remaining Alfredo mixture; spoon half of chicken mixture over spinach mixture. Repeat layers once with remaining spinach mixture and chicken mixture.
4. Bake in preheated oven 30 minutes. Remove from oven, and sprinkle with cheese. Return to oven, and bake until hot and bubbly, about 5 minutes. Top with basil and paprika.

Greek Meatballs with Cucumber–Yogurt Sauce and Rice

This recipe makes enough tender meatballs for sandwiches the next day.

ACTIVE 30 MIN. - TOTAL 40 MIN.
SERVES 4

- 2 lb. ground chuck
- 4 oz. feta cheese, crumbled (about 1 cup)
- 2 Tbsp. chopped fresh oregano
- 1 Tbsp. chopped fresh flat-leaf parsley
- ½ tsp. crushed red pepper
- 1 large egg, lightly beaten
- 2 tsp. kosher salt, divided
- 1 tsp. black pepper, divided
- 1 ½ cups whole milk Greek yogurt (about 12 oz.)
- 1 large cucumber, peeled, seeded, and grated (about ½ cup)
- 3 Tbsp. chopped fresh mint
- 1 Tbsp. chopped fresh dill
- ½ tsp. lemon zest plus 1 Tbsp. fresh juice
- 2 cups cooked basmati rice

1. Preheat broiler with oven rack 6 inches from heat. Place ground chuck, feta cheese, oregano, parsley, crushed red pepper, egg, 1 teaspoon of the salt, and ½ teaspoon of the pepper in large bowl, and gently combine.
2. Shape mixture into 32 meatballs, and place on a large aluminum foil-lined rimmed baking sheet. Broil until meatballs are no longer pink in centers, 8 to 10 minutes.
3. Meanwhile, stir together yogurt, cucumber, mint, dill, lemon zest, lemon juice, and remaining 1 teaspoon salt and ½ teaspoon pepper in a bowl.
4. Reserve 12 meatballs and 1 cup cucumber-yogurt sauce for stuffed pitas (see below). Serve remaining meatballs and cucumber-yogurt sauce with hot cooked rice.

LEFTOVERS Reheat 12 meatballs; stuff 3 meatballs into each of 4 warm pita bread halves. Add lettuce, tomato, and red onion; top with 1 cup cucumber-yogurt sauce.

Sheet Pan Flank Steak, Greens, and Yukon Gold Fries

Marinating the steak the night before makes this one-pan dinner faster and more flavorful.

ACTIVE 5 MIN. - TOTAL 1 HOUR, 7 MIN.
SERVES 4

- 1 ½ lb. flank steak
- 2 garlic cloves, minced
- 2 tsp. chopped fresh rosemary
- 2 tsp. chopped fresh thyme
- 1 tsp. crushed red pepper
- 2 tsp. kosher salt, divided
- 1 tsp. black pepper, divided
- ¼ cup plus 1 Tbsp. extra-virgin olive oil, divided
- 1 lb. Yukon Gold potatoes (about 3 large potatoes), each cut into wedges
- 1 Tbsp. salted butter, melted
- 2 bunches curly kale (about 16 oz.), stemmed, chopped

1. Place flank steak in a large ziplock plastic freezer bag. Stir together garlic, rosemary, thyme, crushed red pepper, 1 teaspoon of the salt, and ½ teaspoon of the black pepper in a small bowl. Whisk in ¼ cup of the olive oil, and pour over steak. Seal bag, and turn to coat. Chill 30 minutes or up to 24 hours.
2. Place top oven rack 6 inches from heat. Preheat oven to 450°F. Stir together potatoes, butter, and remaining 1 tablespoon oil, 1 teaspoon salt, and ½ teaspoon black pepper. Spread in an even layer on a heavy-duty aluminum foil-lined rimmed baking sheet.
3. Bake potatoes in preheated oven 20 minutes. Remove from oven, and move potatoes to outer edges of pan. Place kale in center of pan, and top with steak. Increase oven temperature to broil.
4. Broil 6 minutes. Turn steak, stir vegetables, and broil 6 minutes more or to desired degree of doneness. Remove from oven, and let stand 5 minutes. Cut steak across the grain, and drizzle with pan drippings. Serve steak with kale and potatoes.

Winter Vegetables and Gnocchi

Pillowy store-bought potato gnocchi are a great stand-in for dumplings in this easy and comforting dish. Buy precut butternut squash to save time, but slice any larger pieces of squash in half to ensure that it cooks evenly.

ACTIVE 15 MIN. - TOTAL 30 MIN.
SERVES 4

- 1 (12-oz.) pkg. prechopped fresh butternut squash (about 12 oz.)
- 8 oz. cremini mushrooms, halved
- 1 cup frozen pearl onions, thawed
- 2 Tbsp. extra-virgin olive oil
- 1½ tsp. kosher salt
- ¼ tsp. black pepper
- 1 (16-oz.) pkg. potato gnocchi (such as Gia Russa)
- 2 Tbsp. salted butter, softened
- 2 oz. Parmigiano-Reggiano cheese, shaved (about ½ cup), divided
  Chopped fresh flat-leaf parsley

1. Toss together butternut squash, mushrooms, pearl onions, olive oil, salt, and pepper. Spoon vegetable mixture into a lightly greased 13-x 9-inch baking pan; place pan in oven. Preheat oven to 450°F, leaving pan in oven as it preheats. Bake vegetable mixture in preheated oven until squash is tender and browned, about 20 minutes.
2. Meanwhile, prepare gnocchi according to package directions, reserving 1 cup of the cooking water.
3. Remove vegetable mixture from oven. Stir in gnocchi and softened butter. (Be careful—the pan will be hot.) Gradually add up to 1 cup reserved cooking water, ¼ cup at a time, stirring until a slightly thick sauce begins to form. Stir in ¼ cup of the shredded cheese. Sprinkle top with remaining ¼ cup cheese. Divide the vegetable and dumpling mixture evenly among 4 bowls. Garnish with chopped parsley, if desired, and serve immediately.

Sausage Calzones

ACTIVE 45 MIN. - TOTAL 1 HOUR, 25 MIN.
SERVES 8

- 2 (1-lb.) fresh deli pizza dough pieces
- 3 Tbsp. extra-virgin olive oil, divided
- 2 lb. ground sweet Italian sausage
- 1 (28-oz.) can whole San Marzano tomatoes, drained
- 2 garlic cloves, minced
- 1 Tbsp. chopped fresh basil
- 1 Tbsp. chopped fresh flat-leaf parsley
- 2 tsp. chopped fresh oregano
- 1 tsp. kosher salt
- ½ tsp. black pepper
- 16 oz. preshredded low-moisture part-skim mozzarella
- 2 large eggs, lightly beaten
- 1 tsp. water
  Favorite jarred marinara sauce, for dipping

1. Place 2 large rimmed baking sheets (at least 17 x 11 inches) in oven. Preheat oven to 450°F, leaving pans in oven as it preheats. Place pizza dough pieces on a lightly floured surface, and cover each with plastic wrap. Let stand 20 minutes.
2. Meanwhile, heat 1 tablespoon of the oil in a large skillet over medium-high. Add sausage, and cook, stirring often, until browned and crumbled, about 10 minutes.
3. Stir in tomatoes, crushing with a wooden spoon. Add garlic, basil, parsley, oregano, salt, and pepper, and bring to boil over medium-high. Reduce heat to medium, and simmer 10 minutes. Remove from heat.
4. Cut each pizza dough piece into 4 equal portions. Roll each portion to a 8-inch circle on a lightly floured surface. Transfer 4 of the dough circles to a large piece of parchment paper. Transfer remaining 4 dough circles to another large piece of parchment paper.
5. Spread ¾ cup of sausage mixture over half of each dough circle. Top each with ½ cup shredded mozzarella. Whisk together eggs and water; brush a small amount of egg mixture around edges of each dough circle. Fold dough over filling, pressing and crimping edges to seal.
6. Carefully slide 1 parchment paper piece with unbaked calzones onto a hot baking sheet; repeat with remaining unbaked calzones and hot baking sheet. Brush tops of calzones with remaining 2 tablespoons oil. Bake in preheated oven until dough is golden brown and crisp, 18 to 20 minutes, switching pans top rack to bottom rack halfway through baking. Let stand 5 minutes before serving. Serve with marinara sauce on the side.

10-MINUTE DESSERT

Chocolate Banana Puddings

SERVES 4

Coarsely crush 2 **chocolate wafers** into the bottom of each of 4 (6-ounce) glasses, custard cups, or ramekins. Top evenly with pudding from 2 **pudding cups** and half of the slices from 2 **bananas;** repeat layers. Garnish each pudding with 1 chocolate wafer.

TIME-SAVING TIP
AVOID THE RUNAROUND

It's amazing how multiple trips to the pantry or time spent searching through a spice rack can delay dinner. Store your most-used ingredients— salt, cooking spray, flour—within close reach.

WEEK 2

Sweet Potato Soup

This creamy soup makes excellent leftovers to take to work or anywhere on the go.

ACTIVE 20 MIN. - TOTAL 50 MIN.
SERVES 8

2	Tbsp. olive oil
1 ½	cups chopped yellow onion (from 1 large onion)
1	cup roughly chopped carrots (3 carrots)
1	Tbsp. chopped garlic
3	lb. sweet potatoes, peeled and cut into ½-inch cubes
2	lb. Yukon Gold potatoes, peeled and cut into ½-inch cubes
1 ½	tsp. kosher salt
1	tsp. black pepper
1	tsp. ground cumin
¼	tsp. ground cinnamon
⅛	tsp. cayenne pepper
7	cups chicken stock
2	Tbsp. salted butter
1	cup finely chopped pecans
½	cup plain yogurt
¼	cup torn fresh flat-leaf parsley leaves

1. Preheat oven to 450°F. Heat oil in a large Dutch oven over medium-high. Add onion and carrots, and cook, stirring, until softened, about 5 minutes. Add garlic, and cook, stirring, until fragrant, 1 minute. Add sweet potatoes, Yukon Gold potatoes, salt, black pepper, cumin, cinnamon, and cayenne pepper, and cook, stirring, 1 minute. Add stock; bring to a boil. Reduce heat to medium-low, and simmer until potatoes are very tender, about 30 minutes.
2. Melt butter in a skillet over medium-high. Add pecans, and cook, stirring often, until toasted, about 8 minutes. Transfer to a bowl.
3. Transfer potato mixture, in batches, to a blender. Remove center piece of blender lid (to allow steam to escape); secure lid on blender, and place a clean towel over opening in lid. Process until smooth. (Or process soup in Dutch oven using an immersion blender.)
4. Top servings with 2 tablespoons pecans, 1 tablespoon yogurt, and ½ tablespoon parsley.

Chicken Bog

You'll love our superfast take on this homey dish of chicken and vegetables in creamy rice.

ACTIVE 30 MIN. - TOTAL 30 MIN.
SERVES 4

2	Tbsp. olive oil
1	cup chopped yellow onion (from 1 onion)
1	cup chopped carrots (from about 3 carrots)
2	tsp. chopped garlic
1 ½	cups uncooked long-grain white rice
1	tsp. kosher salt
¾	tsp. black pepper
4	cups chicken stock
1	(4-inch) piece Parmesan cheese rind
4	cups shredded boneless, skinless rotisserie chicken (about 1 rotisserie chicken)
3	Tbsp. chopped fresh flat-leaf parsley
1	Tbsp. fresh lemon juice
1 ½	oz. Parmesan cheese, shaved (about ⅓ cup)

1. Heat oil in a Dutch oven over medium-high. Add onion and carrots, and cook, stirring occasionally, until beginning to soften, about 4 minutes. Add garlic, rice, salt, and pepper, and cook until fragrant and rice begins to toast, about 3 minutes.
2. Stir in stock, and add Parmesan rind; bring to a boil. Reduce heat to low. Cover and simmer until rice is just cooked through, about 18 minutes. Uncover and discard rind; stir in chicken. Cook until chicken is heated through, about 5 minutes.
3. Stir in parsley and lemon juice just before serving, and top with shaved Parmesan.

Cabbage, Mushroom, and Bacon Pasta

ACTIVE 25 MIN. - TOTAL 25 MIN.
SERVES 4

4	thick-cut bacon slices, chopped
12	oz. uncooked bucatini pasta
8	oz. baby portobello mushrooms, sliced
1	tsp. kosher salt
¾	tsp. black pepper
4	cups shredded savoy cabbage (about ½ head of cabbage)
2	oz. cream cheese, softened
2	Tbsp. fresh thyme leaves
1	oz. Parmesan cheese, shredded (about ¼ cup)

1. Bring a large saucepan filled with water to a boil over high.
2. While water comes to a boil, cook bacon in a large skillet over medium, stirring occasionally, until crisp, about 8 minutes. Transfer to a plate lined with paper towels, reserving drippings in skillet.
3. Cook pasta according to package directions. Drain well, reserving 1 cup pasta cooking water.
4. Add mushrooms to skillet, and sprinkle with salt and pepper. Increase heat to medium-high, and cook, stirring occasionally, until golden, about 8 minutes. Add cabbage, and cook until cabbage wilts and just begins to caramelize, about 4 minutes. Add cream cheese and ½ cup of the reserved pasta water, and stir until smooth. Fold in cooked pasta, and cook until heated through, about 2 minutes. (Stir in more cooking water if needed.) Divide evenly among 4 bowls, and top with cooked bacon, thyme, and Parmesan.

TIME-SAVING TIP
SUNDAY PREP

We've all experienced that sinking feeling: It's 6 o'clock on a Tuesday, and—oops!—we forgot to defrost the pork chops. Create your five-day menu on Sunday, and pull out the upcoming week's meat from the freezer to let it defrost safely in the fridge. The payoff will be faster home-cooked dinners all week long.

Fried Pork Chops with Peas and Potatoes

ACTIVE 30 MIN. - TOTAL 30 MIN.
SERVES 4

- 1 ½ lb. Yukon Gold potatoes, quartered
- 1 medium-size yellow onion, quartered
- 3 Tbsp. olive oil, divided
- 1 ½ tsp. kosher salt, divided
- 1 ¼ tsp. black pepper, divided
- ⅓ cup plus 1 Tbsp. all-purpose flour, divided
- 4 (6-oz.) bone-in pork chops (about ½ inch thick)
- 3 Tbsp. unsalted butter, divided
- ¼ cup dry white wine
- 1 cup chicken stock
- 1 (12- or 15-oz.) pkg. microwave-in-bag petite green peas
- 2 Tbsp. chopped fresh flat-leaf parsley

1. Preheat oven to 450°F. Place potatoes and onion in a rimmed baking sheet. Drizzle with 1 tablespoon olive oil, and sprinkle with ½ teaspoon each salt and pepper. Bake in preheated oven until potatoes are golden brown and tender and onions are soft, about 25 minutes.

2. Meanwhile, stir together ⅓ cup flour and ½ teaspoon each salt and pepper in a small, shallow dish. Dredge pork chops in flour mixture, evenly coating all sides. Heat remaining 2 tablespoons olive oil in a large skillet over medium-high. Add pork chops, and cook until golden, about 4 minutes per side. Transfer pork chops to a platter.

3. Melt 2 tablespoons of the butter in skillet. Add 1 tablespoon of the flour, whisking until smooth. Add wine, and cook, stirring and scraping to loosen browned bits from bottom of skillet, until reduced by about one-third, about 2 minutes. Add chicken stock; bring to a boil, and reduce heat to medium-low. Cook, stirring occasionally, until sauce is thickened, about 4 minutes.

4. Cook peas according to package directions; transfer to a bowl. Stir in remaining ½ teaspoon salt, ¼ teaspoon pepper, and 1 tablespoon butter until combined. Serve pork chops with potato mixture, peas, and sauce; sprinkle with parsley just before serving.

10-MINUTE DESSERT

Mini Lemon Cream Pies

SERVES 4

Divide 1 (11.5-oz.) jar high-quality **lemon curd** (such as Stonewall Kitchen) evenly among 4 **mini graham cracker piecrusts** (from a 4-oz. pkg.). Beat ¾ cup **heavy cream** and 2 Tbsp. **powdered sugar** with an electric mixer on high speed until stiff peaks form; spoon over lemon curd in piecrusts. Top with 1 tsp. **lemon zest.**

Sheet Pan Nachos

Kick off the weekend with a fast and fun dinner that's completely customizable.

ACTIVE 20 MIN. - TOTAL 30 MIN.
SERVES 4

- 12 oz. ground chuck
- ½ cup chopped yellow onion (from 1 small onion)
- ½ tsp. ground cumin
- ½ tsp. chili powder
- ½ tsp. kosher salt, divided
- ½ tsp. black pepper, divided
- 9 oz. corn tortilla chips
- 1 (15-oz.) can pinto beans, drained and rinsed
- 12 oz. preshredded Mexican 4-cheese blend (about 3 cups)
- ½ cup minced red onion (about 1 small onion)
- ¼ cup pickled jalapeño slices
- 1 medium-size ripe avocado, diced
- ½ cup sour cream
- ¼ cup chopped fresh cilantro
- 1 cup jarred salsa
- 1 lime, cut into wedges

1. Preheat oven to 400°F. Place ground chuck and onion in a large nonstick skillet over medium. Sprinkle with cumin, chili powder, and ½ teaspoon each of salt and pepper. Cook, stirring often, until meat crumbles and is no longer pink and onions are softened, about 8 minutes. Transfer mixture to a plate lined with paper towels to drain.

2. Line a large rimmed baking sheet with aluminum foil. Spread chips across pan in a single layer with as little overlap as possible. Top chips evenly with meat mixture, beans, and cheese.

3. Bake in preheated oven until cheese melts and just begins to brown in places, about 8 minutes. Remove chips from oven, and top with onion, jalapeño, avocado, sour cream, and cilantro. Serve with salsa and lime wedges.

WEEK 1

WEEK 2

WEEK 3

MONDAY

Creamy Chicken Alfredo Casserole, page 58

TUESDAY

Greek Meatballs with Cucumber-Yogurt Sauce and Rice, page 58

MONDAY

Sweet Potato Soup, page 60

TUESDAY

Chicken Bog, page 60

MONDAY

Quick and Easy Spaghetti Bolognese, page 64

TUESDAY

BBQ Rub Roasted Chickens with Potatoes and Carrots, page 64

WEDNESDAY

Sheet Pan Flank Steak, Greens, and Yukon Gold Fries, page 58

THURSDAY

Winter Vegetables and Gnocchi, page 59

FRIDAY

Sausage Calzones, page 59

WEDNESDAY

Cabbage, Mushroom, and Bacon Pasta, page 60

THURSDAY

Fried Pork Chops with Peas and Potatoes, page 61

FRIDAY

Sheet Pan Nachos, page 61

WEDNESDAY

Chicken and Sausage Jambalaya, page 64

THURSDAY

Hearty Beef and Freezer Veggie Soup, page 65

FRIDAY

Fish Tacos and Topping Bar, page 65

WEEK 3

Quick and Easy Spaghetti Bolognese

A rich and seasoned meat sauce doesn't require a full day of stirring at the stove—all you need is 25 minutes. We love the robust flavor of Italian sausage in this chunky tomato sauce, but you can substitute ground beef or pork too.

ACTIVE 15 MIN. - TOTAL 25 MIN.
SERVES 4

- 1   Tbsp. olive oil
- 1   lb. sweet Italian sausage, casings removed
- ½   cup chopped sweet onion
- ½   cup chopped green bell pepper
- 2   garlic cloves, minced
- 1   (24-oz.) jar tomato and basil pasta sauce (such as Barilla or Classico)
- 1   tsp. granulated sugar
- ½   tsp. kosher salt
- ¼   tsp. black pepper
- 1   (16-oz.) pkg. spaghetti or linguine noodles
- 2   Tbsp. chopped fresh basil
     Shaved Parmesan cheese (optional)

1. Heat oil in a large skillet over medium-high. Add sausage, onion, bell pepper, and garlic, and cook, stirring, until sausage is browned and vegetables are tender, 8 to 10 minutes.
2. Stir in pasta sauce, sugar, salt, and black pepper; bring mixture to a boil over medium-high. Reduce heat to low; simmer 15 minutes.
3. Cook pasta according to package directions, reserving ½ cup cooking water. Stir chopped basil into meat sauce. Stir in up to ½ cup reserved cooking water, adding ¼ cup at a time, if needed, to reach desired consistency. Serve sauce over cooked spaghetti. Garnish with shaved Parmesan cheese, if desired.

BBQ Rub Roasted Chickens with Potatoes and Carrots

ACTIVE 15 MIN. - TOTAL 1 HOUR, 30 MIN.
SERVES 4

- 4   tsp. dark brown sugar
- 1   Tbsp. smoked paprika
- ½   tsp. ground cumin
- ½   tsp. garlic powder
- ½   tsp. onion powder
- 5   tsp. kosher salt, divided
- 2 ½ tsp. black pepper, divided
- 2   (4- to 5-lb.) whole chickens
- 3   Tbsp. olive oil, divided
- 1 ½ lb. small red potatoes, halved
- 1   (8-oz.) pkg. baby carrots
- 1   Tbsp. chopped fresh flat-leaf parsley

1. Preheat oven to 375°F. Stir together first 5 ingredients, 4 teaspoons of the salt, and 2 teaspoons of the pepper. Remove necks and giblets from chickens, and reserve for another use. Pat chickens dry.
2. Sprinkle 1 teaspoon brown sugar mixture inside cavity of each chicken. Rub 1 tablespoon olive oil into skin of each chicken. Sprinkle evenly with remaining brown sugar mixture; rub into skin. Tuck wing tips under.
3. Toss together potatoes, carrots, remaining 1 tablespoon olive oil, remaining 1 teaspoon salt, and remaining ½ teaspoon pepper. Spread potato mixture in a single layer in a 17- x 12-inch rimmed baking sheet. Place chickens, breast side up, facing in opposite directions (for even browning), on top of potato mixture.
4. Bake in preheated oven until a meat thermometer inserted in thickest portion of thigh registers 165°F, 1 hour to 1 hour and 15 minutes. Cover and let stand 10 minutes before slicing. Stir parsley into vegetables.

LEFTOVERS Toss together 2 heads chopped **romaine** lettuce; 1 cup thinly sliced **cucumber;** 2 cups halved **cherry tomatoes;** and 1 **avocado,** cut into wedges. Top with sliced leftover **BBQ Rub Roasted Chicken.** Serve with your favorite **buttermilk dressing.**

Chicken and Sausage Jambalaya

This hearty one-pot meal will transport you to New Orleans on the busiest week-night. Like it spicy? Serve with hot sauce on the side.

ACTIVE 25 MIN. - TOTAL 50 MIN.
SERVES 8

- 1   Tbsp. canola oil
- 2   lb. boneless, skinless chicken thighs, cut into 1 ½-inch cubes
- 1   lb. smoked sausage (such as Conecuh sausage), cut into 1-inch pieces
- 1   large white onion, chopped (about 2 cups)
- 1   large green bell pepper, chopped (about 1 ½ cups)
- 1   cup chopped celery (about 1 stalk)
- 3   garlic cloves, minced
- 2   bay leaves
- 1   Tbsp. Creole seasoning
- 1   tsp. dried thyme
- 1   tsp. dried oregano
- 2   cups uncooked converted rice
- 3   cups chicken broth
- 2   (14.5-oz.) cans diced fire-roasted tomatoes
     Sliced scallions (optional)

1. Heat oil in a Dutch oven over medium-high. Add chicken and sausage, and cook, stirring constantly, until browned on all sides, 8 to 10 minutes. Remove with a slotted spoon to paper towels; blot with paper towels.
2. Add onion, bell pepper, celery, garlic, bay leaves, Creole seasoning, thyme, and oregano to hot drippings; cook over medium-high until vegetables are tender, 5 to 7 minutes. Stir in rice, and cook until fragrant, about 3 minutes. Stir in chicken broth, tomatoes, chicken, and sausage. Bring to a boil over high. Cover, reduce heat to medium, and simmer, stirring occasionally, until rice is tender, about 20 minutes. Garnish with sliced scallions, if desired.

Hearty Beef and Freezer Veggie Soup

ACTIVE 40 MIN. - TOTAL 40 MIN.
SERVES 8

- 1 Tbsp. olive oil
- 1 lb. cubed lean stew meat
- 1 (12-oz.) pkg. frozen seasoning blend (such as Pictsweet)
- 2 garlic cloves, minced
- 2 (32-oz.) cartons vegetable broth
- 2 (14.5-oz.) cans petite diced tomatoes
- 2 cups frozen cut corn
- 1 cup frozen cut okra
- 1 cup frozen baby lima beans
- 1 cup frozen cut green beans
- ½ tsp. black pepper
- ½ tsp. dried thyme
- ½ cup uncooked ditalini pasta
  Refrigerated basil pesto (optional)

1. Heat oil in a Dutch oven over medium-high. Add stew meat, seasoning blend, and garlic, and cook, stirring often, until meat is browned and seasoning blend is tender, about 8 to 10 minutes.
2. Stir in vegetable broth, tomatoes, corn, okra, lima beans, green beans, pepper, and thyme, and bring mixture to a boil over medium-high; reduce heat to low, and simmer, stirring occasionally, until vegetables are tender, 15 to 20 minutes.
3. Stir in pasta, and cook, stirring occasionally, until pasta is tender, 10 to 12 minutes. Top each serving with 1 to 2 tsp. basil pesto, if desired.

TIME-SAVING TIP
TURN UP THE HEAT

Pasta is one of the quickest meals you can make, but there's an easy way to get it on the table even faster: When you're filling your stockpot from the tap, use very hot water to kick-start the boiling process. (Try this to speed up blanching or boiling vegetables too.)

Fish Tacos and Topping Bar

ACTIVE 40 MIN. - TOTAL 55 MIN.
SERVES 8

- 2 lb. firm white fish fillets (such as tilapia, grouper, sea bass, or red snapper)
- 1 tsp. kosher salt
- 1 tsp. black pepper
- 2 large egg whites, lightly beaten
- 1 cup finely ground corn chips (such as Fritos)
- 16 (6-inch) corn or flour tortillas
  Asian Slaw (recipe below)
  Quick Chipotle Cream (recipe below)
  Toppings: chopped tomatoes, shredded iceberg lettuce, sliced avocado, chopped fresh cilantro, lime wedges

1. Preheat oven to 400°F. Pat fish dry with paper towels; sprinkle evenly with salt and pepper. Place egg whites in a shallow dish. Place ground corn chips in a separate shallow dish. Dip each fillet in egg whites, and dredge in ground corn chips, shaking off excess.
2. Arrange fish on a large baking sheet coated with cooking spray. Bake in preheated oven until fish is cooked through, about 15 minutes.
3. Serve fish in tortillas with Asian Slaw, Quick Chipotle Cream, and desired toppings.

Asian Slaw

SERVES 8

Whisk together ⅓ cup **rice vinegar,** 1 Tbsp. granulated **sugar,** 2 tsp. **toasted sesame oil,** 1 Tbsp. **soy sauce,** 1 tsp. grated fresh **ginger,** 1 tsp. **Asian chili-garlic sauce,** ¼ tsp. **kosher salt,** and ¼ tsp. black **pepper.** Stir in 1 (16-oz.) pkg. tri-color **coleslaw mix** and ¼ cup chopped fresh **cilantro.**

Quick Chipotle Cream

SERVES 8

Stir together 1 (8-oz.) container **sour cream,** 1 seeded and minced **chipotle pepper in adobo sauce** (from can), ½ tsp. **lime zest,** 1 Tbsp. fresh **lime juice,** and ¼ tsp. **kosher salt.**

10-MINUTE DESSERT

Ambrosia Meringue Trifles

SERVES 4

Beat 1 cup **heavy cream,** 2 Tbsp. **powdered sugar,** and 1 tsp. **vanilla** extract with an electric mixer on high speed until stiff peaks form. Combine 1 cup refrigerated **orange segments,** drained, and 1 cup refrigerated **grapefruit segments,** drained; divide citrus mixture evenly among 4 (10-oz.) glasses. Drizzle each with 1 ½ tsp. **honey.** Crumble 1 store-bought **vanilla meringue cookie** over fruit in each glass; top evenly with half of whipped cream. Sprinkle each with 1 ½ Tbsp. toasted unsweetened flaked **coconut.** Repeat layers once.

WEEK 4

Steak, Sweet Potato, and Blue Cheese Salad

Salad for dinner usually sounds like a shortcut. Not so fast. Toss together this satisfying, surprisingly hearty mix of sweet and savory ingredients, and serve with a loaf of focaccia on the side.

ACTIVE 40 MIN. - TOTAL 50 MIN.
SERVES 4

      2   sweet potatoes (about 1 lb.), peeled and cut into ¼-inch-thick rounds
      7   Tbsp. olive oil, divided
   1½   tsp. kosher salt, divided
      1   tsp. black pepper, divided
   1½   lb. flank steak
      1   (5-oz.) pkg. mixed baby greens
      4   cups baby arugula (about 2½ oz.)
      ¾   cup thinly sliced red onion (from ½ onion)
      3   oz. blue cheese, crumbled (about ¾ cup)
   2½   Tbsp. balsamic vinegar
      1   tsp. Dijon mustard

1. Preheat oven to 425°F. Place sweet potato slices on an aluminum foil-lined large rimmed baking sheet. Drizzle with 1 tablespoon oil, and sprinkle with ¼ teaspoon each of salt and pepper; toss to coat. Spread potatoes in a single layer. Bake in preheated oven until lightly browned and tender, 12 to 15 minutes. Cool 5 minutes.

2. Meanwhile, brush steak with 1 tablespoon of the oil, and rub with 1 teaspoon of the salt and remaining ¾ teaspoon pepper; let stand 10 minutes. Heat a grill pan over medium-high; brush with 1 tablespoon of the oil. Cook steak 6 to 7 minutes per side for medium-rare, or to desired degree of doneness. Remove steak from pan, and let stand 10 minutes. Cut steak across the grain into thin slices, reserving steak for sandwiches the following day, if desired.

3. Divide baby greens, arugula, red onion, blue cheese, potatoes, and sliced steak among 4 serving plates. Whisk together vinegar, mustard, and remaining ¼ cup oil and ¼ teaspoon salt; drizzle over salads.

Tortellini, White Bean, and Turnip Greens Soup

Looking for a meatless meal that still satisfies? Try this filling soup loaded with pasta, beans, and vegetables. Swap out the tortellini for refrigerated ravioli if you prefer.

ACTIVE 30 MIN. - TOTAL 30 MIN.
SERVES 4

      2   Tbsp. olive oil
      1   cup chopped yellow onion (about 1 small onion)
      ½   cup thinly sliced celery (about 1 stalk)
      ½   cup chopped carrot (about 1 medium carrot)
      1   tsp. minced garlic (about 1 clove)
      6   cups roughly chopped turnip greens
      1   (32-oz.) container vegetable broth
      1   (15.5-oz.) can cannellini beans, drained and rinsed
      1   (14.5-oz.) can diced tomatoes with basil, garlic, and oregano, undrained
      1   (9-oz.) pkg. refrigerated cheese tortellini
      1   oz. Parmesan cheese, shaved

Heat oil in a Dutch oven over medium. Add onion, celery, carrot, and garlic, and cook, stirring often, until onion is tender and celery and carrot are almost tender, about 8 minutes. Add turnip greens, in 2 batches, stirring until wilted after each addition. Stir in broth, beans, and tomatoes, and bring to a boil over medium-high. Add tortellini, and cook until pasta is tender, about 4 minutes. Top with Parmesan.

TIME-SAVING TIP
STOCK YOUR FREEZER

The frozen food section of the supermarket is a time-crunched cook's secret weapon. Stock up on frozen prechopped vegetables, precooked grains (such as quinoa and brown rice), filled pastas (such as ravioli and tortellini), and pizza dough.

Ham and Lima Bean Fried Rice

This delicious Southern twist on fried rice is made with pantry and freezer staples, so you probably already have most of the ingredients on hand.

ACTIVE 30 MIN. - TOTAL 30 MIN.
SERVES 4

   1½   cups frozen baby lima beans
      5   scallions
      3   Tbsp. peanut or canola oil, divided
      2   large eggs, lightly beaten
      ⅛   tsp. kosher salt
      1   cup (about 8 oz.) cubed ham
      ⅔   cup matchstick carrots, roughly chopped
      2   tsp. minced garlic (about 2 cloves)
      2   (8.8-oz.) pouches microwavable white rice (such as Uncle Ben's Ready Rice), prepared according to pkg. directions
      1   Tbsp. toasted sesame oil
      ¼   cup soy sauce

1. Cook lima beans in boiling water to cover in a medium saucepan over medium-high until tender, 15 to 20 minutes. Drain.

2. Meanwhile, thinly slice green parts of scallions, and set aside. Thinly slice white parts of scallions, and set aside.

3. Heat 1 tablespoon of the oil in a large nonstick skillet over medium-high. Pour beaten egg into skillet; sprinkle with salt, and cook, without stirring, until egg is set on top and lightly browned on the bottom, about 1 minute. Flip and cook 20 seconds. Transfer cooked egg to a cutting board; fold in half, and roughly chop.

4. Heat remaining 2 tablespoons oil in skillet over medium-high. Add white scallion slices, ham, carrots, and garlic; cook, stirring constantly, until ham is lightly browned and vegetables are tender, about 4 minutes. Add rice and sesame oil; cook, stirring constantly, until rice is hot, about 2 minutes. Stir in chopped egg, soy sauce, lima beans, and green scallion slices.

Buttermilk Chicken Tenders with Roasted Potatoes and Green Beans

ACTIVE 25 MIN. - TOTAL 55 MIN.
SERVES 4

- 1 cup whole buttermilk
- 3 garlic cloves, pressed
- 1 ½ tsp. kosher salt, divided
- 1 tsp. black pepper, divided
- 1 ½ lb. chicken breast tenders (about 12)
- 1 lb. small red potatoes, cut into ½-inch-thick wedges
- 1 (8-oz.) pkg. haricots verts (French green beans)
- 2 medium shallots, sliced
- 4 Tbsp. olive oil, divided
- 1 ½ cup panko (Japanese-style breadcrumbs)
- 3 Tbsp. chopped fresh flat-leaf parsley, divided
- 3 Tbsp. salted butter, divided

1. Preheat oven to 425°F. Combine buttermilk, garlic, 1 teaspoon of the salt, and ½ teaspoon of the pepper in a large ziplock plastic freezer bag; add chicken, seal bag, and toss to coat. Let stand at room temperature 30 minutes.
2. Combine potatoes, haricots verts, and shallots in a large rimmed baking sheet. Drizzle with 2 tablespoons of the oil, and sprinkle with remaining ½ teaspoon each of salt and pepper. Stir to coat, and spread in a single layer. Bake in preheated oven until potatoes and haricots verts are browned and tender, about 20 minutes, stirring once after 15 minutes.
3. Combine panko and 2 tablespoons of the parsley in a shallow bowl. Remove chicken from plastic bag, discarding any mixture in bag. Dredge chicken tenders in panko mixture, pressing to adhere.
4. Heat 1 tablespoon of the oil and 1 ½ tablespoons of the butter in a large skillet over medium. Add half of chicken; cook until golden brown and done, 3 to 4 minutes per side. Remove to a serving platter; wipe pan, and repeat with remaining 1 tablespoon oil, 1 ½ tablespoons butter, and half of chicken. Serve chicken with potatoes and haricots verts. Top chicken and vegetables with remaining 1 tablespoon parsley.

10-MINUTE DESSERT

Sautéed Apple Crisp
SERVES 4

Melt 3 Tbsp. salted **butter** in a large skillet over medium-high. Add 2 large peeled and thinly sliced **Honeycrisp apples;** increase heat to high, and cook until apples begin to soften, about 3 minutes, stirring once. Sprinkle with ¼ cup packed **light brown sugar** and ½ tsp. ground **cinnamon,** and cook, stirring occasionally, until sugar melts and apples are tender, about 3 minutes. Whisk together ⅓ cup **apple cider** and 1 tsp. **all-purpose flour;** add to skillet, and cook, stirring constantly, until thickened, about 1 minute. Divide apple mixture evenly among 4 bowls; sprinkle each with ¼ cup **maple-pecan granola,** and top with a scoop of vanilla or cinnamon **ice cream.**

BBQ Pork Loaded Baked Potatoes

Set up a top-your-own potato bar at your next family movie or game night.

ACTIVE 45 MIN. - TOTAL 50 MIN.
SERVES 8

- 8 medium-size russet potatoes (about 8 oz. each)
- 2 Tbsp. olive oil
- 1 large yellow onion, thinly sliced
- 1 large red bell pepper, thinly sliced vertically
- ¼ tsp. kosher salt
- ¼ tsp. black pepper
- 8 oz. Monterey Jack cheese, shredded (about 2 cups)
- 1 ½ lb. pulled smoked pork, warmed
- 2 cups corn chips (such as Fritos), coarsely crushed
- 2 small ripe avocados, diced
- 1 ½ cups barbecue sauce
- ¼ cup chopped fresh cilantro
- 1 (14-oz.) pkg. coleslaw mix
- ¾ cup white barbecue sauce

1. Preheat oven to 400°F. Place potatoes on an aluminum foil-lined large rimmed baking sheet. Bake in preheated oven until very tender, about 45 minutes.
2. Meanwhile, heat oil in a large skillet over medium. Add onion slices, and cook, stirring often, until tender and lightly browned, 5 to 7 minutes. Add bell pepper, and cook, stirring often, 5 minutes. Remove from heat, and sprinkle with salt and black pepper.
3. Cut a lengthwise slit down center of each potato (do not cut all the way through); squeeze sides to open. Slightly mash cooked potato pulp, and push toward opening. Top with cheese, pork, onion mixture, corn chips, and avocado; drizzle with barbecue sauce, and sprinkle with cilantro.
4. Toss together coleslaw mix and white barbecue sauce; serve with pork-stuffed potatoes.

WEEK 4

MONDAY

Steak, Sweet Potato, and Blue Cheese Salad,
page 66

TUESDAY

Tortellini, White Bean, and Turnip Greens Soup,
page 66

WEDNESDAY

Ham and Lima Bean Fried Rice, page 66

THURSDAY

Buttermilk Chicken Tenders with Roasted Potatoes
and Green Beans, page 67

FRIDAY

BBQ Pork Loaded Baked Potatoes, page 67

½ tsp. vanilla extract
¾ cup heavy cream
ADDITIONAL INGREDIENT
1 Tbsp. powdered sugar

1. Prepare the Cakes: Combine chopped semisweet chocolate and heavy cream in a small microwave-safe bowl. Microwave on HIGH 30 seconds. Let stand 1 minute; whisk until melted and smooth. Place plastic wrap directly on chocolate mixture (to prevent a skin from forming); chill until firm, about 2 hours. Chocolate mixture can be prepared 1 day in advance; store, covered, in the refrigerator.

2. Preheat oven to 400°F. Grease 4 (8-ounce) ramekins with butter; dust with unsweetened cocoa, and tap out excess. Whisk together flour, cocoa, baking soda, and salt in a medium bowl. Whisk together melted butter, granulated sugar, buttermilk, food coloring, vanilla, vinegar, and egg yolk in a separate bowl. Add butter mixture to flour mixture, and whisk just until blended. Divide batter evenly among prepared ramekins.

3. Using a small (1¼- or 1½-inch) cookie scoop, portion chilled chocolate mixture into 4 balls. Place 1 chocolate ball in center of batter in each ramekin, pressing lightly. (Chocolate will sink into batter as it bakes.) Place ramekins on a baking sheet. Bake in preheated oven until center springs back when lightly pressed, about 18 minutes.

4. Meanwhile, prepare the Cream Cheese Whipped Cream: Stir together cream cheese, powdered sugar, and vanilla in a medium bowl until smooth. Add heavy cream; beat with an electric mixer on medium-high speed until soft peaks form, 30 seconds to 1 minute, scraping down sides of bowl as needed.

5. Remove cakes from oven. Immediately run an offset spatula or thin knife around outer edge of cakes to loosen; invert each cake onto a serving plate. Dust cakes evenly with 1 tablespoon powdered sugar. Top cakes with Cream Cheese Whipped Cream, and serve immediately.

Hit the Sweet Spot

Sink your fork into a mini red velvet cake filled with a gooey chocolate center

Molten Red Velvet Cakes

Sharing dessert is overrated. These single-serving molten cakes are a sweet way to end a Valentine's Day dinner at home. Best part? The chocolate mixture and frosting can be made 1 day in advance, and the cakes take less than 20 minutes to bake.

ACTIVE 20 MIN. - TOTAL 2 HOURS, 35 MIN.
SERVES 4

CAKES
2 oz. semisweet chocolate baking bar, finely chopped
¼ cup heavy cream
1 cup cake flour
1½ tsp. unsweetened cocoa plus more for ramekins
¼ tsp. baking soda
¼ tsp. salt
½ cup salted butter, melted, plus more for ramekins
½ cup granulated sugar
6 Tbsp. buttermilk
1½ tsp. red liquid food coloring
½ tsp. vanilla extract
½ tsp. apple cider vinegar
1 large egg yolk
CREAM CHEESE WHIPPED CREAM
2 oz. cream cheese, softened
3 Tbsp. powdered sugar

COOKING (SL) SCHOOL

PANTRY PRIMER

Choose the Right Kind of Rice

LONG-GRAIN
Slim and long, this rice has a dry, fluffy texture when cooked. Varieties include basmati and jasmine.

MEDIUM-GRAIN
Starchy, plump rice that gets sticky when cooked and is best for risotto. Varieties include Arborio.

SHORT-GRAIN
Fatter and rounder, this rice clumps together and stays tender, even after cooling. Great for sushi.

WILD
This chewy, nutty-tasting rice is actually a type of grass. Often combined with other grains, like white and brown rice.

Master Fluffy Rice

HOW TO

Start with a 2-to-1 ratio of water to rice. Bring water to a boil. Stir in rice; add salt and butter to taste. Reduce heat to low. Cover with a tight-fitting lid, and let simmer. Check on it after about 18 minutes. When rice is tender but still firm, remove from the heat. Cover and let stand 5 to 7 minutes. Fluff with a fork, and serve.

IN SEASON

Why Citrus Zest is Best

Want to add an extra kick to your favorite pasta, cake, or even biscuit recipe? Put the peels of lemons, oranges, grapefruits, or other citrus fruits to work. Here, four bright ideas for incorporating them.

BAKING. Pulse in food processor; then stir into granulated sugar.

DRESSING. Whisk into a vinaigrette for a fruity, aromatic note.

SMEARING. Blend into butter, and spread onto toast or biscuits.

DRIZZLING. Make a tangy marinade for meats or seafood.

KNOW-HOW

Secrets to Three Super Dips

❶
SPINACH DIP
When using cooked greens, wring as much liquid out of the vegetables as possible to prevent a watery dip. Squeeze out excess water with a potato ricer, or press the greens against a fine-mesh strainer.

❷
GUACAMOLE
Prep all of the ingredients, and then mash in the avocado right before serving to keep it from turning brown.

❸
SALSA
Season with salt; then let it stand for 10 minutes so the tomatoes release their juices. Serve at room temperature for the most robust flavor.

PAM LOLLEY
SL Test Kitchen Professional

"To enhance the flavor of a chocolate dessert, dust pan with cocoa powder instead of flour."

March

LET THEM EAT CAKE

Julia Child once famously quipped that a party without cake was just a meeting. Smart lady, that Julia. To make sure your next celebration is party worthy, count on these festive delights for any occasion.

Buttermilk-Lime Mini Cakes with Vanilla-Mascarpone Buttercream

The cakes are brushed twice with a tangy lime syrup (easily made with melted frozen limeade concentrate), once when the sheet cake comes out of the oven and again after the cake has been cut into rounds with a biscuit cutter.

ACTIVE 1 HOUR · TOTAL 2 HOURS, 30 MIN.
SERVES 8

CAKE
- 3 cups cake flour
- 3 tsp. baking powder
- 1 tsp. salt
- ½ cup unsalted butter
- ½ cup canola or vegetable oil
- 2 cups granulated sugar
- 4 large eggs
- 1 Tbsp. vanilla extract
- 1⅓ cups whole buttermilk
- ½ (12-oz.) container frozen limeade concentrate, thawed

BUTTERCREAM
- 1 lb. powdered sugar
- 1 cup unsalted butter, softened
- 1 tsp. vanilla extract
- 8 oz. mascarpone cheese, softened

GARNISHES
White chocolate curls, white nonpareils, edible flowers, fresh raspberries, fresh strawberries, fresh blackberries

1. Prepare the Cake: Preheat oven to 350°F. Coat a 17- x 12-inch half-sheet pan with cooking spray, and line bottom of pan with parchment paper. Sift cake flour, baking powder, and salt in a medium bowl. Set aside.

2. Beat butter and oil in a large bowl with an electric mixer on medium-high speed until smooth and creamy. Add sugar, and beat until light and fluffy, 4 to 5 minutes. Add eggs, 1 at a time, and beat on medium-low speed until well blended after each addition. Beat in vanilla. Add flour mixture, one-third at a time, to butter mixture alternately with buttermilk, beginning and ending with flour mixture. Beat on low just until smooth after each addition. (Do not overbeat or cake will be tough.) Spread batter evenly in prepared sheet pan. Gently tap pan on countertop to release any air bubbles.

3. Bake in center of preheated oven until a wooden pick or cake tester inserted in center of cake comes out clean, 18 to 22 minutes. Place pan on a wire rack.

4. Heat thawed limeade concentrate in a small saucepan over medium just until warmed through, about 3 minutes. Brush cake lightly with about half of the limeade syrup. (Reserve remaining limeade syrup for later use.) Cool cake completely in pan, about 45 minutes. Freeze cooled cake, uncovered, until very cold and very firm, about 30 minutes.

5. Meanwhile, prepare the Buttercream: Beat powdered sugar and butter in a large bowl with an electric mixer on medium-high speed until thick and creamy, 4 to 5 minutes. Beat in vanilla. Add mascarpone cheese, and beat on low speed just until combined, stopping to scrape down sides of bowl as needed. (Do not overmix or the mascarpone will start to break down and the frosting will become too thin.)

6. Fit a large disposable piping bag with a large star tip. Fill piping bag with 3 cups of the Buttercream. Remove cake from freezer. Using a 2 ¾-inch round cutter, carefully cut 16 circles from sheet cake. Use an offset spatula to transfer cake circles to another sheet pan. Discard cake scraps or reserve for another use.

7. Brush top and sides of each cake circle with reserved remaining limeade syrup. Pipe a tight spiral of icing on 8 of the cake layers. Top each frosted layer with unfrosted cake layer to make 8 miniature 2-layer cakes. Hold 1 cake on your fingertips, and, using an offset spatula, carefully swipe sides of cake with a thin layer of Buttercream, barely covering the cake. Repeat with remaining cakes. Pipe a rosette of Buttercream on top of each cake. Garnish with white chocolate curls, white nonpareils, a fresh berry, or edible flower.

DAUGHTER'S BRIDAL SHOWER

How about a party for the bridal party? Your sweet girl is in love, and it's time to honor her, her honey, and her BFFs with as much celebration as you can muster. Make these baby cakes for the young woman who will always be your baby.

SUPPER CLUB

Supper clubs are a Southern institution, a special kind of entertaining where we regularly gather around a common table with devoted friends who feel like family. The steadfast camaraderie matters most, but a killer cake never hurts.

Butter Toffee-Pecan Layer Cake

This buttery vanilla layer cake is swathed in a creamy toffee frosting made extra luscious with the addition of browned butter and lots of toasted pecans.

ACTIVE 1 HOUR · TOTAL 2 HOURS, 40 MIN.

SERVES 8

BROWN BUTTER TOFFEE FROSTING
- 1 cup unsalted butter, divided
- 2 cups packed dark brown sugar
- 1¼ cups heavy cream
- 2 Tbsp. golden cane syrup (such as Lyle's Golden Syrup) or light corn syrup
- ¼ tsp. kosher salt
- 1 Tbsp. bourbon, dark rum, or cognac (optional)
- 3 cups powdered sugar
- 1 tsp. vanilla extract

CAKE
- 2 cups all-purpose flour
- 2 tsp. baking powder
- ¾ tsp. kosher salt
- 2 cups granulated sugar
- 1 cup unsalted butter, softened
- 3 large eggs
- 1 tsp. vanilla extract
- 1 cup whole buttermilk
- 1 cup finely chopped toasted pecans
- ½ cup toffee bits (such as Heath Bits 'O Brickle Toffee Bits)

ADDITIONAL INGREDIENTS
- ½ cup toasted pecan halves
- ¼ tsp. flaky sea salt (such as Maldon), optional

1. Prepare the Frosting: Melt ¾ cup of the butter in a deep, heavy-duty saucepan over low. Increase heat to medium-high, and bring butter to a boil, stirring constantly. Cook, stirring constantly, until butter is fragrant and milk solids start to brown, about 5 minutes.

2. Remove pan from heat, and stir in brown sugar, cream, syrup, salt, and, if desired, bourbon. Return pan to medium heat, and cook, stirring occasionally, until sugar dissolves. Increase heat to medium-high, and bring to a boil. Boil, stirring constantly, exactly 2 minutes. Remove mixture from heat, and pour into bowl of a heavy-duty electric stand mixer fitted with paddle attachment. Beat on low speed until mixture is lukewarm, about 8 to 10 minutes. Gradually add powdered sugar and vanilla, and beat on low speed until combined after each addition. Beat until frosting is completely cool and consistency is thick, creamy, and spreadable, 6 to 10 minutes. Add remaining 4 tablespoons butter, 1 tablespoon at a time, and beat on medium speed until fully incorporated after each addition. Cover frosting, and let stand at room temperature until ready to use.

3. Prepare the Cake: Preheat oven to 350°F. Lightly coat 2 (9-inch-round x 2-inch-deep) cake pans with cooking spray, and line bottoms with parchment paper. Sift together flour, baking powder, and salt in a medium bowl. Set aside.

4. Beat sugar and butter in a large bowl with an electric mixer on medium-high speed until thick and creamy, 4 to 5 minutes. Add eggs, 1 at a time, and beat on medium speed until well blended after each addition. Beat in vanilla. Add flour mixture, one-third at a time, to butter mixture alternately with buttermilk, beginning and ending with flour mixture. Beat on low just until smooth after each addition. (Do not overbeat or the cake will be tough.) Fold in chopped pecans and toffee bits. Divide batter evenly between cake pans, smoothing surface.

5. Bake in preheated oven until a wooden pick or cake tester inserted into center of cake comes out clean, 30 to 35 minutes. Cool in pans on a wire rack 10 minutes. Invert layers onto wire rack, and peel off parchment paper. Cool completely, about 1 hour.

6. Place 1 cake layer on a serving plate; spread evenly with 1 heaping cup of frosting. Chill 15 minutes. Top with remaining cake layer, and frost top and sides of cake with remaining frosting. Sprinkle pecan halves in a ring around top edge of cake. If desired, crush sea salt with your fingers, and sprinkle over pecans. Serve immediately, or store, covered, at room temperature for 3 to 5 days.

Triple-Layer Chocolate-Caramel Cake

This three-tiered beauty is so much easier to make than it looks. The frosting is best made the day before you need to use it, as it sets to the right spreading consistency when left to cool overnight at room temperature. A splash of bourbon enhances the caramel flavors in the creamy frosting, but it can be left out without causing any problems.

ACTIVE 1 HOUR, 15 MIN. - TOTAL 10 HOURS, 30 MIN., INCLUDING 8 HOURS STANDING

SERVES 10 TO 12

CHOCOLATE-CARAMEL GANACHE
- 1 ½ lb. bittersweet (60% cacao) chocolate chips
- ¼ cup light corn syrup
- 2 Tbsp. bourbon (optional)
- 2 cups granulated sugar
- ¼ cup cold water
- ⅛ tsp. cream of tartar
- 2 cups heavy cream
- ⅛ tsp. salt
- ¼ cup unsalted butter

CAKE
- 3 cups cake flour
- 1 cup unsweetened cocoa
- 2 tsp. baking powder
- 1 tsp. baking soda
- 1 tsp. salt
- 3 cups granulated sugar
- 1 cup sour cream
- 1 cup canola or vegetable oil
- 4 large eggs
- 1 Tbsp. vanilla extract
- 1 ½ cups hot, strong coffee

FATHER'S BIRTHDAY

For he is a jolly good fellow, and he deserves a birthday cake—not a bite of yours, but his own. Fill his silver flask with some exceptional Southern bourbon, lift a glass to toast his special day, and add a splash to his cake.

1. Prepare the Chocolate-Caramel Ganache: Stir together chocolate chips, corn syrup, and, if desired, bourbon in a large bowl. Set aside.

2. Stir together sugar, cold water, and cream of tartar in a large, heavy saucepan. Cook over medium, swirling pan occasionally, until sugar dissolves and starts to change color. Increase heat to high, and cook, swirling pan occasionally, until mixture is a rich, golden caramel color, 4 to 5 minutes.

3. Remove pan from heat. Using a long-handled wooden spoon, carefully stir in heavy cream. (Be careful: Hot caramel can spit and bubble as the cream hits it.) Reduce heat to low, and return pan to heat. Cook, stirring constantly, until caramel thickens slightly and any lumps of hardened caramel have melted, about 4 minutes. Pour warm caramel sauce over chocolate chip mixture, covering chips completely. Let stand 1 minute. Stir until mixture is completely smooth. Stir in salt. Add butter, 1 tablespoon at a time, stirring until melted and combined after each addition. Let ganache cool until lukewarm. Cover loosely with plastic wrap, and let stand at room temperature 8 hours or overnight.

4. Prepare the Cake: Preheat oven to 350°F. Lightly coat 3 (9-inch-round x 2-inch-deep) cake pans with cooking spray, and line bottoms with parchment paper. Sift together flour, cocoa, baking powder, baking soda, and salt in a large bowl. Set aside.

5. Beat sugar, sour cream, oil, eggs, and vanilla in a large bowl with an electric mixer on medium speed until thick and smooth, about 2 minutes. Add flour mixture, one-third at a time, to butter mixture. Beat on low speed just until combined after each addition. (Do not overbeat or the cake will be tough.) Add ¾ cup of the hot coffee, and beat just until smooth. Add remaining ¾ cup coffee, and beat just until smooth. Divide batter evenly among prepared pans.

6. Bake in the middle of preheated oven until a long wooden pick or cake tester inserted in center of cake comes out clean, 20 to 25 minutes. Cool in pans on a wire rack 10 minutes. Invert layers onto wire rack, and peel off parchment paper. Cool completely, about 45 minutes.

7. Place 1 cake layer on a serving plate; spread evenly with about 1 heaping cup of Chocolate-Caramel Ganache. Top with second cake layer, and spread evenly with 1 heaping cup of ganache. Top with remaining cake layer, and frost top and sides of cake with remaining ganache. Let stand at room temperature until ready to serve, or cover and refrigerate overnight.

This Banana Pudding Poke Cake is rich and delicious, bursting with fresh banana flavor and big enough to feed a crowd. The banana cake is made with oil instead of butter, which keeps it soft and moist, even when it's cut ice-cold from the refrigerator.

Banana Pudding Poke Cake

ACTIVE 1 HOUR, 10 MIN. - TOTAL 3 HOURS, 45 MIN.

SERVES 16 TO 20

CAKE

- 2 ½ cups all-purpose flour
- 2 tsp. baking powder
- 1 tsp. ground cinnamon
- ¾ tsp. kosher salt
- ¼ tsp. baking soda
- 2 cups granulated sugar
- 3 large eggs
- 1 cup canola or vegetable oil
- ½ cup whole buttermilk
- 1 tsp. vanilla extract
- 1 ½ cups mashed, overripe bananas (about 3 to 4 large bananas)

HOMEMADE VANILLA PUDDING

- ½ cup granulated sugar
- 1 Tbsp. cornstarch
- Pinch of kosher salt
- 2 cups whole milk
- 2 large egg yolks
- 1 Tbsp. vanilla bean paste
- ½ Tbsp. salted butter

ADDITIONAL INGREDIENTS

- 4-5 large, barely ripe fresh bananas, sliced
- 2 cups heavy cream
- ¼ cup powdered sugar
- 1 tsp. vanilla extract
- 20 vanilla wafers, coarsely crushed
- 2 Tbsp. salted butter, melted
- 1 Tbsp. all-purpose flour
- 1 Tbsp. granulated sugar

1. Prepare the Cake: Preheat oven to 350°F. Coat a 13- x 9-inch baking pan with cooking spray. Sift together flour, baking powder, cinnamon, salt, and baking soda in a medium bowl. Set aside.
2. Beat sugar, eggs, oil, buttermilk, and vanilla in a large bowl with an electric mixer on medium speed until combined, about 2 minutes. Add flour mixture to sugar mixture, one-third at a time, and beat on low speed just until smooth after each addition. Fold in mashed bananas, and transfer batter to prepared pan.
3. Bake in middle of preheated oven until a wooden pick or cake tester inserted in center of cake comes out clean, 30 to 35 minutes. Transfer to a wire rack, and cool 10 minutes. Using the handle of a wooden spoon, poke deep holes all over the cake (about 5 across and 6 down, for a total of 30 holes).
4. Prepare the Pudding: Whisk together sugar, cornstarch, and salt in a large saucepan; whisk in milk. Whisk in egg yolks until well blended. Bring to a boil over medium, stirring constantly. Immediately reduce heat to low, and simmer, stirring constantly, just until pudding is thick enough to coat the back of a spoon, 1 to 2 minutes.
5. Pour pudding through a fine wire-mesh strainer into a large bowl. Whisk in vanilla bean paste and butter. Cool, stirring occasionally, until lukewarm, about 15 minutes. Spread pudding evenly over cake. Cover cake with plastic wrap, pressing it directly onto pudding (to prevent a skin from forming). Chill the cake for at least 2 hours but preferably overnight.
6. Preheat oven to 350°F. Remove plastic wrap from cake. Scatter banana slices evenly over pudding. Beat heavy cream, powdered sugar, and vanilla in a large bowl with an electric mixer on medium-high speed until thick and spreadable. Spread over bananas, covering cake in an even layer.
7. Stir together crushed vanilla wafers, melted butter, flour, and granulated sugar in a small bowl. Press mixture with your fingers to form small clumps, and spread on a baking sheet. Bake in preheated oven until crisp and brown, 5 to 6 minutes. Cool completely, about 10 minutes. Sprinkle over whipped cream topping. Serve immediately.

TIME-SAVER

To use instant vanilla pudding instead of homemade, beat 2 (3.4-ounce) packages of instant vanilla pudding, 4 cups whole milk, and 1 tablespoon vanilla extract with an electric mixer on medium-high speed until thick and smooth.

GO AHEAD
AND GIVE IT A POKE

Most cake names don't include the punch line. But yes, true to its name, a poke cake is a cake that is punctured with holes—on purpose. The baker pierces the top of the freshly baked cake and then pours over something that's sweet, either syrupy or creamy, and often colorful to seep into those holes, settle, and soak. The intent is to infuse lots of flavor, and perhaps a little whimsy, into the baked treat. When it's finally time to cut, the rivulets of filling look like stalactites inside a cave in the Big Rock Candy Mountain.

Poke cakes popped up in American kitchens around 1970, first appearing in a print advertisement to increase Jell-O sales. The ad illustrated the quick and simple cleverness of combining convenience foods—cake mix, Jell-O, and Dream Whip or Cool Whip—to create hip and modern desserts. The original poke cake was white, which provided a blank slate for the colorful Jell-O insets in one or more colors, depending on the desired effect. Poke cakes were often inspired by color schemes as much as flavor combinations.

The holey desserts never disappeared from home kitchens, but lately they've been surfing a new wave of popularity and creativity. Instead of sticking with old school rainbows of Jell-O in the traditional rectangular form, bakers are pouring all sorts of unexpected fillings over cakes of different shapes and sizes. Popular choices include pudding, mousse, sweetened condensed milk, pastry cream, pureed fruit, fudge, and flavored syrup. (Here, we chose vanilla pudding.) To customize the appearance of these creations, they bore into the cake with objects of varying diameters, from a thick wooden spoon handle to tiny fork tines. Some of these over-the-top combos turn out so ooey and gooey that instead of a sliceable cake, the end product is essentially a dessert casserole that must be scooped out of the dish with a spoon.

They're easy to make and delightful to serve, whether assembled entirely from boxes or wholly homemade. How could anything called a poke cake be anything less than a good time?
—SHERI CASTLE

Cream Soda Confetti Sheet Cake with Strawberry-Sour Cream Buttercream

If fun is what you're looking for, this simple cake, enlivened with cream soda and confetti sprinkles, will make your day. Freeze-dried strawberries give the icing a naturally pink color and tangy-sweet flavor.

ACTIVE 35 MIN. - TOTAL 55 MIN.

SERVES 15 TO 20

CAKE
- 2 ¼ cups all-purpose flour
- 2 tsp. baking powder
- ½ tsp. kosher salt
- 1 ¾ cups granulated sugar
- 1 cup unsalted butter, softened
- 3 large eggs
- 2 tsp. vanilla extract
- 1 cup cream soda soft drink, at room temperature
- ½ cup pastel sprinkles or pastel rainbow jimmies

STRAWBERRY-SOUR CREAM BUTTERCREAM
- 1 (1.2-oz.) pkg. freeze-dried strawberries
- 1 lb. powdered sugar
- 1 cup unsalted butter, softened
- 4 - 5 Tbsp. sour cream
- 1 - 2 Tbsp. whole milk, if necessary

GARNISHES
Pastel sprinkles, nonpareils, pastel rainbow jimmies

1. Prepare the Cake: Preheat oven to 350°F. Lightly coat a jelly-roll pan with cooking spray. Sift together flour, baking powder, and salt in a medium bowl. Set aside.

2. Beat granulated sugar and butter in a large bowl with an electric mixer on medium speed until light and fluffy, 4 to 5 minutes. Add eggs, 1 at a time, beating well after each addition. Beat in vanilla. Add flour mixture, one-third at a time, to butter mixture alternately with cream soda, beginning and ending with flour mixture. Beat on low speed just until smooth after each addition. Using a spatula, fold in pastel sprinkles. Spread batter in prepared pan. Gently tap pan on countertop to release any bubbles.

3. Bake in preheated oven until a wooden pick or cake tester inserted in center of cake comes out clean, 20 to 25 minutes. Cool completely on a wire rack, about 1 hour.

DAUGHTER'S BIRTHDAY

Sugar and spice and everything nice, plus sprinkles. A daughter's birthday is an extra family holiday each year when we celebrate the joy she brings to our world. As she blows out the candles on this darling cake, whisper an extra wish for all of her dreams to come true as well.

4. Prepare the Strawberry-Sour Cream Buttercream: Remove and discard the packet of desiccant from strawberries. (The desiccant keeps freeze-dried fruit from getting damp.) Process berries in a food processor until crushed to a fine powder, about 1 minute. Beat powdered sugar and butter in a large bowl with an electric mixer on medium speed until well blended. Add crushed strawberries, and beat until fluffy, about 4 minutes. Add sour cream, 1 tablespoon at a time, and beat until just combined after each addition. Beat on medium-high speed until creamy and spreadable, about 3 minutes. (If necessary, beat in up to 2 tablespoons of milk, 1 tablespoon at a time, until spreadable.) Spread buttercream over cake. Garnish with sprinkles. Serve immediately, or cover and refrigerate up to 3 days.

Vanilla Bean-Brownie Ripple Pound Cake

This simple loaf of vanilla pound cake reveals a pretty secret when it's sliced: a ribbon of fudgy brownie swirled right into the batter.

ACTIVE 30 MIN. - TOTAL 2 HOURS, 45 MIN.
SERVES 8

BROWNIE RIPPLE BATTER
- 6 Tbsp. unsalted butter
- 1 oz. unsweetened baking chocolate, coarsely chopped
- ½ cup granulated sugar
- ¼ cup all-purpose flour
- 1 large egg
- ¼ tsp. vanilla extract

POUND CAKE BATTER
- 2 cups all-purpose flour
- ½ tsp. baking powder
- ½ tsp. kosher salt
- 1 ¼ cups granulated sugar
- 1 cup unsalted butter, softened
- 2 Tbsp. vanilla bean paste or 1 Tbsp. vanilla extract
- 4 large eggs
- ½ cup sour cream

1. Prepare the Brownie Ripple Batter: Preheat oven to 325°F. Lightly coat a 9- x 5- x 3-inch loaf pan with cooking spray. Line bottom and 2 long sides of pan with parchment paper, allowing 2 to 3 inches to extend over sides. Combine butter and chocolate in a microwave-sate bowl. Microwave on HIGH until melted, about 1 minute. Stir until smooth. Whisk in sugar, flour, egg, and vanilla to form a loose batter. Set aside to cool slightly while making cake batter.

2. Prepare the Pound Cake Batter: Sift together flour, baking powder, and salt into a medium bowl. Set aside.

3. Beat sugar and butter in a large bowl with an electric mixer on medium-high speed until light and fluffy, 4 to 5 minutes. Beat in vanilla bean paste. Add eggs, 1 at a time, beating well after each addition. Beat in sour cream just until smooth. Add flour mixture, one-third at a time, and beat on low speed just until blended after each addition. Spoon half of the Pound Cake Batter into prepared pan. Spoon Brownie Ripple Batter over Pound Cake Batter, covering it completely. Top with remaining Pound Cake Batter. Using a small offset spatula, smooth batter carefully.

4. Bake cake in middle of preheated oven until a long wooden pick or a cake tester inserted in center of cake comes out clean, about 1 hour and 45 minutes. (If cake seems to be browning too quickly, cover top loosely with foil for last 30 minutes of baking.) Cool cake in pan on a wire rack 30 minutes. Remove cake from pan using parchment paper as handles, and cool completely on wire rack, about 1 hour. Slice and serve.

SERVING TIP

Be sure to let the cake cool completely before slicing so the brownie ripple layer has time to set.

Spring Chicken!

Liven up weeknight meals with an
abundance of colorful produce

CHICKEN FRICASSEE
WITH SPRING
VEGETABLES,
PAGE 83

Grilled Chicken Kebabs with Arugula Pesto

Wake up your grill from winter hibernation with flavorful skewers (chicken, sweet onion, squash, and zucchini) paired with arugula pesto on the side. Serve with plenty of crusty bread to mop up the pesto.

ACTIVE 30 MIN. - TOTAL 30 MIN.
SERVES 4

- 2 cups packed baby arugula leaves
- 1 cup loosely packed basil leaves
- ¼ cup pine nuts, toasted
- 2 small garlic cloves, coarsely chopped
- 1 Tbsp. fresh lemon juice
- 1 tsp. kosher salt
- ½ tsp. black pepper
- 5 Tbsp. extra-virgin olive oil, divided
- 1 small zucchini, cut into ¼-inch-thick slices, then cut into half-moons (about 1½ cups)
- 1 small yellow squash, cut into ¼-inch-thick slices, then cut into half-moons (about 1½ cups)
- 1 small Vidalia or other sweet onion, cut into 8 wedges and separated into pieces (about 1 cup)
- 1 tsp. sherry vinegar
- 1¼ lb. chicken breast tenders, cut crosswise into thirds

1. Place arugula, basil, pine nuts, garlic, lemon juice, salt, pepper, and 4 tablespoons of the oil in the bowl of a mini food processor; pulse until smooth, about 10 times, scraping sides of bowl occasionally.

2. Place zucchini, squash, and onion in a medium bowl; toss with vinegar, 2 tablespoons of the pesto, and remaining 1 tablespoon oil. Place chicken pieces in a separate bowl, and toss with 2 tablespoons of the pesto.

3. Preheat grill to medium-high (about 450°F). Thread chicken and vegetables alternately onto each of 8 (6-inch) bamboo skewers. Place kebabs on oiled grates; grill, uncovered, until chicken is cooked through and vegetables are tender and lightly charred, about 4 minutes per side. Serve chicken-and-vegetable kebabs with remaining pesto.

One-Pan Chicken with Lemon, Olives, and Artichokes

For a fresh, tangy transformation, cook chicken breasts with artichokes, green olives, and lemon.

ACTIVE 20 MIN. - TOTAL 1 HOUR

SERVES 4

- 4 bone-in, skin-on chicken breast halves (about 3 ½ lb.)
- 1 ½ tsp. kosher salt, divided
- ¾ tsp. black pepper, divided
- ¼ cup all-purpose flour, divided
- 3 Tbsp. extra-virgin olive oil, divided
- 2 (14-oz.) cans whole artichokes, drained and halved
- 2 small red onions, vertically sliced
- 1 ½ cups Castelvetrano or picholine olives, pitted and divided
- 3 cups chicken broth
- 1 lemon, thinly sliced
- 2 Tbsp. chopped fresh thyme, divided
- 1 Tbsp. chopped fresh parsley
- 2 cups cooked pearl couscous

1. Preheat oven to 375°F. Pat chicken dry, and sprinkle with 1 teaspoon of the salt and ½ teaspoon of the pepper. Dust chicken with 2 tablespoons of the flour.
2. Heat 2 tablespoons of the oil in a large, enameled cast-iron skillet over medium-high. Add half of chicken to skillet, and cook until browned on both sides, about 6 minutes, turning once. Remove chicken to a platter; keep warm. Repeat procedure with remaining half of chicken. Add artichokes, onion, and 1 cup of the olives to skillet; cook, stirring occasionally, until onion is just softened, 3 to 4 minutes. Add remaining 2 tablespoons flour to skillet; cook, stirring constantly, about 1 minute. Add broth, lemon slices, and 1 tablespoon of the thyme, scraping bottom of skillet to loosen any browned bits. Return chicken to skillet, nestling into sauce. Cover and cook 20 minutes. Uncover and cook until a thermometer inserted in thickest portion of chicken registers 165°F, about 15 minutes.
3. Meanwhile, coarsely chop remaining ½ cup olives. Combine chopped olives, parsley, and remaining 1 tablespoon thyme, 1 tablespoon oil, ½ teaspoon salt, and ¼ teaspoon pepper.
4. Serve chicken, artichoke mixture, and chopped olive-herb mixture over couscous.

Chicken Fricassee with Spring Vegetables

A comforting stew of chicken and vegetables in a velvety pan sauce hits the spot on a cool spring evening. Best of all, it comes together in 45 minutes, and you'll only have to use a single skillet.

ACTIVE 18 MIN. · TOTAL 45 MIN.
SERVES 4

- 8 skinless, bone-in chicken thighs (about 4 lb.)
- 1 ½ tsp. kosher salt, divided
- ¾ tsp. black pepper, divided
- ½ cup all-purpose flour
- 2 Tbsp. olive oil
- 1 (8-oz.) pkg. cremini mushrooms, quartered
- 3 medium carrots, peeled and cut diagonally into ½-inch-thick slices (about 2 cups)
- 1 cup coarsely chopped leek (from 1 medium leek)
- 2 cups chicken stock
- ½ cup dry white wine
- ¼ cup heavy cream
- 8 oz. asparagus, trimmed and cut into 1-inch pieces (about 1 cup)
  Hot cooked egg noodles
  Chopped fresh chives

1. Pat chicken dry, and sprinkle with 1 teaspoon of the salt and ½ teaspoon of the pepper. Place flour in a large ziplock plastic freezer bag; add chicken to bag. Seal bag, and toss to coat with flour. Heat oil in a 12-inch cast-iron skillet over medium-high. Remove chicken from bag, reserving flour in bag. Shake excess flour mixture from chicken, and place, bone side up, in skillet. Cook chicken until deep golden brown, 4 to 5 minutes per side. Remove chicken to a plate, and keep warm.

2. Add mushrooms to hot drippings in skillet; cook, stirring often, until beginning to brown, about 4 minutes. Add carrots and leek; cook about 3 minutes. Add 2 tablespoons of the reserved flour; cook, stirring constantly, about 1 minute. Add chicken stock and wine; cook, stirring often, until sauce thickens slightly, about 6 minutes. Stir in cream and remaining ½ teaspoon salt and ¼ teaspoon pepper; add chicken, bone side down, nestling chicken into sauce mixture.

3. Cover, reduce heat to medium-low, and cook until sauce has thickened slightly and chicken is almost cooked through, about 15 minutes. Uncover and sprinkle with asparagus. Cover and cook until chicken is cooked through and asparagus is tender-crisp, about 10 minutes.

4. Serve chicken, vegetables, and sauce over hot cooked noodles, and garnish with chives, if desired.

Oven-Fried Chicken with Spring Salad

Making crispy, golden-brown chicken is possible on a weeknight if you use the oven instead of the stove-top. Enjoy the contrast between the hot cooked chicken and the tangy caper-and-lemon vinaigrette.

ACTIVE 20 MIN. - TOTAL 40 MIN.
SERVES 4

- 4 (6-oz.) chicken cutlets
- 1 cup all-purpose flour
- 1¼ tsp. kosher salt, divided
- 1 large egg, lightly beaten
- 1 Tbsp. water
- 1½ cups lemon pepper panko (Japanese-style breadcrumbs)
- 2 Tbsp. finely chopped shallots (from 1 medium shallot)
- 1 Tbsp. capers, drained
- 1 Tbsp. fresh lemon juice
- 2 tsp. Dijon mustard
- 1 tsp. honey
- ¼ cup canola oil
- ¼ cup extra-virgin olive oil
- 8 oz. Belgian endive (about 3 heads), diagonally sliced (about 2 cups)
- 1 (5-oz.) pkg. baby spring mix
- 4 oz. multicolored radishes (about 8 radishes), very thinly sliced (about 1 cup)

1. Preheat oven to 400°F. Line a baking sheet with aluminum foil, and place a lightly greased wire rack on the baking sheet.

2. Place chicken between 2 sheets of heavy-duty plastic wrap; pound each cutlet to ¼-inch thickness using the flat side of a meat mallet or small heavy skillet. Place flour and ½ teaspoon of the salt in a large ziplock plastic freezer bag. Combine egg, water, and ½ teaspoon of the salt in a shallow dish. Place panko in a separate shallow dish. Place 1 cutlet in bag; seal bag, and shake to coat with flour mixture. Dip floured cutlet in egg mixture; dredge in panko, pressing gently to coat cutlet completely, and place on wire rack. Repeat procedure with remaining cutlets. Coat cutlets with cooking spray. Bake in preheated oven until cutlets are golden brown and cooked through, 20 to 25 minutes.

3. Meanwhile, place shallots, capers, lemon juice, Dijon mustard, honey, and remaining ¼ teaspoon salt in a mini food processor or blender; pulse until blended, about 5 times. With processor running, slowly pour canola oil and olive oil through food chute, and process until well blended. Combine Belgian endive, spring mix, and radishes in a medium bowl; toss with 3 tablespoons of the vinaigrette. Divide cutlets and salad evenly among 4 serving plates. Drizzle salads with remaining vinaigrette, if desired, and serve immediately.

Creamy Chicken and Bacon with Herbed Puff Pastry

With a rich cheese sauce, crispy bacon, and a buttery puff pastry topper, our latest take on chicken pot pie is even more decadent than the original.

ACTIVE 45 MIN. - TOTAL 1 HOUR
SERVES 4

- 4 boneless, skinless chicken breasts (about 1 ½ lb.)
- 3 cups chicken stock
- 1 tsp. kosher salt, divided
- 1 frozen puff pastry sheet, thawed (½ of 17.3-oz. pkg.)
- 1 large egg, lightly beaten
- 12 parsley leaves
- ¼ tsp. black pepper
- 2 (6-oz.) pkg. steam-in-bag fresh English peas or 3 cups frozen English peas
- 4 bacon slices
- 3 Tbsp. salted butter
- 1 cup chopped Vidalia or other sweet onion (from 1 medium onion)
- ½ cup (¼-inch) diagonally sliced celery (from 1 large stalk)
- ¼ cup all-purpose flour
- ½ cup heavy cream
- 2 oz. fontina cheese, shredded (about ½ cup)

1. Preheat oven to 400°F. Place chicken, stock, and ½ teaspoon of the salt in a large saucepan; bring to a boil over high. Reduce heat to medium-low; cover and cook until chicken is cooked through, about 15 minutes. Remove from heat, and let stand about 20 minutes. Remove chicken from stock, reserving 2 ½ cups of the stock. Coarsely shred chicken.

2. Meanwhile, place puff pastry sheet on a baking sheet lined with parchment paper. Cut pastry sheet into 4 squares; separate squares. Brush squares lightly with egg; top each square with 3 parsley leaves, pressing gently to adhere. Sprinkle with pepper. Bake on oven rack in bottom third of preheated oven until dough is puffed and golden brown, 12 to 14 minutes.

3. Cook peas according to package directions; keep warm.

4. Cook bacon in a large skillet over medium-high until crisp, about 6 minutes. Remove bacon to a paper towel-lined plate, reserving drippings in skillet; crumble bacon. Add butter to hot drippings in skillet, and cook over medium until butter melts, about 1 minute. Add onion and celery; cook, stirring often, until onion is tender and celery is tender-crisp, about 8 minutes. Add flour, and cook, stirring constantly, about 1 minute. Stir in cream and reserved 2 ½ cups stock; bring to a simmer, stirring often. Stir in peas, cheese, chicken, bacon, and remaining ½ teaspoon salt; reduce heat to medium-low, and cook until mixture is thickened and thoroughly heated, about 10 minutes.

5. Divide mixture among 4 shallow bowls, and top each with a puff pastry square. Serve immediately.

A Great Pot of Gumbo

Louisiana's signature dish is a simmering source of debate
for Southerners. The *SL* Kitchen puts our pot to the test.

IF THERE'S a more satisfying meal to make for cool weather, we haven't found it. Gumbo is a stay-inside-and-cook-all-day kind of dish that warms you inside and out. While Louisianans have firm ideas about what goes into a proper gumbo, there are infinite variations—chicken and okra; turkey and sausage; duck, oyster, and sausage—and countless versions, including ones with filé as a thickener and others with okra. So when the *SL* Test Kitchen set out to make a singular recipe, we weighed all of the delicious combinations before landing on shrimp and sausage. Of course, our gumbo has what you'd expect, like bell pepper, onions, and celery, plus a few surprises, such as canned tomatoes (because we think they add a nice touch of acidity). Our end result is a vibrant, cayenne-kissed dish that allows all of the ingredients to shine. Now we wouldn't dare call this the best recipe you've ever tasted—we know that's the one you grew up enjoying. That said, this is the finest pot of gumbo our Test Kitchen has ever turned out, and that's saying a lot.

TIP

Our testers chose a butter-based roux, which cooks over lower heat so it takes a little longer but gives the gumbo a nutty and rich flavor. While some cooks say a roux must be dark brown in color, a butter-based roux should be a deep shade of caramel—you don't want it to taste burned. Turn to page 92 for step-by-step instructions.

TIP

Filé (FEE-lay) powder, a spicy herb made from sassafras leaves, is often sprinkled on individual servings to thicken and season gumbo. While you can certainly serve gumbo without it, we like its earthy, slightly floral flavor. If you can't find filé powder at your local supermarket, you can order it from penzeys.com.

THE ABC'S OF GUMBO

Ⓐ THE TRIFECTA
Chopped onions, celery, and bell pepper are must-haves in Cajun cooking. We also added garlic to the mix.

Ⓑ BROTH
Use a lightly seasoned broth (or stock) instead of water for the boldest flavor—homemade broth is always better if you have it.

Ⓒ RICE
Serve gumbo over steamed white rice. We like Louisiana's fluffy, aromatic Jazzmen Rice (jazzmenrice.com).

Shrimp and Sausage Gumbo

ACTIVE 1 HOUR · TOTAL 4 HOURS

MAKES 12 CUPS

- 1 lb. smoked spicy-hot sausage (such as Conecuh), cut into ½-inch-thick slices
- ½ cup salted butter
- ½ cup all-purpose flour
- 2 medium-size yellow onions, chopped (about 3 cups)
- 1 large green bell pepper, chopped (about 1½ cups)
- 3 large celery stalks, chopped (about 1 cup)
- 3 garlic cloves, minced
- 2 (32-oz.) cartons chicken broth
- 1 lb. fresh okra, trimmed and cut into ½-inch pieces (about 2¾ cups)
- 1 (14.5-oz.) can petite diced tomatoes, undrained
- 3 bay leaves
- 2 tsp. salt
- 2 tsp. Worcestershire sauce
- 2 tsp. hot sauce
- 1½ tsp. dried thyme
- 1 tsp. black pepper
- 2 lb. unpeeled raw medium shrimp, peeled and deveined
- ¼ cup chopped fresh flat-leaf parsley
  Hot cooked rice
  Sliced scallions, filé powder (optional)

1. Place sausage in a large Dutch oven over medium; cook, stirring often, until browned on both sides, about 15 minutes. Using a slotted spoon, remove sausage to drain on paper towels; reserve drippings in pan.

2. Add butter to hot drippings in Dutch oven, stirring until melted. Gradually whisk in all-purpose flour, and cook, whisking constantly, until mixture is caramel colored, 20 to 30 minutes.

3. Add onions, bell pepper, celery, and garlic, and cook, stirring often, until vegetables are very tender, 15 to 18 minutes. Gradually stir in broth. Stir in sausage, okra, tomatoes, bay leaves, salt, Worcestershire sauce, hot sauce, thyme, and pepper.

4. Increase heat to medium-high, and bring mixture to a boil. Reduce heat to low, and simmer, partially covered, stirring occasionally, about 3 hours. Remove and discard bay leaves. Stir in shrimp, and cook until shrimp turn pink, about 5 minutes. Stir in parsley, and remove from heat. Serve gumbo over hot cooked rice. Garnish with sliced scallions and filé powder, if desired.

BEET-AND-ORANGE
SALAD WITH SPICED
PECANS, PAGE 89

Beauty of the Beets

Virginia Willis shares
three delicious new ways
to cook with a sure sign
of spring: fresh beets

BEETS ARE THE OKRA of the root vegetable world—folks either love them or hate them. My mother was firmly in the anti-beet crowd, so we never had beets on our family table. My beet breakthrough came with my very first job cooking as an apprentice to Nathalie Dupree on the set for her PBS cooking series. Her recipe called for chopped cubes of beets sautéed with grated ginger and butter until just tender; then beet leaves were added to the pan and quickly steamed to finish the dish. The cubed beets looked like rubies against the bright green leaves. It was a beautiful, delicious dish and completely mind-opening. While my mother and grandmother taught me cooking fundamentals, Nathalie took me out of my mother's kitchen and exposed me to things I had never seen or tasted, resulting in my newfound love of beets.

There are many types of beets available in the markets today: red, golden, Chioggia beets with their distinctive white-and-red interior circles, and baby ones the size of walnuts. When buying beets, healthy leaves are a sign of freshness, so look for leaves that are vibrant, green, and not wilted. I find it best to purchase them with the leaves and stems on, but if you buy them without, make sure the beets are firm and have no soft spots or bruises. If you're really short on time, precooked beets are increasingly available in produce departments and are great for tossing into salads.

Beets are incredibly versatile and can be grilled, roasted, sautéed, pickled, steamed, juiced, or spiralized. And as you'll see in these recipes, they can be part of your Southern table from breakfast to dessert.

Golden Beet-and-Potato Breakfast Bake

Beets add color and flavor to hash browns in this one-pan breakfast. Squeeze out as much liquid as possible from the beets and potatoes so they crisp up in the pan.

ACTIVE 30 MIN. - TOTAL 40 MIN.
SERVES 4

- 1   lb. Yukon Gold potatoes
- ½   lb. golden beets
- 1   small sweet onion
- 4   thick-cut bacon slices, cut into lardons (small strips or cubes)
- 2   Tbsp. salted butter
- 1   Tbsp. canola oil
- 2   garlic cloves, finely chopped
- 1   tsp. kosher salt, divided
- ½   tsp. black pepper, divided
- 4   large eggs
- 1   Tbsp. chopped fresh flat-leaf parsley

1. Preheat oven to 350°F. Grate potatoes, beets, and onion with the grating blade of a food processor or on the large holes of a box grater. Transfer grated vegetables to a strainer lined with a lint-free towel. Using your hands, squeeze vegetables to remove as much liquid as possible.
2. Cook bacon in a large ovenproof nonstick skillet over medium until crispy, about 5 minutes. Remove bacon with a slotted spoon to a plate lined with paper towels; reserve 1 teaspoon drippings in skillet. Increase heat to high; add butter and oil, and stir until warm. Add garlic to skillet, and cook, stirring often, until fragrant, about 20 seconds. Add grated vegetables; sprinkle with ¾ teaspoon of the salt and ¼ teaspoon of the pepper, and cook, stirring and tossing the vegetables occasionally, until vegetables start to become tender, about 5 minutes. Gently pat vegetables down into an even layer in skillet, and cook 5 minutes. Stir vegetables, and pat down again into an even layer. Cook until a crust forms on bottom, about 8 minutes. Remove from heat.
3. Using the back of a spoon, make 4 indentations (nests) in beet mixture in skillet. Break 1 egg into each indentation. Sprinkle eggs evenly with remaining ¼ teaspoon each salt and pepper. Bake in preheated oven until whites are set and yolks are still runny, about 8 minutes, or to desired degree of doneness. Sprinkle top with bacon and parsley, and serve immediately.

GOLDEN BEET-AND-POTATO
BREAKFAST BAKE

Beet-and-Orange Salad with Spiced Pecans

For this bright, beautiful salad, use ready-to-eat peeled and steamed beets (which cut the cook time down to just 15 minutes), or roast your own.

ACTIVE 15 MIN. - TOTAL 15 MIN.
SERVES 4

Heat 2 tablespoons **canola oil** in a large skillet over medium-low. Add ½ cup chopped **pecans,** ½ teaspoon ground **cumin,** ½ teaspoon ground **coriander,** ¼ teaspoon each of **kosher salt** and **black pepper,** and a pinch of **cayenne pepper.** Cook, stirring often, until pecans are toasted and spices are fragrant, 3 to 5 minutes. Remove from heat, and cool. Place 5 ounces **mixed greens** (such as spinach, arugula, or mâche) in a large bowl. Section 2 **navel oranges** by cutting off the top and bottom ends of each, allowing them to stand upright. Working from top to bottom of orange and following curve of fruit, cut off peel, white pith, and outer membranes from orange to expose segments. Carefully cut orange segments away from membranes. Squeeze any remaining juices from outer membranes of orange over greens. Add orange segments; 1 (8-ounce) **package ready-to-eat peeled and steamed beets,** quartered; 2 tablespoons **sherry vinegar;** and the **spiced pecans with oil.** Sprinkle with 2 ounces crumbled **feta cheese** (about ½ cup), and toss to coat.

Beet Red Velvet Cupcakes

Beets act as a natural food coloring and give these cupcakes a tender crumb. Microwaving the beets and adding lemon juice for acidity helps retain their color, making the cupcakes even more red.

ACTIVE 25 MIN. - TOTAL 1 HOUR, 10 MIN.
MAKES 24 CUPCAKES

- 10 oz. red beets, well scrubbed
- 2 Tbsp. fresh lemon juice (from 1 lemon)
- ¾ cup canola oil
- ¾ cup whole buttermilk
- 4 large eggs
- 2 ½ cups all-purpose flour
- 1 ½ cups granulated sugar
- 3 Tbsp. unsweetened cocoa (not Dutch process)
- 2 tsp. baking powder
- 1 tsp. fine sea salt
- ½ tsp. baking soda

- 1 (8-oz.) pkg. cream cheese, softened
- ¼ cup unsalted butter, softened
- 1 (16-oz.) pkg. powdered sugar
- 1 tsp. vanilla extract
- 1 cup chopped toasted pecans (optional)

1. Preheat oven to 350°F. Wrap beets in parchment paper. Microwave on HIGH until tender, 8 to 10 minutes. Cool beets wrapped in paper until just warm to the touch.

2. Peel beets, and coarsely chop. Process chopped beets and lemon juice in a food processor until finely chopped, stopping to scrape down the sides of the bowl as necessary. Add oil and buttermilk; process until smooth. Add eggs; process until completely combined. Whisk together flour, sugar, cocoa, baking powder, salt, and baking soda in a large bowl; add beet mixture, and whisk just until combined.

3. Line 2 (12-cup) muffin pans with baking liners. Using an ice-cream scoop, a spoon, or a liquid measuring cup, fill liners two-thirds full with batter. Bake in preheated oven until a wooden toothpick inserted in center comes out clean, 15 to 18 minutes. Cool in pans on wire racks 5 minutes. Remove from pans to racks, and cool completely, about 25 minutes.

4. Meanwhile, beat cream cheese and butter in the bowl of a stand mixer fitted with paddle attachment or with a handheld mixer on medium speed until very smooth. Gradually add powdered sugar, beating on low speed until blended and light and fluffy. Beat in vanilla. Spread frosting on cupcakes using an offset spatula. Or spoon frosting into a ziplock plastic freezer bag; snip 1 corner of bag to make a small hole, and pipe frosting on cupcakes. Sprinkle with pecans, if desired.

One Potato, Two Potato

Crispy on the outside, pillowy on the inside, these pan-toasted gnocchi
are pure comfort in a bowl—and about 400 calories per serving

TIP

Instead of boiling the potato dumplings, toast them in a skillet until golden brown. Don't overstir in the pan, because you'll want a nice crisp exterior.

Skillet-Toasted Gnocchi with Peas

ACTIVE 30 MIN. - TOTAL 30 MIN.

SERVES 6

- ¼ cup salted butter, divided
- 1 (16-oz.) pkg. potato gnocchi
- 1 Tbsp. minced garlic (about 1 large garlic clove)
- 2 tsp. chopped fresh thyme
- 1½ cups reduced-sodium chicken broth
- ½ tsp. kosher salt
- ½ tsp. black pepper
- 1 (10-oz.) pkg. frozen sweet peas, thawed, or 1½ cups shelled fresh sweet peas
- 2 Tbsp. chopped fresh flat-leaf parsley
- 1 tsp. lemon zest plus 1 Tbsp. fresh juice (from 1 lemon)
- 2 oz. Parmesan cheese, grated (about ½ cup)

Heat 2 tablespoons of the butter in a large nonstick skillet over medium-high; add gnocchi, and cook, stirring occasionally, until browned all over, about 10 minutes. Add garlic and thyme, and cook, stirring often, until fragrant, about 1 minute. Add broth, salt, and pepper; bring to a simmer, and cook until reduced by about half, 4 to 5 minutes. Add peas, parsley, lemon zest, lemon juice, and remaining 2 tablespoons butter; cook, stirring constantly, until butter melts, about 1 minute. Top with Parmesan, and serve immediately.

Nutritional information (per serving):
Calories: 407 - Protein: 13g - Carbs: 53.19g - Fiber: 6.33g - Fat: 16.27g

COOKING (SL) SCHOOL

KNOW-HOW

The Right Way To Make Roux

Master our foolproof method for the classic base of gravies, sauces, and gumbo

1

Heat fat (butter, oil, or bacon drippings) in a Dutch oven or skillet over medium, and whisk in an equal amount of flour.

2

Cook, whisking constantly, until mixture is smooth and thick, like a wet sand consistency. Continue cooking to desired doneness.

3

Know your colors, which vary by cook time: White is for creamy sauces, blond for gravy, and deep brown for traditional gumbo.

"Swap out a white or yellow onion for a spring onion. You can use the whole thing, cooked or raw, from the green top to the white bulb."

—Robby Melvin
Test Kitchen Director

DIY

Sugared Blooms

Sparkly edible-flower dessert toppers are simple to make.

[A] With a small brush, coat individual petals with a mixture of egg white powder and water. [B] Sprinkle flowers with extra-fine sugar. [C] Let dry overnight.

KITCHEN TRICKS

Beat Beet Stains

Vibrant beets have a reputation for leaving their marks—pesky, hard-to-remove pink ones. Try these tips for quick cleanup.

ON A CUTTING BOARD
Scrub half of 1 lemon and a generous amount of coarse salt into the board. Rinse with cold water; repeat if necessary.

ON CLOTHING
Immediately treat with a spot stain remover (like Dreft); wash in cold water with fabric-appropriate bleach, if needed.

ON HANDS
Over the sink, coat hands with a small amount of baking soda and water. Rub vigorously; then rinse and repeat until the stains are completely gone.

April

A LAID-BACK
Easter Lunch

Gather the whole family for a beautiful spring meal
that celebrates the best seasonal ingredients

THE SOUP

You can make this a day ahead of time, but the color is more vibrant when served immediately.

Spring Lettuce and Leek Soup

Many lettuces are grown in sandy soil, so thoroughly wash and dry your greens to remove any grit. If you don't have an immersion blender, process the soup in batches in a blender until smooth.

ACTIVE 25 MIN. - TOTAL 45 MIN.
SERVES 8

1 large head romaine lettuce
1 large head escarole lettuce
1 head butter lettuce
3 Tbsp. salted butter
2 leeks, white and light green parts only, thinly sliced (about 3 cups)
2 garlic cloves, chopped
¼ cup dry white wine
5 cups chicken stock
1 (15-oz.) can white beans, drained and rinsed
¾ cup sour cream
½ cup firmly packed fresh flat-leaf parsley leaves
2 Tbsp. chopped fresh dill
1 ½ tsp. kosher salt
¼ tsp. black pepper
   Sour cream
   Dill sprigs

1. Rinse romaine, escarole, and butter lettuce well; shake and pat dry. Roughly chop leaves and stems; discard cores.

2. Melt butter in a large Dutch oven over medium. Add leeks and garlic; cook, stirring occasionally, until softened, 4 to 5 minutes. Add wine, and cook 1 minute. Stir in lettuces, stock, and beans. Cover and increase heat to medium-high; bring to a boil, stirring occasionally. Reduce heat to low, and simmer, covered, until lettuce leaves are wilted and stems are softened, 8 to 10 minutes. Remove from heat; stir in sour cream, parsley, and dill.

3. Using an immersion blender, process hot soup until smooth. Stir in salt and pepper. Garnish servings with sour cream and dill sprigs, if desired.

HONEY-PORT
LACQUERED HAM

"CARROT CAKE"
BISCUITS

THE MAIN

Honey-Port Lacquered Ham

This isn't your salty, pink smoked ham that's typical of a holiday event. Covered in a shiny cracklin' shell, it's a showstopper worthy of the center of the table.

ACTIVE 30 MIN. - TOTAL 7 HOURS, 10 MIN.
SERVES 8

- 3 Tbsp. finely chopped fresh rosemary
- 6 large garlic cloves, minced
- 3 Tbsp. plus ¼ tsp. kosher salt, divided
- 6 ¾ tsp. black pepper, divided
- 1 (10- to 12-lb.) bone-in, skin-on pork picnic shoulder roast
- 2-3 cups water
- 2 cups ruby port
- ½ cup honey
- 8 whole cloves
- 3 Tbsp. red wine vinegar, divided
  Whipped Dijon Cream (recipe follows)

1. Stir together rosemary, garlic, 2 tablespoons of the salt, and 1 ½ tablespoons of the pepper in a small bowl. Using a retractable-blade knife, make deep cuts ¼ inch apart through skin and fat of roast. Rub rosemary mixture into cuts in roast and any other openings in the skin. Sprinkle roast with 1 tablespoon of the salt and 2 teaspoons of the pepper. Place roast, skin side up, on a wire rack in a lightly greased roasting pan. Let stand until pork is at room temperature, at least 2 hours.
2. Preheat oven to 350°F. Pour 2 to 3 cups water into roasting pan to cover the bottom of the pan. Bake in preheated oven on lowest oven rack until a meat thermometer inserted in thickest portion registers 175°F, 4 hours to 4 hours and 15 minutes.
3. Meanwhile, combine port, honey, cloves, 2 tablespoons of the vinegar, and remaining ¼ teaspoon each salt and pepper in a medium saucepan over high. Cook, stirring occasionally, until mixture thickens and reduces to a scant 1 cup, 15 to 20 minutes.
4. Remove roast from oven, and brush with half of the port mixture. Return to oven, and bake 10 minutes. Brush with remaining glaze, and bake until skin hardens, about 10 minutes. Remove roast from oven; let stand 20 minutes. Transfer roast to a serving platter. Pour pan drippings into a heatproof measuring cup; skim fat from the top. Combine pan drippings and remaining 1 tablespoon vinegar in a small saucepan over medium-high, stirring until warmed through, about 2 minutes.
5. Before slicing roast, remove hardened, crispy skin from the top of the roast; arrange around roast on the platter. Serve with pan sauce and Whipped Dijon Cream.

Whipped Dijon Cream

ACTIVE 5 MIN. - TOTAL 5 MIN.
MAKES 1 ½ CUPS

Stir together ⅓ cup **mayonnaise** and 3 Tbsp. **Dijon** mustard. Beat ½ cup **heavy cream** with an electric mixer on high speed until peaks begin to form. Fold in mayonnaise mixture until smooth. Serve immediately, or cover and chill up to 4 hours.

"Carrot Cake" Biscuits and Pineapple-Cinnamon Butter

These fluffy, not-too-sweet biscuits are a fun addition to your Easter table. You can freeze and cut the biscuit dough up to 1 week ahead. Bake from frozen as directed, increasing bake time about 3 minutes.

ACTIVE 25 MIN. - TOTAL 40 MIN.
MAKES 20 BISCUITS

- 1 ½ cups firmly packed grated carrots (about 4 medium carrots)
- ⅔ cup golden raisins
- 4 cups all-purpose flour, plus more for dusting
- ⅓ cup firmly packed light brown sugar
- 1 ½ Tbsp. baking powder
- 2 tsp. baking soda
- 1 ½ tsp. kosher salt
- 1 tsp. ground cinnamon
- ¾ cup cold unsalted butter, diced
- 1 ½ cups buttermilk
  Pineapple-Cinnamon Butter (recipe follows)

1. Preheat oven to 450°F. Combine carrots and raisins on a cutting board; roughly chop. Whisk together flour, brown sugar, baking powder, baking soda, salt, and cinnamon in a large bowl. Cut butter into flour mixture with a pastry blender or fork until crumbly. Add carrots and raisins; toss to combine.
2. Stir in buttermilk with a fork until ingredients are just combined and dough forms a ball. Turn dough out onto a floured surface; knead gently 4 to 5 times, sprinkling additional flour as necessary to prevent sticking.
3. Roll or pat dough to ¾-inch thickness. Using a 2 ½-inch round cutter, cut 20 rounds from dough, rerolling dough scraps as necessary. Arrange biscuits 1 inch apart on 2 parchment paper-lined baking sheets. Bake in preheated oven until golden brown, 13 to 15 minutes. Serve warm with Pineapple-Cinnamon Butter.

Pineapple-Cinnamon Butter

ACTIVE 5 MIN. - TOTAL 5 MIN.
MAKES ¾ CUP

Stir together ½ cup softened salted **butter**, 3 Tbsp. well-drained and chopped **crushed pineapple**, 2 Tbsp. **light brown sugar**, and ½ tsp. ground **cinnamon** with a fork until well combined. Serve at room temperature.

THE SPREADS

Artichoke and Spinach Dip

You'll love this healthier, colorful update on a crowd favorite. Leftovers are delicious tossed with hot pasta.

ACTIVE 20 MIN. - TOTAL 2 HOURS, 40 MIN.
MAKES 3 CUPS

- 1 (12-oz.) pkg. frozen artichoke hearts, thawed
- 1 Tbsp. salted butter
- 3 large garlic cloves, minced
- 1 (6-oz.) container fresh baby spinach
- 2 scallions, sliced
- 3 oz. Parmesan cheese, grated (about ¾ cup)
- ⅓ cup toasted pecan halves
- ½ cup extra-virgin olive oil
- 2 tsp. lemon zest plus 3 Tbsp. fresh juice (from 2 lemons)
- ½ tsp. kosher salt
- ¼ tsp. black pepper
  Assorted flatbreads and crudités
  Lemon zest strips

CARROT HUMMUS

ARTICHOKE AND
SPINACH DIP

1. Drain artichokes well, squeezing lightly to release excess moisture. Melt butter in a large skillet over medium-high. Add artichokes; cook, stirring occasionally, until hot, about 3 minutes. Stir in garlic, and remove from heat. Let stand until cool, about 20 minutes.

2. Process spinach and scallions in a food processor, stopping to scrape sides as necessary, until finely chopped. Transfer to a medium bowl. Process artichoke mixture, Parmesan, and pecans until finely chopped. Add artichoke-Parmesan mixture, oil, zest, and juice to spinach mixture in bowl; stir until well combined. Stir in salt and pepper. Cover and chill at least 2 hours or up to 2 days. Serve with flatbreads and crudités. Garnish with lemon zest strips, if desired.

Carrot Hummus

Carrots add a pretty orange hue and subtle sweetness to this smooth and creamy hummus. Choose milder red chiles, such as New Mexico-style or guajillo dried chiles, for heat that's not overpowering.

ACTIVE 20 MIN. - TOTAL 4 HOURS, 35 MIN.
MAKES 3 CUPS

- 1 ½ lb. carrots, peeled and roughly chopped
- 2 cups vegetable stock
- 2 large dried red chiles, stems and seeds removed
- 2 large garlic cloves
- ¼ cup tahini (sesame paste)
- 3 Tbsp. finely chopped fresh mint
- 2 Tbsp. fresh lemon juice (from 1 lemon)
- 1 tsp. ground coriander
- ½ tsp. ground cumin
- ¾ tsp. kosher salt
- ¼ tsp. black pepper
  Extra-virgin olive oil (optional)
  Toasted sesame seeds, chopped fresh parsley (optional)
  Assorted flatbreads and crudités

1. Bring carrots, stock, chiles, and garlic to a boil in a small saucepan over medium-high. Cover and reduce heat to medium-low; simmer until carrots are very tender, 15 to 20 minutes. Drain.

2. Process carrot mixture, tahini, mint, lemon juice, coriander, and cumin in a food processor, stopping to scrape sides as necessary, until very smooth, about 2 minutes. Transfer to a bowl, and stir in salt and pepper. Cover and chill 4 hours or up to 2 days. Before serving, drizzle with olive oil and sprinkle with sesame seeds and fresh parsley, if desired. Serve with flatbreads and crudités.

THE SIDES

Radishes in Warm Herb Butter

Use a colorful mix of Watermelon, French Breakfast, and Easter Egg radishes in this crunchy but warm side. This recipe comes together in minutes, so prep the ingredients in advance and cook it right before serving.

ACTIVE 10 MIN. - TOTAL 15 MIN.
SERVES 8

- 1 tsp. fennel seeds
- 5 Tbsp. cold unsalted butter, diced, divided
- 1 garlic clove, finely grated
- 1¼ lb. assorted radishes, trimmed and quartered (about 4 cups)
- 2 Tbsp. thinly sliced fresh chives
- 2 Tbsp. finely chopped fresh basil
- 1½ tsp. coarse gray sea salt
- ¼ tsp. black pepper

Crush fennel seeds with a rolling pin or heavy skillet. Heat 1 tablespoon of the butter in a large, deep skillet over medium until melted. Stir in crushed fennel seeds and grated garlic; cook, stirring often, until fragrant, about 1 minute. Stir in radishes; cook, stirring constantly, until radishes are warmed through, 2 to 3 minutes. Remove from heat. Add chives, basil, and remaining 4 tablespoons butter; stir until butter is melted. Sprinkle with salt and pepper.

New Potato and Fennel Salad

This bright and tangy potato salad pairs wonderfully with the ham. We prefer buttery Castelvetrano olives if you can find them.

ACTIVE 35 MIN. - TOTAL 55 MIN.
SERVES 8

- 3 lb. baby red potatoes, halved
- 8 cups water
- 1 Tbsp. plus 1 tsp. kosher salt, divided
- 1 fennel bulb
- ¾ cup roughly chopped green olives
- ⅓ cup extra-virgin olive oil
- 3 Tbsp. fresh lemon juice (from 2 lemons)
- 2 scallions, finely chopped
- ⅜ tsp. black pepper

NEW POTATO AND FENNEL SALAD

RADISHES IN WARM HERB BUTTER

TARRAGON ASPARAGUS WITH EGGS

1. Combine potatoes, water, and 1 tablespoon of the salt in a large saucepan. Bring to a boil over medium-high. Reduce heat to medium-low, and simmer until tender, 8 to 12 minutes. Drain, spread potatoes on a baking sheet in a single layer, and let stand until cool, about 20 minutes.
2. Chop fennel fronds to equal ½ cup. Thinly slice fennel bulb. Toss together chopped fronds, sliced fennel, green olives, oil, lemon juice, and scallions in a large bowl. Add cooled potatoes, pepper, and remaining 1 teaspoon salt; gently stir to combine. Serve at room temperature, or cover and chill up to 1 day.

Tarragon Asparagus with Eggs

Choose thick asparagus instead of thin for this dish. The wider spears have an excellent sweet flavor and can stand up to the bold tarragon vinaigrette.

ACTIVE 15 MIN. - TOTAL 15 MIN.
SERVES 8

- ⅓ cup extra-virgin olive oil
- 3 Tbsp. red wine vinegar
- 1½ Tbsp. finely chopped fresh tarragon
- 1½ tsp. Dijon mustard
- ¼ tsp. black pepper
- ⅛ tsp. granulated sugar
- 1 small shallot, finely chopped
- 3 Tbsp. plus ¾ tsp. kosher salt, divided
- 10 cups water
- 3 bunches (about 3 lb.) thick asparagus spears
- 2 boiled and peeled eggs, grated

1. Whisk together olive oil, vinegar, tarragon, mustard, pepper, sugar, shallot, and ¾ teaspoon of the salt.
2. Bring water and remaining 3 tablespoons salt to a boil in a large saucepan over medium-high. Remove and discard tough ends of asparagus spears. Place asparagus in boiling water; cook until tender-crisp, 2 to 3 minutes. Drain and rinse with cool water; pat dry.
3. Arrange asparagus on a serving platter. Drizzle with vinaigrette, and toss lightly to coat. Top with grated eggs. Serve warm or at room temperature.

THE DESSERT

You can easily swap orange
liqueur for the elderflower if
desired—either will be delicious.

Coconut Meringues with Elderflower Strawberries

This heavenly dessert tops airy meringues with pillows of mascarpone cream and fresh, juicy strawberries in an elderflower-mint syrup.

ACTIVE 30 MIN. - TOTAL 14 HOURS, INCLUDING 12 HOURS STANDING

SERVES 8

4	tsp. cornstarch
1¼	cups plus 2 Tbsp. superfine sugar, divided
5	large egg whites, at room temperature
¼	tsp. cream of tartar
⅛	tsp. salt
1	tsp. vanilla extract
1½	pt. strawberries, hulled and quartered or halved (about 4 cups)
¼	cup elderflower liqueur
2	Tbsp. finely chopped fresh mint
1	(8-oz.) container mascarpone cheese
⅓	cup cream of coconut
¾	cup heavy cream
1	cup toasted unsweetened flaked coconut

1. Preheat oven to 225°F. Whisk together cornstarch and 1¼ cups of the sugar. Beat egg whites with an electric stand mixer on medium-high speed 1 minute; add cream of tartar and salt, beating until blended. Very slowly add sugar mixture, 1 tablespoon at a time, beating until mixture is glossy, stiff peaks form, and sugar has dissolved. Add vanilla, beating until incorporated.

2. Spoon mixture into 8 tall mounds on 2 parchment paper-lined baking sheets. Flatten mounds slightly into 4-inch rounds. Using the back of a spoon, make an indentation in center of each to hold filling. Bake in preheated oven until very pale and golden, about 2 hours. Turn oven off; let meringues stand in oven, with door closed and oven light on, 12 hours.

3. Stir together strawberries, elderflower liqueur, mint, and remaining 2 tablespoons of the sugar. Let stand, stirring occasionally, until sugar is dissolved, about 15 minutes. Stir together mascarpone and cream of coconut until smooth. Beat heavy cream on high speed until stiff peaks form, 2 to 3 minutes. Fold whipped cream into mascarpone mixture.

4. Spoon mascarpone cream into center of meringues; top with strawberries and accumulated juices. Sprinkle with coconut.

Eat Your Greens

In the South, that expression usually pertains to collards and the leafy ends of turnips and beets, but spring brings a slew of gorgeous vegetables worth a new look

Pork and Bok Choy Stir-Fry

This comes together quickly in a wok or a large skillet.

ACTIVE 35 MIN. - TOTAL 35 MIN.

SERVES 6

1½ lb. pork tenderloin
¼ tsp. black pepper
1¼ tsp. kosher salt, divided
3 Tbsp. peanut oil, divided
½ lb. bok choy, cut into 1-inch pieces (about 3 cups)
3 cups matchstick carrots
1 small red onion, thinly sliced
1 Tbsp. minced peeled fresh ginger
2 garlic cloves, minced
1½ tsp. cornstarch
¾ cup chicken broth, divided
¼ cup fresh orange juice
2 Tbsp. soy sauce
Hot cooked rice

1. Cut pork into ½-inch-thick slices; cut each slice into 3 to 4 (1-inch-long) pieces. Season with pepper and ½ teaspoon of the salt.

2. Heat 1 tablespoon of the oil in a large skillet or wok over high. Add half of pork; cook, stirring, until browned, 2 to 3 minutes. Remove from skillet. Repeat with 1 tablespoon of the oil and remaining pork.

3. Heat remaining 1 tablespoon oil in skillet. Add bok choy, carrots, onion, ginger, and garlic; cook, stirring, until vegetables are tender-crisp, 3 to 4 minutes.

4. Whisk together cornstarch and 1 tablespoon of the broth in a bowl; set aside. Stir together orange juice, soy sauce, and remaining broth in a separate bowl. Pour orange juice mixture over vegetables in skillet; bring to a simmer over medium-high. Add pork and remaining ¾ teaspoon salt; simmer until meat is just done, 1 to 2 minutes. Add cornstarch mixture; cook, stirring, until thickened, about 1 minute. Serve stir-fry over hot cooked rice.

TIP

Roasting broccoli gives the florets delightfully crispy, frizzled edges. The key is cooking it in a hot oven (400°F) until the broccoli is browned and slightly charred.

Crispy Oven–Fried Chicken Cutlets with Roasted Broccoli

If your family's favorite side dish is broccoli drenched in cheese sauce, try this spicy new spin with a tangy Parmesan Cream Sauce.

ACTIVE 15 MIN. - TOTAL 35 MIN.
SERVES 4

- ½ cup salted butter, melted
- 2 Tbsp. Dijon mustard
- 1½ tsp. kosher salt, divided
- 1 tsp. black pepper, divided
- ⅔ cup panko (Japanese-style breadcrumbs)
- ½ cup crushed cornflakes cereal
- 2 oz. Parmesan cheese, grated (about ½ cup)
- 4 chicken breast cutlets (about 1¼ lb.)
- 3½ Tbsp. olive oil
- 3 garlic cloves, minced
- 1 tsp. crushed red pepper
- 1 lb. fresh broccoli florets (about 8 cups)
Parmesan Cream Sauce (recipe follows)

1. Preheat oven to 400°F. Stir together butter, mustard, and ½ teaspoon each of the salt and black pepper in a medium bowl. Stir together panko, cornflakes, and Parmesan in a second shallow bowl. Dip chicken in butter mixture; dredge in panko mixture, pressing to adhere. Place on a baking sheet lined with aluminum foil. Bake in preheated oven until chicken is browned and done, about 17 minutes.
2. Meanwhile, stir together oil, garlic, crushed red pepper, and remaining 1 teaspoon salt and ½ teaspoon black pepper in a large bowl. Add broccoli, and toss to coat. Transfer to a rimmed baking sheet, and roast at 400°F until broccoli is browned and tender, about 17 minutes. Serve chicken and broccoli with Parmesan Cream Sauce.

Parmesan Cream Sauce

ACTIVE 15 MIN. - TOTAL 15 MIN.
MAKES 1 CUP

Melt 2 Tbsp. salted **butter** in a 3-quart saucepan over medium-high. Whisk in 1 Tbsp. all-purpose **flour;** cook, whisking constantly, 1 minute. Gradually whisk in 1 cup whole **milk.** Bring to a boil, and cook, whisking constantly, until thickened, 1 to 2 minutes. Whisk in 1 oz. grated **Parmesan** cheese (about ¼ cup), 1 tsp. fresh **lemon juice,** ¼ tsp. **kosher salt,** and ¼ tsp. black **pepper.** Serve immediately.

TIP

Mild fresh spinach can be slipped into just about any recipe. Simply wilt it in a pan with a little water or oil until it cooks down. Let the spinach cool; then wring out any excess moisture. Add it to pastas, top a pizza, or whisk it into scrambled eggs.

Turkey and Spinach Meatball Sandwiches

Sautéed spinach makes these meatballs extra tender. Layer sliced leaves on hearty sandwiches for an extra dose of color and nutrients.

ACTIVE 40 MIN. - TOTAL 40 MIN.
SERVES 4

- 1 (8-oz.) pkg. fresh baby spinach, divided
- 1 Tbsp. extra-virgin olive oil
- 1½ tsp. minced garlic
- ½ tsp. kosher salt, divided
- ½ tsp. black pepper, divided
- ½ lb. ground turkey (with dark meat)
- ½ lb. spicy Italian turkey sausage, casings removed
- ½ cup fine, dry breadcrumbs
- ⅓ cup minced onion (from 1 small onion)
- 1½ oz. Parmesan cheese, grated (about ⅓ cup)
- 2 large eggs, lightly beaten
- 1½ cups jarred marinara sauce
- ¼ cup water
- 4 oz. provolone cheese, shredded (about 2 cups)
- 4 French hoagie rolls

1. Thinly slice 1 cup of the spinach; set aside. Heat oil in a Dutch oven over medium. Add garlic; cook until lightly browned and fragrant, about 1 minute. Stir in remaining spinach; cook, stirring constantly, until wilted, about 2 minutes. Add ¼ teaspoon each of the salt and pepper; cook, stirring often, 2 minutes. Drain well, and finely chop spinach mixture.

2. Stir together ground turkey, sausage, breadcrumbs, onion, Parmesan cheese, eggs, chopped spinach mixture, and remaining ¼ teaspoon each salt and pepper in a large bowl until well blended. Gently shape mixture into 20 (1-inch) balls.

3. Bring marinara sauce and water to a boil in a large skillet over medium, stirring occasionally. Reduce heat to medium-low, and maintain at a simmer. Add meatballs, and cook until meatballs are cooked through, 6 to 8 minutes. Reduce heat to low; cover and cook 10 minutes.

4. Remove from heat; sprinkle with provolone cheese. Let stand, covered, until cheese melts, 1 to 2 minutes. Divide meatballs and sauce among hoagie rolls. Top evenly with reserved sliced spinach. Serve immediately.

TIP

Naturally sweet snap peas are great eaten raw, but pickling gives the pods a vinegary punch while preserving their crunchy texture. Toss into salads, or serve on a cheese platter.

Poached Salmon Salad with Pickled Snap Peas

Crunchy Pickled Snap Peas bring welcome texture to this salad. Make the pickles 1 day in advance; store in the refrigerator up to 3 weeks.

ACTIVE 30 MIN. - TOTAL 40 MIN.
SERVES 4

3 ½ cups dry white wine (about 1 [750-milliliter] bottle)
2 cups water
2 cups thinly sliced yellow onion (about 1 large onion)
¼ cup fresh lemon juice
2 dill sprigs
4 (6-oz.) skin-on salmon fillets (about 1 inch thick)
12 oz. baby Yukon Gold potatoes, halved
3 tsp. kosher salt, divided
1 cup firmly packed fresh basil leaves
½ cup whole buttermilk
½ cup mayonnaise
½ cup sour cream
1 small shallot, sliced
2 Tbsp. apple cider vinegar
¼ tsp. black pepper
1 (5-oz.) pkg. fresh baby spinach Pickled Snap Peas (recipe follows)

1. Combine first 5 ingredients in a large, high-sided skillet; bring to a boil over medium-high. Reduce heat to medium; cover and simmer 10 minutes. Add salmon in a single layer; cook, uncovered, until opaque or to desired degree of doneness, about 7 minutes. Using a slotted spoon, transfer fish and onions to a plate; discard dill and liquid. Break fish into large pieces.
2. Place potatoes and 2 teaspoons of the salt in a medium saucepan. Add water to cover, and bring to a boil over high. Reduce heat to medium, and simmer until tender, about 10 minutes. Drain and cool 5 minutes.
3. Process basil, buttermilk, mayonnaise, sour cream, shallot, vinegar, pepper, and remaining 1 teaspoon salt in a blender or food processor until smooth. Combine potatoes, spinach, and 3 tablespoons of the dressing in a bowl; toss to coat.
4. Divide potato mixture among 4 plates. Top each with flaked salmon and Pickled Snap Peas. Drizzle each salad with remaining dressing.

Pickled Snap Peas

ACTIVE 15 MIN. - TOTAL 1 DAY, 15 MIN.
SERVES 4

Bring 1 ¼ cups **apple cider vinegar,** 1 ¼ cups **water,** 1 Tbsp. granulated **sugar,** and 1 Tbsp. **kosher salt** to a boil in a small saucepan over high, stirring to dissolve sugar and salt. Remove from heat. Stir in 2 sliced **garlic** cloves, 2 **dill** sprigs, and ⅛ tsp. **crushed red pepper;** cool 20 minutes. Place 1 (8-oz.) pkg. fresh **sugar snap peas,** stems and strings removed, in an airtight container; pour vinegar mixture over peas. Cover; chill 1 day.

TIP

There are so many ways to cook fresh or frozen sweet peas, but their creamy texture makes them an excellent addition to pesto. Swap out some or all of the basil for other tender fresh herbs like tarragon, mint, and parsley—peas complement them all.

Pea Pesto Flatbread

ACTIVE 30 MIN. - TOTAL 55 MIN.

SERVES 6

- 1 (11-oz.) pkg. refrigerated thin-crust pizza dough
- 1 cup plus 2 Tbsp. fresh basil leaves, divided
- 1 cup frozen sweet peas, thawed
- ½ cup firmly packed fresh flat-leaf parsley leaves
- ¼ cup extra-virgin olive oil
- 3 Tbsp. fresh lemon juice (from 1 large lemon)

- 2 garlic cloves
- 1 tsp. kosher salt
- 6 oz. fresh mozzarella cheese, shredded (about 1½ cups)
- 6 bacon slices, cooked crisp and crumbled

1. Preheat oven to 425°F. Press pizza dough into a 15- x 11-inch rectangle on a lightly greased (with cooking spray) rimmed baking sheet.

2. Bake on lower rack in preheated oven until lightly browned and crisp, about 12 minutes. Increase oven temperature to broil with oven rack 3 inches from heat.

3. Pulse 1 cup basil, peas, parsley, oil, lemon juice, garlic, and salt in a food processor until smooth, about 5 times. Spread pesto over crust, and top evenly with mozzarella.

4. Broil the flatbread until cheese is melted, about 2 minutes. Top evenly with cooked crumbled bacon and 2 tablespoons basil leaves. Slice the flatbread into pieces, and serve immediately.

TIP

Tenderize hardy greens like kale by blanching them in a large stockpot of boiling water. Cook the kale in salted water until tender, and then drain the kale and pat dry with paper towels. Look for bags of prewashed and chopped kale to save prep time.

Creamy Kale and Pasta Bake

Even self-professed kale haters will fall in love with this cheesy baked pasta with crispy breadcrumbs. Round out the meal with a simple side of roasted carrots.

ACTIVE 20 MIN. - TOTAL 30 MIN.
SERVES 6

4 qt. water
¼ cup plus 1 ½ tsp. kosher salt, divided
1 (16-oz.) pkg. chopped fresh kale
4 cups whole milk
6 Tbsp. cold salted butter, cut into pieces
1 cup chopped yellow onion (from 1 onion)
6 Tbsp. all-purpose flour

1 (8-oz.) pkg. preshredded Monterey Jack cheese (about 2 cups)
1 tsp. hot sauce (such as Tabasco)
½ tsp. black pepper
8 oz. uncooked medium-size shell pasta, cooked according to package directions
½ cup panko (Japanese-style breadcrumbs)
1 Tbsp. olive oil

1. Preheat broiler with oven rack 8 to 9 inches from heat. Bring 4 quarts water and ¼ cup of the salt to a boil in a Dutch oven over high. Add chopped kale; cook until tender, 5 to 7 minutes. Drain and pat dry with paper towels. Cool 10 minutes.
2. Meanwhile, place milk in a 1-quart

glass measuring cup. Cover with plastic wrap, and microwave on HIGH 3 minutes.
3. Melt butter in Dutch oven over medium. Add onion, and cook, stirring occasionally, until tender, about 6 minutes. Add flour, and cook, whisking constantly, 2 minutes. Whisk in hot milk. Increase heat to medium-high, and bring to a low boil, whisking often. Cook, whisking often, until thickened, about 6 minutes. Remove from heat; whisk in cheese, hot sauce, pepper, and remaining 1 ½ teaspoons salt. Roughly chop kale. Fold kale and cooked pasta into cheese sauce. Pour into a greased 11- x 7-inch baking dish.
4. Stir together panko and 1 tablespoon olive oil; sprinkle over pasta mixture. Broil until panko is golden brown, 1 to 2 minutes. Serve immediately.

Spring Slow-Cooker Soup

A leftover Easter ham bone is the foundation for this easy, hearty meal

Ham-and-Bean Soup

A pan of cornbread is the perfect companion to this comforting and rich Southern-style recipe.

ACTIVE 15 MIN. - TOTAL 6 HOURS, 15 MIN.
SERVES 8

- 6 cups unsalted chicken stock
- 1 lb. dried Great Northern beans, sorted of debris and rinsed
- 1 Tbsp. chopped fresh thyme
- 1½ tsp. kosher salt
- ½ tsp. black pepper
- 3 garlic cloves, chopped (about 1 Tbsp.)
- 3 celery stalks, cut into ½-inch pieces (about ½ cup)
- 2 large carrots, cut into ½-inch pieces (about 1 cup)
- 1 small yellow onion, cut into ½-inch pieces (about 1 cup)
- 1 large, meaty ham bone (about 4 lb.)

Stir together chicken stock, beans, thyme, salt, pepper, garlic, celery, carrots, and onion in a 5- to 6-quart slow cooker. Place ham bone in the center of mixture; cover and cook on HIGH until beans are tender, about 6 hours. Remove ham bone; let stand until cool enough to handle. Remove meat from bone; discard fat, gristle, and bone. Shred meat, and stir into soup.

PREP TIP

Be sure to cut the celery, carrots, and onion as uniformly as possible for the most even cooking and tenderest results.

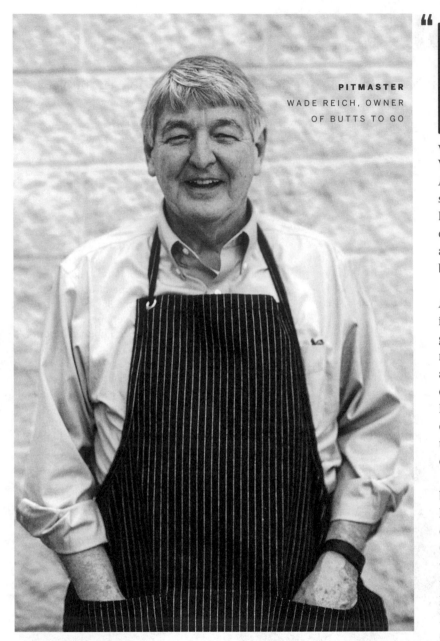

PITMASTER
WADE REICH, OWNER
OF BUTTS TO GO

The South's Best Butts

Our latest book shares the stories and secrets behind the Barbecue Belt's most beloved pitmasters

BY **MATT MOORE**

"KEPT SEEING television spots with Cindy Crawford every 15 minutes advertising Rooms To Go, so I thought, why not have some fun and name our little joint Butts To Go?" That's the promotional and humorous workings from the mind of pitmaster Wade Reich in Pell City, Alabama. As we sit inside a Texaco service station, it's just one of many lines I learn from Wade—and I soon find out that his savvy promotional awareness stretches far beyond the byways of I-20.

Born and raised in Gadsden, Alabama, Wade was brought up in the hospitality business. His great-grandfather David Reich, a merchant-turned-hotelier, owned and ran the Printup Hotel until he died in 1914. His grandfather Adolph Philip Reich, "Poppo," took over the cherished hotel, while also building the Reich Hotel, among several others.

Wade got an early start in the business working odd jobs in the hotel. After earning a marketing degree at the University of Alabama (wait for it . . . Roll Tide), he returned to Gadsden to remodel the lobby of the Printup and create "Poppo's," his own restaurant named in honor of family patriarchs. Wade credits his father, Bobby, for teaching him the way around the kitchen—that know-how combined with a mix of both Southern and Creole cooking shows.

Then there's the second phase of Wade's career. Long before the SkyMiles-esque loyalty programs of today, supermarkets would reward shoppers with free dishware, for example, for their loyalty. Such promotions were a hit with stores and consumers—and not just in Alabama. Wade spent nearly two decades dividing his time between homes in London and Paris, running such promotions throughout Europe.

After Wade returned to the States, a friend invited him to go in on a local service station. A few years later, they acquired the Texaco in Pell City, Alabama. So what about the barbecue? Well, with all his Southern-gentleman charm, Wade tells me, "The gas business got so bad that it made the food business look good."

His place serves as a quick in-and-out eatery for families and hungry road warriors to literally get their butts to go. Within an off-hour on a weekday, I notice at least a dozen or so folks coming in to request their previously placed orders for smoked butts. Other people are scattered about the convenience store, digging into their food. I can't imagine a more unpretentious environment for such a well-traveled, humble, and honestly cool cat to serve such delicious food. It's entirely fitting.

Dry-Rubbed Smoked Chicken Wings

Butts ain't the only item highly demanded by Wade's clientele. His wings are equally delicious. They come on and off the smoker throughout the day just to keep up with demand. The low-and-slow method ensures that the meat remains super moist and fall-off-the-bone tender, with a deliciously melded skin that is heavily seasoned with an in-house rub. I'm beginning to think these wings might play a part in the success of Wade's alma mater on game day.

ACTIVE 10 MIN. - TOTAL 1 HOUR, 40 MIN., INCLUDING RUB

SERVES 2

Prepare smoker according to manufacturer's instructions with an area cleared of coals to create an indirect-heat area, bringing internal temperature to 215°F; maintain temperature 15 to 20 minutes. Toss 1 lb. **chicken wings** and **drumettes** in 2 Tbsp. **Butts To Go Wing Rub** (recipe follows) until liberally coated. Smoke chicken over indirect heat, maintaining temperature inside smoker around 215°F until done, 1 ½ to 2 hours.

Butts To Go Wing Rub

Paprika, along with a good bit of salt, plays the dominant role in this fragrant, orange-hued rub, which works great with poultry.

Stir together ½ cup **paprika,** ¼ cup **kosher salt,** ¼ cup **freshly ground black pepper,** ¼ cup **garlic powder,** 2 ½ Tbsp. **dried oregano,** and 2 Tbsp. **cayenne pepper** in a bowl. Use immediately, or store in an airtight container up to 1 year. Makes about 2 cups.

Proud Mary

One taste of our made-from-scratch Bloody Mary mixer and you'll never go back to the bottled stuff again

FOR THE BEST FLAVOR, MAKE THE MIXER A DAY IN ADVANCE AND STORE IN THE REFRIGERATOR.

WHILE THE SOUTH can't lay claim to the Bloody Mary (even cocktail experts can't agree on where or when it was first made), it's such a fixture at weekend brunches and afternoon tailgates that it might as well have originated here. Like many Southern recipes, the cocktail appears simple, but it's deceptively complex. Tomato juice and vodka are essential–from there, spices and seasonings vary as much as the person making the drink. We tested all sorts of add-ins (some traditional, some not so much) to make a spicy, pungent base that's just right when mixed with your favorite vodka and served over ice in a sturdy glass. As for garnishes, some bars and restaurants are all about the show-manship, from steamed oysters to boiled shrimp, but we prefer a simpler approach with celery, pickled vegetables, and–to gild the lily–a bacon salt rim. Maybe the Bloody Mary is more Southern than we thought. . . .

How Do You Like Your Bloody Mary?

Half the fun of a Bloody Mary is the built-in snack. Here are three options.

NAKED
Celery stick

HALFWAY
Celery stick and skewer of garnishes

ALL-IN
Celery stick, skewer of garnishes, bacon salt rim, and okra

SECRETS OF A GREAT MIXER

Ⓐ

VEGETABLE JUICE
We prefer juice sold in a plastic container; the canned kind leaves a metallic aftertaste.

Ⓑ

ROASTED RED PEPPERS
This unexpected ingredient thickens the mix and balances the tomato juice flavor.

Ⓒ

LEMON AND LIME JUICES
A mix of two citrus juices adds brightness and acidity.

SET UP
A MIX-YOUR-OWN BLOODY MARY BAR

Spicy Bloody Mary Mixer

ACTIVE 10 MIN. - TOTAL 10 MIN.

MAKES 7 CUPS

- 1 (46-oz.) container plain vegetable juice (such as V8 Original)
- ⅓ cup drained roasted red peppers
- ½ cup roughly chopped scallion tops
- ¼ cup drained cocktail onions
- 1 tsp. lemon zest plus ¼ cup fresh juice (from 1 large lemon)
- ¼ cup fresh lime juice (from 2 limes)
- 2 Tbsp. Old Bay seasoning
- 2 tsp. hot sauce (such as Tabasco or Crystal)
- 2 tsp. prepared horseradish
- 2 tsp. Worcestershire sauce
- 1 tsp. celery salt
- ¼ tsp. granulated sugar

Process all ingredients in a blender until smooth. Refrigerate in an airtight container up to 4 days.

Bloody Mary Bacon Salt

ACTIVE 5 MIN. - TOTAL 5 MIN.

MAKES 1 CUP

Cook 3 thick-cut **bacon** slices until crisp. Drain on paper towels and blot dry; then crumble (making about ¼ cup). Pulse crumbled bacon, ½ Tbsp. **kosher salt,** 1 ½ Tbsp. **Old Bay** seasoning, 1 ½ Tbsp. ground **coriander,** and 1 tsp. **celery salt** in a mini food processor until ingredients are uniformly ground, 6 to 8 times. Store in an airtight container at room temperature up to 1 week.

Southern Living Bloody Mary

ACTIVE 5 MIN. - TOTAL 5 MIN.

MAKES 1 SERVING

Rub a **lime** wedge on the rim of 1 (16-oz.) glass. Spread **Bloody Mary Bacon Salt** in a saucer; dip glass rim in salt. Fill glass with ice. Squeeze 1 lime wedge and 1 **lemon** wedge into glass, and add 2 oz. **vodka.** Top with 7 oz. **Spicy Bloody Mary Mixer;** stir to combine. Garnish with a **pickled okra** pod, **celery** stick, or bamboo pick threaded with **olives** and **cocktail onions.**

---

4 Spins on the Classic

BLOODY MARIA
Replace the vodka with tequila; serve as directed.

MICHELADA
Top off light beer with Bloody Mary mixer; serve with a lime wedge.

VIRGIN MARY
Hold the vodka. Add more citrus juice to taste; serve as directed.

BLOODY CAESAR
Equal parts Bloody Mary mixer and bottled clam juice; serve as directed.

TIP

Israeli couscous (also called pearl couscous) really soaks up the tangy dressing, but you can also substitute a cooked, cooled whole grain like quinoa or bulgur.

Lickety-Split Shrimp

This tasty dish comes together faster than it takes to set the table

Garlic Shrimp and Herbed Couscous Salad

ACTIVE 15 MIN. - TOTAL 27 MIN.

SERVES 4

- 1 cup uncooked Israeli couscous
- ¼ cup olive oil, divided
- 1 lb. peeled and deveined raw small shrimp
- 1 Tbsp. minced garlic
- ½ tsp. black pepper
- ¾ tsp. kosher salt, divided
- 1 tsp. lemon zest plus 2 ½ Tbsp. fresh juice (from 1 lemon), divided
- 2 tsp. chopped fresh oregano
- 2 tsp. chopped fresh thyme
- 1 cup chopped English cucumber
- 2 oz. crumbled feta cheese
- 1 Tbsp. chopped fresh flat-leaf parsley
  Lemon wedges

1. Bring a pot of salted water to a boil; add couscous. Boil, stirring occasionally, until tender, 5 to 6 minutes. Drain and rinse under cold water. Place couscous in a large bowl.

2. Heat 1 tablespoon of the olive oil in a large skillet over medium-high. Add shrimp, and cook, stirring often, 2 minutes. Stir in garlic, pepper, and ½ teaspoon of the salt; cook until shrimp are opaque, about 1 more minute. Remove from heat, and stir in 1 ½ teaspoons of the lemon juice, tossing to coat. Cool 5 minutes.

3. Meanwhile, whisk together oregano, thyme, lemon zest, and remaining 3 tablespoons olive oil, 2 tablespoons lemon juice, and ¼ teaspoon salt. Drizzle over couscous. Add cucumber and feta, and toss to combine. Top with shrimp and parsley. Serve with lemon wedges.

Nutritional information (per serving):
Calories: 437 - Protein: 24g - Carbs: 44g - Fiber: 2g - Fat: 18g

TIP To help the cupcakes rise nice and high in the pan, make sure the eggs are at room temperature and don't overwhip them.

Cupcakes à la Mode

A scoop of ice cream turns a fudgy flourless chocolate cupcake into a celebration worthy dessert

Flourless Chocolate Cupcakes

These tasty cakes have crisp edges and intensely rich centers. Make them for a Passover dinner or for your favorite chocoholic who's going gluten-free.

ACTIVE 20 MIN. - TOTAL 1 HOUR
SERVES 12

1 1/4 cups dark chocolate chips (8 oz.)
6 Tbsp. unsalted butter
1/2 tsp. vanilla extract
1/8 tsp. salt
5 large eggs, at room temperature, separated
1/4 tsp. cream of tartar
1/3 cup granulated sugar
4 cups fudge ripple or fudge swirl ice cream
3/4 cup jarred caramel topping
3/4 cup chopped toasted pecans

1. Preheat oven to 275°F. Line a 12-cup muffin pan with baking liners; lightly coat liners with cooking spray.
2. Place chocolate and butter in a large microwave-safe bowl. Microwave on HIGH until mixture is melted, about 1 minute, stirring every 15 seconds. Stir in vanilla and salt. Cool slightly. Stir in egg yolks.
3. Place egg whites and cream of tartar in a large bowl; beat with an electric mixer fitted with a whisk attachment on medium-low speed until foamy. Increase speed to high, and beat until medium peaks form, about 2 minutes. Decrease speed to medium; beat in sugar 1 tablespoon at a time, scraping down sides of bowl as needed. Increase speed to high, and beat until stiff peaks form, about 1 minute.
4. Stir one-third of egg white mixture into chocolate mixture. Gently fold in remaining egg white mixture. Divide batter evenly among prepared muffin cups. Bake in preheated oven until set in center, 25 to 27 minutes. Let cupcakes stand in pan until completely cool, about 20 minutes.
5. To assemble dessert, remove liners from cupcakes. Place cupcakes on serving plates; top each with about 1/3 cup ice cream. Drizzle with 1 tablespoon caramel topping, and sprinkle with 1 tablespoon toasted pecans.

Ham Primer

If it's the centerpiece of your Easter menu, then now is the time to–ahem–bone up on this beloved Southern meat

FULLY COOKED
Often referred to as "city ham," this ready-to-eat ham is most likely the type you'll purchase for holiday meals. Opt for the shank end of the ham instead of the sirloin end–it has one straight bone for easier slicing. Though the meat needs no additional cooking, you can heat it and add a glaze or sauce for more flavor.

FRESH
This is the same cut (a leg) as other hams but has not been cured, smoked, or brined. Think of it as a very big pork roast.

DRY-CURED
Also called country ham, this cured and smoked beauty can take about a year to age to its full potential. Slice it thinly, and serve with biscuits.

Southern Hams Worth the Splurge

 1

SPIRAL-CUT
Kentucky-based Father's Country Hams delivers big flavor (and easy slicing) with its brown sugar-glazed spiral-cut ham. $55 for a bone-in half ham; *fatherscountry hams.com*

 2

COUNTRY HAM
You don't get called the "king of country ham" for nothing. Tennessee's Allan Benton is a favorite for his distinctively salty and smoky aged hams. $71 for a whole aged country ham; *bentons countryham.com*

 3

HONEY-GLAZED
The hickory-smoked ham from Edwards Virginia Smoke-house is flavored with a honey, brown sugar, and orange glaze. $96 for a bone-in half ham; *edwardsvaham.com*

"For the lightest, most tender meatballs, gently roll the meat into a ball shape in your hands. Don't pack it tightly."

—**Robby Melvin**
Southern Living Test Kitchen Director

All About Asparagus

Three pointers for making the most of those springy green spears

SIZE MATTERS Thin stalks are best blanched or served raw. Thicker stalks are good for roasting or grilling.

TRIM WISELY Line up asparagus on a cutting board, and slice where the stalks start to turn woody. And don't bother peeling them–it's usually unnecessary.

STORAGE SMARTS Asparagus is technically a lily, so treat spears like fresh flowers. Stand them up in a glass of water, and place in the refrigerator.

May

CHEERS *to* MOM

STRAWBERRY MIMOSAS
AND SHORTCAKE
DESSERT BAR

**TREAT THE SPECIAL WOMEN IN YOUR LIFE TO A
DELICIOUS, TOTALLY DOABLE MOTHER'S DAY
BRUNCH OF SWEET AND SAVORY FINGER FOODS**

Snickerdoodle Doughnut Hole Muffins

These little muffins are dangerously good, combining the spice of snicker-doodles and the richness of doughnuts.

ACTIVE 25 MIN. - TOTAL 37 MIN.
MAKES 2 DOZEN

MUFFINS
- ½ cup sour cream
- ¼ cup vegetable oil
- 1 large egg, at room temperature
- 1 tsp. vanilla extract
- ½ cup granulated sugar
- 1 cup all-purpose flour
- ½ tsp. baking soda
- ¼ tsp. kosher salt
- ½ tsp. ground cinnamon
- ¼ tsp. freshly grated nutmeg

COATING
- ½ cup salted butter, melted
- 1 cup granulated sugar
- 1½ tsp. ground cinnamon
- ½ tsp. freshly grated nutmeg

1. Prepare the Muffins: Preheat oven to 350°F. Lightly grease a 24-cup miniature muffin pan with cooking spray. Stir together sour cream, oil, egg, vanilla, and ½ cup sugar in a small bowl. Whisk together flour, baking soda, salt, ½ teaspoon cinnamon, and ¼ teaspoon nutmeg in a medium bowl. Whisk sour cream mixture into flour mixture. (Batter will be very thick.) Spoon 1 tablespoon of batter into each prepared muffin cup, keeping batter rounded on top.

2. Bake in preheated oven until golden and springy when touched lightly on top, 10 to 12 minutes. Cool in pan 5 minutes. Remove from pan to a wire rack; cool completely, about 15 minutes.

3. Prepare the Coating: Place melted butter in a small bowl. Whisk together 1 cup sugar, 1½ teaspoons cinnamon, and ½ teaspoon nutmeg in another small bowl.

4. Dip 1 Muffin in butter; immediately dredge in sugar mixture, and place on a serving platter. Repeat with remaining Muffins, butter, and sugar mixture.

Shortcake Dessert Bar

Let everyone help themselves to a build-your-own-shortcake station with a spread of fresh toppings.

ACTIVE 15 MIN. - TOTAL 40 MIN.
SERVES 8

SHORTCAKE CREAM BISCUITS
- 3 cups all-purpose flour
- ¼ cup granulated sugar
- 4 tsp. baking powder
- 1 tsp. kosher salt
- ¾ cup cold unsalted butter, cut into small cubes
- 1 tsp. vanilla extract
- 1¼ cups heavy cream, divided
- 2 Tbsp. turbinado or Demerara sugar

LEMON CREAM FILLING
- 1 pt. cold whipping cream
- 1 cup premium lemon curd (such as Dickinson's)
- 1 Tbsp. Grand Marnier (optional)

ADDITIONAL INGREDIENTS
- 1½ cups sliced fresh strawberries
- 1½ cups sliced fresh peaches
- 1½ cups whole fresh raspberries
- 1½ cups whole fresh blackberries

1. Prepare the Biscuits: Preheat oven to 400°F. Stir together flour, granulated sugar, baking powder, and salt in a large bowl. Using your hands or a pastry blender, gently combine flour mixture and butter until mixture resembles small peas. Stir in vanilla and 1 cup and 3 tablespoons of the heavy cream. (Mixture will be crumbly.) Turn out dough carefully onto a lightly floured surface, and gently pat into 1-inch-thick disk. Using a 2 ½-inch round cutter, cut 8 Biscuits, gathering and patting scraps as needed.

2. Transfer Biscuits to a baking sheet lined with parchment paper or a silicone baking mat. Brush tops lightly with remaining 1 tablespoon heavy cream, and sprinkle with turbinado sugar. Bake in preheated oven until golden and resistant to the touch, 20 to 25 minutes. Cool on a wire rack about 30 minutes.

3. Meanwhile, prepare Filling: Beat whipping cream with an electric mixer with chilled beaters on high speed in a large chilled bowl until stiff peaks form, about 4 minutes. Gently fold in lemon curd, and if desired, Grand Marnier.

4. Split Biscuits, and place on a serving platter. Serve with Filling and fresh fruit.

MASTER THE MIMOSA

A fizzy mimosa pairs well with every dish on this menu. Serving a simple two-ingredient signature cocktail means anyone can be a successful bartender.

Just-Right Mimosas

MAKES 1 COCKTAIL

Pour 2 oz. freshly squeezed **orange juice,** strained and chilled, in a fluted wineglass. Slowly add 2 oz. freshly opened **Champagne.** Serve immediately.

CUSTOMIZE YOUR MIMOSA

Instead of orange juice, use grapefruit, cranberry, pineapple, pomegranate, or mango juice.

Swap the juice with fresh fruit puree or sorbel, such as peach, strawberry, or raspberry.

Replace the Champagne with another type of sparkling wine, such as Prosecco, Cava, blanc de blancs, or sparkling rosé. When in doubt, ask a wine seller to guide you to a wine as dry or sweet as you like.

To create a refreshing orange-cream cocktail, add a small splash of chilled heavy cream.

Shrimp and Bacon Salad Sliders

A hint of fresh orange juice and zest in this shrimp salad is a delightful addition.

ACTIVE 20 MIN. - TOTAL 20 MIN.
SERVES 6

- ⅓ cup mayonnaise
- 1 Tbsp. chopped fresh basil
- 1 ½ tsp. fresh lemon juice (from 1 lemon)
- ½ tsp. orange zest, plus 1 ½ tsp. fresh juice (from 1 orange)
- ¾ tsp. Old Bay seasoning
- ¾ lb. chilled cooked shrimp, peeled and cut into ½-inch pieces
- 6 bacon slices, cooked crisp and diced
- ¼ tsp. kosher salt
- ¼ tsp. black pepper
- 6 slider buns
- 1 ½ Tbsp. salted butter, at room temperature
- 18 large fresh basil leaves
- 1-2 plum tomatoes, thinly sliced

1. Preheat broiler with oven rack 8 to 10 inches from heat. Stir together first 5 ingredients in a medium bowl. Fold in shrimp, bacon, salt, and pepper.
2. Split slider buns, and spread butter evenly on cut sides of buns. Place halves, butter side up, on a baking sheet; broil until light golden brown, about 3 minutes. Spoon about ¼ cup shrimp mixture on each bottom half; top each with 3 basil leaves and 1 or 2 tomato slices. Top with top slider bun halves, and serve.

Deviled Egg Salad and Asparagus Tartines

Everyone will love this fresh take on finger sandwiches. If you want more heat in the egg salad, add extra hot sauce or a dash of cayenne pepper.

ACTIVE 30 MIN. - TOTAL 30 MIN.
SERVES 8

- 6 hard-cooked eggs, peeled
- 3 Tbsp. mayonnaise
- 1 Tbsp. Dijon mustard
- 1 ½ tsp. finely chopped fresh dill
- 1 ½ tsp. finely chopped fresh chives
- 2 scallions, finely chopped
- 2 tsp. dill pickle brine or fresh lemon juice
- 1 tsp. hot sauce
- ½ tsp. kosher salt
- ¼ tsp. black pepper
- 1 lb. asparagus
- 3 Tbsp. salted butter, at room temperature
- 8 white sandwich bread slices, crusts removed, toasted

1. Using a fork, finely crush eggs in a medium bowl. Stir in next 9 ingredients.
2. Bring a medium saucepan of salted water to a boil over high. Fill a large bowl with ice water. Cut tip ends of asparagus spears into 4-inch lengths (the same length as bread slices); reserve remaining spears for another use. Cook asparagus tips in boiling water until tender-crisp, 30 seconds to 1 minute; drain. Place in ice water; drain and pat dry.
3. Spread butter evenly on toasted bread slices; cut bread slices in half lengthwise. Spread egg mixture evenly over butter; top with 2 or 3 asparagus tips. Serve immediately, or cover with damp paper towels, and chill up to 1 hour.

Avocado Fritters with Lime Cream

You'll love these crispy-on-the-outside and creamy-on-the-inside fried avocados. The Lime Cream also tastes fabulous over fish.

ACTIVE 30 MIN. - TOTAL 30 MIN.
SERVES 10 TO 12

LIME CREAM
- 1 cup sour cream
- 3 Tbsp. green hot sauce (such as Tabasco Green Jalapeño Pepper Sauce)
- ¾ tsp. lime zest
- Pinch of kosher salt

FRITTERS
- ½ cup all-purpose flour
- 1 Tbsp. chili powder
- ½ tsp. black pepper
- 2 ¼ tsp. kosher salt, divided
- 3 large eggs, beaten
- 1 ½ cups panko (Japanese-style breadcrumbs)
- 3 medium-size firm-ripe Hass avocados, peeled and cut into ½-inch-thick slices
- Vegetable oil

1. Prepare the Lime Cream: Whisk together all the ingredients. Chill until ready to serve.

2. Prepare the Fritters: Stir together flour, chili powder, pepper, and 2 teaspoons of the salt in a shallow dish. Place beaten eggs in a second shallow dish. Place panko in a third shallow dish. Dredge avocado slices, in batches, in flour mixture; dip in eggs, shaking off excess. Dredge in panko, pressing to adhere.
3. Pour oil to depth of ¼ inch in a large nonstick skillet. Heat over medium-high. Test oil by sprinkling in a pinch of panko; it should begin to sizzle immediately without the oil popping. Fry coated avocado slices, in batches, in hot oil until crisp and deep golden, about 1 minute on each side. Transfer Fritters to a wire rack, and sprinkle evenly with remaining ¼ teaspoon salt. Skim any loose panko crumbs from oil, and let oil return to temperature between batches. Serve immediately with Lime Cream.

Bite-Size Potatoes O'Brien

We turned a beloved breakfast hash into a fun finger food. If you can't find Broccolini, use broccoli and finely cut the stems.

ACTIVE 15 MIN. - TOTAL 40 MIN.
SERVES 10 TO 12

- 2 lb. fingerling potatoes
- 1 Tbsp. olive oil
- ¼ tsp. black pepper
- 1 tsp. kosher salt, divided
- 2 Tbsp. salted butter
- 4 red, yellow, or orange mini bell peppers, finely chopped
- 3 Broccolini stalks, chopped
- 2 large shallots, diced

1. Preheat oven to 425°F. Drizzle potatoes with oil, and rub to coat. Sprinkle with pepper and ¾ teaspoon of the salt. Spread in a single layer on a baking sheet, and bake until skins are slightly crispy and potatoes are tender when pierced, about 25 minutes.
2. Meanwhile, melt butter in a medium skillet over medium. Add bell peppers, Broccolini, and shallots, and cook, stirring occasionally, until tender-crisp, about 3 minutes. Stir in remaining ¼ teaspoon salt. Slit each potato lengthwise. Gently push the ends toward the center to split them open, like miniature baked potatoes. Spoon about 2 teaspoons bell pepper mixture into each potato. Serve warm.

CLOCKWISE FROM TOP LEFT:

SHRIMP AND BACON SALAD SLIDERS

DEVILED EGG SALAD AND ASPARAGUS TARTINES

AVOCADO FRITTERS WITH LIME CREAM

BITE-SIZE POTATOES O'BRIEN

CLOCKWISE FROM TOP LEFT:

BAKED FINGERLING POTATOES

CHEESE PUFFS WITH HAM SALAD

BREAKFAST SAUSAGE MEATBALLS

SNICKERDOODLE DOUGHNUT HOLE MUFFINS, *page 117*

Baked Fingerling Potatoes with Smoked Salmon and Capers

Fingerling potatoes vary in size, so make sure they are all cooked through, or use small red potatoes.

ACTIVE 15 MIN. - TOTAL 35 MIN.
SERVES 10 TO 12

- 2 lb. fingerling potatoes
- 1 Tbsp. olive oil
- ¾ tsp. kosher salt
- ¼ tsp. black pepper
- ½ cup sour cream
- 4 oz. thinly sliced smoked salmon, cut into thin strips
- 2 Tbsp. drained capers
- 1 large shallot, finely chopped
- 3 ½ Tbsp. fresh lemon juice (from 1 large lemon)
  Dill sprigs

1. Preheat oven to 425°F. Drizzle potatoes with oil, and rub to coat. Sprinkle with salt and pepper. Spread in a single layer on a baking sheet, and bake until skins are slightly crispy and potatoes are tender when pierced, about 25 minutes.
2. Slit each potato lengthwise. Gently push the ends toward the center to split them open, like miniature baked potatoes. Spoon about 1 teaspoon sour cream into each potato. Tuck in strips of salmon, and top with capers and shallots. Drizzle about ½ teaspoon lemon juice over each potato. Garnish with dill, if desired. Serve warm.

Cheese Puffs with Ham Salad

These light and airy puffs are delicious on their own and even better filled with tangy Ham Salad.

ACTIVE 1 HOUR - TOTAL 1 ½ HOURS
SERVES 10

- 1 cup all-purpose flour
- ½ tsp. kosher salt
- ½ tsp. dry mustard
- ½ tsp. cayenne pepper
- 1 cup water
- ½ cup unsalted butter
- 4 large eggs, at room temperature
- 6 oz. Gruyère cheese, grated (about 1 ½ cups)
  Ham Salad (recipe follows)

1. Preheat oven to 450°F. Whisk together flour, salt, dry mustard, and cayenne in a small bowl. Bring water and butter to a boil in a medium saucepan over medium-high, stirring to melt butter. Remove from heat; add flour mixture all at once, and stir vigorously until mixture is smooth and thick, like mashed potatoes. Transfer to large bowl, and let stand 3 minutes. Beat dough with an electric mixer on low speed until dough no longer steams and is just warm to the touch, about 1 minute. Add eggs, 1 at a time, beating on medium-high speed until dough is smooth and creamy after each addition. Add cheese, and beat until combined.
2. Line a baking sheet with parchment paper or a silicone baking mat. Use a ½-ounce ice-cream scoop or 2 spoons to portion dough into walnut-size mounds (about 1 tablespoon) 1 inch apart onto prepared baking sheet.
3. Bake at 450°F for 10 minutes. Reduce heat to 350°F, and continue baking until Cheese Puffs are puffed, deep golden brown, and dry to the touch, 15 to 20 more minutes. (They should sound hollow when tapped on the bottom.)
4. Cool on baking sheet 3 minutes; split with a serrated knife. Spoon about 1 tablespoon Ham Salad into each, and replace the tops. Serve warm or at room temperature.

MAKE AHEAD: Reheat baked Cheese Puffs in a 300°F oven 5 to 10 minutes before filling and serving, or freeze unbaked mounds until solid; then transfer to ziplock plastic freezer bag. Bake frozen Cheese Puffs at 350°F, increasing baking time by 5 to 10 minutes.

Ham Salad

Make up to 3 days in advance, and then cover and refrigerate. Serve at room temperature.

ACTIVE 10 MIN. - TOTAL 10 MIN.
MAKES 2 CUPS

- 4 oz. cream cheese, at room temperature
- 2 scallions, finely chopped
- 2 Tbsp. finely chopped fresh flat-leaf parsley
- 1 Tbsp. Creole mustard
- ¼ tsp. cayenne pepper
- ¼ tsp. black pepper
- 8 oz. smoked fully cooked ham, finely chopped

Stir together cream cheese, scallions, parsley, mustard, cayenne, and black pepper in a medium bowl. Fold in ham.

Breakfast Sausage Meatballs with Apple Butter Dipping Sauce

These pork sausage meatballs are more festive than sausage patties.

ACTIVE 20 MIN. - TOTAL 1 HOUR.
SERVES 12

MEATBALLS
- 1 lb. hot ground pork breakfast sausage (such as Jimmy Dean)
- 1 large egg, beaten
- ¼ cup grated apple
- ¼ cup grated onion (from ½ medium onion)
- 1 oz. Parmesan cheese, finely grated (about ¼ cup)
- 2 tsp. finely chopped fresh sage
- ½ cup fine, dry breadcrumbs, divided

DIPPING SAUCE
- ½ cup apple butter
- 3 Tbsp. sharp honey mustard

GARNISH
Fresh flat-leaf parsley

1. Prepare the Meatballs: Preheat oven to 400°F. Coat a 24-cup miniature muffin pan with cooking spray. Place sausage in a large bowl, and let stand at room temperature 15 minutes. Gently stir in egg, apple, onion, Parmesan, sage, and ¼ cup of the breadcrumbs. (Mixture should be well combined but not overworked.) Using gloves or hands dipped in ice water, gently shape sausage mixture into 24 (1 ½-inch) balls. Coat balls lightly in remaining ¼ cup breadcrumbs; place 1 ball in each prepared muffin cup.
2. Bake in preheated oven until browned on the bottom and beginning to sizzle around the edges, about 10 minutes. Remove from oven, and, using tip of a knife, turn Meatballs over. Return to oven, and bake until cooked through and well browned, about 10 minutes. Remove from oven, and let stand 5 minutes.
3. Meanwhile, prepare the Dipping Sauce: Stir together apple butter and mustard in a small bowl. Place Meatballs on a serving platter, and, if desired, garnish with parsley. Serve warm with Dipping Sauce.

Cinco de Mayo San Antonio Style

On May 5, Texas chef Johnny Hernandez celebrates with his favorite things: tacos, tequila, and a table surrounded by good friends

JOHNNY HERNANDEZ

Johnny Hernandez is in the kitchen of his San Antonio home slicing melon, pineapple, and papaya into perfectly symmetrical strips when the memory of his first restaurant job makes him laugh out loud. It's a warm, rich laugh that surfaces easily and often—and it's contagious. "When I was 14, I got hired at a Marriott downtown to cut up fruit for their brunch buffet," he recalls. "I thought I was a big deal because I was finally getting to wear a starched white chef's coat and tall hat. I was so proud; I would even wear the uniform home!"

It might have been his first time in a toque, but Hernandez had already spent most of his life in restaurants. When he was growing up in San Antonio, his parents ran a small one that served "a wonderful combination of Mexican and Texas comfort foods," he explains. His earliest memories involve the foods and fragrances that surrounded him: chorizo frying with eggs, chiles toasting, and tortillas cooking on a comal (a flat Mexican griddle). So it's no surprise that he was seduced by a career in the kitchen.

After graduating from The Culinary Institute of America in New York and working several high-end cooking stints around the country, he was pulled back home by a yearning for family. Since returning, he has created a growing empire and become a driving force in the city's red-hot culinary scene. His restaurants have distinct identities, but they're all anchored in the heart and soul of Mexico. La Gloria serves street food like Tacos al Pastor; El Machito is Hernandez's shrine to wood-fire grilled meat; and The Frutería riffs on Mexico's colorful produce stands with fruity cocktails (served along with tostadas and tortas).

With more projects on the horizon, the chef shows no sign of slowing down. But he always makes time to toast Cinco de Mayo at his historic hacienda. His menu is typical of both the holiday and host: colorful, casual, and fun. He says, "I love to cook, but there is something more meaningful to it when you're cooking for friends in your home."

Queso Fundido with Mushrooms and Chiles

Hernandez tops this molten three-cheese dip with a mouthwatering mixture of toasted garlic, mushrooms, and green chiles.

ACTIVE 15 MIN. - TOTAL 40 MIN.
SERVES 10

- 1 lb. Monterey Jack cheese, grated (about 4 cups)
- 8 oz. Muenster cheese, grated (about 2 cups)
- 8 oz. queso fresco (fresh Mexican cheese), grated (about 2 cups)
- ½ lb. Anaheim chiles
- ¼ cup olive oil, divided
- 3 garlic cloves, sliced
- 1 lb. white mushrooms, sliced Tortilla chips

1. Preheat oven to 400°F. Gently stir together Monterey Jack, Muenster, and queso fresco in a large bowl.
2. Spread chiles in an even layer on a rimmed baking sheet, and drizzle with 1 tablespoon of the oil. Bake in preheated oven until chiles have softened and skins have blistered, 20 to 25 minutes. Remove chiles from oven; do not turn off oven. Peel and seed chiles under cool running water. Chop chiles, and set aside.
3. Brush a 12-inch cast-iron skillet with 1 tablespoon of the oil, and add cheese mixture to skillet. Bake until cheese has melted and top is golden brown, 20 to 25 minutes.
4. Meanwhile, heat remaining 2 tablespoons olive oil in a large sauté pan or skillet over medium. Add garlic, and cook, stirring often, until slightly browned, about 1 minute. Add mushrooms, and cook, stirring often, until mushrooms have softened and liquid has almost completely evaporated, 6 to 7 minutes. Add roasted chiles, and cook, stirring often, until mixture is hot, 1 to 2 minutes.
5. Carefully remove the hot skillet from oven. Top cheese with mushroom mixture. Serve with tortilla chips.

PAPAYA-STRAWBERRY COCKTAIL

Guacamole with Jicama

Crunchy cubes of jicama and a little orange zest make this guacamole especially good. This recipe can be easily doubled or tripled, which we recommend—it tends to disappear quickly.

ACTIVE 15 MIN. - TOTAL 15 MIN.
SERVES 6

- 2 firm, ripe avocados, halved
- ½ cup chopped peeled jicama
- 2 Tbsp. fresh lime juice (from 2 limes)
- 2 Tbsp. minced fresh cilantro
- 1 Tbsp. minced jalapeño chile (about 1 chile)
- 2 tsp. orange zest (from 1 orange)
- ½ tsp. kosher salt

Mash avocados in a medium bowl. Stir in jicama, lime juice, cilantro, jalapeño, and orange zest. Stir in salt; cover and chill until ready to serve.

Fruits and Vegetables with Lime and Chile Powder

Slice the produce into big spears and chunks so it can be eaten with bare hands or toothpicks.

ACTIVE 20 MIN. - TOTAL 20 MIN.
SERVES 8

Stir together 3 lb. coarsely chopped **assorted fruits and vegetables** (such as jicama, cucumber, watermelon, mango, cantaloupe, honeydew, pineapple, and carrots) in a large bowl. Cover and chill until ready to serve (up to 8 hours). When ready to serve, add ¼ cup fresh **lime juice**, 1 tsp. kosher **salt,** and ½ tsp. **chile powder,** and gently stir using a rubber spatula. Transfer to a serving platter. Top with 1 Tbsp. lime juice and ⅛ tsp. each salt and chile powder.

Papaya-Strawberry Cocktail

Instead of the usual margaritas, mix up a pitcher of these fresh, fruity cocktails. Use a light tequila, such as Herradura Silver.

ACTIVE 20 MIN. - TOTAL 20 MIN.
SERVES 6

Place 24 (1-inch) cubes fresh **papaya,** 6 hulled and quartered fresh **strawberries,** and 6 fresh **mint** leaves in a large glass measuring cup, and gently muddle to release flavors. Add 1 ½ cups fresh **orange juice,** 1 cup plus 2 Tbsp. **tequila blanco,** ¾ cup **simple syrup,** and ¾ cup fresh **lime juice;** stir to combine. Pour into a 4-quart pitcher, and chill until ready to serve. Serve over ice. Garnish with **orange slices** and mint leaves.

Grilled Chicken Tacos

A simple citrus marinade keeps the chicken tender and infuses it with bright, sunny flavor. Achiote paste is a fragrant, deep red spice mixture that includes oregano, cumin, and allspice.

ACTIVE 30 MIN. - TOTAL 3 HOURS, 45 MIN.
SERVES 8

- 2-3 lb. boneless, skin-on chicken thighs
- 3 cups fresh orange juice
- ½ cup fresh lime juice
- 4 garlic cloves
- 1 Tbsp. kosher salt
- 3 Tbsp. minced fresh cilantro
- 1 (7-oz.) container achiote paste
- 1 fresh pineapple, peeled, cored, and cut into ½-inch-thick slices
- 1 cup firmly packed fresh cilantro leaves
- 1 (1 ½-lb.) jicama, peeled and diced (about 2 cups)
- 8 (6-inch) corn or flour tortillas
  Lime wedges
  Salsa

1. Place chicken thighs in a large ziplock plastic freezer bag. Process orange juice, lime juice, garlic, salt, minced cilantro, and achiote paste in a blender until smooth. Pour over chicken; seal bag, and turn to coat. Chill 3 hours.
2. Preheat grill to medium (350°F to 450°F). Place pineapple slices on oiled grates, and grill, uncovered, until slightly charred, 2 to 3 minutes per side. Chill 30 minutes.
3. Meanwhile, remove chicken from marinade; discard marinade. Place chicken on oiled grates, and grill, covered, until a thermometer inserted in thickest portion registers 165°F, 6 to 7 minutes per side. Remove from grill; cover with foil while pineapple chills.
4. Dice grilled pineapple; toss with cilantro leaves and jicama.
5. Slice chicken, and divide among warmed tortillas; top tacos with pineapple mixture. Serve with limes and salsa.

Grilled Sirloin Tacos

This steak is tender and deeply flavored with a simple blender marinade of onion, garlic, jalapeños, and beer.

ACTIVE 30 MIN. - TOTAL 4 HOURS, 45 MIN.
SERVES 8

- 2-3 lb. boneless (½-inch-thick) top sirloin steaks
- 1 lb. white onions (about 1 ½ large onions), chopped
- 6 garlic cloves
- 2 jalapeño chiles, seeded and chopped
- 2 Tbsp. kosher salt
- 1 tsp. cracked black pepper
- 6 oz. Mexican beer (such as Corona)
- ½ cup water
- 1 cup firmly packed fresh cilantro leaves
- 2 small red onions, thinly sliced
- 8 (6-inch) corn or flour tortillas
  Lime wedges
  Salsa

1. Place sirloin steaks in a large ziplock plastic freezer bag. Process white onions, garlic cloves, seeded and chopped jalapeños, kosher salt, black pepper, beer, and water in a blender until smooth. Pour over steaks; seal bag, and turn to coat. Chill 3 hours.
2. Preheat grill to medium-high (about 450°F). Remove steak from marinade; discard marinade. Place steak on oiled grates, and grill sirloin, uncovered, until a thermometer inserted in thickest portion registers 145°F or to desired degree of doneness, 5 to 6 minutes per side for medium-rare. Let steak stand 3 minutes before diagonally slicing across the grain.
3. Toss together cilantro leaves and red onion slices. Heat tortillas on a comal (flat griddle) or according to package directions.
4. Divide steak among tortillas; top with cilantro mixture. Serve with limes and salsa.

Paletas

Kids and adults will melt over these refreshing Mexican frozen pops. You'll want a stash of them in your freezer all summer long—especially the cucumber-chile flavor, which won rave reviews in our Test Kitchen.

ACTIVE 15 MIN. - TOTAL 5 HOURS, 15 MIN.
SERVES 6 (SERVING SIZE: 1 PALETA)

STRAWBERRY-COCONUT PALETAS

Process 3 ¾ cups halved, hulled fresh **strawberries** in a blender until smooth. Pour strawberry puree through a fine wire-mesh strainer into a bowl, and press to extract juice from solids; discard solids. Add ⅓ cup granulated **sugar**, ¼ cup unsweetened **coconut flakes,** and 1 Tbsp. fresh **lemon juice** to strawberry puree; stir until sugar is dissolved. Pour mixture evenly into 6 (2 ½-oz.) plastic frozen pop molds. Top with lids, and insert pop sticks, leaving 2 inches of each stick exposed. Freeze paletas until firm, 3 to 5 hours or overnight.

TART MANGO PALETAS

Process 2 ½ cups fresh **mango** chunks (from 1 ½ [1-lb.] mangoes), ¼ cup granulated **sugar,** and 3 Tbsp. fresh **lime juice** (from 2 limes) in a blender until smooth. Pour mixture evenly into 6 (2 ½-oz.) plastic frozen pop molds. Top with lids, and insert pop sticks, leaving 2 inches of each stick exposed. Freeze paletas until firm, 3 to 5 hours or overnight.

CUCUMBER-CHILE PALETAS

Process 2 (11- to 12-oz.) **cucumbers,** peeled, seeded, and cut into chunks, ⅔ cup granulated **sugar,** ⅓ cup fresh **lemon juice** (from 2 lemons), and 1 **jalapeño chile,** seeded and rinsed, in a blender until smooth. Pour cucumber mixture through a fine wire-mesh strainer into a bowl, and press to extract juice from solids; discard solids. Pour mixture evenly into 6 (2 ½-oz.) plastic frozen pop molds. Top with lids, and insert pop sticks, leaving 2 inches of each stick exposed. Freeze paletas until firm, 3 to 5 hours or overnight.

GRILLED
SIRLOIN
TACOS

QUESO
FUNDIDO
WITH
MUSHROOMS
AND CHILES,
PAGE 123

GUACAMOLE
WITH JICAMA,
PAGE 123

GRILLED
CHICKEN
TACOS

Pasta Night!

Six crowd-pleasing suppers that dress up your favorite noodles with fresh, flavorful summertime produce

Shrimp Boil Pasta

Two summertime staples—pasta salads and shrimp boils—combine in this fun family-style meal. The tangy sauce, flavored with scallions, Old Bay seasoning, lemon, and thyme, is truly delicious.

ACTIVE 25 MIN. - TOTAL 35 MIN.
SERVES 6

- 1 lb. uncooked gemelli or casarecce pasta
- 16 oz. smoked sausage, cut into ½-inch-thick slices
- 2 cups chicken broth
- 2 cups fresh corn kernels (about 3 ears)
- 2 lb. raw peeled and deveined large shrimp
- 2 ½ tsp. Old Bay seasoning
- 1 bunch scallions, sliced (about 1 cup)
- 2 Tbsp. fresh lemon juice (from 1 lemon)
- 1 Tbsp. fresh thyme leaves

1. Cook pasta in salted water according to package directions. Drain and transfer to a large serving bowl; cover to keep warm.

2. While pasta cooks, cook sausage in a Dutch oven over medium-high, stirring occasionally, until browned, about 5 minutes. Drain and discard pan drippings. Stir in broth and corn. Bring to a boil; reduce heat to medium-low, and simmer until corn is tender-crisp, about 5 minutes.

3. Add shrimp and Old Bay to sausage mixture; stir to combine. Cover and cook until shrimp are done, 2 to 4 minutes. Remove from heat, and stir in scallions and lemon juice.

4. Add shrimp mixture to pasta; toss gently to combine. Sprinkle with thyme.

SAUSAGE SWAP
YOU CAN USE PORK,
TURKEY, CHICKEN, OR
VEGGIE SAUSAGE AS
LONG AS IT'S SPICY

Sweet Pepper Pasta with Sausage

Any sweet peppers will work in this dish, but we like colorful, tender baby bell peppers.

ACTIVE 20 MIN. - TOTAL 30 MIN.
SERVES 6

- 1 lb. uncooked orecchiette pasta
- 1 lb. hot Italian sausage, casings removed
- 3 Tbsp. unsalted butter, divided
- 1 lb. multicolored sweet baby bell peppers, thinly sliced cross-wise
- 2 Tbsp. red wine vinegar
- 1½ tsp. kosher salt
- 1 garlic clove, minced
- ⅓ cup coarsely chopped fresh oregano
- 1¼ oz. Pecorino Romano cheese, finely shredded (about ½ cup)
- ¼ cup torn fresh basil

1. Cook pasta in salted water according to package directions. Drain, reserving 1½ cups cooking water.
2. While pasta cooks, cook sausage in a large nonstick skillet over medium-high, stirring to break into bite-size pieces, until cooked through, 5 to 7 minutes.

Transfer to a plate lined with paper towels. Discard drippings.
3. Add 2 tablespoons of the butter to skillet, stirring and scraping to loosen browned bits from bottom of skillet. Add peppers, and cook, stirring occasionally, 3 minutes. Stir in vinegar, salt, and garlic; cook 1 minute. Stir in pasta, sausage, and remaining 1 tablespoon butter. Stir in cooking water, ¼ cup at a time, until sauce is smooth and coats pasta. Discard any remaining cooking water. Stir in oregano.
4. Top servings evenly with cheese and basil.

TIP

Broil the vegetables before you add them to the pasta to keep them from releasing too much water as the pasta bakes.

EXTRA CHEESE
TWO LAYERS OF RICOTTA MAKE THIS ZITI EXTRA TASTY.

Baked Ziti with Summer Vegetables

We lightened up the usual baked pasta with loads of in-season squash and tomatoes—this is a delicious way to use up your farmers' market haul.

ACTIVE 25 MIN. - TOTAL 50 MIN.
SERVES 8

- 1 lb. uncooked ziti pasta
- 2 ½ lb. yellow squash and zucchini, sliced into ½-inch-thick rounds and half-moons
- 2 pt. red grape tomatoes
- 2 garlic cloves, minced
- 3 Tbsp. extra-virgin olive oil, divided
- 2 tsp. kosher salt, divided
- 1 tsp. black pepper, divided
- 2 cups ricotta cheese
- 2 oz. Romano cheese, grated (about ½ cup)
- ⅓ cup chopped fresh basil
- 1 tsp. white wine vinegar
- 1 (12-oz.) jar marinara sauce
- 6 oz. mozzarella cheese, shredded (about 1 ½ cups)
  Fresh basil leaves

1. Cook pasta in salted water according to package directions. Drain and cool slightly, about 10 minutes.
2. While pasta cooks, preheat broiler with oven rack 6 inches from heat. Toss together squash, zucchini, tomatoes, garlic, 2 tablespoons of the oil, 1 teaspoon of the salt, and ½ teaspoon of the pepper on an aluminum foil-lined rimmed baking sheet. Spread in a single layer; broil until charred and tender, about 10 minutes.
3. Preheat oven to 350°F. Stir together ricotta, Romano, basil, vinegar, and remaining 1 tablespoon oil, 1 teaspoon salt, and ½ teaspoon pepper in a small bowl.
4. Combine pasta, cooked vegetables, and marinara sauce in a large bowl; gently stir to combine. Spoon half of pasta mixture into a 13- x 9-inch baking dish. Dollop 1 cup of ricotta mixture evenly on pasta mixture. Repeat with remaining pasta mixture and ricotta mixture. Top evenly with mozzarella.
5. Bake at 350°F until lightly browned and bubbly, about 25 minutes. Let stand 5 minutes before serving. Sprinkle with basil.

ADD PROTEIN
TOP PASTA WITH
GRILLED SHRIMP
OR CHICKEN.

Spaghetti with Pecan Pesto and Garlicky Breadcrumbs

A zingy pesto and buttery breadcrumbs make this simple pasta anything but ordinary.

ACTIVE 20 MIN. - TOTAL 30 MIN.
SERVES 6

- 16 oz. uncooked thin spaghetti
- 3 cups loosely packed fresh basil leaves
- 3 cups loosely packed fresh flat-leaf parsley leaves
- 6 oz. Parmesan cheese, grated (about 1 ½ cups), plus more for serving
- 1 cup olive oil
- ½ cup pecan halves (about 2 oz.)
- 3 Tbsp. fresh lemon juice (from 2 lemons)
- 2 garlic cloves
- 1 tsp. kosher salt
- 2 Tbsp. unsalted butter
  Garlicky Breadcrumbs (recipe follows)

1. Cook pasta in salted water according to package directions. Drain, reserving 1 ½ cups cooking water. Transfer pasta to a large serving bowl; cover to keep warm.
2. While pasta cooks, process basil, parsley, Parmesan, oil, pecans, lemon juice, garlic, and salt in a food processor until smooth, stopping to scrape down sides as necessary.
3. Add pesto and butter to hot pasta; toss gently until pasta is coated. Stir in cooking water, ¼ cup at a time, until sauce reaches desired consistency. Discard any remaining cooking water. Top with Garlicky Breadcrumbs and Parmesan.

Garlicky Breadcrumbs

- 4 garlic cloves
- 5 oz. sourdough or other crusty bread, crust removed, cut into 1-inch pieces (about 2 cups)
- 1 tsp. lemon zest (from 1 lemon)
- ½ tsp. kosher salt
- ¼ tsp. black pepper
- ¼ cup olive oil

1. Pulse garlic cloves in a food processor until finely chopped. Add bread and lemon zest, and pulse until coarse crumbs form. Stir in salt and pepper.
2. Heat oil in a Dutch oven over medium. Add breadcrumb mixture, and cook, stirring often, until golden brown and crisp, about 5 minutes. Using a slotted spoon, transfer breadcrumb mixture to a small bowl.

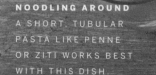

NOODLING AROUND
A SHORT, TUBULAR PASTA LIKE PENNE OR ZITI WORKS BEST WITH THIS DISH.

Penne with Mushrooms, Corn, and Thyme

Cream cheese and half-and-half meld together to make this wonderfully luscious sauce.

ACTIVE 25 MIN. - TOTAL 35 MIN.
SERVES 6

- 16 oz. uncooked penne pasta
- 3 Tbsp. unsalted butter, divided
- 2 Tbsp. extra-virgin olive oil, divided
- 1 ½ lb. cremini mushrooms, quartered
- 2 ½ cups fresh corn kernels (4 ears)
- 6 oz. cream cheese, softened
- ¾ cup half-and-half
- 1 ½ Tbsp. fresh thyme leaves
- 1 tsp. kosher salt
- ½ tsp. black pepper
- ¼ cup fresh chives, cut in 1-inch pieces (about 3 oz.)

1. Cook pasta in salted water according to package directions. Drain pasta, reserving 1 ½ cups cooking water.

2. Heat 1 ½ tablespoons of the butter and 1 tablespoon of the oil in a large Dutch oven over medium-high. Add half of the mushrooms, and cook, stirring occasionally, until lightly browned, about 6 minutes. Transfer mushrooms to a plate. Repeat process with remaining butter, oil, and mushrooms. Return mushrooms to Dutch oven. Add corn; cook, stirring often, until corn is tender, about 5 minutes. Add cream cheese, half-and-half, thyme, salt, and pepper. Cook, stirring constantly, until cream cheese is melted and mixture is smooth. Add pasta, and stir to combine. Stir in reserved cooking water, ¼ cup at a time, until sauce reaches desired consistency. Discard any remaining cooking water.

3. Top servings evenly with chives.

The Secret to the Best Pasta Sauce

● **FORGET ABOUT THE FANCY** olive oil or expensive Parmesan cheese. The key to a great bowl of pasta is probably what you're pouring down the kitchen drain: the pasta water. This salty, starchy liquid seasons the sauce, gives it a silky texture, and helps it cling to the noodles. And the best pasta water starts with salt—you need about 2 tablespoons of kosher salt for a large stockpot of water. Once the noodles are cooked to your liking, reserve a few cups of cooking water before draining the pasta. (Don't rinse the cooked noodles, or you'll wash away more precious starch.) Add the pasta water to the sauce, just a splash or two at a time, until it's rich and smooth.

PERFECT PAIRING
SERVE WITH A LIGHT,
CRISP WHITE WINE
LIKE PINOT GRIGIO
OR VINHO VERDE.

TIP
Don't worry about the raw egg yolks in this recipe. The heat of the pan and hot pasta water "cook" them, making a rich, silky sauce.

Tomato Carbonara

Give this indulgent pasta dish more of an Italian flair by using prosciutto or pancetta instead of bacon. Cherry tomatoes add pops of summery brightness and color.

ACTIVE 35 MIN. - TOTAL 35 MIN.
SERVES 6

- 12 oz. uncooked dried fettuccine
- 1 cup chopped bacon (about 9 oz.)
- 2 pt. multicolored cherry tomatoes
- 2 shallots, thinly sliced (about ½ cup)
- 2 garlic cloves, minced
- 3 large egg yolks
- 2 oz. Parmesan cheese, grated (about ½ cup), plus more for serving
- 3 Tbsp. chopped fresh chives
- 3 Tbsp. chopped fresh flat-leaf parsley
- ½ tsp. black pepper

1. Cook pasta in salted water according to package directions. Drain, reserving 1 ½ cups cooking water.
2. While pasta cooks, cook bacon in a large skillet over medium-high until crisp, 5 to 6 minutes. Transfer bacon to a plate lined with paper towels to drain; reserve 2 tablespoons drippings in skillet.
3. Add tomatoes to skillet, and cook, stirring often, until slightly softened, about 3 minutes. Add shallots, and cook, stirring often, until shallots and tomatoes are softened, 3 to 4 minutes. Add garlic; cook, stirring constantly, 1 minute. Add 1 cup of the reserved cooking water; bring to boil. Remove from heat, and stir in pasta. Stir in egg yolks, 1 at a time, until thoroughly combined.
4. Return skillet to medium-low, and cook, stirring constantly, until sauce is slightly thickened and creamy, 2 to 3 minutes. Remove from heat; stir in bacon, cheese, chives, parsley, and pepper until cheese melts and sauce is smooth, adding remaining ½ cup cooking water if necessary to reach desired consistency.
5. Top servings evenly with grated Parmesan.

TIP

A wire rack isn't just for cooling cookies—use it to make a double-decker sheet pan supper.

Drumsticks, Please

A chicken-and-squash sheet pan supper bursting with flavor

Sweet-and-Spicy Chicken Drumsticks with Squash

Choose red pepper jelly, rather than green, to make this glistening glaze.

ACTIVE 15 MIN. - TOTAL 1 HOUR

SERVES 4

- 2 medium-size yellow squash, diagonally cut into ⅓-inch-thick slices
- 2 medium zucchini, diagonally cut into ⅓-inch-thick slices
- 1½ Tbsp. olive oil
- 1¼ tsp. kosher salt, divided
- ½ tsp. black pepper, divided
- ¾ cup hot pepper jelly
- 1 Tbsp. Dijon mustard
- 1 Tbsp. apple cider vinegar
- 1 Tbsp. honey
- 1 tsp. hot sauce (such as Tabasco)
- 8 chicken drumsticks (about 2½ lb.)
- 2 Tbsp. chopped fresh flat-leaf parsley

1. Preheat oven to 400°F with an oven rack in center of oven and another oven rack 6 inches from broiler.
2. Toss together squash, zucchini, olive oil, ½ teaspoon of the salt, and ¼ teaspoon of the pepper. Place on an aluminum foil-lined rimmed baking sheet in a single layer.
3. Microwave hot pepper jelly in a large microwave-safe bowl on HIGH until melted, about 1½ minutes, stirring every 30 seconds. Whisk in mustard, vinegar, honey, hot sauce, and remaining ¾ teaspoon salt and ¼ teaspoon pepper. Remove and reserve ¼ cup of the pepper jelly mixture.
4. Add chicken to remaining pepper jelly mixture in bowl; toss to coat. Fit a wire rack over squash on baking sheet; place chicken on rack. Bake in center of preheated oven until browned on top, 20 to 25 minutes. Turn chicken, and bake until browned on top and a meat thermometer inserted into thickest portion registers 165°F, about 20 minutes. Remove wire rack and chicken; brush with reserved pepper jelly mixture.
5. Increase oven temperature to broil. Transfer squash to upper oven rack; broil until tender and lightly browned, about 4 minutes. Top with parsley.

TIP

Add a handful of mixed greens for extra volume, or swap out the bulgur wheat for another hearty whole grain like quinoa or farro.

Whole-Grain Goodness

This filling vegetarian dish comes together in less than 30 minutes

Black-Eyed Pea and Grain Salad

Texas caviar, the classic combo of black-eyed peas, peppers, cilantro, and scallions, inspired this zesty main dish salad.

ACTIVE 10 MIN. - TOTAL 25 MIN.
SERVES 4

- ½ cup uncooked bulgur wheat
- 1 cup water
- ⅓ cup olive oil
- ¼ cup Champagne vinegar
- 1 tsp. hot sauce (such as Tabasco)
- 1 tsp. kosher salt
- ½ tsp. granulated sugar
- ¼ tsp. black pepper
- 2 (15-oz.) cans black-eyed peas, drained and rinsed
- 1 cup fresh corn kernels (about 2 medium ears)
- ¾ cup chopped red bell pepper (from 1 medium bell pepper)
- ½ cup sliced scallions (about 3 scallions)
- 2 Tbsp. chopped fresh cilantro
- 1 small jalapeño chile, seeds removed, diced (about 2 Tbsp.)
- 2 oz. queso fresco, crumbled (about ½ cup)

1. Bring bulgur and water to a boil in a small saucepan over high. Reduce heat to low; cover and simmer until tender, about 5 minutes. Spread bulgur in an even layer on a baking sheet, and cool 10 minutes.

2. Meanwhile, whisk together olive oil, vinegar, hot sauce, salt, sugar, and black pepper.

3. Toss together black-eyed peas, corn, bell pepper, scallions, cilantro, jalapeño, cooked bulgur, and dressing. Top with queso fresco.

Nutritional information (per serving):
Calories: 479 - Protein: 24g - Carbs: 54g - Fiber: 11g - Fat: 27g

CORNMEAL CAKE
TRY DRESSING UP THIS
HOMEY DESSERT WITH
WHIPPED CREAM.

Juicy Little Gems

It's peak season for sweet Southern blueberries

THERE'S SOMETHING INCREDIBLY satisfying about harvesting your own fruits and vegetables. I love blueberries so much that I went to great lengths to grow them in my own backyard—including draping the bushes with netting to prevent birds from enjoying the fruit before I did. Every now and then, a bird would get caught in a net; it was a bit traumatic for everyone involved, even though I was able to free all of the attempted robbers. I love viewing birds from afar but not up close and personal. As if that weren't terrifying enough, last year's crop attracted baby garden snakes, which promptly ended my foray into blueberry growing. There are lots of folks who are better at farming than I am—like farmers. From mid-April through August, you can find pints of Southern-grown blueberries at farmers' markets and grocery stores. (My home state of Georgia is one of the top producers of blueberries in the entire United States.) Or make a day of it by taking advantage of the numerous you-pick farms dotted across the South. Whether "you-pick" or "you-buy," make sure to have blueberries on your table this summer.

Meringue Pillows with Blueberry-Mint Compote

Light and airy meringues make an elegant dessert when topped with juicy blueberries.

ACTIVE 15 MIN. - TOTAL 10 HOURS, 15 MIN.
SERVES 6

MERINGUES
- 4 large egg whites
- ½ tsp. cream of tartar
- ½ tsp. fine sea salt, divided
- 1 cup granulated sugar
- 1 tsp. vanilla extract

BLUEBERRY COMPOTE
- ½ cup granulated sugar
- ½ cup water
- 1 Tbsp. lemon zest, plus 1 ½ Tbsp. fresh juice (from 1 medium lemon), divided
- 2 cups fresh blueberries (about 10 oz.)
- 2 Tbsp. finely chopped fresh mint
  Pinch of fine sea salt

GARNISHES
- Mint leaves
- Whipped cream

1. Prepare the Meringues: Preheat oven to 400°F. Line 2 rimmed baking sheets with silicone baking sheets or parchment paper; set aside. (If you are using parchment paper, butter and flour the parchment. Before shaping the Meringues, dab a little bit of meringue at each corner of the paper to secure it to the baking sheet.)

2. Beat the egg whites, cream of tartar, and a pinch of the sea salt with a heavy-duty electric mixer fitted with the whisk attachment on high speed until frothy. Gradually add the granulated sugar, vanilla, and remaining sea salt, beating on high speed until stiff, glossy peaks form, about 3 minutes.

3. Using a rubber spatula or large ice-cream scoop, spoon 3 (¾-cup) blobs of meringue onto each prepared baking sheet, leaving 2 to 3 inches of space between blobs. Using an offset spatula, smooth the top of each blob.

4. Reduce oven temperature to 175°F. Place the baking sheets in the oven; bake at 175°F until Meringues are crisp on the outside but interiors are still slightly wet, about 2 hours. (Check the consistency by poking into the bottom of 1 Meringue with your finger.) Turn on the oven light; turn off the oven, and leave the Meringues in the oven until fully dried, about 8 hours or overnight. (Poke again to make sure they are dry.)

5. Prepare the Blueberry Compote: Stir together sugar, water, and lemon zest in a 1-quart heavy saucepan, and bring to a boil over high. Boil, stirring occasionally, 5 minutes. Stir in the fresh blueberries; reduce heat to medium, and simmer, stirring occasionally, until the blueberries begin to burst, about 4 minutes. Remove from heat, and stir in finely chopped mint, lemon juice, and a pinch of sea salt.

6. When you are ready to serve, spoon about ¼ cup warm or room temperature Blueberry Compote over each Meringue; garnish with mint leaves and a dollop of whipped cream.

MERINGUE PILLOWS WITH BLUEBERRY-MINT COMPOTE

Blueberry-Cornmeal Cake

This moist, berry-studded cake gets its texture from medium-grind cornmeal.

ACTIVE 20 MIN. - TOTAL 1 HOUR, 30 MIN.
SERVES 8

- ½ cup unsalted butter, softened, plus more for greasing pan
- 1 cup granulated sugar
- 2 large eggs
- 1 Tbsp. lemon zest (from 2 lemons)
- 1 ½ cups all-purpose flour
- ½ cup medium-grind yellow cornmeal
- 2 tsp. baking powder
- ½ tsp. baking soda
- ½ tsp. fine sea salt
- ⅔ cup buttermilk
- 1 ½ cups fresh blueberries (about 7 oz.)

1. Preheat oven to 350°F. Butter an 8-inch springform pan. Set aside.

2. Beat sugar and butter with a heavy-duty electric stand mixer on medium-high speed until light and fluffy, about 2 minutes. Add eggs, 1 at a time, beating well after each addition. Add lemon zest, and beat on medium speed just until combined.

3. Stir together flour, cornmeal, baking powder, baking soda, and sea salt; add to butter mixture alternately with buttermilk, beginning and ending with flour mixture. Beat on medium-low speed just until combined after each addition. Pour batter into prepared cake pan, and sprinkle with fresh blueberries.

4. Bake in preheated oven until the cake starts to pull away from the sides of the pan and springs back when lightly pressed in the center with a fingertip, 45 to 50 minutes. Transfer to a wire rack, and cool in pan 10 minutes. Remove cake from springform pan; serve warm or at room temperature.

Blueberry Overnight Oatmeal

When blueberries are in season, this easy, hearty oatmeal is my go-to breakfast at least once a week.

ACTIVE 8 MIN. - TOTAL 8 HOURS, 8 MIN., INCLUDING 8 HOURS CHILLING
SERVES 1

Place ½ cup uncooked regular rolled **oats,** 1 cup 2% reduced-fat **milk,** ¼ cup fresh **blueberries,** a dash of **cinnamon,** and a pinch of **salt** in a 1-pint canning jar; cover with lid, and shake to combine. Chill until the oats are tender and moist, about 8 hours. Remove from refrigerator; uncover and microwave on HIGH until warmed, about 3 minutes. Stir in 1 Tbsp. chopped toasted **pecans** and 1 tsp. **flax seeds.** Drizzle with **honey** or pure maple syrup; serve immediately.

Pound Cake Perfection

Southerners enjoy this old-time favorite at breakfast, for dessert, and with afternoon tea

A POUND CAKE'S beauty is its simplicity. It isn't as showy as a tall, frosted layer cake or as dramatic as a fruit-crowned upside-down cake or as cute as a cupcake. But this humble, comforting treat rises to nearly every setting, occasion, and crowd, whether served on a paper plate or on grandmother's heirloom china.

We've all tasted dense, breadlike versions of pound cake that have lived up to its weighty name, which was coined in the 1700s for the ingredients—1 pound each of flour, sugar, butter, and eggs. Over time, cooks have tweaked the ratio of ingredients to make the cake lighter in texture as well as smaller in size.

In March 1966, we featured our first-ever pound cake recipe, the One-Two-Three-Four Pound Cake, and since then, pound cakes have appeared in countless forms and flavors. This spring, the *SL* Test Kitchen set out to perfect this Southern classic by retesting them all, from the Buttermilk Pound Cake to the seven-ingredient Million Dollar Pound Cake, devoting hours—and untold pounds of butter—to fine-tuning this recipe. Taste and see how this one stacks up against all the rest.

(TIP)

Creaming the butter, sugar, and cream cheese is key, because it will give the batter its volume. Using an electric stand mixer, beat the ingredients for 5 to 7 minutes on medium-high speed until mixture is light, fluffy, and almost white in color. Gradually add in the flour, and avoid overmixing, which will deflate the batter and make the cake tough.

A SWEET TOUCH
GIVE THIS CAKE
A DUSTING OF
POWDERED SUGAR.'

BATTER BASICS

1

SUGAR
While granulated sugar works well for this batter, we prefer superfine sugar for the most even texture and tender crumb.

2

HALF-AND-HALF
It adds more richness than whole milk and is more fluid than heavy cream.

3

VANILLA
Just 2 teaspoons will give you a hint of vanilla without overpowering this cake's buttery flavor.

TIP
Leave the eggs, butter, and cream cheese out at room temperature for about an hour before mixing. This is important because adding cold eggs to softened butter and cream cheese will create a lumpy batter.

Classic Southern Pound Cake

ACTIVE 20 MIN. - TOTAL 3 HOURS, 55 MIN.
SERVES 12

- 3 cups superfine or granulated sugar
- 1½ cups unsalted butter, at room temperature
- 6 oz. cream cheese, at room temperature
- 4 large eggs, at room temperature
- 2 large egg yolks, at room temperature
- ¼ cup half-and-half
- 2 tsp. vanilla extract
- 3 cups all-purpose flour
- 1 tsp. salt

1. Preheat oven to 300°F with oven rack in center of oven. Grease and flour a 10-inch (14-cup) Bundt pan.
2. Beat sugar, butter, and cream cheese with a heavy-duty electric stand mixer fitted with paddle attachment on medium-high speed until very fluffy and pale in color, 5 to 7 minutes. Add eggs, 1 at a time, beating on low speed just until yellow disappears after each addition. Add egg yolks, half-and-half, and vanilla, and beat on low speed just until blended.
3. Stir together flour and salt in medium bowl; gradually add to butter mixture in 3 batches, beating on low speed just until blended after each addition, stopping to scrape down sides of bowl as needed. Remove bowl from stand,

and scrape batter from paddle. Using a spatula, stir batter once by hand, scraping sides and bottom to incorporate any unmixed batter. Spoon batter into prepared pan, and gently tap pan on counter to release any large air bubbles.
4. Bake in preheated oven until cake is golden and a long wooden pick inserted in center comes out clean, 1 hour and 20 minutes to 1 hour and 30 minutes. Cool cake in pan on a wire rack 15 minutes; remove cake from pan, and cool completely on wire rack before slicing and serving, about 2 hours.

COOKING (SL) SCHOOL

Chile vs. Chili Powder

Yes, there's a difference. Chile powder is made of pure ground dried chiles; chili powder is a blend of chile powder and other spices, like cumin and oregano. Here are three of our favorite chile powders.

CHIPOTLE
Dried, smoked jalapeños give this powder its rich, smoky aroma while also adding a moderate dose of heat.

ANCHO
Made from the sweetest dried chile, ancho powder has a slightly fruity flavor with only a mild amount of heat.

CAYENNE
Spicy, pungent cayenne is a good way to increase the heat factor in dishes. Use it in any recipe that calls for "ground red pepper."

2-Ingredient Marinades

Add a splash of neutral cooking oil (like canola) to equal parts of these kitchen staples

PEACH PRESERVES + GRAINY MUSTARD
Slather on pork before cooking, or use as a condiment.

SOY SAUCE + SESAME OIL
Drizzle just a little on fish for a savory and toasty flavor.

DIJON MUSTARD + SRIRACHA CHILI SAUCE
Spice up a lean cut of beef, like flank steak.

APPLE CIDER VINEGAR + HONEY
Flavor salmon or pork tenderloin with this tangy duo.

Slice a Pineapple Like a Pro

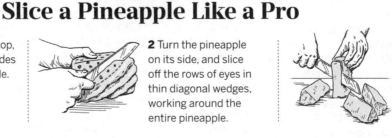

1 Slice off the top, bottom, and sides of the pineapple.

2 Turn the pineapple on its side, and slice off the rows of eyes in thin diagonal wedges, working around the entire pineapple.

3 Cut the pineapple into quarters. Trim out the core from each quarter, and slice cored quarters into wedges.

June

A SOUTHERN LIVING GUIDE

(A)	(B)	(C)	(D)
BABY BACK RIBS	BEEF BACK RIBS	ST. LOUIS-STYLE RIBS	SHORT RIBS

STICK TO THE RIBS

FIRE UP THE SMOKER (OR GRILL, OR OVEN, OR SLOW COOKER), AND MAKE A RACK OF THE SOUTH'S JUICIEST CUTS

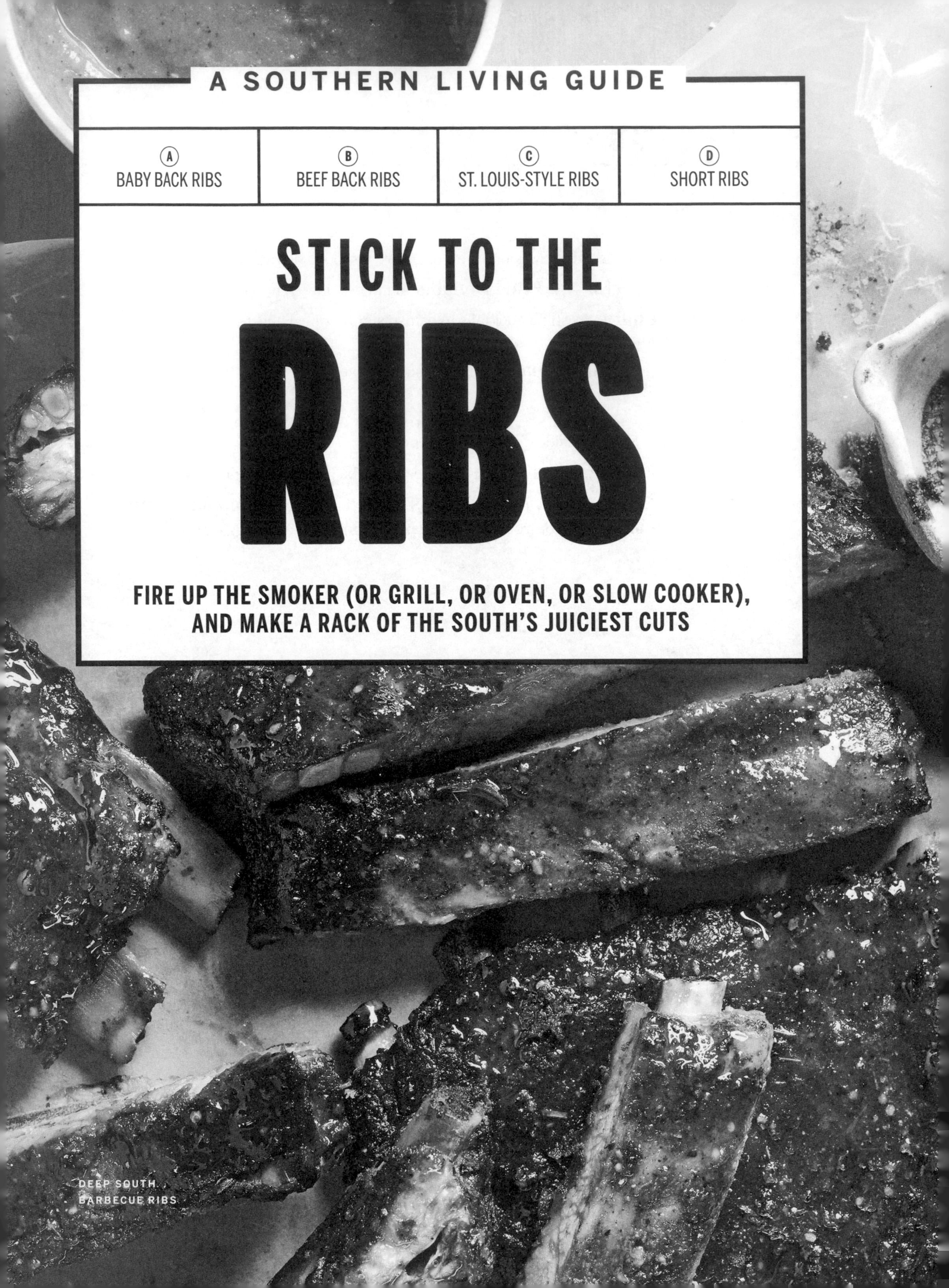

DEEP SOUTH BARBECUE RIBS

Deep South Barbecue Ribs

These tender, oven-roasted ribs are basted with our Melting Pot Barbecue Sauce, a sweet and tangy mix of several regional Southern sauces. The recipe at right includes tomatoes, light brown sugar, vinegar, and yellow mustard. It may not be for pit-loving purists, but it's undeniably good.

ACTIVE 45 MIN. - TOTAL 3 HOURS, 30 MIN.
SERVES 6

- 2 (2 ½- to 3-lb.) slabs St. Louis-style pork ribs (about 10 bones each)
- ¾ cup Southern Barbecue Dry Rub (recipe follows)
- 1 qt. Melting Pot Barbecue Sauce (recipe follows)

1. Preheat oven to 350°F. Pat both sides of slabs dry with paper towels. Using a sharp knife, remove thin membrane from back of each slab by slicing into it and pulling it off with a paper towel. Divide Southern Barbecue Dry Rub evenly between slabs, rubbing on both sides of each. Press gently to adhere. Place slabs, meaty side up, on a wire rack on an aluminum foil-lined baking sheet, and let stand at room temperature 30 minutes.
2. Bake in preheated oven until meat begins to pull away from bones but is not yet tender, about 1 hour and 30 minutes. Increase oven temperature to 450°F (Do not remove ribs from oven.)
3. Brush both sides of ribs with 1 cup Melting Pot Barbecue Sauce. Bake until ribs are very tender and caramelized, 35 to 45 minutes, brushing with another cup of sauce halfway through baking. Remove ribs from oven, and let stand at least 10 minutes. Serve ribs with remaining 2 cups sauce.

Southern Barbecue Dry Rub

ACTIVE 10 MIN. - TOTAL 10 MIN.
MAKES ABOUT 1 ¼ CUPS

Combine ⅓ cup **kosher salt,** 3 Tbsp. **black pepper,** 2 Tbsp. **smoked paprika,** 2 Tbsp. **chili powder,** 2 Tbsp. **onion powder,** 2 Tbsp. **garlic powder,** 2 Tbsp. **light brown sugar,** 2 tsp. **dried oregano,** and 1 tsp. **cayenne pepper** in a medium bowl.

Melting Pot Barbecue Sauce

ACTIVE 20 MIN. - TOTAL 1 HOUR, 15 MIN.
MAKES ABOUT 1 QT.

Heat a large (12-inch) cast-iron skillet over medium-high. Add 1 ½ lb. **cherry tomatoes,** and cook, stirring often, until skins begin to split and char, 5 to 7 minutes. Add 3 cups chopped **yellow onions** (about 2 medium onions) and 2 **garlic cloves,** minced, and cook, stirring often, 5 minutes. Add 3 Tbsp. **salted butter** to pan, and cook until melted, about 1 minute. Stir in ½ cup packed **light brown sugar.** Cook, without stirring, until edges start to caramelize, 2 to 3 minutes. Stir in 1 ½ cups **white vinegar,** ¼ cup **yellow mustard,** 2 Tbsp. **Worcestershire sauce,** 2 tsp. **kosher salt,** and 1 tsp. **black pepper;** reduce heat to medium-low, and cook until tomatoes break down and mixture is slightly thickened, about 45 minutes. Remove from heat; carefully transfer to a blender. Remove center piece of blender lid (to allow steam to escape); process on high until almost smooth, about 1 minute. Cool completely, about 30 minutes. Store in an airtight container in refrigerator up to 2 weeks.

Slow-Cooker Ginger, Sweet Tea, and Whiskey Short Ribs

Short ribs are thought of as a cold-weather dish, but we gave them a summer makeover with a bright sauce and fresh herbal topping. You can also serve these ribs atop grits, mashed potatoes, or egg noodles.

ACTIVE 45 MIN. - TOTAL 8 HOURS
SERVES 4

- 4 (12-oz.) bone-in beef short ribs, trimmed
- ½ tsp. black pepper
- 2 ¼ tsp. kosher salt, divided
- 2 Tbsp. canola oil
- 3 medium-size yellow onions, sliced (about 5 cups)
- 4 garlic cloves, minced (about 1 ½ Tbsp.)
- 1 (3-inch) piece fresh ginger, sliced
- ¾ cup (6 oz.) plus 1 Tbsp. (½ oz.) rye whiskey, divided
- 1 cup sweet tea
- 1 cup beef broth
- 1 Tbsp. sherry vinegar
- 1 Tbsp. cornstarch
- 1 Tbsp. warm water
- ½ cup chopped fresh flat-leaf parsley
- ½ cup chopped scallions (about 4 scallions)
- 2 Tbsp. lemon zest, plus 2 tsp. fresh juice (from about 2 lemons)
- 1 tsp. extra-virgin olive oil

1. Sprinkle short ribs with pepper and 1 teaspoon of the salt. Heat canola oil in a large (12-inch) cast-iron skillet over medium-high. Add ribs, and cook until well browned, about 10 minutes, turning once. Transfer to a 6-quart slow cooker.
2. Add onions, garlic, ginger, and ½ teaspoon of the salt to skillet, and cook over medium-high, stirring often, until onions are very tender, 8 to 10 minutes. Add ¾ cup of the whiskey, and cook 1 minute. Stir in tea and broth, and bring to a simmer, about 3 minutes. Pour onion mixture over ribs in slow cooker. Cover and cook on LOW until meat is very tender and falling off the bone, about 7 hours.
3. Remove ribs, and set aside. Pour mixture from slow cooker through a fine wire-mesh strainer into a medium saucepan; discard solids. Cook liquid in pan over medium-high until reduced by half (about 1 ½ cups), 10 to 12 minutes. Add sherry vinegar, ½ teaspoon of the salt, and remaining 1 tablespoon whiskey. Stir together cornstarch and warm water; stir into mixture in pan, and bring to a simmer, 2 to 3 minutes. Remove from heat.
4. Combine parsley, scallions, lemon zest, lemon juice, olive oil, and remaining ¼ teaspoon salt in a small bowl. Serve ribs in whiskey sauce topped with parsley mixture.

MEMPHIS DRY-RUBBED
BABY BACK RIBS

Memphis Dry-Rubbed Baby Back Ribs

These smoked ribs are surprisingly easy to make, even for a first-timer. A Memphis-style dry rub forms a delicious crust around the meat, and a vinegar wash with an extra sprinkling of dry rub at the end of the cooking process adds another layer of flavor—no sauce necessary.

ACTIVE 30 MIN. - TOTAL 4 HOURS
SERVES 4

- 2 (2 ½- to 3-lb.) slabs baby back pork ribs
- ⅓ cup kosher salt
- ¼ cup packed dark brown sugar
- 3 Tbsp. paprika
- 1 Tbsp. black pepper
- 1 Tbsp. garlic powder
- 1 Tbsp. onion powder
- 1 Tbsp. dry mustard
- 1 Tbsp. chili powder
- 1 Tbsp. ground cumin
- 1 Tbsp. ground allspice
- 1 Tbsp. herbes de Provence
- 1 cup apple cider vinegar, divided
- 1 cup water, divided
- 2 handfuls wood chunks for smoking (hickory, oak, or pecan)

1. Pat both sides of slabs dry with paper towels. Using a sharp knife, remove thin membrane from back of each slab by slicing into it and pulling it off with a paper towel. (This will make ribs more tender and allow meat to absorb the rub better.) Combine salt, brown sugar, paprika, pepper, garlic powder, onion powder, dry mustard, chili powder, cumin, allspice, and herbes de Provence in a medium bowl. Rub ¾ cup mixture evenly over both sides of slabs, and let stand at room temperature 30 minutes.
2. Prepare a charcoal fire in smoker according to manufacturer's instructions, substituting a mixture of ¾ cup each of the vinegar and water in drip pan. Bring internal temperature to 250°F to 275°F, and maintain for 15 to 20 minutes. Place wood chunks on coals. Place slabs on smoker, meaty side up; cover with lid.
3. Smoke ribs, maintaining inside temperature between 250°F and 275°F, until meat is tender to the touch and pulls away from bones on the ends, 3 hours to 3 hours and 30 minutes. Remove ribs, and place on a baking sheet. Stir together remaining ¼ cup each of vinegar and water. Spritz or brush vinegar-water mixture on both sides of ribs to thoroughly moisten. If desired, rub remaining ½ cup brown sugar mixture on both sides of ribs. Slice ribs between the bones, and serve.

Cola-and-Coffee Beef Ribs

A sweet barbecue sauce balances out the earthy, peppery dry rub on these amazingly rich smoked ribs.

ACTIVE 45 MIN. - TOTAL 5 HOURS, 45 MIN.
SERVES 8

- 2 (3 ½-lb.) racks beef back ribs
- ⅓ cup kosher salt
- ¼ cup finely ground medium-roast coffee beans
- 3 Tbsp. black pepper
- 2 Tbsp. paprika
- 2 Tbsp. chili powder
- 2 handfuls wood chunks for smoking (oak, hickory, or mesquite)
  Cola-Coffee Barbecue Sauce (recipe follows)

1. Pat both sides of slabs dry with paper towels. Using a sharp knife, remove thin membrane from back of each slab by slicing into it and pulling it off with a paper towel. (It can be difficult to remove the membrane from beef ribs, so you might want to have the butcher do it for you.)
2. Combine salt, coffee, pepper, paprika, and chili powder in a bowl; rub evenly over both sides of each rack, and let stand at room temperature 30 minutes.
3. Prepare a charcoal fire in smoker according to manufacturer's instructions, bringing internal temperature to 250°F to 275°F. Maintain temperature for 15 to 20 minutes. Place wood chunks on coals.
4. Place ribs, meaty side up, on smoker; cover with lid. Smoke ribs, maintaining inside temperature between 250°F and 275°F, until meat begins to pull away from bones but is not yet tender, about 3 hours. Brush about ½ cup Cola-Coffee Barbecue Sauce over both sides of ribs. Cover and smoke until a meat thermometer inserted in between the rib bones registers 205°F and rib meat is very tender, about 1 hour and 30 minutes, brushing with about ¼ cup barbecue sauce every 30 minutes. Remove ribs from the smoker; brush with ¼ cup barbecue sauce. Serve with remaining barbecue sauce.

Cola-Coffee Barbecue Sauce

ACTIVE 10 MIN. - TOTAL 1 HOUR, 10 MIN.
MAKES ABOUT 2 CUPS

Combine 1 cup **cola soft drink,** 1 cup **ketchup,** ½ cup **brewed coffee,** ¼ cup **dark molasses,** 2 Tbsp. **sherry vinegar,** 2 Tbsp. **Worcestershire sauce,** ½ tsp. **chili powder,** ½ tsp. **kosher salt,** ⅛ tsp. **garlic powder,** and ⅛ tsp. **onion powder** in a medium saucepan over medium-low. Cook, stirring occasionally, until heated through and flavors meld, about 30 minutes. Remove from heat, and cool completely, about 30 minutes. Transfer to an airtight container, and store in the refrigerator up to 2 weeks.

COLA-AND-COFFEE
BEEF RIBS

7 SECRETS TO BETTER RIBS

1. SHOP WISELY Whether you're buying baby backs or beef ribs, choose pink meat with uniform size and marbling, which will help them cook more evenly. Avoid ribs that have been "enhanced" or "basted" with a liquid sodium solution—this can lead to overly salty ribs once you add a rub or sauce.

2. CLEAN YOUR GRILL OR SMOKER Yes, we know this is obvious, but a greasy grill or smoker grate can ruin a batch of ribs—no matter how amazing your sauce.

3. GET THE RIGHT GEAR You'll need long-handled tongs and a grill basting brush if you're adding a sauce (silicone models are easiest to clean). We also like having a cheap squirt bottle on hand to add a vinegar wash.

4. REMOVE EXCESS MOISTURE Before you cook your ribs, pat them dry with paper towels to absorb surface moisture, which will keep them from browning.

5. LET THE RUB STAND If you're using a dry rub, coat ribs evenly and press the rub into the meat so it forms a crust. For the most flavor, let the rub sit on the meat for 30 minutes before cooking.

6. DON'T PEEK Whether you're cooking ribs on the grill, in a smoker, or in the oven, you want to maintain a constant tempera-ture, so keep the door or lid shut as much as possible.

7. TEST FOR DONENESS It can be hard to tell if a rack of ribs is done just by looking at it. A good test is whether you can easily pull apart two ribs with a pair of tongs. Once the meat is cooked, let it rest at least 10 minutes before serving so the juices can redistribute.

Sweet Chili-and-Mustard Baby Back Ribs

This tangy-sweet glaze is a tasty change of pace from the usual sauce. Keep an eye on the heat when grilling these ribs— you don't want the coals to be too hot for the initial sear. If your charcoal grill doesn't have a temperature gauge, you can insert an instant-read thermometer into a vent in the grill lid.

ACTIVE 45 MIN. - TOTAL 4 HOURS, 50 MIN.
SERVES 6

- 2 (2 ½- to 3-lb.) slabs baby back pork ribs
- ¼ cup kosher salt
- 2 Tbsp. ground cumin
- 2 Tbsp. dry mustard
- 2 tsp. cayenne pepper
- ½ cup sweet chili sauce (such as Mae Ploy)
- ½ cup Dijon mustard
- ¼ cup honey
- ¼ cup rice vinegar
- 2 Tbsp. soy sauce

1. Pat both sides of slabs dry with paper towels. Using a sharp knife, remove thin membrane from back of each slab by slicing into it and pulling it off with a paper towel. (This will make ribs more tender and allow meat to absorb the rub better.) Combine salt, cumin, dry mustard, and cayenne in a small bowl; rub evenly over both sides of slabs, and let stand at room temperature 30 minutes. Combine sweet chili sauce, Dijon mustard, honey, vinegar, and soy sauce.

2. Prepare a charcoal fire on bottom grate of a large charcoal grill. When coals are covered with gray ash, push to 1 side of grill. Maintain an inside temperature of about 300°F. (If the temperature drops below 300°F, add more charcoal as needed.) Brush both sides of ribs with ¼ cup sweet chili sauce mixture. Place ribs on top oiled grate of grill directly over hot coals, and grill, covered, 10 minutes per side. Brush both sides of ribs again with ¼ cup sweet chili sauce mixture, and place on grate over side without the coals. Grill, covered, 40 minutes.

3. Brush both sides again with ¼ cup sweet chili sauce mixture, and grill, covered, until meat is tender to the touch and pulls away from bones on the ends, about 2 hours, brushing with ¼ cup sweet chili sauce mixture after 1 hour. Remove ribs from grill, and brush with remaining sweet chili sauce mixture.

Fried Delights

Flaky, fruit-filled pastries for a festive outdoor get-together

Fried Blueberry-Ginger Hand Pies

Fresh ginger (or ⅛ teaspoon ground ginger) gives the jammy berry filling a hint of heat. Assemble the pies one day in advance, and refrigerate until you're ready to fry

ACTIVE 40 MIN. - TOTAL 1 HOUR, 10 MIN.
SERVES 12

FILLING

- ½ cup granulated sugar
- 2 Tbsp. cornstarch
- ½ cup water
- 1 tsp. grated fresh ginger
- ⅛ tsp. salt
- 2 cups fresh blueberries (about 10 oz.)
- 2 tsp. fresh lemon juice

DOUGH

- 5 cups all-purpose flour, plus more for surface
- 2 tsp. salt
- 10 Tbsp. cold vegetable shortening, cubed
- 6 Tbsp. cold unsalted butter, diced
- ½ cup plus 3 to 6 Tbsp. ice water
  Vegetable oil
  Powdered sugar

1. Prepare the Filling: Whisk together sugar and cornstarch in a saucepan. Whisk in ½ cup water, ginger, and salt; bring to a boil over medium-high, whisking often. Cook, whisking constantly, until thickened, about 1 minute. Remove pan from heat. Stir in blueberries and lemon juice, lightly crushing half of the blueberries; let stand until completely cool, about 30 minutes.

2. Prepare the Dough: Place flour and salt in the bowl of a food processor; pulse until combined, about 3 times. Scatter shortening and butter over top of flour mixture; pulse until mixture resembles coarse crumbs, 6 to 7 times. Add ½ cup of the ice water; pulse until mixture just starts to clump together, about 8 times, adding additional water, 1 tablespoon at a time, if necessary. Scrape out onto a lightly floured surface. Knead until it comes together, 2 to 3 times. Divide in half, and shape each half into a flat disk; wrap disks with plastic wrap, and chill about 30 minutes.

3. Roll one Dough disk to ⅛-inch thickness; cut 6 (5-inch) circles, and discard scraps. Repeat procedure with remaining disk. Scoop about 1 rounded tablespoon Filling into center of each circle. Moisten edge of half of each circle with water; fold circles in half, and crimp edges to seal. Cover and chill until ready to fry.

4. Pour vegetable oil to a depth of 1 inch in a large, deep skillet; heat oil to 360°F. Place 3 to 4 pies in hot oil, and fry until golden brown on both sides, 6 to 7 minutes, turning occasionally. Remove pies to paper towels to drain; sprinkle with powdered sugar. Repeat procedure with remaining pies and powdered sugar. Serve warm or at room temperature.

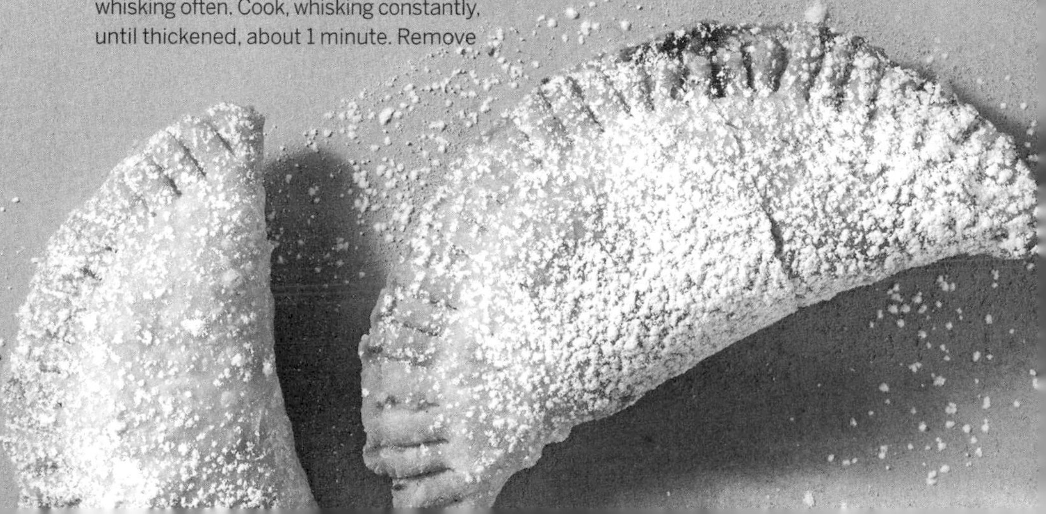

1
CANTALOUPE-
MINT AGUA
FRESCA

2
WATERMELON-
TOMATO
COOLER

MAKE A DOUBLE BATCH!

JUST CHILL

FEELING FESTIVE? ENJOY THESE REFRESHING TWISTS ON SUMMER COCKTAILS

(1)
Cantaloupe–Mint Agua Fresca

SERVES 8
ACTIVE 15 MIN. · TOTAL 4 HOURS, 45 MIN.

Combine ½ cup **granulated sugar,** 1 cup **water,** and 5 **mint** sprigs in a small saucepan. Bring to a boil over medium-high, stirring until sugar is dissolved. Remove from heat, and cool completely (about 30 minutes). Discard mint sprigs. Process 6 cups chopped **cantaloupe** (from 1 [3-lb.] melon) and ½ cup water in a blender until smooth, about 1 minute, stopping to scrape down sides as needed. Pour mixture through a fine wire-mesh strainer into a pitcher, discarding solids. Stir in mint syrup, ¼ cup fresh **lemon juice** (from 1 large lemon), 2 cups cold water, 1¼ cups **tequila,** and 5 mint sprigs. Chill until very cold, about 4 hours. Serve over ice, and garnish with mint sprigs and cantaloupe.

3

CARROT-
GINGER
BEER

4

CHERRY-
BASIL
FIZZ

(2)
Watermelon-Tomato Cooler

SERVES 4
ACTIVE 25 MIN. · TOTAL 6 HOURS, 25 MIN.

Process 6 cups cubed **seedless watermelon;** 3 cups **red heirloom tomatoes,** seeded and chopped (about 1½ lb.); 2 **Persian cucumbers,** peeled and sliced; and ¼ cup **granulated sugar** in a blender until very smooth, about 1 minute, stopping to scrape down sides as needed. Pour mixture through a fine wire-mesh strainer lined with cheese-cloth into a large pitcher; discard solids. Stir in ¼ cup fresh **lime juice** (from about 2 limes); ¾ to 1 cup **tequila** or **vodka;** and, if desired, 1 small **jalapeño chile,** sliced. Chill until very cold, about 6 hours. Stir well, and serve over ice. Garnish with cucumber or watermelon wedges and fresh **cilantro** sprigs.

(3)
Carrot-Ginger Beer

SERVES 4
ACTIVE 15 MIN. · TOTAL 2 HOURS, 45 MIN.

Combine 1 cup **water,** ½ cup packed **dark brown sugar,** and 6 large **mint** sprigs in a small saucepan. Bring to a boil over medium-high, stirring just until sugar is dissolved. Remove from heat, and cool completely (about 30 minutes). Discard mint sprigs. Combine mint syrup, ½ cup cold-pressed **carrot juice,** and ¼ cup fresh **lime juice** (from about 2 limes) in a pitcher, and chill until very cold, about 2 hours. For each serving, pour 6 Tbsp. of the mixture over ice in a 12-oz. glass, and stir in 3 Tbsp. **spiced rum.** Top each with ¾ cup chilled **ginger beer.** Garnish with mint sprigs and shaved **carrots.**

(4)
Cherry-Basil Fizz

SERVES 8
ACTIVE 20 MIN. · TOTAL 3 HOURS, 20 MIN.

Combine 2½ cups fresh pitted **cherries,** 1 cup **granulated sugar,** ¼ cup **water,** and 3 large **basil** sprigs in a medium saucepan. Bring to a boil over medium-high, stirring until sugar is dissolved. Remove from heat, and cool completely (about 1 hour). Pour syrup through a fine wire-mesh strainer into a pitcher, discarding solids. (Yield should equal about 1 cup.) Cover and chill until very cold, about 2 hours. For each serving, pour 2 Tbsp. of the syrup over ice in a 12-oz. glass, and stir in 3 Tbsp. **vodka.** Top each with about 1 cup plain, chilled **kombucha** (like GT's Classic Organic Raw Kombucha, original flavor). Garnish with cherries and basil sprigs.

Full of Flavor

Stuff summer's best vegetables for a fresh spin on weeknight meals

Stuffed Peppers with Grits and Sausage

Cheesy grits and Italian pork sausage create a satisfying filling for tender bell peppers. A serrated tomato corer or melon baller makes an easy job of hollowing out the peppers.

ACTIVE 15 MIN. - TOTAL 1 HOUR, 5 MIN.
SERVES 6

- 3 large red bell peppers (about 20 oz.)
- 1 Tbsp. canola oil
- 3 hot Italian pork sausage links, casings removed
- 1 cup chopped sweet onion
- ½ cup coarse cornmeal (such as McEwen & Sons)
- 1½ cups chicken broth
- 1 cup whole milk
- 1 tsp. kosher salt, divided
- ¼ cup chopped fresh flat-leaf parsley
- 3 oz. mozzarella cheese, shredded (about 1 cup), divided
- 3 Tbsp. extra-virgin olive oil
- 2 Tbsp. white wine vinegar
- ¼ tsp. black pepper
- 2 cups heirloom grape tomatoes, halved
- ½ cup basil leaves

1. Preheat oven to 350°F. Microwave bell peppers on HIGH 2 minutes to soften slightly. Cut bell peppers in half through the stem. Remove seeds and white membranes using a serrated tomato corer or melon baller, leaving stem intact. Discard seeds and membranes.
2. Heat canola oil in a large skillet over medium-high. Add sausage to skillet; cook 4 minutes, stirring to break into small pieces. Add onion to skillet; cook, stirring occasionally, until sausage is cooked and onion is tender, about 3 minutes. Remove sausage mixture from pan. Add cornmeal to skillet; cook 1 minute, stirring constantly. Add broth, milk, and ¾ teaspoon of the salt to skillet; bring to a boil. Cover, reduce heat to medium, and cook, stirring occasionally, until liquid is absorbed, about 20 minutes. Stir in parsley, sausage mixture, and half of the cheese. Divide mixture evenly among bell pepper halves. Place side by side on a baking sheet. Sprinkle with remaining mozzarella cheese.
3. Bake in preheated oven until cheese is browned and peppers are tender, about 30 minutes.
4. Whisk together olive oil, vinegar, black pepper, and remaining ¼ teaspoon salt in a medium bowl. Add tomatoes and basil; toss to coat. Serve over peppers.

TIP

This recipe can also be made with yellow zucchini or summer squash. Can't tell the difference? Summer squash (also called yellow or crookneck squash) is curved with a narrow neck; yellow zucchini is long and straight, like the green kind.

Cornbread-Stuffed Zucchini

Choose squash that are uniform in shape so they will cook evenly. The best kind for this recipe are long, straight, and not too skinny.

ACTIVE 20 MIN. - TOTAL 55 MIN.
SERVES 4

- 3 cups coarsely crumbled cornbread (about 10 oz.)
- 4 (12-oz.) zucchini
- 3 Tbsp. canola oil, divided
- 1 tsp. kosher salt, divided
- 16 oz. ground chicken
- ½ cup chopped red onion
- 4 garlic cloves, minced (about 2 Tbsp.)
- 1 tsp. paprika
- ½ tsp. black pepper
- 6 oz. white Cheddar cheese, shredded (about 1 ½ cups)
- ½ cup fresh corn
- 3 Tbsp. chopped fresh flat-leaf parsley

1. Preheat oven to 375°F. Spread cornbread in an even layer on one end of a baking sheet. Cut zucchini in half lengthwise. Using a serrated tomato corer or melon baller, scoop out zucchini pulp to equal 3 cups pulp, leaving a ½-inch shell intact. Coarsely chop 1 ½ cups of pulp; reserve remaining pulp for another use. Brush zucchini shells with 2 tablespoons of the canola oil. Place zucchini shells on baking sheet with cornbread, and sprinkle with ¼ teaspoon of the salt. Bake zucchini and cornbread at 375°F until cornbread is lightly browned, 8 to 10 minutes. Reduce oven temperature to 350°F.

2. Heat remaining 1 tablespoon oil in a large skillet over medium-high. Add ground chicken to skillet; cook, stirring to crumble, until browned, 5 to 6 minutes. Add onion, garlic, paprika, pepper, reserved 1 ½ cups zucchini pulp, and remaining ¾ teaspoon salt to skillet; cook, stirring occasionally, until onion is tender, about 3 minutes. Transfer mixture to a large bowl, and stir in cornbread, white Cheddar cheese, corn, and parsley. Divide chicken mixture evenly among zucchini shells. Place shells on a baking sheet.

3. Bake stuffed zucchini at 350°F until filling is lightly browned and zucchini is tender, 25 minutes.

Stuffed Pattypan Squash with Beef and Feta

Feta cheese and fresh dill add a Greek accent to stuffed squash. Pattypan squash make cute, round vessels for this tasty filling, but you can also use zucchini or summer squash.

ACTIVE 35 MIN. - TOTAL 1 HOUR, 25 MIN.

SERVES 10

- 10 large pattypan squash (4 to 6 inches wide)
- ¼ tsp. kosher salt
- 4 oz. chopped bacon (about 5 slices)
- 1 lb. 90% lean ground beef
- ½ cup chopped red onion
- 1 Tbsp. minced garlic
- 8 oz. baby spinach
- 2 large eggs, lightly beaten
- ⅔ cup cooked white rice
- ½ tsp. black pepper
- ¼ cup chopped fresh dill, divided
- 5 oz. feta cheese, crumbled (about 1 ¼ cups)

1. Preheat oven to 350°F. Cut off top third of each squash, and scoop out pulp, using a serrated corer or melon baller, leaving a 1-inch shell intact. Coarsely chop pulp; reserve 1 cup of chopped pulp, and discard remaining pulp. Place squash bowls in an 13- x 9-inch baking dish, and sprinkle with salt. Bake in preheated oven 10 minutes.
2. Place bacon in a large nonstick skillet over medium-high, and cook, stirring occasionally, until starting to brown, about 5 minutes. Add beef to skillet, and cook, stirring to crumble, until starting to brown, about 6 minutes. Add onion, garlic, and reserved 1 cup chopped squash pulp to skillet, and cook, stirring occasionally, until tender, about 3 minutes. Stir in spinach; cover and cook until spinach is wilted, about 2 minutes. Uncover and cook until liquid is almost evaporated, about 1 minute. Transfer beef mixture to a medium bowl; cool 10 minutes.
3. Stir eggs, cooked rice, pepper, and 3 tablespoons of the dill into beef mixture. Gently stir in cheese. Spoon mixture into baked squash bowls.
4. Bake squash in preheated oven until tops begin to brown and squash is tender, about 30 minutes. Sprinkle squash with remaining 1 tablespoon dill.

Stuffed Tomatoes with Pesto Rice

Hull the tomatoes as gently as possible. If you break the skin, they will over-soften while baking and could fall apart.

ACTIVE 25 MIN. - TOTAL 40 MIN.

SERVES 4

- 8 (6-oz.) tomatoes
- ¾ tsp. kosher salt, divided
- 2 Tbsp. salted butter
- 2 cups chopped yellow onion
- 5 oz. baby spinach
- 1 (8.8-oz.) pouch microwavable long-grain white rice (such as Uncle Ben's Ready Rice)
- ½ cup chopped fresh basil
- ½ cup refrigerated pesto (such as Buitoni), divided
- 1 ½ oz. pecorino Romano cheese, shaved (about ¾ cup)

1. Preheat oven to 350°F, with oven rack 6 to 9 inches from top. Cut about ½ inch off tops of tomatoes; discard tops. Cut a small (⅛-inch) slice off bottoms of tomatoes so they will sit flat in baking dish. Carefully scoop out tomato pulp, using a serrated tomato corer or melon baller, leaving a ½-inch shell intact. Sprinkle shells with ¼ teaspoon of the salt. Place pulp in a wire-mesh strainer over a bowl; press to remove ⅓ cup tomato juice. Reserve juice; discard pulp.
2. Melt butter in a large skillet over medium-high. Add onion to skillet; cook, stirring occasionally, until starting to soften, about 4 minutes. Add spinach to skillet; cover and cook until wilted, 2 to 3 minutes. Add rice and reserved ⅓ cup tomato juice to skillet; cook until warmed through, about 1 minute. Remove from heat. Stir in basil, ⅓ cup of the pesto, and remaining ½ teaspoon salt. Divide mixture evenly among tomato shells. Place shells in an 11- x 7-inch baking dish.
3. Bake in preheated oven until tomatoes are tender, about 15 minutes. Top with cheese and remaining pesto.

> **TIP** Pair with garlic bread: Mix 4 Tbsp. melted butter and 2 cloves grated garlic in a bowl. Cut 1 French bread loaf in half lengthwise, and brush with butter-garlic mixture. Bake at 350°F for 15 minutes. Top with Parmesan and chopped fresh parsley.

Stuffed Eggplant Parmesan

Our Test Kitchen made eggplant Parmesan easier (and healthier!) without sacrificing any of the comforting flavor of the original home-cooked dish.

ACTIVE 20 MIN. - TOTAL 1 HOUR, 40 MIN.
SERVES 4

- 2 (10-oz.) eggplants
- 2 Tbsp. canola oil, divided
- 1 cup chopped sweet onion
- 1 Tbsp. chopped fresh thyme
- 1 Tbsp. minced garlic
- 1 tsp. kosher salt
- 1 small tomato, chopped (about 1 cup)
- 2 large eggs, lightly beaten
- ½ cup chopped fresh basil
- 2 oz. mozzarella cheese, shredded (about ¾ cup)
- ¾ cup Italian-seasoned panko (Japanese-style breadcrumbs), divided
- 1½ cups jarred pasta sauce, divided
- 2 oz. fresh mozzarella cheese, torn into small pieces (about ½ cup)
- 1½ oz. Parmesan cheese, shredded (about ½ cup)
- Small fresh basil leaves, for topping

1. Preheat oven to 350°F. Partially peel eggplants in 1-inch strips, using a vegetable peeler. Cut eggplants in half lengthwise. Score eggplant pulp in a crosshatch pattern. (Do not cut through the skin. This will make it easier to remove pulp after it is baked.) Brush eggplants with 1 tablespoon of the canola oil, and place in a 13- x 9-inch baking dish. Bake in preheated oven 40 minutes. Remove pulp from eggplants, using a serrated tomato corer or melon baller, leaving a ½-inch shell intact. Set shells aside. Coarsely chop pulp, and place in a medium bowl.

2. Heat remaining 1 tablespoon oil in a small skillet over medium-high. Add onion to skillet; cook, stirring occasionally, until tender, 5 to 6 minutes. Add thyme, garlic, and salt to skillet; cook, stirring constantly, 1 minute.

3. Add onion mixture and chopped tomato to eggplant pulp. Add eggs, basil, shredded mozzarella, and ½ cup of the breadcrumbs; toss to coat. Coat a 13- x 9-inch baking dish with cooking spray. Spread ½ cup of the pasta sauce in bottom of dish. Place eggplant shells in dish. Divide tomato mixture evenly among eggplant shells. Top with remaining 1 cup pasta sauce and ¼ cup breadcrumbs. Sprinkle with torn mozzarella and Parmesan.

4. Bake eggplants in preheated oven until cheese is melted and top is browned, 35 to 40 minutes. Top eggplants with basil leaves.

ONLY 372
CALORIES
PER SERVING

A New Spin on Succotash

Adding chicken turns this traditional side into a light summer meal

Chicken and Charred Succotash Salad

ACTIVE 25 MIN. - TOTAL 25 MIN.

SERVES 4

- 4 (6-oz.) boneless, skinless chicken breasts
- ½ tsp. black pepper
- 1½ tsp. kosher salt, divided
- 5 Tbsp. olive oil, divided
- 4 oz. fresh green beans, cut into 1-inch pieces (about 1 cup)
- ½ cup fresh yellow corn kernels (from 1 ear)
- 2 medium scallions, thinly sliced
- 1 cup chopped red bell pepper (from 1 medium bell pepper)
- 1 cup half-moon sliced zucchini (from 1 small zucchini)
- 1 cup cherry tomatoes, halved
- 1 Tbsp. white wine vinegar
- 2 tsp. chopped fresh tarragon

1. Preheat oven to 400°F. Sprinkle chicken with pepper and ¾ teaspoon of the salt. Heat 1 tablespoon of the oil in a large cast-iron skillet over medium-high until shimmering; add chicken, and cook until browned on both sides, 3 to 4 minutes per side. Transfer to a baking sheet, and bake in preheated oven until a thermometer inserted in thickest part registers 165°F, 12 to 13 minutes.

2. Meanwhile, add 2 tablespoons of the oil to skillet; swirl to coat. Add green beans, corn, and scallions; cook, stirring occasionally, until beans are bright green and slightly charred, about 4 minutes.

Add red bell pepper; cook, stirring occasionally, until slightly softened, about 2 minutes. Add zucchini; cook until charred and tender-crisp, about 4 more minutes. Remove from heat, and stir in tomatoes and ½ teaspoon of the salt.

3. Remove chicken from oven, and let stand 5 minutes. Meanwhile, combine vinegar, tarragon, and remaining ¼ teaspoon salt in a small bowl. Whisk in remaining 2 tablespoons oil until combined. Slice chicken, and serve over salad. Drizzle with dressing.

Nutritional information (per serving):
Calories: 372 - Protein: 34g - Carbs: 11g - Fiber: 3g - Fat: 21g

Easy as Peach Pie

Beat the heat with this sweet freeze-ahead dessert

Peach Melba Ice-Cream Pie

This summer pie looks difficult, but thanks to store-bought ice cream and a press-in cookie crust, it's a cinch to assemble. All you need is enough time for it to freeze so the layers look nice and neat.

ACTIVE 25 MIN. - TOTAL 12 HOURS, 55 MIN., INCLUDING 12 HOURS FREEZING

SERVES 8

- 1 (5.25-oz.) pkg. thin almond cookies (such as Anna's)
- 1 cup salted roasted almonds
- 3 Tbsp. granulated sugar
- ¼ tsp. kosher salt
- 6 Tbsp. unsalted butter, melted
- 4 cups vanilla ice cream, softened and divided
- 2 medium peaches, divided
- 1 pint raspberry sorbet, softened
- 1 cup fresh raspberries (about 4 oz.)

1. Preheat oven to 350°F. Place cookies, almonds, sugar, and salt in the bowl of a food processor; process until finely ground, about 15 seconds. Drizzle butter over top of mixture; pulse until combined, 5 to 6 times.

2. Press crumb mixture into bottom and up sides of a lightly greased 9 ½-inch deep-dish glass or ceramic pie plate. Bake in preheated oven until browned, about 12 minutes. Place on a wire rack, and cool completely, about 30 minutes.

3. Place 2 cups of the ice cream in a bowl. Peel and dice 1 of the peaches; stir diced peach into ice cream. Spread ice-cream mixture over crust. Freeze about 2 hours.

4. Spread sorbet over ice-cream mixture; freeze about 2 hours.

5. Spread remaining 2 cups vanilla ice cream over sorbet. Freeze 8 hours or overnight.

6. To serve, let pie stand at room temperature about 10 minutes. Meanwhile, peel and slice remaining peach into ¼-inch-thick slices. Arrange peach slices around edge of pie. Mound raspberries in center of pie.

TIP

For the best flavor and most impressive presentation, top the pie with fresh raspberries and sliced peaches just before serving.

KNOW-HOW

Pie Problems, Solved!

Because the season is too short for making any baking mistakes

1
PROBLEM Bubbled-over fruit filling
FIX Leaks happen, especially with lattice pies. Crimp the edges of the pie tightly, and if it has a double crust, add steam vents. Be sure to bake the pie on a parchment-lined baking sheet to catch any drips.

2
PROBLEM Crumbly cookie crust
FIX When making a cookie crust for an icebox pie, make sure the cookie crumbs are coated evenly with melted butter and are not too dry. For a nice thick crust, press into a pie pan with a measuring cup.

3
PROBLEM Weeping meringue
FIX Top the pie with meringue when the filling is still hot. This "cooks" the bottom of the meringue and prevents beads of liquid from rising to the top. Overbaking may also cause weeping.

4
PROBLEM Runny fruit filling
FIX Baked fruit can release a lot of liquid. Make sure that your pie filling includes a thickener (such as flour, cornstarch, or quick-cooking tapioca) and that the pie is baked for long enough.

IN SEASON

The Scoop on Summer Vegetables

Tips for hollowing out our favorite produce. *(Turn to page 148 for tasty recipes.)*

TOMATO
Core with a paring knife, and then scoop out the seeds and pulp with a teaspoon.

EGGPLANT
Slice in half lengthwise, and then run a paring knife around the edge of the eggplant, leaving a ¼-inch border. Use the knife to score the flesh in a crosshatch pattern. Scrape out the flesh with a teaspoon.

SQUASH
Slice in half lengthwise, and then scoop out the flesh with a melon baller.

July

THE 5-INGREDIENT

Farmers' Market Cookbook

The most delicious recipes begin with the ripest ingredients. Buying at-peak fruits and vegetables is the next best thing to growing your own. Celebrate summer's vibrant flavors with these dishes, made with just five ingredients and a few pantry staples. And cheers to the farmers who share their bounties with us!

"At least once each summer, we fill up a stockpot with overripe tomatoes and cook them down all day, stirring occasionally. Then we freeze them in freezer bags. In the winter, when we have more time, we add in garlic, herbs, and onions and make the best tomato sauce ever."

—Margaret Ann Toohey, Snow's Bend Farm, Tuscaloosa, Alabama

Tomato, Peach, and Corn Salad

SERVES 4
ACTIVE 15 MIN. · TOTAL 15 MIN.

Cut 2 **beefsteak tomatoes** into wedges. Combine with 1 diced **peach** and 1 cup fresh **corn kernels** in a medium bowl. Sprinkle with ¼ tsp. **kosher salt.** Drizzle with ¼ cup **Honey Vinaigrette** (recipe, page 195); toss to coat. Serve on a large platter. Top with 2 oz. **feta cheese,** crumbled (about ½ cup), and sprinkle with ¼ tsp. **black pepper.**

Tomatoes

Green Zebra, Cherokee Purple, Kellogg's Breakfast–if the names of novelty and heirloom tomatoes don't make you smile, their eye-popping shapes, vibrant colors, and robust flavors will. When tomatoes are at their peak, a sprinkle of flaky salt is all they need. But if you want to spice it up, try these almost-as-easy recipes.

Cherry Tomato Fondue

SERVES 6
ACTIVE 10 MIN. · TOTAL 10 MIN.

Combine 2 pt. **cherry tomatoes** and 4 Tbsp. **olive oil** in a cast-iron skillet over high. Cook, stirring often, until tomatoes begin to burst, about 5 minutes. Reduce heat to medium-high; cook, stirring often, until tomatoes are mostly broken down, about 5 minutes. Stir in ½ cup cold **unsalted butter** and ½ tsp. **kosher salt** until melted. Remove from heat. Serve hot with sliced **crusty bread,** and top with torn fresh **basil.**

TOASTED
COUSCOUS AND
TOMATO SALAD

THE SAUCE OF SUMMER

DRIZZLE THIS FRESH HERB CONDIMENT ON JUST ABOUT ANYTHING

Summer Sauce

MAKES 1 CUP
ACTIVE 10 MIN. · TOTAL 10 MIN.

Process 2 cups packed fresh **basil leaves,** ¾ cup **extra-virgin olive oil,** ½ cup loosely packed fresh **flat-leaf parsley leaves,** ¼ cup loosely packed fresh **mint leaves,** 1 Tbsp. **lemon zest,** plus 2 tsp. fresh **lemon juice** (from 1 lemon), 1 tsp. **kosher salt,** and 1 **garlic clove** in a food processor or blender until smooth. Add additional kosher salt or lemon juice, if desired. Cover and chill until ready to use. Use within 2 days.

Toasted Couscous and Tomato Salad

SERVES 4
ACTIVE 15 MIN. · TOTAL 40 MIN.

- 1 pt. cherry or grape tomatoes
- 1 tsp. kosher salt
- 1 tsp. black pepper
- 2 Tbsp. extra-virgin olive oil, divided
- 1 cup uncooked Israeli couscous
- 1½ cups water
- 2 Tbsp. Honey Vinaigrette (recipe, page 195)
- ⅓ cup chopped fresh flat-leaf parsley or other herb
- 1 oz. Parmesan cheese, shaved (about ½ cup)

1. Preheat oven to 425°F. Toss together tomatoes, salt, pepper, and 1 tablespoon of the olive oil on a rimmed baking sheet. Bake in preheated oven until tomatoes burst and caramelize, about 15 minutes.
2. Heat remaining 1 tablespoon oil in a saucepan over medium-high. Add couscous, and cook, stirring often, until couscous turns golden and smells toasty, 4 to 5 minutes. Add water, and bring to a boil. Reduce heat to medium-low; cover and simmer until couscous is tender, 10 to 13 minutes.
3. Transfer couscous to a serving bowl. Add Honey Vinaigrette; toss to coat. Gently stir in roasted tomatoes and parsley. Top with Parmesan.

Tomato Tea Sandwiches

SERVES 6
ACTIVE 25 MIN. · TOTAL 25 MIN.

Stir together 6 Tbsp. **cream cheese,** softened; 2 ½ tsp. **Summer Sauce** (recipe at left); ¾ tsp. **black pepper;** and ½ tsp. **kosher salt** in a small bowl until combined. Spread cream cheese mixture on 1 side of 12 **thin white bread slices,** toasted. Place 1 **tomato** slice and about ¼ cup thinly sliced **red onion** on each of 6 bread slices. Sprinkle evenly with ¼ tsp. salt. Cover with remaining 6 bread slices. Cut sandwiches in half; serve immediately.

Squash Tart
SERVES 4
ACTIVE 20 MIN. · TOTAL 50 MIN.

- ½ (17.3-oz.) pkg. frozen puff pastry sheets, thawed
- 2 medium zucchini or yellow squash, shaved into thin slices (about 1 cup)
- 3 Tbsp. Summer Sauce, divided (recipe at left)
- ½ oz. Parmesan cheese, grated (about ¼ cup)
- ¼ tsp. kosher salt
- ¼ tsp. black pepper

1. Preheat oven to 400°F. Place a sheet of parchment paper on a rimmed baking sheet. Place puff pastry on parchment, and roll pastry into a 14- x 11-inch rectangle. Fold pastry edges to create a ¾-inch border; prick pastry beside border evenly with a fork. Place a sheet of parchment over the pastry, and place pie weights evenly over pastry inside border. Bake pastry in preheated oven until golden brown, about 30 minutes. Remove pie weights, and discard top sheet of parchment.
2. Toss shaved zucchini with 2 tablespoons of the Summer Sauce. Top pastry evenly with zucchini, Parmesan, and remaining 1 Tbsp. Summer Sauce. Sprinkle tart with kosher salt and black pepper.
3. Cut tart into 12 pieces and serve.

Squash

Whether you have an overproductive vegetable garden or there was a three-for-one special at the supermarket, summer squash and zucchini tend to pile up this time of year. Looking for new ways to prepare them? Here are some recipes to grill them, sauté them, and enjoy these beauties raw.

Grilled Ratatouille Skewers

SERVES 4 TO 6

ACTIVE 45 MIN. · TOTAL 1 HOUR

- 8-12 wooden skewers
- 2 medium-size yellow squash, cut into 1½-inch cubes
- 2 red bell peppers, cut into 2-inch pieces
- 1 large eggplant, cut into 1½-inch cubes
- 1 large sweet onion, cut into 2-inch pieces
- ½ tsp. kosher salt
- ¼ tsp. black pepper
- ½ cup Summer Sauce (recipe, page 158)

1. Soak wooden skewers in water 30 minutes. Meanwhile, preheat grill to medium-high (about 450°F). Thread vegetables alternately onto skewers. Sprinkle with salt and pepper, and brush with Summer Sauce until coated.
2. Grill, uncovered, turning occasionally and brushing with Summer Sauce, until vegetables are tender and charred in spots, 15 to 20 minutes.

CORNBREAD
PANZANELLA
WITH SQUASH

Cornbread Panzanella with Squash

SERVES 6

ACTIVE 15 MIN. · TOTAL 20 MIN.

- 2 Tbsp. olive oil
- 2 cups yellow squash, cut into 1-inch cubes (about 2 medium squash)
- ½ tsp. kosher salt
- ¼ tsp. black pepper
- 15 oz. store-bought cornbread, cubed and toasted (do not use sweet cornbread)
- 1 cup diced zucchini (from 1 zucchini)
- 4 oz. fresh mozzarella cheese, torn
- ½ cup Honey Vinaigrette (recipe, page 195)

1. Heat oil in a medium saucepan over medium. Add yellow squash, salt, and pepper. Cook, stirring occasionally, until tender, about 5 minutes. Remove from heat.
2. Toss together cornbread, zucchini, and mozzarella in a large bowl. Add cooked yellow squash, and drizzle with Honey Vinaigrette. Toss gently to combine. Serve immediately.

Squash and Halloumi Salad

SERVES 4

ACTIVE 50 MIN. · TOTAL 50 MIN.

- 1 lb. yellow squash, cut into ½-inch-thick slices
- 1 (8-oz.) pkg. Halloumi cheese, cut into ½-inch-thick slices
- 1 Tbsp. olive oil
- ½ tsp. kosher salt
- ½ tsp. black pepper
- 1 Tbsp. Summer Sauce (recipe, page 158)
- 2 Tbsp. fresh basil leaves

1. Preheat grill to medium (350°F to 450°F). Brush squash and Halloumi with oil; season with salt and pepper. Grill, uncovered, until squash is tender and Halloumi has grill marks, 2 to 3 minutes on each side.
2. Stir together squash, Halloumi, and Summer Sauce in a medium bowl. Top with basil.

SQUASH AND
HALLOUMI SALAD

PEACH MELBA ICE CREAM PIE
(PAGE 153)

CLOCKWISE FROM TOP LEFT:

- CORNBREAD-STUFFED ZUCCHINI (PAGE 149)
- STUFFED EGGPLANT PARMESAN (PAGE 151)
- STUFFED PEPPERS WITH GRITS AND SAUSAGE (PAGE 148)
- MEMPHIS DRY-RUBBED BABY BACK RIBS (PAGE 142)

GRILLED CLAMBAKE FOIL
PACKETS WITH HERB BUTTER
(PAGE 211)

TOMATO, PEACH, AND
CORN SALAD (PAGE 157)

CLOCKWISE FROM TOP LEFT:
- PEACH ICEBOX CAKE (PAGE 204)
- CHILLED SWEET CORN SOUP (PAGE 217)
- WATERMELON GAZPACHO (PAGE 197)
- PEACHES-AND-CREAM PANCAKES (PAGE 205)

FIG FLATBREAD
(PAGE 201)

FIG AND LEMON REFRIGERATOR
JAM (PAGE 201)

CLOCKWISE FROM TOP:
- CRAB CAKES WITH CREAMY FENNEL-AND-RADISH SLAW (PAGE 213)
- CHICKEN, WHITE BEAN, AND SPINACH SALAD (PAGE 233)
- OLD-SCHOOL SQUASH CASSEROLE (PAGE 237)

SALTED CARAMEL-PECAN MILK SHAKE,
BANANA PUDDING MILK SHAKE,
PEANUT BUTTER PIE MILK SHAKE
(PAGE 241)

CLOCKWISE FROM TOP LEFT:

- BLACKBERRY GELATO (PAGE 231)
- SHAVED CUCUMBER SALAD WITH PICKLED BLACKBERRIES (PAGE 229)
- GRILLED PORK LOIN WITH BLACKBERRY GLAZE (PAGE 229)
- BLACKBERRY, BROWNED BUTTER, AND ALMOND TART (PAGE 230)

SUMMER COBBLER
COCKTAIL (PAGE 231)

LEMON-OLIVE OIL CAKE WITH
WHIPPED MASCARPONE
(PAGE 224)

ROSEMARY FOCACCIA WITH
STEWED GRAPES AND OLIVES
(PAGE 225)

**TANGY POTATO-GREEN
BEAN SALAD (PAGE 239)**

RANCH TURKEY
BURGERS (PAGE 238)

LIGHTER PAN-FRIED
CHICKEN WITH GREEN
BEANS AND TOMATOES
(PAGE 251)

THE BIG CINNAMON ROLL
(PAGE 248)

BEEF STEW WITH BUTTERY
GARLIC BREAD (PAGE 250)

FUDGY FLOURLESS
CHOCOLATE-PECAN
COOKIES (PAGE 261)

CLOCKWISE FROM TOP LEFT:

- OATMEAL-CARAMEL CREAM PIES (PAGE 299)
- ITALIAN-STYLE GRITS AND GREENS (PAGE 283)
- BACON-AND-CHIVE GRIT FRIES WITH SMOKY HOT KETCHUP (PAGE 283)

BUTTERMILK
STONE-GROUND
GRITS (PAGE 280)

BRUSSELS SPROUT-AND-LEEK
SLAW WITH BACON AND
PECANS (PAGE 286)

ROASTED BEET-AND-
CITRUS SALAD WITH
HONEY-ORANGE
VINAIGRETTE
(PAGE 286)

SWEET POTATO-AND-
COLLARD GREEN GRATIN
(PAGE 329)

TURKEY-AND-COLLARD
GREEN STEW (PAGE 328)

SECRETS TO CRISPY,
GOLDEN TURKEY (PAGE 330)

SAVORY CORN PUDDING
(PAGE 309)

187

OLD-SCHOOL GREEN BEAN
CASSEROLE (PAGE 308);
ANGEL BISCUITS (PAGE 308);
CANDIED YAMS (PAGE 307);
CRANBERRY SALAD (PAGE 307)

CORNBREAD DRESSING (PAGE 304)

CARAMEL TART WITH
BRANDY WHIPPED CREAM
(PAGE 326)

CUSHAW PIE WITH VANILLA BEAN
CUSTARD SAUCE (PAGE 323)

Field Pea, Corn, and Bacon Salad

SERVES 4
ACTIVE 20 MIN. · TOTAL 25 MIN.

Cook 4 **bacon slices,** chopped, in a skillet over medium until crisp. Transfer bacon to a plate lined with paper towels; reserve 1 Tbsp. drippings in skillet. Reduce heat to medium. Add 1½ cups uncooked shelled fresh **Lady Cream peas,** 1 cup fresh **corn kernels,** ½ cup **sweet onion,** and ½ cup **water** to skillet. Cook until peas are tender, about 7 minutes. Stir in bacon and 2 Tbsp. **Summer Sauce** (recipe, page 158). Serve warm.

SHOPPING TIP

Knowing how many pounds of unshelled field peas to buy at the market can be a challenge. Depending on the type of legume (some pods contain more peas than others), ¾ pound of unshelled pods will yield roughly 1 cup of field peas.

Field Peas

Black-eyed, crowder, purple hull, lady, and cream—those are just a few of the kinds you'll find at the market. Shelling peas on the back porch on a summer afternoon is practically a rite of passage in the South. Fresh field peas also freeze beautifully, so buy plenty and don't forget to dig into your stash all year long.

ASK A FARMER

WHAT'S THE DIFFERENCE BETWEEN WHITE AND BROWN EGGS?

"There is no major difference in the nutritional value, quality, or flavor between brown and white eggs. Their color depends on the breed of the hens. White eggs come from hens with white feathers and earlobes, and brown eggs come from hens with red feathers and earlobes."

—Alex Simpson, Simpson's Eggs, Monroe, North Carolina

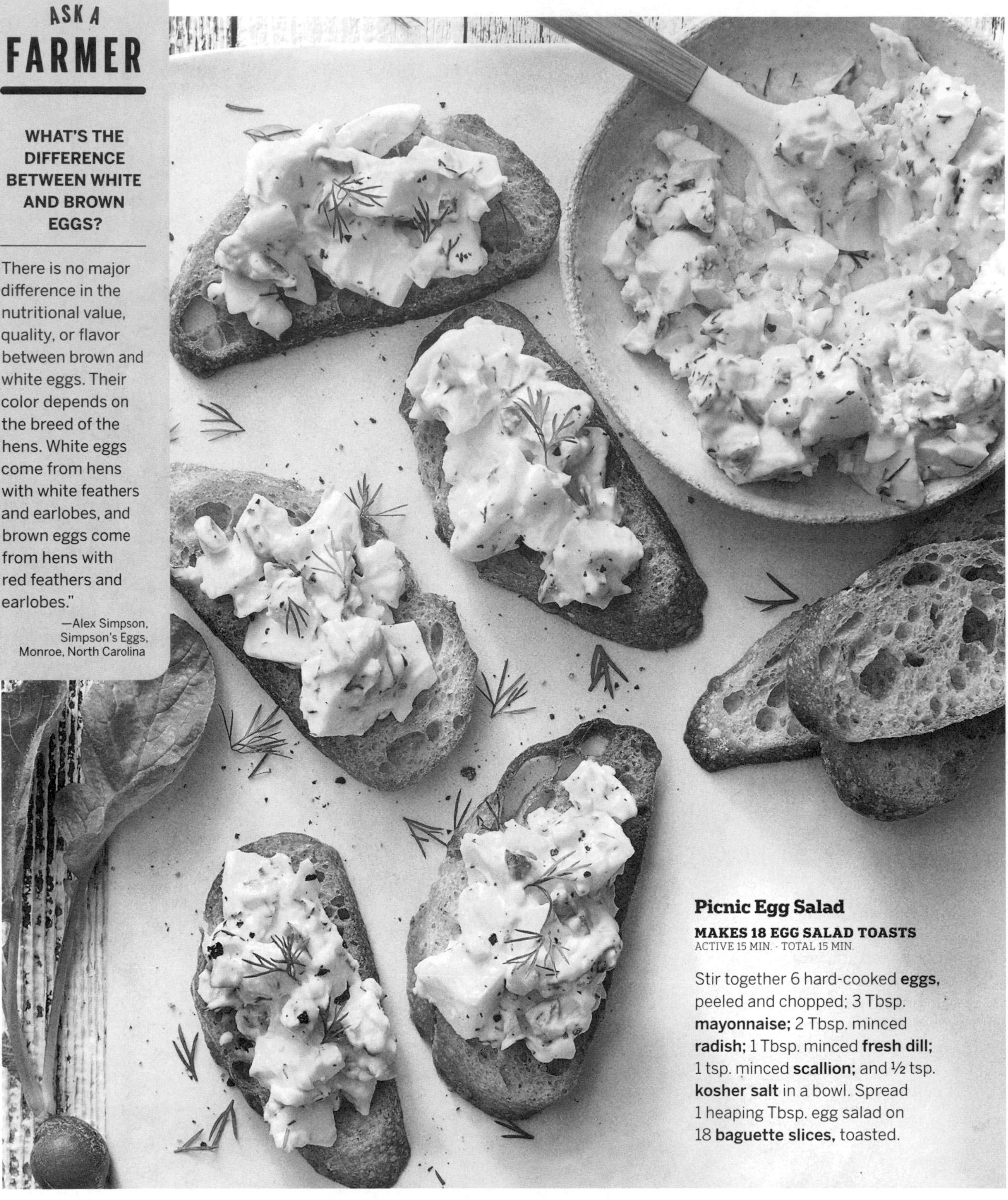

Picnic Egg Salad

MAKES 18 EGG SALAD TOASTS
ACTIVE 15 MIN. - TOTAL 15 MIN.

Stir together 6 hard-cooked **eggs,** peeled and chopped; 3 Tbsp. **mayonnaise;** 2 Tbsp. minced **radish;** 1 Tbsp. minced **fresh dill;** 1 tsp. minced **scallion;** and ½ tsp. **kosher salt** in a bowl. Spread 1 heaping Tbsp. egg salad on 18 **baguette slices,** toasted.

Eggs

Long gone are the days when the only decision we had to make was between brown and white. Strolling through the farmers' market today, you'll be amazed by the rainbow of beautiful blue, green, and yellow hues—all of which work equally well in this fresh take on egg salad.

Bee's Knees

SERVES 1
ACTIVE 5 MIN.
TOTAL 5 MIN.

Combine ¼ cup **gin**, 2 Tbsp. **honey**, and 2 Tbsp. fresh **lemon juice** in a cocktail shaker filled with **ice**. Shake until chilled. Strain into a coupe glass.

THE DRESSING OF SUMMER

SHAKE UP SALADS WITH THIS TANGY 5-MINUTE VINAIGRETTE

Honey Vinaigrette

MAKES 1 CUP
ACTIVE 5 MIN.
TOTAL 5 MIN.

Combine ½ cup **canola oil**, ⅓ cup **white balsamic vinegar**, 2 Tbsp. **honey**, 2 tsp. minced **red onion** or shallot, ¼ tsp. **kosher salt**, and ¼ tsp. **black pepper** in a clean jar. Cover with lid, and shake until blended. Use immediately, or chill until ready to use.

Honey Barbecue Sauce

MAKES 1½ CUPS
ACTIVE 5 MIN.
TOTAL 35 MIN.

Bring 1 cup **ketchup**, ⅓ cup **honey**, ¼ cup **unsalted butter**, 2 Tbsp. fresh **lemon juice**, and 1 Tbsp. **Worcestershire sauce** to a boil in a small saucepan over medium. Reduce heat to low, and add 2 **lemon slices**. Simmer 30 minutes. Remove sauce from heat, and discard lemon slices; let cool.

Honey

Fruits and vegetables get all the glory at the farmers' market, but savvy shoppers know to look for jars of this golden, locally produced liquid that's far superior to anything at the supermarket. Whether you find wildflower, blueberry, or clover honey, stock up and add it to more than just hot tea.

Spiked Watermelon Lemonade

SERVES 1
ACTIVE 15 MIN. · TOTAL 15 MIN.

Combine ½ cup fresh **watermelon juice**, ½ cup (or to taste) **simple syrup**, ¼ cup **vodka**, and 3 Tbsp. fresh **lemon juice** in a cocktail shaker. Cover and shake vigorously, about 15 seconds. Strain into a glass filled with ice. Garnish with **mint sprig**.

ASK A FARMER

HOW CAN I TELL IF A WATERMELON IS RIPE?

"Check the stem. A green stem means it is fresh and has not been off the vine for too long. The watermelon should also be fat for its length and have a shiny, green exterior with well-defined stripes."

—Lee Wroten, Global Produce Sales, Inc., Lakeland, Florida

Watermelon

What's more refreshing than juicy watermelon by the slice? Watermelon by the glass. Or—even more fun—as an ice pop. Whip up a batch of fresh watermelon juice, and serve it as a signature cocktail, chilled soup, smoothie, or afternoon treat.

Watermelon Gazpacho

SERVES 5
ACTIVE 15 MIN.
TOTAL 45 MIN.

Process 5 cups cubed **watermelon** (from 1 watermelon); 1 cup peeled, seeded, and diced **cucumber**; ¼ cup chopped **red onion**; and ½ **jalapeño chile**, seeded and minced, in a blender until smooth. Stir in 2 Tbsp. **apple cider vinegar** and 1 tsp. **kosher salt.** Cover and chill at least 30 minutes. Serve in small bowls or glasses.

Watermelon Smoothies

SERVES 4
ACTIVE 15 MIN.
TOTAL 15 MIN.

Process 2 cups fresh **watermelon juice**; 1 cup **ice**; ½ cup plain **yogurt**; 1 cup **fresh strawberries**, hulled; and 1 Tbsp. **honey** in a blender until smooth. Pour mixture evenly into 4 glasses.

Watermelon-Lime Pops with Chile Dipping Salt

SERVES 12
ACTIVE 15 MIN. · TOTAL 4 HOURS, 15 MIN.,
INCLUDING 4 HOURS FREEZING

- 4 cups fresh watermelon juice (from 1 watermelon)
- 5 Tbsp. fresh lime juice (from 4 limes)
- ¼ cup simple syrup
- 2 Tbsp. granulated sugar
- 1 tsp. kosher salt
- ⅛ tsp. chile powder

1. Stir together watermelon juice, lime juice, and simple syrup. Pour into 12 (3-ounce) plastic pop molds. Insert plastic or wooden pop sticks, and freeze until completely frozen, 4 hours or overnight.
2. Stir together sugar, salt, and chile powder in a small bowl; serve with Watermelon-Lime Pops for dipping.

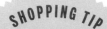

Eggplant

With its bold purple (or white or yellow or green) shades and curvaceous shapes, the eggplant is one of the most eye-catching vegetables at the market. It's also probably the most underused. Contrary to popular belief, you don't need special skills to master cooking it—just a few foolproof recipes like these.

EGGPLANT ROLLUPS

EGGPLANT-YOGURT DIP

Eggplant Rollups

SERVES 6
ACTIVE 20 MIN. · TOTAL 1 HOUR, 10 MIN.

- 2 eggplants, cut lengthwise into 12 (¼-inch-thick) slices
- ¾ tsp. kosher salt, divided
- 6 Tbsp. extra-virgin olive oil, divided
- 1 (10-oz.) container whole-milk ricotta cheese
- ½ cup fresh basil leaves, finely chopped, plus more basil for serving
- ¾ tsp. black pepper
- 1¼ cups marinara sauce
- 1 oz. Parmesan cheese, shaved (about ½ cup)

1. Preheat oven to 425°F. Sprinkle eggplant slices on both sides with ¼ teaspoon of the salt, and place in a colander to drain 15 minutes. Rinse well, and press between 2 clean, absorbent towels to dry. Arrange eggplant slices in a single layer on greased baking sheets. Rub eggplant slices on both sides with 3 tablespoons of the oil. Bake in preheated oven until just beginning to brown, 13 to 15 minutes. Remove eggplant from oven, and reduce oven temperature to 375°F.
2. While eggplant is baking, stir together ricotta, chopped basil, pepper, and remaining 3 tablespoons oil and ½ teaspoon salt in a medium bowl. Pour 1 cup of the marinara into an 11- x 7-inch baking dish. Place 1 tablespoon ricotta mixture on 1 eggplant slice, and roll up from 1 short end. Place rollup, seam side down, in baking dish. Repeat with remaining ricotta mixture and eggplant

slices. Top evenly with remaining ¼ cup marinara.
3. Bake at 375°F until sauce is bubbly and warm and tops of rollups are very lightly browned, 15 to 20 minutes. Top with shaved Parmesan cheese and basil. Serve immediately.

Eggplant-Yogurt Dip

SERVES 4
ACTIVE 15 MIN. · TOTAL 55 MIN., INCLUDING 20 MIN. COOLING

- 1 medium eggplant (about 10 oz.)
- 1 Tbsp. olive oil
- ½ tsp. black pepper
- ½ tsp. kosher salt, divided
- 1 garlic clove
- ¾ cup plain yogurt
- 2 Tbsp. Summer Sauce, plus more for serving (recipe, page 158)
- ½ tsp. ground cumin
  Vegetables or bread for dipping

1. Preheat oven to 450°F. Cut eggplant in half lengthwise, and make a few shallow cuts into eggplant flesh. Brush eggplant flesh with oil; sprinkle with pepper and ¼ teaspoon of the salt. Place eggplant, cut side down, on a rimmed baking sheet with garlic clove. Bake in preheated oven until browned and tender, 20 to 25 minutes. Cool to room temperature, about 20 minutes. Roughly chop eggplant.
2. Process eggplant, garlic, yogurt, Summer Sauce, ground cumin, and remaining ¼ teaspoon salt in a food processor until combined. Transfer mixture to a serving bowl. Top with a

swirl of Summer Sauce. Serve with vegetables or bread for dipping.

Pasta with Eggplant, Burrata, and Mint

SERVES 4
ACTIVE 25 MIN. · TOTAL 35 MIN.

- ¼ cup extra-virgin olive oil
- 1 Tbsp. crushed red pepper
- 2 garlic cloves, thinly sliced
- 1 large eggplant, cut into 1-inch cubes (about 2 cups)
- 1 lb. uncooked rigatoni, ziti, or orecchiette pasta
- 8 oz. fresh Burrata or mozzarella cheese
- ½ cup torn fresh mint, plus more for serving
- 1 tsp. lemon zest, plus 1 Tbsp. fresh lemon juice (from 1 lemon)

1. Heat oil in a large skillet over medium. Add crushed red pepper and garlic; cook until fragrant, about 2 minutes. Add eggplant, and cook, stirring occasionally, until browned, about 20 minutes.
2. Meanwhile, cook pasta in boiling salted water according to package directions for al dente. Drain pasta, reserving 1 cup cooking water. Place cooked pasta in a serving bowl; add eggplant mixture. Slowly add reserved cooking water, tossing to coat. Tear fresh Burrata into pieces over the bowl (to catch any cream from the cheese), and add torn fresh mint, lemon zest, and lemon juice. Toss to combine. Add salt to taste, if desired. Top servings with additional mint.

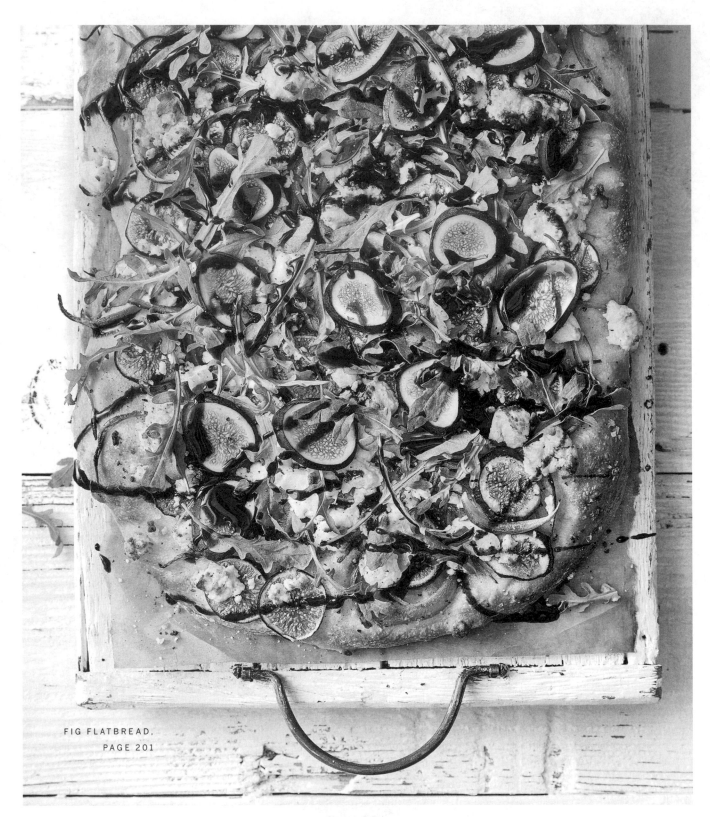

FIG FLATBREAD,
PAGE 201

Figs

Soft, not squishy, is the key when choosing good figs. Because their season is short and the fruit
is perishable, there should be a holiday dedicated to celebrating this syrupy summertime treat. Load up on a
few pounds of them at the farmers' market, and try this easy jam and sweet-savory flatbread.

Fig Flatbread

SERVES 4
ACTIVE 10 MIN. · TOTAL 30 MIN.

- 1 Tbsp. olive oil
- 1 small red onion, sliced
- ½ tsp. kosher salt, divided
- ½ tsp. black pepper, divided
- 14 oz. store-bought fresh pizza dough
- 6 figs, thinly sliced crosswise, divided
- 8 oz. goat cheese, crumbled (about 2 cups)
- ¼ cup balsamic vinegar
- 1 cup loosely packed arugula

1. Preheat oven to 450°F. Heat oil in a saucepan over medium. Add red onion and ¼ teaspoon each of the kosher salt and pepper. Cook, stirring, until tender, 2 minutes.
2. Roll pizza dough into a ¼-inch-thick, 17- x 11-inch rectangle. Place on a large baking sheet lined with parchment paper. Sprinkle with remaining ¼ teaspoon each salt and pepper. Top evenly with cooked onions, one-third of the fig slices, and cheese. Bake until crust is lightly browned and done, 15 to 20 minutes.
3. Meanwhile, cook balsamic vinegar in a small saucepan over medium-high until reduced by half, about 5 minutes. Top flatbread with remaining figs, arugula, and balsamic reduction.

Fig and Lemon Refrigerator Jam

MAKES 2 CUPS
ACTIVE 40 MIN. · TOTAL 1 HOUR

Stir together 1 lb. **figs,** chopped into ¼-inch pieces; ⅓ cup **granulated sugar;** and 2 Tbsp. **lemon zest** in a saucepan. Let stand until figs are juicy and sugar is mostly dissolved, about 15 minutes. Add ⅓ cup fresh **lemon juice** (from 3 lemons) and ⅓ cup **water;** bring to a boil over medium. Reduce heat to low; simmer, stirring occasionally, until figs are tender and broken down and syrup coats the back of a spoon, about 25 minutes. Cool completely, about 20 minutes. Store in an airtight container in refrigerator up to 3 months.

the SWEET spot

PEARSON FARM IS GEORGIA'S GIFT
THAT KEEPS ON GIVING, AND NOW
MORE THAN JUST THE LOCALS CAN
ENJOY THEIR FRESHLY PICKED PEACHES

PEACHES-
AND-CREAM
PANCAKES,
PAGE 205

Stephen and Jessica Rose

GROWING UP IN FORT VALLEY, GEORGIA,
Stephen Rose thought all peaches were as *gloriously sweet and juicy* as the kind grown *down the road* at Pearson Farm.

The Pearsons were family friends, so Stephen spent many of his childhood days at the farm enjoying peach ice cream. "It was summer in a small town, and that was what you did," he says. But it wasn't until he was an adult living in Nashville that he realized that Pearson peaches weren't the norm; They were the delicious exception.

Tender, super-juicy, skin-on, ready-to-eat peaches depend on many factors: trees, mineral-rich clay soil, extremely hot weather—all of which can be found in Fort Valley. Add in experienced pickers and the knowledge gained from five generations of farming the same land, and you reap sweet rewards—that is if nature cooperates, of course. Al Pearson, the current patriarch at the helm (his son, Lawton, became a partner in 2008), says that even after many years of planting and picking, a good harvest still seems like a miracle. "Peaches really are stressful to grow, but it's in our blood," says Al.

When Stephen took his wife, Jessica, back home for her first Pearson Farm peach, it was an eye opener for her too. Determined to bring this natural goodness back to Nashville, the couple teamed up with the Pearsons to launch The Peach Truck, named for the 1964 Jeep the Roses use to deliver and sell tree-ripened peaches. And it's obvious Music City adores the Georgia gems as much as Pearson Farm's hometown fans do. Since 2012, the Roses have sold over 4.5 million pounds of peaches (they now ship nationwide) and earned a cult following among the farmers' market faithful and Southern chefs alike.

The Peach Truck sells about 40 kinds of peaches, including the iconic Elberta and the fragrant White Lady, but don't ask Al or Stephen to choose a favorite, because they will give the same answer: "The one in my hand." Once you eat their peaches, either out of hand or in one of the recipes that follow, we think you'll agree.

PEACH ICEBOX CAKE

One delicious warm-weather treat, two ways to serve it: Make it in a glass trifle dish and scoop out helpings, or prepare it in a large cake pan and serve by the slice.

ACTIVE 20 MIN. - TOTAL 4 HOURS, 20 MIN., INCLUDING 4 HOURS CHILLING

SERVES 10 TO 12

- 3 cups heavy cream
- ¾ cup granulated sugar
- 2 tsp. vanilla extract
- ½ tsp. almond extract
- 8 oz. mascarpone cheese
- 1 (5.3-oz.) container vanilla Greek yogurt
- 6 fresh peaches (about 2 lb.)
- 1 (14.4-oz.) pkg. graham crackers (about 27 crackers)
  Fresh mint sprig

1. Beat cream, sugar, vanilla extract, and almond extract with an electric mixer on high speed until stiff peaks form.
2. Beat mascarpone cheese and yogurt in a separate bowl on medium speed until smooth. Fold into whipped cream mixture, and set aside.
3. Gently rub peaches under running water to remove fuzz. Cut into ⅛-inch-thick slices. (You will have about 8 cups.)
4. Spread a thin layer of cream mixture in the bottom of a trifle dish. Cover the cream with a single layer of graham crackers, breaking some crackers to fill in gaps. Add a layer of peach slices to completely cover the crackers. Repeat layers, ending with cream mixture. Cover and chill 4 to 12 hours.
5. Top with any remaining broken cracker pieces; garnish with mint, if desired. Serve cold.

Peaches-and-Cream Pancakes

These thin, crêpe-like pancakes are gluten free, but you can swap out the gluten-free flour for an equal amount of all-purpose flour.

ACTIVE 20 MIN. - TOTAL 20 MIN.
SERVES 2

- 2 fresh peaches (about ⅔ lb.)
- ¼ cup pure maple syrup
- 4 large eggs
- 1 Tbsp. granulated sugar
- ½ tsp. vanilla extract
- ½ cup gluten-free flour
- ½ cup cottage cheese
- 1 Tbsp. salted butter
  Sweetened whipped cream

1. Gently rub peaches under running water to remove fuzz. Thinly slice peaches, and cut in half. Toss together peach slices and maple syrup in a medium bowl.
2. Whisk together eggs, sugar, and vanilla in a medium bowl until combined. Whisk in flour until smooth. Add cottage cheese, and stir to combine.
3. Heat a 9-inch nonstick skillet over medium-high. Add ½ teaspoon of the butter to skillet. Spoon ⅓ cup of pancake batter into melted butter in skillet, swirling to evenly distribute batter in a thin layer. Cook until the batter begins to firm up, about 1 minute. Flip pancake, and cook until firm, about 1 more minute. Transfer to a baking sheet, and keep warm in a 200°F oven. Repeat with remaining butter and batter.
4. To serve, layer 3 pancakes and peaches on each of 2 plates; top with whipped cream.

Freezer Peach Pie

What's better than peach pie in summer? Peach pie in winter! Try this genius freezing method to get your pie fix anytime.

ACTIVE 10 MIN. - TOTAL 9 HOURS, INCLUDING 8 HOURS FREEZING
SERVES 8

- 1 ½ lb. fresh peaches, peeled and sliced (about 3 cups)
- ½ cup granulated sugar
- 1 Tbsp. plus 2 tsp. cornstarch
- ¼ tsp. ground ginger
- ¼ tsp. ground cardamom
- ¼ tsp. ground cinnamon
- 1 (14.1-oz.) pkg. refrigerated piecrusts

FREEZER PEACH PIE

1. Toss together fresh peaches, sugar, cornstarch, ground ginger, ground cardamom, and ground cinnamon in a large bowl, making sure spices are distributed throughout. Line a 9-inch pie pan with aluminum foil, and transfer peach mixture to the pie pan. Cover and freeze 8 to 12 hours. Remove frozen peach filling from pan, discard foil, and place filling in a ziplock plastic freezer bag. Return to freezer until ready to use. Peach filling will keep up to 6 months in the freezer.
2. To make pie, preheat oven to 450°F. Unroll 1 piecrust, and fit into the same 9-inch pie pan. Fold edges under, and crimp. Place frozen filling on crust.
3. Unroll second piecrust on a lightly floured surface, and cut into 8 (1-inch-wide) strips. Arrange strips in a lattice design over filling; gently press ends of strips, sealing to bottom piecrust. Shield crust edge with foil to prevent crust from burning.
4. Bake in preheated oven 10 minutes. Reduce oven temperature to 350°F, leaving edges covered with foil, and continue to bake until top crust is browned and filling is bubbly, about 40 minutes.

Peach Fried Pies

Canned biscuits make easy work of these irresistible hand pies with a spiced, jammy filling.

ACTIVE 1 HOUR - TOTAL 1 HOUR, 30 MIN.
MAKES ABOUT 16 PIES

- 2 fresh peaches (about ⅔ lb.)
- ½ cup granulated sugar
- 1 Tbsp. fresh lemon juice
- ½ tsp. ground cardamom
- 1 Tbsp. cornstarch
- 1 Tbsp. water
- 1 Tbsp. cold salted butter
  All-purpose flour (for dusting)
- 2 (16.3-oz.) cans refrigerated large Southern-style biscuits
- 2 cups shortening
  Powdered sugar (optional)

1. Bring a small saucepan of water to a boil. Make a small, shallow X in the bottom of each peach, just to break the skin. Place each peach in the boiling water for 10 seconds; immediately plunge into a bowl of ice water. Peel the skin with a paring knife. Remove the pits, and cut the peaches into slices.
2. Place the peach slices, sugar, lemon juice, and cardamom in a saucepan. Bring to a boil over high; reduce heat to low. Cover and simmer 5 minutes. Stir together cornstarch and water; stir into simmering peach mixture. Increase heat to high, and bring to a boil; boil until thickened, about 1 minute. Remove from heat, and stir in butter. Transfer to a bowl, and chill until ready to use.
3. Sprinkle a work surface with flour. Generously flour both sides of biscuits, and roll each into a 5 ½-inch circle (about ⅛ inch thick). Place a heaping table-spoon of the chilled filling in the center of each dough circle, leaving a 1-inch border around the edge. Do not overfill. Using a brush or your finger, dampen the edge of the circle with water. Carefully fold the dough in half, pressing the edges together to make a half-moon shape. Press edges with a fork to seal.
4. Melt shortening in a Dutch oven over medium; heat to 325°F. Fry pies, in batches, until deep golden brown, 4 to 5 minutes on each side, turning as necessary to ensure even browning. Remove and drain on paper towels; if desired, dust with powdered sugar.

Peach Bread Pudding with Bourbon Caramel

A spiked caramel sauce makes this bread pudding truly spectacular. Resist the urge to stir the caramel as it cooks, and watch it closely. Once it starts to brown, it can easily turn too dark and become bitter.

ACTIVE 15 MIN. - TOTAL 9 HOURS, 30 MIN., INCLUDING 8 HOURS CHILLING

SERVES 10 TO 12

BREAD PUDDING
- 5 large eggs, separated
- 1 cup whole milk
- 1 Tbsp. vanilla extract
- ½ tsp. ground cinnamon
- ¼ tsp. kosher salt
- 2 cups heavy cream
- ⅔ cup granulated sugar
- 1 (16-oz.) challah bread loaf, cut into 1-inch cubes (about 11 ½ cups)
- 3-4 fresh peaches
- 4 Tbsp. salted butter, cut into small pieces, plus more for dish

BOURBON CARAMEL
- 2 Tbsp. unsalted butter
- ¼ cup water
- 1 cup granulated sugar
- 1 cup heavy cream, at room temperature
- 2 oz. (¼ cup) bourbon

1. Prepare the Bread Pudding: Whisk together egg yolks, milk, vanilla extract, cinnamon, salt, 2 cups heavy cream, and ⅔ cup granulated sugar in a large bowl until thoroughly combined. Add bread pieces, and toss to coat pieces evenly. Cover and chill 8 to 12 hours to allow bread to absorb the liquid.
2. Preheat oven to 350°F. Gently rub peaches under running water to remove fuzz, and chop peaches. (You will have about 6 ½ cups.) Beat egg whites with an electric mixer on high speed until soft peaks form. Remove soaked bread from refrigerator; stir in 4 tablespoons salted butter pieces and chopped peaches. Fold in whipped egg whites until combined. Transfer mixture to a well-greased (with butter) 13- x 9-inch baking dish or a large cast-iron skillet. Cover loosely with aluminum foil, and bake in preheated oven until it puffs in the center, about 45 minutes. Remove foil, and bake until the top is lightly browned, 25 to 30 minutes.
3. Prepare the Bourbon Caramel: Melt 2 tablespoons unsalted butter in a medium saucepan over medium-high; stir in water and 1 cup granulated sugar. Cook, without stirring, until mixture is a medium shade of brown, 4 to 6 minutes. Carefully whisk in 1 cup heavy cream. (Mixture will bubble up as the cream is added.) Remove from heat, and whisk in bourbon. Serve Bourbon Caramel warm with the Bread Pudding.

Peach–Ricotta Cheesecake with Pecan Crust

This silky peach-topped cheesecake is made with another Georgia staple: pecans. For the smoothest texture, make this gluten-free dessert a day in advance and store in the refrigerator before serving.

ACTIVE 25 MIN. - TOTAL 13 HOURS, 30 MIN., INCLUDING 8 HOURS CHILLING AND 4 HOURS COOLING

SERVES 8 TO 10

- 1 (32-oz.) container whole-milk ricotta cheese
- 3 cups chopped pecans
- 3 Tbsp. light brown sugar
- ¼ tsp. kosher salt
- 3 Tbsp. tapioca starch or gluten-free flour, divided
- 1 egg white, whisked until frothy
- 4 fresh peaches, divided
- 1 (8-oz.) pkg. cream cheese, at room temperature
- 1 cup granulated sugar
- 2 large eggs
- 1 tsp. lemon zest, plus 2 Tbsp. fresh juice (from 1 lemon), divided
- 1 tsp. vanilla extract
- ¼ tsp. fine sea salt
- ¼ tsp. almond extract
- Fresh mint

1. Place ricotta cheese in a cheesecloth-lined colander. Set colander in a bowl, and cover colander and bowl with plastic wrap. Chill 8 to 12 hours to drain.
2. Preheat oven to 350°F. Spread chopped pecans in a single layer on a rimmed baking sheet, and bake in preheated oven until fragrant and lightly toasted, about 10 minutes. Remove from oven, and cool on baking sheet 20 minutes. Process pecans in a food processor until finely ground. Transfer to a medium bowl. Add brown sugar, kosher salt, and 1 tablespoon of the tapioca starch; whisk to combine. Add beaten egg white, and whisk just until blended. Using dampened fingers, press pecan mixture onto bottom and up sides of a lightly greased 9-inch springform pan, making crust about ⅛ inch thick.
3. Place a large pan of water on the bottom rack of the oven. Transfer the drained ricotta to a food processor. Peel 1 peach, cut in half, and remove pit. Add peach to ricotta. Process 30 seconds; scrape down sides. Add cream cheese, granulated sugar, eggs, and remaining 2 tablespoons tapioca starch. Process 30 seconds; scrape down sides. Add lemon zest, vanilla extract, fine sea salt, almond extract, and 1 tablespoon of the lemon juice. Process until smooth, stopping occasionally to scrape down sides. Transfer batter to prepared crust, and place on the center rack of the oven, above the pan of water.
4. Bake in preheated oven until top puffs up and begins to brown and center of cheesecake seems mostly set (it will jiggle a little), about 1 hour and 10 minutes. Transfer cheesecake to a wire rack, and cool 4 hours (or cover and refrigerate overnight). The cheesecake will settle slightly as it cools.
5. Gently rub the 3 remaining peaches under running water to remove fuzz, and thinly slice peaches. Toss together peach slices and remaining 1 tablespoon lemon juice in a large bowl. Top cheesecake with sliced peaches, and garnish with fresh mint, if desired.

Easy Peach Cobbler

This deliciously simple recipe from Jessica and Stephen Rose will serve six people.

ACTIVE 10 MIN. - TOTAL 55 MIN.

SERVES 6

- 1 ¾ lb. fresh peaches
- ½ cup (4 oz.) salted butter
- 1 cup self-rising flour
- 1 cup granulated sugar
- 1 cup whole milk
- 1 tsp. vanilla extract

1. Preheat oven to 350°F. Gently rub the peaches under running water to remove fuzz, and slice peaches. (You will have about 4 cups.) Place butter in an 11- x 7-inch baking dish; place dish in oven until butter melts. Stir together flour, sugar, milk, and vanilla in a bowl, and pour onto melted butter. (Do not stir.) Spoon peaches over mixture. (Do not stir.)
2. Bake in preheated oven until browned and bubbly, 45 to 50 minutes.

EASY PEACH
COBBLER,
PAGE 206

PEACH FRIED
PIES, PAGE 205

PEACH BREAD PUDDING
WITH BOURBON CARAMEL,
PAGE 206

PEACH-
RICOTTA
CHEESECAKE
WITH PECAN
CRUST,
PAGE 206

Fresh Peach Coffee Cake with Pecan Streusel

If you like coffee cake that's heavy on the crumb topping (who doesn't?), you'll love this recipe. Bake it on a Friday night, and snack on it all weekend long.

ACTIVE 10 MIN. · TOTAL 2 HOURS, 10 MIN.
SERVES 8 TO 10

PECAN STREUSEL
- 1 **cup chopped pecans**
- ½ **cup packed light brown sugar**
- 1 **tsp. ground cinnamon**
- 1 **tsp. kosher salt**
- ¾ **cup all-purpose flour**
- ½ **cup granulated sugar**
- 1 **tsp. ground cardamom**
- ½ **cup cold unsalted butter, cut into pieces**

CAKE
- 2 **tsp. baking powder**
- 1½ **cups all-purpose flour, plus more for pan**
- ¾ **cup granulated sugar**
- ½ **tsp. ground cardamom**
- ¾ **cup heavy cream**
- 2 **tsp. vanilla extract**
- 1 **large egg**
- 4 **Tbsp. unsalted butter, melted**
- 2-3 **ripe peaches**

1. Prepare the Pecan Streusel: Preheat oven to 350°F. Stir together chopped pecans, brown sugar, cinnamon, salt, ¾ cup flour, ½ cup granulated sugar, and 1 teaspoon ground cardamom in a medium bowl. Add ½ cup cold butter pieces, and, using your fingers or a pastry blender, combine until a sandy texture is achieved.
2. Prepare the Cake: Sift together baking powder, 1½ cups flour, ¾ cup granulated sugar, and ½ teaspoon cardamom. Beat cream, vanilla, egg, and 4 tablespoons melted butter with an electric mixer on medium-high speed until frothy, about 1 minute. Fold in the flour mixture with a spatula until blended. Do not overmix.
3. Gently rub peaches under running water to remove fuzz, and slice each into 8 wedges. Transfer the batter to a lightly greased and floured 9-inch springform pan, and smooth the surface. Arrange the peach slices evenly over the batter, pressing them into the batter just a bit. Cover the top evenly with the Pecan Streusel, pressing lightly.
4. Bake in preheated oven until a toothpick inserted in the center comes out clean, about 1 hour. Cool in pan on a rack 1 hour. Remove sides of pan before serving.

ONLY 446
CALORIES
PER SERVING

Skirt Steak Soft Tacos with Avocado–Corn Salsa

Warm corn tortillas and a colorful, chunky salsa transform simple grilled skirt steak into a fantastic—and surprisingly light—summer meal.

ACTIVE 25 MIN. - TOTAL 35 MIN.
SERVES 6

- 1 Tbsp. chili powder
- 1½ tsp. ground cumin
- ¼ tsp. black pepper
- ½ tsp. kosher salt, divided
- 1 Tbsp. olive oil
- 1½ lb. skirt steak
- 2 cups fresh corn kernels (about 4 ears)
- 2 ripe avocados, cut into ½-inch pieces
- ¼ cup chopped fresh cilantro
- 1 tsp. lime zest, plus 3 Tbsp. fresh juice (from 2 limes)
- 6 scallions
- 12 (6-inch) corn tortillas, warmed
    Lime wedges

1. Preheat grill to medium-high (about 450°F). Stir together chili powder, cumin, pepper, and ¼ teaspoon of the salt. Rub oil over steak, and coat with spice mixture. Let stand 10 minutes.
2. Meanwhile, to make the salsa, stir together corn kernels, avocados, chopped cilantro, lime zest, lime juice, and remaining ¼ teaspoon salt.
3. Place steak on oiled grate, and grill, uncovered, to desired degree of doneness (2 to 3 minutes on each side for medium-rare). Let stand 5 minutes.
4. Place scallions on grate, and grill, uncovered and turning occasionally until charred and tender, about 2 minutes.
5. Cut steak across the grain into strips, and divide evenly among corn tortillas. Chop scallions, and sprinkle over steak. Top with salsa, and serve with lime wedges.

Nutritional information (per serving):
Calories: 446 - Protein: 29g - Carbs: 31g - Fiber: 7g - Fat: 25g

Sizzling Steak Tacos

Lighten up your weeknight fiesta with a side of fast, foolproof salsa

GRILLED CLAM-BAKE FOIL PACKETS WITH HERB BUTTER, PAGE 211

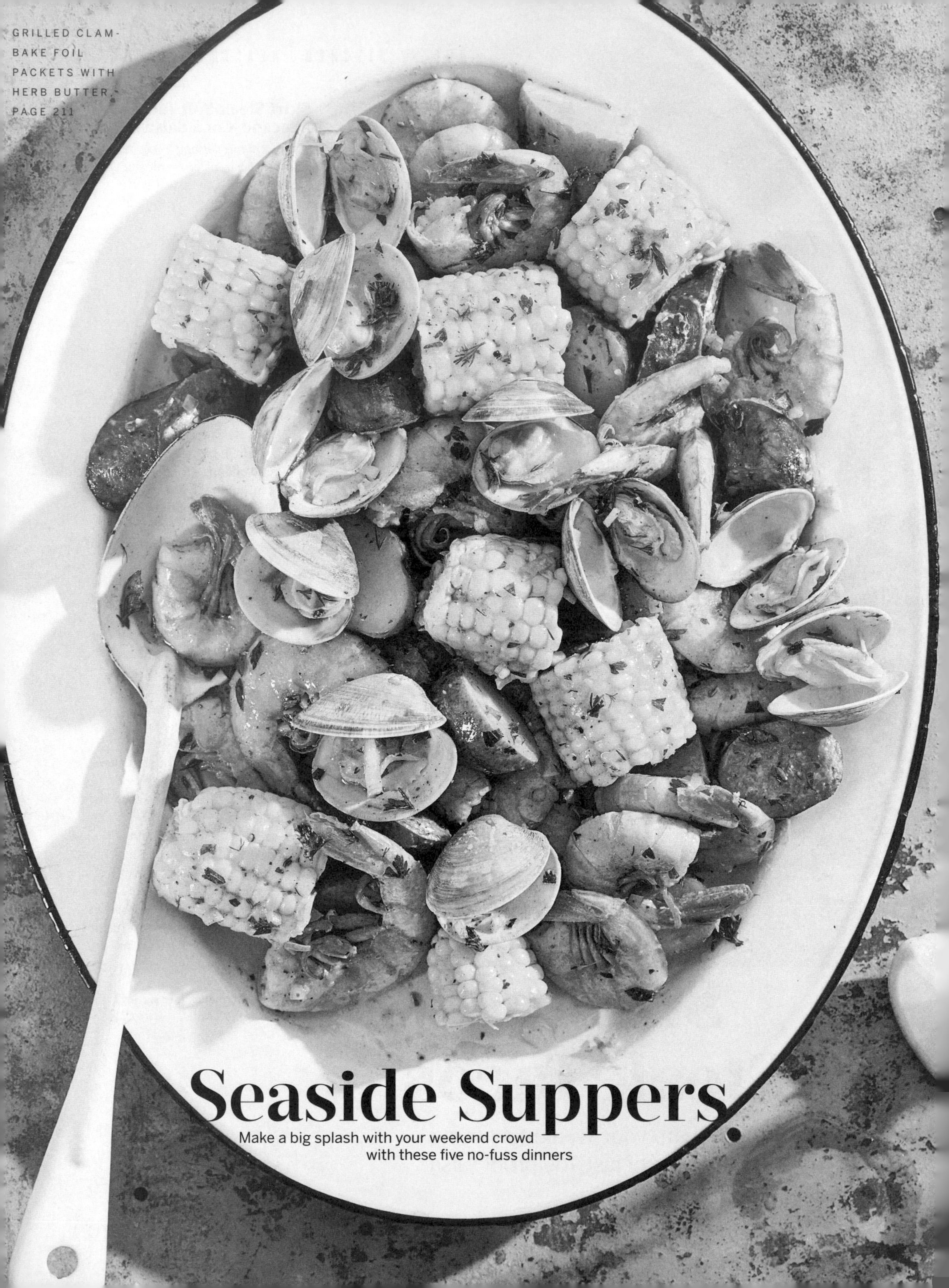

Seaside Suppers

Make a big splash with your weekend crowd with these five no-fuss dinners

Grilled Clambake Foil Packets with Herb Butter

Mesh bags are often used at clambakes, but we prefer foil packets for this recipe. The foil pouches concentrate the flavors of this summery seafood meal and its seasoned, buttery sauce.

ACTIVE 20 MIN. - TOTAL 40 MIN.
SERVES 6

- 1½ cups (12 oz.) unsalted butter, softened
- ¼ cup finely chopped shallot (about 1 shallot)
- 2 Tbsp. chopped fresh flat-leaf parsley
- 1 Tbsp. chopped fresh dill
- 1½ tsp. lemon zest (from 1 lemon)
- 3 Tbsp. Old Bay seasoning, divided
- 12 small red potatoes (about 2 lb.), cut into ½-inch wedges
- ¼ cup water
- 3 ears corn, husks removed, each ear cut into 4 pieces
- 24 unpeeled raw medium shrimp (about ⅔ lb.)
- 24 littleneck clams in shells, scrubbed (about 1 lb., 3 oz.)
- 1 lb. smoked sausage (such as Conecuh), cut diagonally into 1-inch-thick slices
- 3 lemons, cut into quarters
- 6 thyme sprigs
  Grilled French bread

1. Stir together butter, shallot, parsley, dill, lemon zest, and 1 tablespoon of the Old Bay seasoning in a medium bowl until well blended.
2. Combine potatoes and water in a medium-size microwavable bowl; cover with plastic wrap. Microwave on HIGH until tender and a knife can be inserted easily in center of potatoes, about 5 minutes. Drain and let stand 5 minutes.
3. Preheat a grill to medium (400°F to 450°F). Cut 12 (12-inch) square pieces of heavy-duty aluminum foil. Place 6 squares of the foil in a single layer on work surface. Divide potato wedges and corn evenly among foil sheets. Top each with 4 shrimp and 4 clams. Top evenly with sausage slices and lemon wedges. Dollop each with about ¼ cup butter mixture. Top each with 1 thyme sprig, and sprinkle each with 1 teaspoon Old Bay. Top each with 1 foil square, and crimp all sides to seal tightly.

SEARED SCALLOPS WITH FRESH TOMATO-BASIL SAUCE AND ORZO

4. Grill packets, covered, until shrimp are done and clams open, 8 to 10 minutes, rotating packets on grill halfway through cooking time. Discard any clams that do not open. Serve with grilled French bread.

Seared Scallops with Fresh Tomato-Basil Sauce and Orzo

Jumbo scallops (or sea scallops) are up to three times larger than bay scallops and have a sweet, delicate flavor. Dry-packed scallops are sold without extra water or preservatives, which helps them brown nicely. They have a shorter shelf life than wet-packed scallops, so cook them on the same day you buy them.

ACTIVE 10 MIN. - TOTAL 30 MIN.
SERVES 4

- ¼ cup olive oil, divided
- 1 cup thinly sliced sweet onion (from 1 large onion)
- 1½ Tbsp. minced garlic (about 6 cloves)
- 2 pt. cherry tomatoes
- ¼ cup thinly sliced fresh basil, divided
- 1¼ tsp. kosher salt, divided
- ¾ tsp. black pepper, divided
- 16 dry-packed jumbo scallops (about 1 lb.)
- 1½ cups uncooked orzo pasta
- ¼ cup salted butter
- 2 Tbsp. chopped fresh flat-leaf parsley

1. Heat 2 tablespoons of the oil in a 10-inch cast-iron skillet over medium-high. Add onion; cook, stirring occasionally, until softened and beginning to brown, 3 to 4 minutes. Add garlic; cook, stirring constantly, 1 minute. Add tomatoes, 2 tablespoons of the basil, 1 teaspoon of the salt, and ½ teaspoon of the pepper; cook, stirring occasionally, until tomatoes burst and release their juices, 6 to 7 minutes. Continue to cook, stirring occasionally, until sauce thickens slightly, 1 to 2 minutes. Transfer to a bowl; cover and keep warm.
2. Wipe skillet clean. Pat scallops dry with paper towels, and season with remaining ¼ teaspoon each salt and pepper. Heat remaining 2 tablespoons oil in skillet over high. Add scallops, and cook until golden brown, about 1 minute and 30 seconds per side. (Do not overcook.)
3. Cook orzo according to package directions; drain. Stir in butter and parsley.
4. Divide orzo among serving plates; top each with about ⅔ cup tomato sauce and 4 scallops. Sprinkle evenly with remaining 2 tablespoons basil.

Chicken-and-Shrimp Kebabs with Summer Vegetables and Basil Oil

The fragrant basil oil also makes a great dipping sauce for crusty bread.

ACTIVE 25 MIN. - TOTAL 50 MIN.

SERVES 6

- 12 (10-inch) wooden skewers
- 2 cups water
- 2 cups loosely packed fresh basil leaves (about 1 oz.)
- 1 Tbsp. white balsamic vinegar
- ¾ cup olive oil, divided
- 2 tsp. kosher salt, divided
- 1 tsp. black pepper, divided
- 2 lb. boneless, skinless chicken breasts, cut into 36 (1-inch) cubes
- 2 medium-size red bell peppers, cut into 24 (1-inch) pieces
- 2 medium-size yellow bell peppers, cut into 24 (1-inch) pieces
- 1 medium-size red onion, cut into 36 (1-inch) pieces
- 1 medium-size zucchini, cut into 24 (½-inch-thick) half-moons
- 36 peeled and deveined raw medium shrimp (about 12 oz.)

1. Soak wooden skewers in water 30 minutes; drain. Meanwhile, bring 2 cups water to a boil in a small saucepan over high. Add fresh basil, and cook, stirring constantly, until leaves wilt. Drain and pat leaves dry with a paper towel. Place basil, vinegar, ½ cup of the olive oil, 1 teaspoon of the salt, and ½ teaspoon of the black pepper in a blender. Process until smooth, 2 to 3 minutes.
2. Preheat grill to medium (350°F to 400°F). Thread 6 chicken cubes, 2 red bell pepper pieces, 2 yellow bell pepper pieces, 3 onion pieces, and 2 zucchini pieces alternately onto each of 6 skewers. Repeat procedure with remaining 6 skewers, threading each with 6 shrimp, 2 red bell pepper pieces, 2 yellow bell pepper pieces, 3 onion pieces, and 2 zucchini pieces. Drizzle skewers evenly with remaining ¼ cup olive oil, and sprinkle evenly with remaining 1 teaspoon salt and ½ teaspoon black pepper.
3. Grill, uncovered, until chicken and shrimp are done and vegetables are lightly charred, 3 to 5 minutes per side. (Shrimp kebabs will cook more quickly than chicken kebabs.) Transfer kebabs to a serving platter as they finish cooking. Brush evenly with half of the basil oil. Serve with remaining basil oil for dipping or drizzling.

Shrimp Perloo

Medium-size (not large) shrimp are the key here. The heat from the rice mixture cooks the shrimp to tender perfection in only 3 to 5 minutes.

ACTIVE 20 MIN. - TOTAL 40 MIN.

SERVES 6

- 4 thick-cut bacon slices (about 6 oz.), chopped
- 2 cups chopped sweet onion (from 1 large onion)
- 1 ½ cups chopped celery (about 2 large stalks)
- 1 cup chopped red bell pepper (from 1 medium bell pepper)
- 3 Tbsp. minced garlic (4 to 6 large cloves)
- ½ tsp. black pepper
- 3 tsp. kosher salt, divided
- ½ cup dry white wine
- 2 (14.5-oz.) cans fire-roasted diced tomatoes, drained well
- ½ tsp. crushed red pepper
- 7 cups seafood stock
- 3 cups uncooked basmati rice
- 3 Tbsp. unsalted butter
- 1 ½ lb. raw medium shrimp, peeled and deveined
- ¼ cup chopped fresh flat-leaf parsley

1. Cook bacon in a Dutch oven over medium, stirring often, until crisp, 8 to 10 minutes. Transfer bacon with a slotted spoon to a plate lined with paper towels to drain, reserving ¼ cup of the bacon drippings in Dutch oven.
2. Increase heat to medium-high. Add onion, celery, and bell pepper to Dutch oven; cook, stirring often, until vegetables soften but haven't begun to brown, about 5 minutes. Add garlic, black pepper, and 1 teaspoon of the salt; cook, stirring often, until fragrant, about 1 minute. Add wine, stirring and scraping to loosen browned bits from bottom of skillet. Add tomatoes and crushed red pepper; cook, stirring often, until most of the liquid has evaporated, about 3 minutes. Stir in stock, rice, and butter; bring to a boil. Reduce heat to low; cover and cook until rice is just tender, 10 to 12 minutes.
3. Remove from heat. Working quickly, gently stir in shrimp; cover and let stand until shrimp are cooked through, 3 to 5 minutes. Stir in remaining 2 teaspoons salt. Top servings evenly with parsley and bacon.

Crab Cakes with Creamy Fennel-and-Radish Slaw

Succulent jumbo lump crabmeat is worth the extra pennies when you're making crab cakes. Claw meat, the "dark meat" of the crab, is less expensive because it's easier to remove from the crab, but the pieces are smaller and not as tender as jumbo lump.

ACTIVE 30 MIN. - TOTAL 45 MIN.
SERVES 6

- 2 lb. fresh jumbo lump crabmeat, drained and picked
- 2 cups soft, fresh French bread-crumbs (from about 6 oz. bread)
- ½ cup sliced scallions (4 to 5 scallions)
- 2 large eggs, lightly beaten
- 2 tsp. lemon zest, plus 3 Tbsp. fresh juice (from 2 lemons), divided
- 1 cup mayonnaise, divided
- ½ cup chopped fresh flat-leaf parsley (about ½ oz.), divided
- 2 tsp. kosher salt, divided
- 1 tsp. black pepper, divided
- 1 fennel bulb with fronds (about 12 oz.)
- 1 (10-oz.) pkg. angel hair coleslaw
- 2 cups thinly sliced radishes (about 6 large radishes)
- 2 Tbsp. drained capers, chopped
- 1 Tbsp. caper brine from jar
- 1 tsp. honey
- 6 Tbsp. canola oil
   Lemon wedges

1. Gently stir together crabmeat, breadcrumbs, scallions, eggs, lemon zest, ½ cup of the mayonnaise, ¼ cup of the parsley, 1 ¼ teaspoons of the salt, and ½ teaspoon of the pepper in a medium bowl. (Do not break up the larger pieces of crabmeat.) Shape mixture into 12 (3-inch-wide) patties (about ½ cup per patty). Place patties on a baking sheet lined with aluminum foil; cover and chill 15 minutes.

2. Meanwhile, separate fennel stalks from bulb. Pick fronds from stalks; discard stalks. Chop fronds to equal 3 tablespoons. Trim top and bottom of fennel bulb; discard ends. Thinly slice fennel bulb to equal about 2 cups.

3. Combine sliced fennel bulb, chopped fennel fronds, angel hair coleslaw, thinly sliced radishes, and remaining ¼ cup parsley in a medium bowl. Stir together chopped capers, caper brine, honey, lemon juice, and remaining ½ cup mayonnaise, ¾ teaspoon salt, and ½ teaspoon pepper in a small bowl. Pour caper mixture over fennel mixture; toss to coat.

4. Heat 3 tablespoons of the oil in a large nonstick skillet over medium-high. Place 6 of the crab cakes in skillet; cook until golden brown, 3 to 4 minutes per side. Repeat with remaining 3 tablespoons oil and 6 crab cakes. Serve crab cakes with slaw and lemon wedges.

SEASONAL SIDE
PAIR THIS GRILLED
ZUCCHINI WITH
ANY PROTEIN.

Using All That Squash

This summertime vegetable is more versatile than you think

DIGGING IN THE DIRT is one of my family's favorite traditions. When I was growing up, Mama always had a little patch for planting squash, okra, and tomatoes in the backyard, while my grandfather's garden was nearly the size of a football field. He came of age during the Depression and, like many Southerners of that generation, was accustomed to growing much of his own food. He was an amazing gardener; we used to say he could put a stick in the ground and it would grow.

When it came to harvesting, he'd pick the butter beans and okra when they were young and tender. With zucchini, however, his thrifty sensibilities took over. He considered baby vegetables a waste of potential, so he picked zucchini and yellow squash only when they were fully grown. He grew them in large mounds so the vines could spread and produce as much as possible. On some occasions, a squash would slip by unnoticed and grow to the size of a Little League baseball bat. Regardless of my grandfather's "bigger is better" philosophy, I recommend choosing medium zucchini (about 8 inches long) for best results with these simple, flavorful recipes.

Zucchini Noodle Salad

If you don't own a spiralizer, you can use a julienne peeler. Some grocery stores now sell premade zucchini noodles.

ACTIVE 15 MIN. - TOTAL 25 MIN.
SERVES 4

Spiralize 1 ¼ lb. **zucchini** (about 3 medium zucchini) into noodles (about 6 cups), and place in a large bowl. Add 1 cup cooked **lady peas,** ½ very thinly sliced sweet **onion,** 1 very finely chopped **garlic** clove, and 2 Tbsp. chopped fresh flat-leaf **parsley** to bowl. Combine 4 oz. of crumbled **feta** cheese (about 1 cup), ¼ cup **buttermilk,** the zest of 1 **lemon,** and ¼ tsp. black **pepper** in a small bowl; stir until smooth. Just before serving, toss together zucchini noodle mixture and buttermilk dressing. Season with additional pepper and **salt,** if needed, and serve immediately.

Grilled Zucchini with Tomatoes and Mint

Mint is often relegated to dessert, but its bright, fresh flavor is also fantastic in savory dishes and salads. It grows prolifically in the South and is in season at the same time as tomatoes and zucchini, lending credence to the expression "What grows together goes together."

ACTIVE 30 MIN. - TOTAL 45 MIN. FOR GRILL PAN, 1 HOUR, 15 MIN. FOR OUTDOOR GRILL
SERVES 8

- 1½ lb. tomatoes (preferably heirloom), cored, seeded, and roughly chopped
- 1 Tbsp. sherry vinegar
- 1 tsp. minced fresh garlic
- 5 Tbsp. extra-virgin olive oil, divided
- 1 Tbsp. sherry (optional)
- 2 lb. zucchini (about 4 zucchini), cut lengthwise into ¼-inch-thick slices
- ½ tsp. kosher salt
- ½ tsp. black pepper
- 4 small fresh mint sprigs, plus extra leaves for garnish
  Crusty bread

1. Prepare a charcoal fire using about 6 pounds of charcoal briquettes; let burn until the coals are completely covered with a thin coating of light gray ash, 20

POTLUCK PICK
TAKE THIS TASTY "PASTA" SALAD TO A COOKOUT.

to 30 minutes. Spread the coals evenly over the grill bottom; place grate on grill, and heat until hot. (It is hot when you can hold your hand 5 inches above the grill surface for no longer than 3 or 4 seconds.) Or, preheat a gas grill to high (450°F to 550°F). Or, lightly grease a grill pan, and place over medium-high until hot, about 2 minutes.
2. Meanwhile, combine tomatoes; sherry vinegar; garlic; 4 tablespoons of the oil; and, if desired, sherry in a medium bowl. Let stand 15 minutes.
3. Brush both sides of zucchini slices with remaining 1 tablespoon oil; sprinkle evenly with salt and pepper. Arrange

zucchini slices on grill grate or in grill pan, and grill, uncovered, until charred and just tender, 3 to 5 minutes per side. Remove grilled zucchini to a platter, and cover with aluminum foil to keep warm. (The foil will also trap steam and result in delicious zucchini juices.)
4. Just before serving, chop or tear mint leaves from sprigs, and add to tomato mixture. (If you chop mint too far ahead, it will turn black.) Stir to combine; add salt and pepper, if needed, and immediately pour tomato salad and juices over warm zucchini. Garnish, if desired, and serve immediately with crusty bread to sop up the juices.

Zucchini Rice Gratin

Inspired by Julia Child's classic recipe for Tian de Courgettes au Riz (zucchini gratin), my version is comforting yet fresh and clean—it's not overloaded with heavy cream or cheese.

ACTIVE 15 MIN. - TOTAL 1 HOUR, 15 MIN.
SERVES 10

- ¼ cup panko (Japanese-style breadcrumbs)
- 2 oz. Parmigiano-Reggiano cheese, grated (about ¾ cup), divided
- 2 Tbsp. pure olive oil
- 1 large yellow onion, chopped (about 2 cups)
- 1 tsp. finely chopped garlic
- 2 Tbsp. all-purpose flour
- 2 lb. fresh zucchini, roughly chopped
- 2 cups 2% reduced-fat milk
- ½ cup uncooked long-grain rice
- 1 tsp. chopped fresh thyme
- ⅛ tsp. cayenne pepper (or to taste)
- 1 tsp. kosher salt
- ½ tsp. black pepper

1. Preheat oven to 425°F. Combine panko and ¼ cup of the Parmigiano-Reggiano in a small bowl, and set aside.
2. Heat oil in a large skillet over medium. Add onions, and cook, stirring often, until golden brown, 5 to 7 minutes. Add garlic, and cook, stirring constantly, until fragrant, 45 to 60 seconds. Add flour, and stir to combine. (Mixture will be dry.) Gently stir in zucchini. Add milk, rice, thyme, cayenne, and remaining ½ cup Parmigiano-Reggiano, and stir to combine. Spoon mixture into a lightly greased 13- x 9-inch baking dish. Sprinkle with salt and black pepper. (Or, you can start with a large ovenproof skillet and then bake the gratin in it instead of in a baking dish.)
3. Bake in preheated oven until set and liquid is absorbed, about 40 minutes. Remove gratin from oven. Increase oven temperature to broil with oven rack 6 inches from heat. Sprinkle top of gratin with panko-cheese mixture, and broil until golden brown, about 5 minutes. Serve immediately.

The Soup of Summer

Nothing beats this refreshing appetizer when temps rise

PESTO
Add a swirl of store-bought or homemade **pesto** to each serving.

BACON
Top every serving with 1 tsp. each **sour cream** and chopped cooked thick-cut **bacon** and ½ tsp. sliced **scallions.**

SPICY CORN RELISH
Combine ½ cup fresh **corn** kernels, 2 tsp. minced red **Fresno chile,** 1½ tsp. extra-virgin **olive oil,** ½ tsp. fresh **lemon juice,** and a pinch of **salt.** Divide mixture among servings.

Chilled Sweet Corn Soup

For the brightest color, use yellow corn, not white or bicolored. Scrape as much liquid from the cobs as possible—the "corn milk" adds extra flavor and creaminess.

ACTIVE 20 MIN. - TOTAL 4 HOURS, 20 MIN.
SERVES 6

- 3 ears fresh sweet yellow corn, shucked
- 2 Tbsp. unsalted butter
- ½ cup chopped yellow onion (from 1 medium onion)
- 1 tsp. chopped garlic (about 2 garlic cloves)
- ¾ tsp. kosher salt
- ½ tsp. black pepper
- 1 cup water
- 2 Tbsp. extra-virgin olive oil
- 1 tsp. white wine vinegar
  Toppings: bacon, pesto, or Spicy Corn Relish

1. Cut kernels from corncobs; place in a bowl. Using the large holes of a box grater, scrape liquid and pulp from cobs into another bowl. Discard cobs.
2. Melt butter in a medium saucepan over medium-high. Add onion, and cook, stirring often, until tender, about 4 minutes. Stir in corn kernels, garlic, salt, and pepper; cook, stirring occasionally, 3 minutes. Add water and reserved corn liquid and pulp. Bring to a boil over medium-high. Reduce heat to medium-low, and simmer 4 minutes. Transfer to a blender, and add olive oil. Remove center piece of blender lid (to let steam escape); secure lid on blender, and place a clean towel over opening in lid. Process until smooth, 2 minutes.
3. Pour mixture through a fine wire-mesh strainer into a bowl; press with the back of a spoon to extract as much liquid as possible. Discard solids. Stir in vinegar; cover and chill 4 to 8 hours. Pour into 6 (4-ounce) glasses; add toppings.

Caprese with a Twist

Chicken and pasta give a new spin to this classic

Chicken Caprese Pasta

This dish is a great way to use up a bumper crop of tomatoes and herbs. Tender fresh linguine works well with the pesto, but you can use dried pasta as well.

ACTIVE 15 MIN. - TOTAL 20 MIN.
SERVES 4

- 1 (9-oz.) pkg. fresh linguine
- 2 Tbsp. kosher salt
- 2 Tbsp. olive oil
- 2 pt. cherry tomatoes
- 1 shallot, thinly sliced (about 1 oz.)
- 2 garlic cloves, minced
- 4 cups shredded rotisserie chicken

- Fresh Herb Pesto (recipe follows)
- ¼ cup small fresh basil leaves
- 4 oz. fresh mozzarella cheese, torn into ½-inch pieces

1. Cook pasta according to package directions in a large Dutch oven, adding salt once water comes to a boil. Drain pasta, reserving 1 ½ cups cooking water.
2. Wipe Dutch oven clean, and add olive oil. Heat oil over medium-high. Add tomatoes to hot oil, and cook, stirring often, until slightly softened, about 2 minutes. Add shallot, and cook, stirring often, until softened, about 2 minutes. Stir in garlic; cook, stirring constantly, 1 minute.

3. Add chicken, pasta, Fresh Herb Pesto, and ½ cup of reserved cooking water to tomato mixture, stirring to combine. Gradually stir in remaining cooking water, ¼ cup at a time, until desired consistency is reached.
4. Transfer to a serving platter, and sprinkle with basil and mozzarella. Serve immediately.

Fresh Herb Pesto

ACTIVE 10 MIN. - TOTAL 10 MIN.
MAKES ¾ CUP

Process 4 ½ oz. finely shredded **Parmesan** cheese; 1 ½ cups loosely packed fresh **basil** leaves; 1 ½ cups loosely packed fresh flat-leaf **parsley;** ¾ cup fresh **chives,** cut into ½-inch pieces; ⅓ cup **olive oil;** 2 Tbsp. fresh **lemon juice;** and 1 ¼ tsp. **kosher salt** in a food processor until well combined, 1 to 2 minutes. Use immediately, or cover and chill up to 1 day.

Red, White & Berry Bars

Sweeten up your Fourth of July festivities with these make-ahead treats

Red, White, and Blue Cheesecake Bars

Want to be the star of the summer potluck? Make a batch of these crowd-pleasing cookie bars up to two days in advance.

ACTIVE 30 MIN. - TOTAL 6 HOURS, 10 MIN., INCLUDING 4 HOURS CHILLING

SERVES 24

- 2 (6.75-oz.) pkg. crisp, sweet cookies (such as Pepperidge Farm Bordeaux cookies)
- ¼ cup salted butter, melted
- 1 cup fresh or frozen raspberries (about 5 oz.)
- ¾ cup plus 2 Tbsp. granulated sugar, divided
- 2 Tbsp. water, divided
- 1 cup fresh or frozen blueberries (about 5 ½ oz.)
- 3 (8-oz.) pkg. cream cheese, softened
- ¼ tsp. table salt
- 2 large egg whites
- 1 large egg
- ¼ cup sour cream
- 2 Tbsp. all-purpose flour
- 2 tsp. fresh lemon juice (from 1 lemon)
- 2 tsp. vanilla extract

1. Preheat oven to 350°F. Process cookies in a food processor until finely ground, about 1 minute. Drizzle melted butter over cookie crumbs; pulse until well combined, 3 to 4 times. Press crumb mixture onto bottom of a lightly greased 13- x 9-inch baking dish. Bake in preheated oven until lightly browned, about 10 minutes. Cool completely, about 30 minutes. Reduce oven temperature to 325°F.

2. Meanwhile, combine raspberries and 1 tablespoon each of the sugar and water in a small saucepan over medium. Bring to a boil, and cook, stirring frequently to mash raspberries, until thickened, 6 to 8 minutes. Place raspberry mixture in a fine wire-mesh strainer over a bowl; press mixture until there are about 3 tablespoons raspberry puree in bowl. Discard solids in strainer. Cool puree completely. Repeat procedure with blueberries, 1 tablespoon sugar, and remaining 1 tablespoon water.

3. Beat softened cream cheese, salt, and remaining ¾ cup sugar with an electric mixer on medium-low speed until smooth, 1 to 2 minutes. Add egg whites and egg, 1 at a time, beating well after each addition. Add sour cream, all-purpose flour, fresh lemon juice, and vanilla extract, and beat at low speed until smooth, 1 to 2 minutes. Pour batter into prepared baking dish; smooth top.

4. Drop level teaspoonfuls of raspberry and blueberry purees all over top of batter; gently swirl with a knife.

5. Bake at 325°F until cheesecake is almost set (center will still jiggle slightly when dish is touched), 25 to 28 minutes. Run a knife or offset spatula around edge of dish to loosen sides of cheesecake. Cool on wire rack at room temperature 1 hour. Cover and chill 4 hours or overnight. Cut into bars.

COOKING (SL) SCHOOL

PRODUCE PRIMER

The Best Way To Freeze Peaches

Three simple steps for enjoying this summer star all year long

[A] Toss 1 lb. of peeled, sliced **peaches** with 1 Tbsp. fresh **lemon juice.**

[B] Place the peaches in a single layer on a parchment paper-lined baking sheet. Freeze until solid, about 4 hours or overnight.

[C] Transfer the frozen peach slices to a freezer bag, and remove as much air from the bag as possible before sealing.

IN SEASON

8 Ways with Summer Sauce

All you need are 10 minutes and five fresh ingredients to whip up our versatile mixture (recipe, page 158).

1. Add to plain yogurt to make a chicken or seafood sauce.
2. Replace tomato sauce on a pizza.
3. Stir into scrambled eggs.
4. Toss with roasted vegetables.
5. Drizzle over hummus or white bean dip.
6. Dress potato salad.
7. Serve with grilled steak.
8. Use as a sauce to dip pieces of warm, crusty bread.

KNOW-HOW

Tomato Myths, Debunked

Three surprising truths about these seasonal beauties

MYTH Never refrigerate tomatoes.

MYTH Store tomatoes stem-side up.

MYTH To ripen tomatoes, leave them uncovered.

Store at room temperature unless they are very, very ripe. To halt the ripening process, you can refrigerate them one to two days at most.

Though it might look a little weird, storing your fresh tomatoes stem-side down can help prevent bruises.

Place underripe tomatoes in one layer in a paper bag, and close it loosely. Leave in a warm, dry spot, and check daily for ripeness.

"Use dried pasta for rich, hearty toppings. Fresh pasta is great for recipes with delicate components like herbs and light sauces."

—**Robby Melvin**
Test Kitchen Director

August

Under The Texan Sun

**STROLL THROUGH OLIVE ORCHARDS,
TASTE THE OIL, AND ENJOY
A MEDITERRANEAN ADVENTURE
IN THE HILL COUNTRY**

Maybe you wouldn't expect to find

an Italophile in San Antonio, but here I am—an Alabama transplant who loves my adopted Texas home but still dreams of making a return trip to Tuscany. As it turns out, there's a Lone Star version of the Mediterranean nestled in the arid Hill Country, where local olive growers are thriving.

Wind your way over the rise and fall of rural roads toward Bella Vista Ranch in Wimberley, Texas, and you'll be lulled into a relaxed Tuscan state of mind. In Italy, no one's in a hurry—certainly not the olive growers and vineyard owners who cultivate their crops with patience. Those guys don't usually wear cowboy hats, but Jack Dougherty, Bella Vista's proud owner, does. He was the first commercial grower of Texas olives and is the maker of award-winning olive oil produced by his business, First Texas Olive Oil Company.

"I tell people that a visit here is like going on a day trip to Italy but without the expensive airfare," says Dougherty. He's right. Italian cypress trees stand near sprawling live oaks and frame the property's olive-oil tasting room. A newer project on the ranch is the vineyard, a small battalion of neatly cultivated grapevines. And then there's the olive orchard: 1,200 trees strong with row upon row of silvery green branches studded with olives. "I know every tree," Dougherty says.

On weekends, visitors enjoy walks through the shady orchard. Inside the tasting room, much like that of a vineyard, they sip and savor—only it's olive oil instead of wine. If sipping oil seems foreign to you, don't worry. Right there on-site, Dougherty will help you appreciate the nuances of the oils that his company presses: three kinds of extra-virgin olive oil along with citrus-infused varieties pressed with blood oranges, Meyer lemons, and limes. Dougherty also offers sips of balsamic vinegars sourced directly from Italy. Thick and sweet, the Blackberry Pear Balsamic Vinegar makes a delicious marinade for strawberries, he says. Just add a dollop of mascarpone cheese and a sprinkle of bittersweet chocolate for an instant dessert.

Fascinated by California's agritourism, Dougherty planted his olive trees back in 1998, hoping quality oils would attract food-minded travelers. He aimed to emulate an Italian-style family farm—growing olive trees, blackberries, and grapes in close proximity. When a county Extension agent told him that olives wouldn't grow in Texas, Dougherty set out to prove otherwise, though the quest did have its challenges. "It seems very romantic, but there is no romance involved," he says. "It's hard to grow olives. It's hard to make olive oil."

Dougherty uses ancient Roman techniques to grow his olive trees, which have matured quickly. Planted less than 20 years ago, they're now equivalent in size to 50-year-old trees. He won a Gold Award for his 2013 Estate Grown Coratina Olive Oil at an international competition in New York. And the Coratina oil made from his 2015 harvest sold out by April 2016. "I've had Italian visitors come here and buy a case of olive oil," he says, highlighting the authenticity. His daughter, Colleen Peters, with whom he shared his techniques, helps manage the business.

In nearby Dripping Springs, Texas, another father-daughter pair, John and Cara Gambini, operate Texas Hill Country Olive Company, established in 2008. Here, an Italianate facility with a red-tile roof enhances the Tuscan-like views, while a cozy bistro offers lunch. Cara enjoys educating tourists in the orchard, the elegant tasting room, and the mill. "Most people have never really tasted [authentic] extra-virgin olive oil," she says. "Once you know what the good stuff tastes like, you're not going to want the bad."

She tells me that tourists are often surprised to learn that green and black olives are the same fruit; the two are just picked at different times or altered by different brining recipes. Limestone in the Hill Country soil gives it a similar alkalinity to Tuscan soil, she explains, while sloping hillsides in both locales provide the drainage olive trees need—both reasons why Texas is now the second-largest producer of olive oil in the U.S., behind California, with the Texas Olive Oil Council monitoring industry growth.

You won't be thinking about industry stats when you visit though. You'll be too busy savoring the rich oils, tasting local wines, and wandering olive groves drenched in Texas sunlight that's as golden as an old Roman coin.

— Jennifer Chappell Smith

Bella Vista owner, Jack Dougherty

THE RECIPES

Cook Your Own Tuscan Feast

Pasta with Beans, Blistered Tomatoes, and Breadcrumbs

Lemon-Olive Oil Cake with Whipped Mascarpone

Pasta with Beans, Blistered Tomatoes, and Breadcrumbs

ACTIVE 30 MIN. - TOTAL 45 MIN.
SERVES 8

- 1 cup roughly torn fresh bread-crumbs
- ½ cup lightly packed fresh sage leaves, divided
- ½ cup olive oil, divided, plus more for serving
- ½ tsp. kosher salt, divided
- 2 pt. cherry or grape tomatoes
- 1 lb. uncooked orecchiette or other short pasta
- 2 ½ cups finely chopped yellow onion (from 1 large onion)
- 4 garlic cloves, finely chopped
- 2 (15-oz.) cans butter, cannellini, or gigante beans, drained and rinsed
- 1 cup chicken or vegetable broth
- ¼ tsp. black pepper

1. Preheat oven to 400°F. Toss together fresh breadcrumbs, ¼ cup of the fresh sage leaves, 2 tablespoons of the oil, and ¼ teaspoon of the salt on a rimmed baking sheet. Bake in preheated oven until breadcrumbs are golden and sage leaves are crisp, about 5 minutes. Set aside.

2. Increase oven temperature to broil with oven rack 6 inches from heat. Toss together tomatoes and 1 tablespoon of the oil on a rimmed baking sheet. Broil until tomatoes are blistered and beginning to collapse, 5 to 7 minutes, shaking sheet halfway through broiling.

3. Meanwhile, bring a large pot of salted water to a boil. Cook pasta until al dente, about 8 minutes. Drain, reserving 1 cup cooking water.

4. Heat 1 tablespoon of the oil in a very large skillet over medium. Add onion and garlic; cook, stirring occasionally, until soft and golden, about 10 minutes. Add beans, broth, and remaining ¼ cup each sage leaves and oil; bring to a simmer. Cook, stirring occasionally, 10 minutes. Gently stir in blistered tomatoes. Simmer, stirring occasionally, 10 minutes.

5. Add cooked pasta and reserved cooking water to bean mixture; toss gently to combine. Stir in pepper and remaining ¼ teaspoon salt. Cook, stirring often, until liquid thickens slightly, about 4 minutes. Top with crispy breadcrumb mixture. Drizzle with oil, and serve immediately.

Lemon-Olive Oil Cake with Whipped Mascarpone

ACTIVE 20 MIN. - TOTAL 2 HOURS
SERVES 8

CAKE
- ½ cup extra-virgin olive oil, plus more for greasing pan
- 1 cup all-purpose flour, plus more for dusting pan
- ½ cup fine cornmeal
- 1 tsp. baking powder
- ½ tsp. baking soda
- ½ tsp. kosher salt
- 1 cup granulated sugar
- 4 oz. (½ cup) mascarpone cheese
- 3 large eggs
- 1 Tbsp. lemon zest, plus 1 ½ Tbsp. fresh juice (from 2 lemons)

WHIPPED MASCARPONE
- 4 oz. (½ cup) mascarpone cheese
- 1 Tbsp. granulated sugar
- 1 tsp. fresh lemon juice

1. Prepare the Cake: Preheat oven to 350°F. Lightly oil a 9-inch round baking pan. Line with parchment paper, and lightly oil parchment. Dust parchment lightly with flour, tapping out excess.

2. Whisk together flour, cornmeal, baking powder, baking soda, and salt in a large bowl. Whisk together oil, sugar, mascarpone cheese, eggs, lemon zest, and lemon juice in a second large bowl until completely smooth and incorporated. Pour oil mixture into dry ingredients, and stir until evenly moistened and no lumps remain.

3. Pour batter into prepared baking pan; smooth top. Bake in preheated oven until Cake is golden, has risen, and just starts to pull away from the edge of the pan, about 30 minutes. Cool in pan 30 minutes. Transfer to a wire rack; cool completely, about 1 hour. (Cake can be made, unfrosted, up to 3 days in advance. Store at room temperature tightly wrapped with plastic wrap.)

4. Prepare the Whipped Mascarpone: Whisk together all Whipped Mascarpone ingredients in a medium bowl until slightly thickened. Spread mixture on cake.

Rosemary Focaccia with Stewed Grapes and Olives

ACTIVE 25 MIN. - TOTAL 1 HOUR, 55 MIN.
SERVES 10

- 1 (¼-oz.) envelope active dry yeast
- 1 cup warm water
- 1 Tbsp. honey
- 1 cup whole milk, slightly warmed
- 4 tsp. kosher salt
- ½ cup plus 2 Tbsp. olive oil, divided
- 5 cups all-purpose flour
- 2 Tbsp. fresh rosemary leaves
- 1 tsp. flaky or coarse sea salt
  Stewed Grapes and Olives (recipe follows)

1. Place yeast in a large bowl. Add water and honey; let stand until foamy, 5 to 10 minutes. Add milk, kosher salt, and ¼ cup of the oil to yeast mixture; stir to combine. Add flour; stir with a wooden spoon until no dry spots remain and a shaggy dough forms. (You may need to knead gently with your hands to help the dough stick together.) Cover bowl with a clean dish towel or plastic wrap; set aside in a warm place free from drafts until doubled in size, about 1 hour.

Rosemary Focaccia with Stewed Grapes and Olives

Bitter Greens Salad with Lemon and Pecorino

2. Preheat oven to 425°F with oven rack in middle of oven. Place ¼ cup of the oil in a rimmed baking sheet. Turn dough out onto prepared pan; turn to coat dough in oil. Using your fingertips, gently spread dough toward edges of pan. (Dough will not reach all the way to edges.) Let stand 15 minutes.

3. Using your fingertips, press dough gently toward edges of pan. (Dough should almost fit.) Sprinkle dough evenly with rosemary leaves and flaky sea salt. Bake in preheated oven until golden brown, 18 to 20 minutes. Transfer focaccia to a wire rack; brush with remaining 2 tablespoons oil. Cut into squares, or tear into pieces. Serve with Stewed Grapes and Olives.

Stewed Grapes and Olives

ACTIVE 25 MIN. - TOTAL 1 HOUR, 25 MIN.
SERVES 10

- 4 cups seedless black grapes
- ¼ cup water
- 2 Tbsp. granulated sugar
- 1 tsp. kosher salt
- ½ tsp. black pepper
- 1 cup pitted Kalamata olives

Combine grapes, water, sugar, salt, and pepper in a medium saucepan. Bring to a boil over medium-high. Reduce heat to medium-low; simmer, stirring occasionally, until grapes have burst and mixture reduces slightly, 15 to 20

minutes. Stir in olives. Cool to room temperature, about 1 hour. Store tightly covered in refrigerator up to 4 days.

Bitter Greens Salad with Lemon and Pecorino

ACTIVE 5 MIN. - TOTAL 5 MIN.
SERVES 8

- 2 tsp. lemon zest, plus 3 Tbsp. fresh juice (from 2 lemons)
- 2 tsp. honey
- ½ tsp. kosher salt
- ½ tsp. black pepper
- ⅓ cup olive oil
- 1 shallot, finely chopped
- 1 head radicchio, quartered and cored, leaves separated
- 1 head escarole, leaves torn into large, bite-size pieces
- 1 romaine heart, roughly chopped
- 2 oz. Pecorino Romano cheese, shaved or grated

Whisk together lemon zest, lemon juice, honey, salt, and pepper in a large bowl until honey dissolves. Whisk in oil and shallot. Add radicchio, escarole, and romaine; toss to coat. Top with Pecorino Romano.

BLACKBERRY SEASON

If you need inspiration to cook with berries this summer, look to Tennessee's elegant Blackberry Farm and the visionaries behind it

Clockwise from bottom left: Sam and Mary Celeste Beall in the garden; Lila, the couple's youngest child, with a bowlful of blackberries; Shaved Cucumber Salad with Pickled Blackberries

As you drive along West Millers Cove Road in Walland, Tennessee, you'll wind up the mountain past scattered houses and barns, the Memories of Ole Tearoom, an honor system farm stand, and Millers Cove Primitive Baptist Church. You're in the foothills of the Great Smoky Mountains, passing cows, horses, and fields that have been farmed for generations, with the occasional rusty tractor to show for it. Keep going for a while, and you'll come to a well-maintained white fence, shaded by tall pines, that runs along both sides of the road. There's a groomed meadow on your left and a stately red barn on your right, and then after a few more turns, you'll see a pair of stone pillars and a simple wooden sign marking the entrance to Blackberry Farm.

If it's summertime, you won't have to look hard to find the wild blackberries that gave the resort its name. As the story goes, the first owner of the farm, Florida Lasier, a Chicago doyenne who bought the place with her husband in the 1930s, snagged her silk stockings on a blackberry bramble soon after arriving. Today, the prickly bushes are more contained, but you'll still find them sprinkled around the property, growing on fencerows or in the sun on the edges of the woods. Their season is short, intense, and greeted with excitement by everyone in the region, from local chefs to gardeners to kids who pick them before breakfast.

Though it's hidden in these hills about 45 minutes south of Knoxville, Blackberry Farm is now recognized as one of the preeminent resorts in the world, especially when it comes to food. Bought in 1976 as a family home by Kreis and Sandy Beall (who founded the Ruby Tuesday restaurant chain), the farm evolved into a seasonal bed-and-breakfast with a handful of cottages and an ambitious menu. While Sandy managed the business, Kreis was the early visionary, not to mention the cook, decorator, and hostess. They hired chefs like Robert Carter and John Fleer, who put Blackberry Farm on the culinary map with a new kind of cooking called Foothills Cuisine. It was all about local ingredients and old Southern methods. Every dish was somehow connected to the farm, using seasonal fruits and vegetables such as sugar snap peas, hen of the woods mushrooms, heirloom string beans, and, yes, blackberries.

But it was the Bealls' food-obsessed son Sam who took the reins from his parents in 2003 and ultimately harnessed the farm's potential. He had grown up hanging out in the kitchen—sometimes taking plates out to guests in his pajamas. After attending Hampden-Sydney College and spending a couple of years in California, where he went to culinary school and spent most of his free time exploring farmers' markets, Sam couldn't wait to get back to his Tennessee backyard.

From left: Blackberry-Oat Crumble Bars; The Barn, which houses one of two restaurants on the property; Blackberry Gelato

He returned to Blackberry Farm with his wife, Mary Celeste, to build a home, raise a family, and dream up plans for a business that he always knew he would run. Sam worked in every department, from maintenance to housekeeping to the kitchen. He also spent time in the garden, learning all about seeds and heirloom selections from Master Gardener John Coykendall. Even as his responsibilities grew, he found time to pick fruits and vegetables, many of which he'd experiment with in his own kitchen. When the blackberries were at their peak, he would use them for everything—smoothies, waffles, cobblers, cocktails—often picking them early in the morning or just as the sun went down.

Sam also inherited his mother's gift for entertaining, creating over-the-top menus and experiences for his guests. Whenever he greeted a big crowd of people, which I saw him do several times, he would say, "Welcome to my family's home"–and his plans for that home were always growing. In 13 years as the proprietor, he added dozens of rooms and cottages, built a spa, launched an award-winning brewery, started a kids' camp, and opened a concert venue. Sam wanted everyone to drink his best wine (they have 160,000 bottles in the cellar), eat the best meal they'd ever had, sleep in the world's most comfortable four-poster bed, and, of course, come back for more.

Tragically, Sam's life was cut short in February 2016, when he was killed in a Colorado skiing accident at the age of 39. Mary Celeste was left with five children and a family of over 400 employees to manage. They had built their dream home together, a two-story stone house with clapboard siding, on a hill that looked out over the mountains. Now, Mary Celeste is carrying on Sam's legacy, trying to juggle the day-to-day challenges of being a mom and the proprietor of a 4,200-acre resort that hosts a couple hundred guests around the clock, not to mention weddings, outdoor concerts, and culinary programs.

"This has been a really hard year," she told me recently over a lunch at the farm, "losing him, being a single parent, and balancing doing something you love. But the time being involved at Blackberry in this way has also been so healing because it's kept me focused and forward-thinking and feeling really close to Sam."

Like their father, most of the kids (Cameron, 19; Sam, 14; Rose, 12; Josephine, 8; and Lila, 4) have become avid cooks. They have grown up harvesting morels with their dad, picking squash in the garden, and gathering buckets of blackberries from around the property–which they sometimes sold to the kitchen. The Bealls' son, Sam, can grill vegetables and make omelets and even roasted a lamb for Easter. Rose is more interested in sweets and recently made a lemon curd cake with strawberries on top. It helps to have so many cooks in the family with six mouths to feed and almost always a few guests.

"They all know how to do the basics–peel an onion, chop garlic–and they all contribute toward the big effort," explains Mary Celeste. "There's a lot of teamwork."

The resort is running much the same way with a crew of loyal employees making things happen, many of whom have worked here for 10 or 15 years. They all seem to share Sam's excitement for the arrival of a new season, especially when new fruits and vegetables come into the kitchen. They love the unique things that come only from these hills and speak reverently about the man who helped make the farm such a vibrant place.

"We all laugh about him, we cry about him, and we are keeping his spirit alive–and that's just the closest thing I'll get," says Mary Celeste. "Sam's goal–and my goal–has always been, 'How can we carry Blackberry on for generations?' And it's really just our job not to mess it up."

–Sid Evans

Shaved Cucumber Salad with Pickled Blackberries

"This salad was inspired by a basket of onions, blackberries, cucumbers, and mint that showed up in the kitchen one day," says Sarah Steffan, executive chef of The Dogwood restaurant at Blackberry Farm.

ACTIVE 25 MIN. - TOTAL 2 DAYS, 55 MIN., INCLUDING 2 DAYS CHILLING

SERVES 6

PICKLED BLACKBERRIES AND BLACKBERRY VINEGAR

- 1 cup granulated sugar
- 1 cup Champagne vinegar
- 1 cup water
- 3 tarragon sprigs
- 1 Tbsp. black peppercorns
- 2 cups fresh blackberries

SHAVED CUCUMBER SALAD

- 2 large English cucumbers
- 1 small Vidalia or other sweet onion
- 2 Tbsp. torn fresh mint leaves
  Pickled Blackberries
- ¼ cup high-quality extra-virgin olive oil
- 2 Tbsp. Blackberry Vinegar
- ½ tsp. kosher salt
- ⅛ tsp. black pepper

1. Prepare the Pickled Blackberries and Blackberry Vinegar: Combine sugar, Champagne vinegar, water, tarragon sprigs, and peppercorns in a medium saucepan; bring to a boil over medium-high, stirring occasionally to dissolve sugar. Remove from heat, and let stand 15 minutes. Place blackberries in a large bowl. Pour vinegar mixture through a fine wire-mesh strainer over blackberries; discard tarragon and peppercorns. Cover blackberry mixture, and cool completely, about 30 minutes. Refrigerate blackberry mixture at least 2 days and up to 1 week. Transfer Pickled Blackberries to a separate container. Reserve Blackberry Vinegar.

2. Prepare the Shaved Cucumber Salad: Thinly slice cucumbers and onion using a mandoline. Place cucumber and onion slices, mint, and Pickled Blackberries in a medium bowl. Whisk together oil, Blackberry Vinegar, salt, and pepper; pour over cucumber mixture, and toss gently. Reserve remaining Blackberry Vinegar for another use. Refrigerate in an airtight container up to 1 month.

GRILLED PORK LOIN WITH BLACKBERRY GLAZE

Grilled Pork Loin with Blackberry Glaze

"Bone-in pork rack is one of my favorite things ever," says Cassidee Dabney, executive chef at The Barn at Blackberry Farm. "When you make the glaze, cook it down and strain out all the seeds so you have this sticky, unctuous mixture. When the pork fat hits it, it's magic."

ACTIVE 1 HOUR, 30 MIN - TOTAL 2 HOURS

SERVES 8

- 2 Tbsp. chopped fresh rosemary
- 1 Tbsp. grapeseed oil
- 4 garlic cloves, minced
- 1 (4 ½-lb.) bone-in pork loin rack, frenched
- 1½ tsp. kosher salt
- ¾ tsp. black pepper
  Hickory wood chunks or 1 split hickory log
- ⅓ cup Blackberry Glaze (recipe follows)

1. Stir together rosemary, oil, and garlic; rub mixture all over pork, and sprinkle with salt and pepper. Let stand at room temperature about 30 minutes.

2. Preheat a charcoal grill to medium-high (about 450°F). When briquettes are covered in gray ash, push them to one side, and scatter hickory wood chunks over coals. Place pork, fat side down, on oiled grate directly over coals, and grill, covered, until browned, about 10 minutes. Turn pork, and move to side without coals. Grill pork, covered, 30 minutes, turning twice. Brush with Blackberry Glaze, and grill, covered, until a thermometer inserted in thickest portion of pork (away from bone) registers 145°F, about 25 minutes, turning and brushing with glaze twice. Remove pork from grill, and let rest about 10 minutes. Slice into chops, and serve immediately.

Blackberry Glaze

ACTIVE 10 MIN. - TOTAL 35 MIN.

MAKES 2 ½ CUPS

Stir together 4 cups blackberries, 2 cups white balsamic vinegar, 2 cups water, 1 cup granulated sugar, and 6 thyme sprigs in a medium saucepan. Bring to a boil over medium-high; reduce heat to medium-low, and simmer until blackberries have broken down, about 15 minutes. Remove from heat; cool 10 minutes. Remove and discard thyme sprigs. Transfer mixture to a blender. Remove center piece of blender lid (to allow steam to escape); secure blender lid on blender. Place a clean towel over opening in lid (to avoid splatters). Process until smooth. Pour pureed mixture through a fine wire-mesh strainer; discard solids. Stir in 1 ½ tsp. kosher salt and ¾ tsp. black pepper.

Blackberry, Browned Butter, and Almond Tart

"It's like a cookie on the outside and a cake on the inside with pockets of juicy blackberries," says Steffan.

ACTIVE 25 MIN. - TOTAL 1 HOUR, 50 MIN.
SERVES 12

- 1 ½ cups (12 oz.) unsalted butter, plus more for pan
- 8 large egg whites
- 3 ¼ cups unsifted powdered sugar, plus more for dusting
- 1 ½ cups almond flour
- 1 cup plus 1 Tbsp. all-purpose flour, divided, plus more for pan
- 1 Tbsp. vanilla bean paste
- 1 ½ cups fresh blackberries

1. Preheat oven to 325°F. Grease and flour a 12-inch round tart pan with removable bottom; place tart pan on a rimmed baking sheet lined with parchment paper. Melt butter in a saucepan over medium-high, and cook, stirring often, until butter releases a nutty aroma and milk solids are golden brown, about 8 minutes. Immediately transfer butter to a bowl; cool slightly, about 10 minutes.

2. Beat egg whites with a heavy-duty electric stand mixer on medium speed until frothy, about 30 seconds. Gradually add powdered sugar; beat until light and fluffy. Gradually add almond flour and 1 cup of the all-purpose flour; beat on medium-low speed until incorporated. Add vanilla bean paste and browned butter; beat on medium-low speed until incorporated. Spread batter in prepared pan. Toss blackberries with remaining 1 tablespoon all-purpose flour, and sprinkle over batter.

3. Bake in preheated oven until golden brown and a wooden pick inserted in center comes out clean, 42 to 45 minutes. Cool in pan on a wire rack 15 minutes. Remove sides of pan, and cool 30 more minutes. Dust with powdered sugar before serving.

BLACKBERRY, BROWNED BUTTER, AND ALMOND TART

Blackberry-Oat Crumble Bars

"These oat bars are a Blackberry Farm classic," says Steffan. *"The recipe changes a lot with the seasons—we do it with peaches, strawberries, apples, you name it. The secret? Lots of butter."*

ACTIVE 20 MIN. - TOTAL 2 HOURS, 50 MIN.
SERVES 24

CRUST
- 6 cups regular rolled oats
- 2 ¼ cups packed light brown sugar
- 2 ¼ cups all-purpose flour
- 2 cups unsalted butter, melted, plus more for pan
- 1 tsp. kosher salt
- 1 tsp. baking soda

FILLING
- 9 cups fresh blackberries
- 1 cup granulated sugar
- ½ cup fresh lemon juice (from 3 lemons)
- ¼ cup cornstarch

1. Prepare the Crust: Preheat oven to 350°F. Stir together oats, brown sugar, flour, butter, salt, and baking soda. Remove 3 cups of the oat mixture, and set aside. Press remaining oat mixture in an even layer in an aluminum foil-lined and buttered 12- x 17-inch rimmed baking sheet. Bake in preheated oven until golden brown, about 20 minutes. Cool completely, about 30 minutes.

2. Prepare the Filling: Stir together blackberries, sugar, lemon juice, and cornstarch in a large saucepan. Cook over medium, stirring occasionally, until syrup thickens and is bubbly, about 8 minutes. Pour over prepared Crust, and crumble reserved 3 cups oat mixture evenly over Filling. Bake at 350°F until topping is golden brown, 30 to 35 minutes. Cool completely, about 2 hours. Cut into 24 pieces.

SUMMER COBBLER
COCKTAIL

BLACKBERRY-LEMON
GRIDDLE CAKES

Blackberry-Lemon Griddle Cakes

ACTIVE 25 MIN. - TOTAL 25 MIN.

SERVES 4

- 1 cup all-purpose flour
- ¼ cup granulated sugar
- 1½ tsp. baking powder
- ½ tsp. baking soda
- ½ tsp. table salt
- 1 cup whole buttermilk
- 2 large egg yolks
- 1 Tbsp. lemon zest (from 2 lemons)
- 1½ tsp. vanilla extract
- 3 large egg whites
- 3 Tbsp. salted butter, melted
- 1½ cups fresh blackberries

1. Sift together first 5 ingredients in a large bowl. Whisk together buttermilk, egg yolks, lemon zest, and vanilla in a separate bowl; add to flour mixture, and stir just until moistened. Beat egg whites with an electric mixer on high speed until soft peaks form; fold gently into batter.

2. Heat an electric griddle to 350°F; brush with melted butter. Drop batter by ¼-cupfuls onto hot griddle; top each with 3 to 4 blackberries. Cook until edges are set and bubbles begin to appear, 2 to 3 minutes. Turn with a wide spatula, and cook until golden brown, 1 minute.

Blackberry Gelato

This recipe makes 12 cups of lusciously smooth gelato—perfect for summer parties. The berry puree can be made several days in advance and refrigerated. One key step: Be sure to strain the seeds.

ACTIVE 25 MIN. - TOTAL 2 DAYS, 3 HOURS, 5 MIN., INCLUDING 2 DAYS CHILLING

SERVES 24

- 4 cups whole milk
- 2 cups heavy cream
- 1⅔ cups granulated sugar
- ⅓ cup instant nonfat dry milk
- 2 Tbsp. vanilla bean paste
  Blackberry Puree (recipe follows)
  Fresh blackberries

1. Place whole milk, heavy cream, sugar, milk powder, vanilla bean paste, and Blackberry Puree in a large saucepan; bring to a low simmer over medium. Remove from heat; cool completely, about 1 hour. Place in an airtight container, and chill 2 days.

2. Pour mixture into freezer can of a 4-quart ice-cream freezer; proceed according to manufacturer's instructions. (Instructions and times will vary.) Transfer gelato to an airtight freezer-safe container; freeze until firm, about 2 hours. Garnish servings with fresh blackberries.

Blackberry Puree

ACTIVE 10 MIN. - TOTAL 10 MIN.

MAKES ABOUT 1 ½ CUPS

Process 4 cups fresh blackberries, ¼ cup granulated sugar, and 1 Tbsp. fresh lemon juice in a blender until smooth. Pour mixture through a fine wire-mesh strainer to remove seeds, pressing gently with a rubber spatula; discard solids.

Summer Cobbler Cocktail

ACTIVE 5 MIN. - TOTAL 5 MIN.

SERVES 1

Combine 3 Tbsp. (1 ½ oz.) white whiskey, 1 ½ Tbsp. (¾ oz.) Grand Marnier or other orange-flavored liqueur, 1 Tbsp. fresh lime juice, 1 ½ tsp. Blackberry Farm Blackberry Preserves, and 3 fresh blackberries in an ice-filled cocktail shaker. Cover with lid, and shake until mixed and thoroughly chilled, about 45 seconds. Strain whiskey mixture into an old-fashioned glass filled with crushed ice. Garnish with fresh blackberries and lime peel twists.

CHICKEN, WHITE
BEAN, AND
SPINACH SALAD,
PAGE 233

5 Slow-Cooker Suppers

Keep your cool this summer with these easy, oven-free meals

Braised Chicken Thighs with Slow-Cooked Marinara

This dish is a great way to use less-than-perfect summer tomatoes. A Parmesan cheese rind makes the chunky sauce extra savory and delicious.

ACTIVE 30 MIN. - TOTAL 2 HOURS, 30 MIN.
SERVES 6

- 1½ lb. ripe tomatoes, cored and chopped (about 5 cups)
- 2 garlic cloves, crushed
- ½ cup chopped yellow onion (from 1 small onion)
- 3 Tbsp. tomato paste
- 1 (3-inch) piece Parmesan cheese rind
- 1 bunch fresh basil stems, plus ¼ cup basil leaves
- 6 boneless, skinless chicken thighs (about 2 lb.)
- ½ tsp. black pepper
- 2 tsp. kosher salt, divided
- 1 Tbsp. olive oil
- 1 lb. uncooked fettuccine, cooked according to package directions
- ¼ cup grated Parmesan cheese

1. Combine tomatoes, garlic, onion, tomato paste, Parmesan rind, and basil stems in a 5- to 6-quart slow cooker. **2.** Sprinkle chicken thighs evenly with pepper and 1 teaspoon of the salt. Heat oil in a large skillet over medium-high.

Add chicken to skillet, and cook until golden brown, about 2 minutes per side. Transfer to slow cooker, and nestle into tomato mixture. Cover and cook on LOW until tomatoes have broken down and chicken is very tender and done, 2 to 3 hours.
3. Transfer chicken to a cutting board to cool slightly. Remove and discard basil stems and Parmesan rind from slow cooker. Stir in remaining 1 teaspoon salt. Process mixture using an immersion blender until mostly smooth, about 30 seconds. Shred chicken into 1-inch pieces, and stir into slow cooker.
4. Toss pasta with tomato-chicken mixture, and divide evenly among 6 bowls. Top with basil leaves and grated Parmesan.

Chicken, White Bean, and Spinach Salad

ACTIVE 30 MIN. - TOTAL 8 HOURS, 30 MIN.
SERVES 6

- 1 lb. dried white beans
- 4 cups unsalted chicken stock
- 1 Tbsp. chopped garlic
- ½ tsp. smoked paprika
- 1½ tsp. kosher salt, divided
- 1¼ tsp. black pepper, divided
- 4 skinless, bone-in chicken breasts
- ½ cup plus 1 Tbsp. olive oil, divided
- 3 oranges
- 4 Tbsp. Champagne vinegar
- 2 Tbsp. finely chopped shallots
- 4 oz. fresh baby spinach
- ¼ cup slivered almonds, toasted
- 4 oz. goat cheese, crumbled (about 1 cup)

1. Combine first 4 ingredients and ½ teaspoon each of the salt and pepper in a 5- to 6-quart slow cooker. Cover and cook on LOW 6 hours.
2. Sprinkle chicken with ½ teaspoon each of the salt and pepper. Heat 1 tablespoon of the oil in a large skillet over medium-high; add chicken, and cook until golden, 2 minutes per side. Nestle chicken into beans in slow cooker at the end of the 6-hour bean cook time. Cover; cook until chicken and beans are tender and done, about 2 hours. Transfer chicken to a cutting board; remove meat from bones and shred. Remove 3 cups of beans; drain. (Save remaining beans for another use.) Let chicken and beans cool.
3. Squeeze juice from 1 orange to equal ¼ cup. Peel remaining 2 oranges; cut into segments. Whisk together orange juice, vinegar, shallots, and remaining ½ teaspoon salt and ¼ teaspoon pepper in a large bowl. Add remaining ½ cup oil in a steady stream, whisking until incorporated. Add spinach, shredded chicken, beans, orange segments, almonds, and cheese, and toss with the dressing.

Slow-Cooker Pork Tacos with Fresh Tomato Salsa

This spiced pork is also a great topping on nachos or baked potatoes. Brown the sliced pork shoulder in a cast-iron skillet before adding it to the slow cooker to boost its flavor.

ACTIVE 25 MIN. - TOTAL 8 HOURS, 25 MIN.
SERVES 6

- 1 (4- to 5-lb.) boneless pork shoulder roast
- 1 Tbsp. ancho chile powder
- 1 Tbsp. black pepper
- 1 tsp. ground cumin
- ½ tsp. ground cloves
- ½ tsp. granulated sugar
- 1 Tbsp. plus ½ tsp. kosher salt, divided
- 2 Tbsp. canola oil
- ¼ cup apple cider vinegar
- 4 oregano sprigs
- 1 cup chopped tomato (about 1 large)
- ¼ cup chopped red onion (from 1 small onion)
- 1 Tbsp. fresh lime juice (from 1 lime)
- 1 jalapeño chile, seeded and finely chopped (about 2 Tbsp.)
- 12 (6-inch) flour tortillas
- 1 Tbsp. smoked paprika
- ½ tsp. cayenne pepper
- ¼ cup chopped fresh cilantro

1. Cut pork shoulder into 2 (4- to 5-inch-thick) pieces. Combine chile powder, black pepper, cumin, cloves, sugar, and 1 tablespoon of the salt in a small bowl. Sprinkle mixture over all sides of pork pieces. Heat oil in a large cast-iron skillet over high. Add pork pieces, and cook until deep golden brown on all sides, about 2 minutes per side. Place pork in a 5- to 6-quart slow cooker; add vinegar and oregano.

2. Cover and cook on LOW until pork falls apart easily when shredded with a fork, 8 to 10 hours.

3. Stir together tomato, red onion, lime juice, jalapeño, and remaining ½ teaspoon salt in a bowl. Chill at least 2 hours or up to 24.

4. Heat tortillas according to package directions. Shred pork in slow cooker with 2 forks; stir in paprika and cayenne. Serve pork on tortillas topped with salsa and cilantro.

SQUASH AND GREEN CHILE CASSEROLE

SLOW-COOKER CORN CHOWDER

Squash and Green Chile Casserole

Filled with fresh zucchini and squash, this casserole doesn't require the oven.

ACTIVE 15 MIN. - TOTAL 5 HOURS, 15 MIN.
SERVES 6

- 4 tomatillos (about 7 oz.), husked and quartered
- 2 (4-oz.) cans chopped green chiles
- 10 cilantro sprigs, leaves and stems separated
- 2 garlic cloves, smashed
- 2 Tbsp. apple cider vinegar
- 1½ tsp. kosher salt
- 1 tsp. black pepper
- 1½ cups uncooked long-grain white rice
- 1½ lb. yellow squash (about 3 medium squash), sliced
- ½ lb. zucchini (about 1 medium), sliced
- ½ cup sour cream
- 1 (16-oz.) block Monterey Jack cheese, shredded (about 4 cups), divided

1. Process tomatillos, green chiles, cilantro stems, garlic, vinegar, salt, and pepper in a blender until mostly smooth, about 15 seconds.
2. Place rice on bottom of a 5- to 6-quart slow cooker. Top with squash, zucchini, and tomatillo sauce. Cover and cook on LOW until squash is tender and rice is cooked, about 5 hours.
3. Reduce slow-cooker heat to WARM; add sour cream and 3 cups of the cheese, and stir until cheese is melted. Sprinkle with cilantro leaves and remaining 1 cup cheese just before serving.

Slow-Cooker Corn Chowder

This creamy soup makes an indulgent but not too heavy meal on a hot summer day. Pick the freshest sweet corn you can find.

ACTIVE 25 MIN. - TOTAL 6 HOURS, 25 MIN.
SERVES 6

- 14 ears fresh yellow corn (about 3 lb.), divided
- 2½ cups chicken stock
- 2 medium-size russet potatoes (about 1½ lb.), peeled and chopped
- 1 small yellow onion (about 5 oz.), chopped
- 4 thyme sprigs
- 3 garlic cloves, smashed
- 2 tsp. kosher salt
- 1 tsp. black pepper
- 4 thick-cut bacon slices, cooked and crumbled
- ½ cup finely chopped red onion (from 1 small onion)
- 2 Tbsp. chopped fresh chives
- 2 Tbsp. fresh lime juice (from 1 large lime)
- 1 cup heavy cream

1. Cut corn kernels from cobs using a sharp knife. Reserve 1 cup corn kernels. Place remaining corn kernels in a 5- to 6-quart slow cooker. Working over a rimmed pan, use the back of the knife to scrape cobs to release all juices from cobs. Add corn milk, stock, potatoes, yellow onion, thyme sprigs, garlic, salt, and pepper to slow cooker.
2. Cover and cook on LOW until potatoes are very tender and chowder has thickened slightly, about 6 hours.
3. Meanwhile, stir together reserved 1 cup corn kernels, bacon, red onion, chives, and lime juice in a small bowl. Chill until ready to serve, up to 6 hours ahead.
4. Remove half of chowder, and set aside. Process remaining chowder in slow cooker using an immersion blender until smooth. (Or transfer half of chowder to a blender, and remove center piece of blender lid to allow steam to escape. Secure lid; place a clean towel over opening in lid, and process until smooth.) Stir together reserved and pureed chowder in slow cooker. Stir in heavy cream. Divide evenly among 6 bowls; top evenly with fresh corn topping.

Simply the Best Squash Casserole

It's prime time to enjoy one of the South's most requested make-and-take dishes

THERE'S A common cliché about Southern food: that our vegetables are smothered in butter, cream, and cheese. Some clichés are true—and mighty delicious. Only in the South will you dig into a vegetable side dish that's richer than most desserts. And while yellow squash is at the center of this old-school casserole, it's the outrageously creamy sauce (traditionally made with cheese, mayonnaise, and sour cream) and the crunchy, buttery topping that have folks requesting seconds.

This summer, we set out to develop our best-ever squash casserole by revisiting recipes from the *Southern Living* archives as well as trying a variety of different versions of the classic at popular meat 'n' three diners (including Johnny's Restaurant, a local Birmingham favorite). And we even improved the recipe to prevent the most common pitfall: overcooked, mushy squash. (Spoiler: Sautéing rather than boiling the squash helps remove excess water while retaining the right texture.) Our Test Kitchen raved about the results, saying that the entire casserole was polished off in 15 minutes at the tasting table—after all, Southerners do love their vegetables.

SIZE MATTERS
Choose squash on the smaller side, which tend to be less seedy and more tender.

DRAIN MOISTURE
Strain the squash to remove excess water and to cool it slightly before adding it to the casserole.

DON'T OVERCOOK
Sauté the squash until just tender in the center. Remember that it will be baked as well.

HANDLE GENTLY
Avoid breaking or mashing the cooked squash when folding it into the egg-cheese mixture.

4 SECRETS TO SQUASH CASSEROLE

1

SWISS CHEESE
Cheddar is necessary, but we also added some Swiss cheese for tanginess.

2

MAYONNAISE
It's the traditional binder for the casserole. Don't go overboard—a half cup is all you need.

3

BLACK PEPPER
Freshly cracked black pepper adds a bit of heat that cuts through the richness of the dish.

4

CRUSHED CRACKERS
A crunchy topping provides a nice textural contrast to the soft, creamy casserole.

Old-School Squash Casserole

ACTIVE 25 MIN. - TOTAL 1 HOUR, 5 MIN.
SERVES 8

- 6 Tbsp. unsalted butter, divided
- 3 lb. yellow squash, sliced ¼ inch thick (from 5 medium squash)
- 1 medium-size yellow onion, chopped (about 1 ½ cups)
- 2 tsp. kosher salt, divided
- 2 large eggs, lightly beaten
- 1 (8-oz.) container sour cream
- 4 oz. sharp Cheddar cheese, shredded (about 1 cup)
- 2 oz. Swiss cheese, shredded (about ½ cup)
- ½ cup mayonnaise
- 2 tsp. chopped fresh thyme
- ½ tsp. black pepper
- 2 sleeves round buttery crackers (such as Ritz), coarsely crushed
- 1 oz. Parmesan cheese, shredded (about ¼ cup)

1. Preheat oven to 350°F. Melt 3 tablespoons of the butter in a large skillet over medium-high. Add squash, onion, and 1 teaspoon of the salt; cook, stirring often, until center of squash is just tender and liquid has evaporated, about 10 minutes. Transfer mixture to a colander set over a bowl. Drain 5 minutes; discard any liquid.

2. Stir together eggs, sour cream, Cheddar and Swiss cheeses, mayonnaise, thyme, pepper, and remaining 1 teaspoon salt in a large bowl. Gently fold in squash mixture. Spoon into a lightly greased 11- x 7-inch (2-quart) baking dish.

3. Microwave remaining 3 tablespoons butter in a medium-size microwavable bowl on HIGH until melted, about 25 seconds. Toss together crackers, Parmesan cheese, and melted butter until combined; sprinkle over casserole. Bake in preheated oven until golden brown, about 20 minutes.

Turkey Burger Time

Take a break from beef and gobble these up

ONLY 484 CALORIES
PER SERVING

Ranch Turkey Burgers

A mix of reduced-fat sour cream, mayonnaise, and buttermilk keeps the patties moist, while a few spice staples add the ranch flavor everyone loves.

ACTIVE 15 MIN. - TOTAL 20 MIN.
SERVES 4

- 1 ¼ lb. ground turkey
- ½ tsp. garlic powder
- ½ tsp. onion powder
- ½ tsp. dried dill
- ¼ cup reduced-fat sour cream, divided
- ¼ cup canola mayonnaise, divided
- 3 Tbsp. reduced-fat buttermilk, divided
- ¾ tsp. kosher salt, divided
- ¾ tsp. black pepper, divided
- 1 Tbsp. olive oil
- 1 tsp. apple cider vinegar
- 4 (1.5-oz.) hamburger buns, toasted
  Romaine lettuce heart leaves, thin tomato slices, and red onion slices for topping

1. Combine turkey, garlic powder, onion powder, dill, and 1 tablespoon each of sour cream, mayonnaise, and buttermilk in a medium bowl. Divide turkey mixture into 4 (5-ounce) portions; shape into 1-inch-thick patties. Sprinkle patties with ½ teaspoon each of the salt and pepper.
2. Heat oil in a large nonstick skillet over medium-high. Add burgers to skillet; cover and cook until bottoms are browned, about 4 minutes. Turn burgers; cover and cook until browned and a meat thermometer inserted in thickest portion registers 165°F, about 3 minutes.
3. Stir together apple cider vinegar and remaining 3 tablespoons each of sour cream and mayonnaise, 2 tablespoons buttermilk, and ¼ teaspoon each of salt and pepper in a small bowl. Spread about 1 tablespoon of the mixture on each bun half. Place 1 patty on each bottom half of bun; top each with lettuce, tomato, and red onion slices and other half of bun.

Nutritional information (per serving):
Calories: 484 - Protein: 38g - Carbs: 26g - Fiber: 2g - Fat: 25g

TIP Swap out the ground turkey for ground chicken if you prefer its lighter flavor.

Potluck Potato Salad

Hold the mayo. Replace the usual creamy dressing with this lively lemon–dill vinaigrette

Tangy Potato-Green Bean Salad

Party bound? Chill cooked potatoes and green beans in the dressing for 30 minutes. Then assemble the salad (with the radishes, dill, chives, and remaining dressing) on a platter just before serving.

ACTIVE 20 MIN. - TOTAL 1 HOUR, 20 MIN.
SERVES 8

- 3 lb. baby red potatoes (quartered or halved, depending on size)
- ¼ cup plus 1 tsp. kosher salt, divided
- 8 oz. haricots verts (French green beans), trimmed and cut into 1 ½-inch pieces
- 1 tsp. lemon zest, plus ¼ cup fresh juice (from 2 lemons)
- 1 Tbsp. minced shallot (from 1 shallot)
- 1 Tbsp. white wine vinegar
- 1 Tbsp. Dijon mustard
- ¼ tsp. black pepper
- 1 cup loosely packed fresh dill, chopped and divided
- ⅔ cup olive oil
- ½ cup thinly sliced radishes (about 3 radishes)
- 2 Tbsp. thinly sliced chives

1. Bring potatoes, water to cover, and ¼ cup of the salt to a boil in a large Dutch oven over medium-high. Reduce heat to medium-low, and cook until just fork-tender but not falling apart, about 8 minutes. Add haricots verts, and cook until beans are tender-crisp, about 1 minute. Drain well; cool completely, about 30 minutes. Transfer to a large bowl and cover with plastic wrap; chill until ready to use.

2. Whisk together lemon zest and lemon juice, shallot, vinegar, mustard, pepper, remaining 1 teaspoon salt, and 1 tablespoon of the chopped dill in a medium bowl; gradually add olive oil in a slow, steady stream, whisking until smooth.

3. Gently toss together potato-green bean mixture and ½ cup of the dressing, and let stand 30 minutes. Before serving, gently stir in radishes, remaining fresh dill, and remaining dressing. Sprinkle with chives.

SKIP THE SHRIMP
FOR A HEARTY
VEGETARIAN MEAL.

Summer Stir-Fry

Fix a lighter, brighter skillet supper in under 30 minutes

Shrimp Fried Rice

The best fried rice is made with day-old rice because it's drier and not so sticky. If you don't have any leftovers on hand, you can spread freshly cooked grains on a baking sheet and place in the refrigerator for 30 minutes or until the rice has cooled.

ACTIVE 25 MIN. - TOTAL 25 MIN.
SERVES 4

1 lb. raw medium shrimp, peeled and deveined
2 Tbsp. canola oil, divided
½ tsp. kosher salt, divided
4 oz. haricots verts (French green beans), trimmed and cut into 1-inch pieces
4 scallions, white and green parts chopped separately
2 garlic cloves, chopped
½ tsp. finely chopped peeled fresh ginger
4 cups cooked long-grain white rice, cooled
2 large eggs, lightly beaten
⅓ cup small basil leaves
3 Tbsp. soy sauce
1 tsp. toasted sesame oil

1. Heat a wok or large cast-iron skillet over high. Add shrimp, 1 tablespoon of the canola oil, and ¼ teaspoon of the salt; cook, stirring occasionally, until shrimp are opaque, about 2 minutes. Remove shrimp, and set aside.
2. Add green beans, white parts of scallions, garlic, ginger, and remaining 1 tablespoon canola oil; cook, stirring constantly, until beans are just tender, about 1 minute. Add rice and remaining ¼ teaspoon salt, tossing to coat and break up clumps; cook, stirring occasionally, until rice begins to crisp, about 4 minutes.
3. Push rice mixture to 1 side of wok; add eggs to other side, and cook, stirring often, until scrambled, about 1 minute. Combine eggs and rice. Add shrimp, basil, soy sauce, and sesame oil; cook, stirring constantly, just until combined and heated through, about 1 minute. Sprinkle with green parts of scallions.

Shake Up Dessert

Turn plain old vanilla ice cream into three creamy, dreamy Southern-style milk shakes

Salted Caramel–Pecan Milk Shake

ACTIVE 10 MIN. - TOTAL 10 MIN.
SERVES 4

Place 2 Tbsp. jarred **caramel topping** in the bottom of each of 4 chilled glasses, and sprinkle with ¼ tsp. flaky **sea salt.** Process 1 pt. **vanilla ice cream,** softened; 1 pt. **butter-pecan ice cream,** softened; and ⅔ cup whole **milk** in a blender until foamy and thick, 3 to 4 minutes. Divide milk shake evenly among prepared glasses; top with **whipped cream,** and drizzle each with 1 Tbsp. caramel topping. Sprinkle each with ¼ tsp. flaky sea salt, and top with 1 Tbsp. chopped toasted **pecans.** Serve immediately.

Banana Pudding Milk Shake

ACTIVE 10 MIN. - TOTAL 10 MIN.
SERVES 4

Process 2 sliced extra-ripe **bananas** (about 2 cups); 2 pt. **vanilla ice cream,** softened; and ½ cup whole **milk** in a blender until foamy and thick, about 3 minutes. Divide milk shake evenly among 4 chilled glasses. Top each with **whipped cream,** 1 Tbsp. crushed **vanilla wafers,** and 2 banana slices. Serve immediately.

Peanut Butter Pie Milk Shake

ACTIVE 10 MIN. - TOTAL 10 MIN.
SERVES 4

Drizzle 1 Tbsp. **chocolate syrup** down the inside of a chilled glass using a squeeze bottle or spoon. Repeat with 3 more chilled glasses. Process 2 pt. **vanilla ice cream,** softened; 1 cup creamy **peanut butter;** ½ cup whole **milk;** and 2 Tbsp. jarred **caramel topping** in a blender until foamy and thick, about 3 to 4 minutes. Divide milk shake evenly among prepared glasses. Top each with **whipped cream.** Sprinkle each with ¼ cup crumbled **chocolate wafer cookies** and 2 Tbsp. chopped honey-roasted **peanuts.** Serve immediately.

COOKING (SL) SCHOOL

TIPS AND TRICKS FROM THE SOUTH'S MOST TRUSTED KITCHEN

Better Burger Blends

Build your signature patty with these tasty add-ins

BEEF
Add 6 oz. ground, uncooked bacon (use your food processor) to 1 lb. ground beef.

PORK
Combine ½ lb. ground pork with ½ lb. hot or sweet Italian sausage.

LAMB
Add 1 Tbsp. minced fresh oregano, 2 minced garlic cloves, and 2 Tbsp. minced red onion to 1 lb. ground lamb.

TURKEY
Add ½ cup cooked, cooled, chopped caramelized onions; 2 Tbsp. mayonnaise; and 2 Tbsp. fresh minced chives to 1 lb. ground turkey.

"When making a milk shake, let the ice cream get slightly soft before adding it to the blender. If it's frozen solid, you'll add too much milk and end up with a runny shake."

—**Robby Melvin,** *Southern Living* Test Kitchen Director

Kitchen Power Tools

These handy gadgets make prep work a breeze

①

Chef'n StemGem Strawberry Huller, $7.95; *amazon.com*

WHAT IT DOES
Quickly removes the white cores and stems from fresh strawberries

WHY WE LOVE IT
Takes the hassle out of the process of hulling ripe strawberries

②

OXO Good Grips Corn Stripper, $13.95; *amazon.com*

WHAT IT DOES
Slices corn kernels straight off the cob into a half-cup container

WHY WE LOVE IT
Protects fingers and keeps kernels from flying all over your kitchen

③

SCI Cuisine Red Shrimp Deveiner, $4.90; *amazon.com*

WHAT IT DOES
Cleans and peels shrimp in one simple swipe

WHY WE LOVE IT
Removes the unappetizing veins quickly so you can prep pounds of raw shrimp in minutes

September

CAST-IRON COOKBOOK

It's the hardest-working pan in any Southern cook's kitchen. Here are 11 delicious ways to put it to use, from breakfast to dessert

POTATO-BACON HASH

This colorful, hearty hash is even better topped with a fried egg. Use a skillet with a lid so you can cover and uncover the pan to make tender-on-the-inside, toasted-on-the-outside potatoes (recipe, page 248).

LIGHTER PAN-FRIED CHICKEN WITH GREEN BEANS AND TOMATOES

Cast iron is excellent for frying, but you don't always have to deep-fry. Quickly pan-fry the chicken to get a crispy, golden exterior; then pop it in the oven until it's cooked through. Add some tangy green beans and tomatoes to make this a winning meal (recipe, page 251).

BEEF STEW WITH BUTTERY GARLIC BREAD

A Dutch oven is ideal for cooking this satisfying stew. As it simmers, grab your skillet to make the irresistibly good garlic bread (recipe, page 250).

MYTH

RUST MEANS IT'S RUINED

Cast iron is like a chalkboard—you can almost always wipe it clean and start fresh. Unless your pan is cracked or rusted all the way through, scrub off the rust with steel wool, rinse the pan, dry it, and reseason it. (See page 251 for instructions.)

TEXAS SKILLET CAKE

This dense, fudgy dessert combines the ease of a Texas sheet cake with the richness of a brownie. We suggest topping slices with vanilla ice cream, but it's pretty hard not to eat the entire cake straight out of the skillet (recipe, page 251).

The Big Cinnamon Roll

SERVES 16

ACTIVE 1 HOUR · TOTAL 11 HOURS, INCLUDING
8 HOURS CHILLING

- 1 (¼-oz.) envelope active dry yeast
- ¼ cup warm water (100°F to 110°F)
- 1 cup plus 1 tsp. granulated sugar, divided
- 2 large eggs, lightly beaten
- 1 cup plus 2 Tbsp. whole milk, divided
- 1¼ cups unsalted butter, softened, divided
- 5 cups bread flour, divided
- 1¾ tsp. kosher salt, divided
- ½ cup firmly packed light brown sugar
- 2 tsp. ground cinnamon
- 4 oz. cream cheese, softened
- 2 cups powdered sugar

1. Stir together yeast, warm water, and 1 teaspoon of the granulated sugar in the bowl of a heavy-duty stand mixer fitted with paddle attachment. Let stand until foamy, about 5 minutes. Add eggs, 1 cup of the milk, ½ cup of the granulated sugar, ½ cup of the butter, 2 cups of the flour, and 1 teaspoon of the salt to bowl. Beat on low speed just until dough comes together, about 1 minute. Replace paddle attachment with dough hook, and add 2 cups of the flour to bowl. Beat on low speed until dough is smooth but still very sticky, about 5 minutes. Turn dough out onto a surface floured with remaining 1 cup flour, and knead until elastic and almost no stickiness remains and all flour is incorporated. Transfer dough to a lightly greased large bowl, turning once to grease top. Cover with a damp towel, and let rise in a warm place (80°F to 85°F) until doubled in size, about 1 hour.

2. Stir together brown sugar, cinnamon, ½ teaspoon of the salt, and remaining ½ cup granulated sugar in a small bowl. Turn dough out onto a lightly floured surface, and roll out into a 20- x 14-inch rectangle. Spread ½ cup of the softened butter over top of dough rectangle; sprinkle with brown sugar mixture. Starting at 1 long end, roll dough into a long rope, stretching dough back to a 20-inch length, if necessary. Starting in center of a 12-inch cast-iron skillet, wrap dough rope into a tight coil, working outward. Using a sharp paring knife, cut slits through top layers of dough at 1-inch intervals. Cover with plastic wrap, and chill 8 hours or overnight.

3. Place a large bowl of very hot water in oven, and let stand 5 minutes. Place skillet with chilled dough in oven, and let rise until doubled in size, about 1 hour. Remove skillet and bowl of water from oven. Preheat oven to 350°F.

4. Place skillet on an aluminum foil-lined baking sheet, and bake in preheated oven until deep golden brown, about 30 minutes. Cover with foil, and bake until dough in center is cooked through and a thermometer inserted in center registers 190°F, 20 to 30 minutes. Cool in skillet 10 minutes before cutting.

5. Meanwhile, beat cream cheese and remaining ¼ cup butter with an electric mixer on medium-high speed until fluffy. Add powdered sugar and remaining 2 tablespoons milk and ¼ teaspoon salt, and beat until smooth. Drizzle icing over warm cinnamon roll. Serve warm or at room temperature.

Potato-Bacon Hash

SERVES 4

ACTIVE 30 MIN. · TOTAL 40 MIN.

- 6 thick-cut bacon slices (about 5½ oz.)
- 1½ lb. russet potatoes (about 2 medium potatoes), peeled and cut into ½-inch pieces
- 1 cup chopped yellow onion (about 1 medium onion)
- 1 cup chopped red bell pepper (about 1 medium pepper)
- 1 tsp. chopped garlic
- 1 tsp. kosher salt
- ½ tsp. black pepper
- 4 cups baby spinach (about 4 oz.)
    Hot sauce

1. Cook bacon in a large cast-iron skillet over medium until crispy, 10 to 12 minutes, turning often. Transfer to a plate lined with paper towels, reserving drippings in skillet.

2. Add potatoes, onion, and bell pepper to reserved drippings in skillet, and spread in an even layer. Cover and cook over medium until potatoes soften, about 5 minutes. Uncover and cook, without stirring, until potatoes are just browned and beginning to crisp, about 5 minutes. Stir in garlic, salt, and pepper. Cook, without stirring, in 6 (2-minute) intervals, stirring in between each 2-minute interval, until potatoes are browned and crisp.

3. Crumble bacon; add bacon and spinach to skillet. Remove skillet from heat, and stir until spinach wilts, about 2 minutes. Serve with hot sauce.

LUNCH

Grilled Cheese, 4 Ways

SERVES 1

ACTIVE 15 MIN. - TOTAL 15 MIN.

- 2 (1-oz.) sourdough bread slices
- 1 Tbsp. mayonnaise
- 2 American cheese slices
- 2 oz. sharp Cheddar cheese, shredded (about ½ cup)

1. Spread 1 side of each bread slice evenly with mayonnaise. Place 1 bread slice, mayonnaise side down, on a sheet of parchment paper or wax paper. Top with American cheese slices and shredded Cheddar cheese. Cover with remaining bread slice, mayonnaise side up. Place a second sheet of parchment paper or wax paper on top of sandwich, and press gently.

2. Heat a large cast-iron skillet over medium. Remove sandwich from bottom piece of parchment paper, leaving top piece in place, and transfer to hot skillet. Place a small, heavy skillet on top of sandwich, and press. Cook until cheese melts and bread is golden brown on bottom, about 2 minutes. Remove small skillet; turn sandwich, and cook, without pressing, until golden brown on bottom, about 2 minutes.

Caramelized Onion Grilled Cheese

Prepare recipe as directed, substituting 2 oz. (½ cup) shredded fontina cheese, 1 oz. (2 Tbsp.) creamy goat cheese, and ¼ cup caramelized yellow onion (from ½ cup sliced onion) for American cheese slices and shredded sharp Cheddar cheese.

Ham and Dijon Grilled Cheese

Prepare recipe as directed, substituting 2 oz. (½ cup) shredded Gruyère cheese, 2 oz. sliced deli ham, and 1 Tbsp. Dijon mustard for American cheese slices and shredded sharp Cheddar cheese.

Brie, Fig, and Arugula Grilled Cheese

Prepare recipe as directed, substituting 2 oz. thinly sliced Brie, 1 ½ Tbsp. fig preserves, and ¼ cup loosely packed arugula for American cheese slices and shredded sharp Cheddar cheese.

GRILLED CHEESE

Two skillets are better than one for making this popular sandwich. Using a second skillet to weigh down the bread during the first half of the cooking process is the best way to toast it and melt the cheese. Enjoy a classic grilled cheese, or try three tasty new variations.

Cast Iron 101

CLEANING

If your pan is well seasoned, all you need is hot water and a scrub brush to clean it. To remove any stuck-on food, a small amount of mild dish soap won't cause damage. Water is cast iron's real enemy, so thoroughly dry the pan, and then rub the inside and outside with a little vegetable oil.

STORING

Keep cast-iron cookware in a cool, dry place. If you stack your pans, place a paper towel, small piece of cardboard, or even an old oven mitt in between each layer to absorb any extra moisture and prevent scratches or damage.

USING

Cast iron heats up slowly, so preheat your pan in the oven or on the stove-top with some oil before adding anything else to it. Preheating prevents food from sticking to the pan, creates a nice crust on cornbread and meat, and also helps build up more layers of seasoning. You can use the same pan to make both sweet and savory dishes, but thoroughly clean it between uses to avoid transferring any leftover flavors—you don't want your peach cobbler to taste like a batch of fried fish.

DINNER

Cast-Iron Pork Cacciatore

SERVES 4

ACTIVE 30 MIN. - TOTAL 30 MIN.

- 4 (1-inch-thick) bone-in pork chops (about 2 ½ to 3 lb.)
- 1 ½ tsp. kosher salt, divided
- 1 tsp. black pepper, divided
- 2 Tbsp. unsalted butter
- 8 oz. sliced cremini mushrooms
- 1 cup chopped red onion (about 1 medium onion)
- 1 cup chopped green bell pepper (about 1 large pepper)
- ¼ cup chopped carrot (from 1 medium carrot)
- 2 Tbsp. tomato paste
- 1 tsp. chopped garlic (about 1 garlic clove)
- ¼ cup dry white wine
- 1 (28-oz.) can whole peeled tomatoes
- ½ cup unsalted chicken stock
- 1 rosemary sprig
- 1 bay leaf
- ½ cup pitted Castelvetrano olives, halved
- 6 cups hot cooked bucatini pasta (12 oz. uncooked)
- 2 Tbsp. chopped fresh flat-leaf parsley

1. Preheat oven to 400°F. Sprinkle pork chops evenly with 1 teaspoon of the salt and ¾ teaspoon of the pepper. Melt butter in a large cast-iron skillet over high. Add pork to skillet, and sear until deep golden brown, about 3 minutes per side. Transfer to a rimmed baking sheet, and bake in preheated oven until a thermometer inserted into thickest portion registers 145°F, about 10 minutes. Let pork rest 5 to 10 minutes.

2. Meanwhile, add mushrooms, onion, bell pepper, and carrot to skillet. Spread in an even layer, and cook over high, without stirring, until vegetables begin to brown, about 2 minutes. Stir and cook until browned, about 2 minutes more. Add tomato paste, garlic, and remaining ½ teaspoon salt and ¼ teaspoon pepper, and cook, stirring constantly, 1 minute. Add wine, and simmer until reduced by half, about 30 seconds. Add tomatoes, and break apart using a wooden spoon. Add stock, rosemary, and bay leaf to skillet, and bring to a simmer.

3. Reduce heat to medium; add olives, and cook until liquid is reduced slightly and sauce is thickened, 10 to 15 minutes. Remove and discard rosemary sprig and bay leaf. Serve pork and sauce over cooked pasta. Sprinkle with parsley.

Beef Stew with Buttery Garlic Bread

SERVES 6

ACTIVE 40 MIN. - TOTAL 2 HOURS, 15 MIN.

- 2 Tbsp. canola oil
- 2 lb. boneless chuck roast, cut into ¾-inch pieces
- 2 tsp. kosher salt, divided
- 1 tsp. black pepper, divided
- 12 oz. cremini mushrooms, quartered
- 2 medium carrots, chopped (about 1 cup)
- 1 ½ cups frozen pearl onions, thawed
- ¼ cup all-purpose flour
- 2 tsp. chopped garlic (about 2 garlic cloves)
- ¾ cup brown ale beer
- 3 cups unsalted beef stock
- 6 sourdough bread slices
- 1 large garlic clove, halved lengthwise
- ¼ cup salted butter

1. Heat oil in a large cast-iron Dutch oven over medium-high. Add beef, and sprinkle with 1 teaspoon of the salt and ½ teaspoon of the pepper. Cook, stirring occasionally, until browned on all sides, about 6 minutes.

2. Add mushrooms, carrots, and onions, and cook over medium-high, stirring often, until vegetables begin to soften, about 5 minutes. Add flour and garlic, and cook, stirring constantly, 1 minute. Add beer, and simmer until reduced by about half, about 2 minutes. Add stock and remaining 1 teaspoon salt and ½ teaspoon pepper, and bring to a boil. Reduce heat to medium-low; cover and simmer until beef is very tender, about 1 ½ hours.

3. Rub both sides of sourdough bread slices with cut sides of garlic clove. Melt 2 tablespoons of the butter in a large cast-iron skillet over medium-high. Once butter begins to foam, add 3 bread slices, turning immediately to ensure both sides are coated with melted butter. Cook until bottom is golden, about 1 minute. Turn bread slice, and cook until bottom is golden, about 1 minute. Repeat with remaining 2 tablespoons butter and 3 bread slices. Serve Buttery Garlic Bread immediately with Beef Stew.

CAST-IRON PORK CACCIATORE

This recipe is quick enough to whip up on a weeknight but impressive enough to serve to company. Pair it with a salad and your favorite bottle of red wine.

Lighter Pan-Fried Chicken with Green Beans and Tomatoes

SERVES 8

ACTIVE 25 MIN. - TOTAL 8 HOURS, 45 MIN., INCLUDING 8 HOURS CHILLING

- 2 cups whole buttermilk
- 2 large eggs, beaten
- 3 garlic cloves, smashed
- 4 ¾ tsp. kosher salt, divided
- 2 ½ tsp. black pepper, divided
- 2 lb. bone-in, skinless chicken thighs (about 8)
- 2 lb. boneless, skinless chicken breasts (about 4), cut in half
- 2 cups canola oil
- 3 cups all-purpose flour
- 2 Tbsp. cornstarch
- 1 lb. trimmed fresh green beans
- 1 large shallot, thinly sliced (about ½ cup)
- 1 pt. cherry tomatoes
- 2 tsp. fresh lemon juice (from 1 lemon)

1. Whisk together buttermilk, eggs, garlic cloves, 2 teaspoons of the salt, and 1 teaspoon of the pepper in a large bowl. Place chicken in a large ziplock plastic freezer bag; pour buttermilk mixture over chicken. Seal bag, removing as much air as possible. (Or combine in a large bowl, and cover with a tight-fitting lid.) Chill 8 to 24 hours.

2. Preheat oven to 425°F. Pour oil into a large cast-iron skillet, and heat over medium-high.

3. Drain chicken well; discard buttermilk mixture. Whisk together flour, cornstarch, 2 teaspoons of the salt, and 1 teaspoon of the pepper in a large bowl. Working with 1 piece at a time, dredge chicken in flour mixture until well coated. Place coated chicken pieces on a large piece of aluminum foil, and let stand to allow coating to dry out, about 15 minutes.

4. Fry chicken, in batches, 4 pieces at a time, in hot oil until golden, about 3 minutes per side. Transfer browned chicken to a wire rack in a large rimmed baking sheet. Bake in preheated oven until chicken is deep golden brown and cooked through, about 10 minutes.

5. Meanwhile, let skillet rest off heat about 5 minutes while chicken bakes. Carefully pour all of the frying oil into a metal bowl; allow flour to settle to bottom of bowl. Wipe skillet clean.

6. Add 2 tablespoons of the frying oil to skillet, and place over medium-high. Add green beans and shallot, and cook, without stirring, until beginning to brown, about 4 minutes. Stir in tomatoes, and cook, without stirring, until beans and shallot are charred and tomatoes begin to burst, about 2 minutes. Stir in remaining ¾ teaspoon salt and ½ teaspoon pepper. Transfer vegetables to a serving platter, and toss with lemon juice. Serve the vegetables immediately with the fried chicken.

TEST KITCHEN TIPS

The Best Way To Season a Skillet

"Break in" a new cast-iron pan or reseason an old one in three steps.

①

CLEAN IT

Scrub the pan well in hot, soapy water, and dry it thoroughly.

②

COAT IT WITH OIL

Spread a thin layer of vegetable oil or shortening over the entire pan–inside and outside.

③

BAKE IT

Place pan upside down on the middle oven rack. Put a sheet of aluminum foil on the lower rack to catch any drips. Bake at 350°F for 1 hour; let it cool in the oven.

DESSERT

Texas Skillet Cake

SERVES 16

ACTIVE 25 MIN. - TOTAL 1 HOUR, 5 MIN.

CAKE
- 1 ½ cups semisweet chocolate chips (about 10 oz.)
- ¾ cup unsalted butter
- 4 large eggs
- 1 cup granulated sugar
- 1 cup packed light brown sugar
- 2 cups all-purpose flour
- ¼ cup unsweetened cocoa
- 1 ½ tsp. baking powder
- ½ tsp. kosher salt

FROSTING
- 1 cup granulated sugar
- ½ cup unsalted butter
- ½ cup whole milk
- ¼ cup unsweetened cocoa
- 2 Tbsp. all-purpose flour
- ½ tsp. kosher salt
- 1 tsp. vanilla extract

ADDITIONAL INGREDIENTS
- 1 cup toasted pecan halves, chopped

  Ice cream

1. Prepare the Cake: Preheat oven to 350°F. Combine chocolate chips and butter in a medium-size microwavable glass bowl. Microwave on HIGH until melted and smooth, about 2 minutes, stirring every 30 seconds. Cool 10 minutes.

MYTHS

YOU SHOULD NEVER COOK ACIDIC FOODS IN A CAST-IRON SKILLET

Acidic ingredients like tomatoes, lemons, and wine can be cooked in a well-seasoned pan for short amounts of time. You can sauté cherry tomatoes in cast iron, but don't try making a long-simmering tomato sauce. If you recently purchased your skillet and it still needs to be "broken in," acidic ingredients can erode the seasoning and even make foods taste metallic.

THERE'S NO SUCH THING AS TOO MUCH SEASONING

Seasoning cast iron involves oil (it has nothing to do with salt, pepper, or other spices), and if you apply too much to the pan, it may develop a sticky film. A teaspoon of oil should be enough to coat the interior and exterior of a 10-inch skillet.

2. Beat eggs, granulated sugar, and light brown sugar in the bowl of a heavy-duty stand mixer fitted with whisk attachment on medium speed until thick and creamy, about 5 minutes. Whisk together flour, cocoa, baking powder, and salt. Add flour mixture and melted chocolate mixture to egg mixture in batches, beginning and ending with flour mixture. Beat on low speed just until each is incorporated. Pour batter into a 12-inch cast-iron skillet.

3. Bake in preheated oven until a wooden pick inserted in center comes out with a few moist crumbs, about 40 minutes. Place on a wire rack to cool slightly.

4. Prepare the Frosting: Combine granulated sugar, butter, milk, cocoa, flour, and salt in a small saucepan over medium. Cook, stirring constantly, until mixture comes to a boil, about 5 minutes. Cook, stirring constantly, until slightly thickened, about 1 minute (it will still be a bit thin). Remove pan from heat, and stir in vanilla extract. Pour into a medium-size heatproof bowl, and let cool slightly, about 15 minutes. Pour warm Frosting over warm Cake. Sprinkle with chopped pecans. Serve warm or at room temperature with ice cream.

Skillet Caramel Apple Pie

SERVES 8

ACTIVE 1 HOUR - TOTAL 5 HOURS, 30 MIN.

- 1 (14.1-oz.) pkg. refrigerated piecrusts
- 1 cup packed light brown sugar
- ½ cup unsalted butter
- 3 Tbsp. half-and-half
- 1 tsp. kosher salt
- 1 tsp. vanilla extract
- 1 Tbsp. bourbon (optional)
- 3 lb. Fuji apples (about 4 ½ medium apples), peeled and cut into ½-inch-thick slices
- 2 ½ Tbsp. cornstarch
- 1 large egg yolk, lightly beaten
- 1 Tbsp. water

1. Fit 1 piecrust on bottom and press up sides of a 9-inch cast-iron skillet. Transfer skillet to refrigerator, and let chill while assembling caramel sauce and apple filling.

2. Preheat oven to 425°F. Stir together light brown sugar, butter, half-and-half, and salt in a medium saucepan over medium-high. Cook, stirring, until butter melts and mixture begins to bubble, about 5 minutes. Cook, stirring, until mixture begins to thicken, about 2 more minutes. Remove from heat; stir in vanilla extract, and, if desired, bourbon. Let caramel sauce cool to almost room temperature, about 30 minutes.

3. Toss apples with cornstarch in a large bowl. Pour ⅓ cup caramel sauce over apples, and toss to coat. Reserve remaining caramel sauce for serving. Pour apple filling into prepared skillet.

4. Place remaining piecrust over apple filling. Crimp edges of bottom and top crusts together. Using a sharp knife, cut 6 to 8 (1-inch) slits in top crust for steam to escape. Whisk together egg yolk and water in a small bowl; brush over crust.

5. Bake pie in preheated oven on bottom oven rack until crust is golden, apples are tender, and filling is bubbly, about 55 minutes to 1 hour, shielding loosely with aluminum foil after about 40 minutes to prevent excessive browning, if necessary. Transfer pie to a wire rack, and cool completely, about 3 hours. Serve with reserved caramel sauce.

MYTHS

A SKILLET THAT COMES SEASONED DOESN'T NEED TO BE SEASONED

While you can cook immediately with a preseasoned skillet, it will get the job done better after it acquires a few more layers of seasoning—achieved either through regular use or additional seasoning time in the oven.

YOU CAN'T USE ANY METAL UTENSILS WITH CAST IRON

Unlike nonstick pans, cast-iron cookware doesn't have a chemical coating that will flake off. If the pan's seasoning gets a little scraped, it can simply be seasoned again.

SKILLET CARAMEL APPLE PIE

A bourbon-spiked caramel sauce takes this apple pie filling over the top, and using a cast-iron skillet prevents the bottom crust from getting soggy.

FAMILY TREES

A FIFTH-GENERATION PECAN FARMER CARRIES ON A PASSION FOR THE SOUTH'S MOST BELOVED FALL TREAT

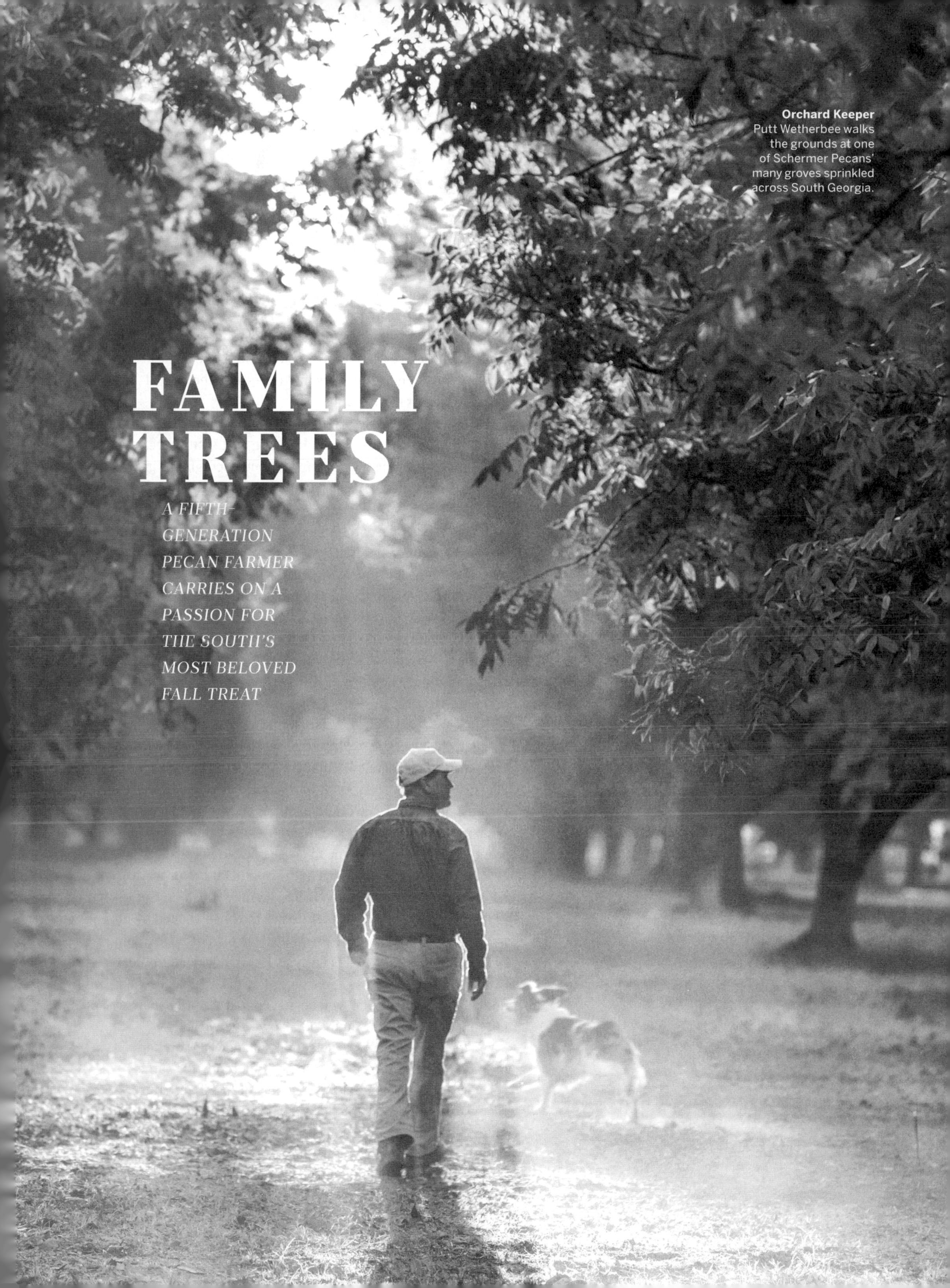

Orchard Keeper Putt Wetherbee walks the grounds at one of Schermer Pecans' many groves sprinkled across South Georgia.

Above: Putt surveys his crop with dogs Rocky and Buster. Below: It's time to harvest at this pecan orchard outside Albany, Georgia.

Pick Up Some Pecans

Order Schermer's fresh-from-the-orchard nuts for yourself—or for a fall hostess gift. Buy them raw or roasted (or glazed or chocolate covered!) at *schermerpecans.com*.

TAKE A DRIVE

along the back roads that cut across the southern half of Georgia, and sooner or later, you're bound to happen upon a pecan orchard—you'll know it by the tidy rows of sprawling pecan trees planted by the hundreds. Many of these date back more than 100 years, and harvest after harvest, these Georgia groves make the state the largest pecan producer in the nation.

No one knows these orchards, or the ins and outs of the South's beloved tree nut, better than Putt Wetherbee, a fifth-generation pecan grower from South Georgia. He grew up watching his father, Frank Wetherbee, revolutionize the industry—boldly introducing new practices in pecan farming and meticulously researching new selections. "If you wanted to spend any time with Dad, you went to work with him," Putt explains. "They didn't have much pecan equipment back then, so he was constantly trying to figure out the best way to do things. We were always inventing or tweaking technology." In the late sixties, Frank became the first farmer in Georgia to irrigate a pecan orchard. "People actually laughed at him," Putt says. "But today, no one would plant an orchard without irrigating."

After too many summers spent atop one of only two mechanical harvesters in the state (yet another of his father's endeavors), Putt set out to pursue a different path. He attended college in Charleston, South Carolina, and started a career in the business world. "I worked a lot, got an MBA, and learned what misery was," he says. "Little did I know, those 20 years were paving the way for me to come back to pecans."

And so as it often happens in the South, Putt returned to his roots—ones that figuratively and literally run deep. Some of the very trees he harvests from are the ones planted by his namesake—his great-great-great-uncle, a planter by the name of Francis Flagg Putney—as early as 1905. In 2014, Putt took over the family business—Schermer Pecans, which grows and packages fresh-like-you've-never-had-before pecans for consumers in the South and all over the world.

As technology evolves, selections change, and orchards grow and shrink, the pecan remains inherently the same— a savory and versatile Southern staple that's a fixture in so many dishes and desserts like the ones on the pages that follow. "It's something significant we can still get our hands on that ties us back to our traditions," he says. "Our grandparents and great-grandparents did this, and it's how they made their living. It's where we come from."

DOUBLE-CHOCOLATE PECAN PIE

Want a rich and powerful flavor combination? Enjoy this dark chocolate piecrust (made with cocoa powder) with the decadent, sweet, and sticky chocolate-pecan filling (recipe, page 257).

PUTT'S BUTTER PECAN SUNDAE

Putt Wetherbee shares his family's recipe for toasted-pecan ice cream and an incredibly rich praline sauce.

ACTIVE 30 MIN. - TOTAL 5 HOURS, INCLUDING 4 HOURS CHILLING

SERVES 6

ICE CREAM
- 3 cups water, divided
- 1 cup whole milk
- 1 cup heavy cream
- ¾ cup packed light brown sugar
- ¼ tsp. kosher salt
- 2 large eggs, lightly beaten
- 2 Tbsp. unsalted butter
- 1 tsp. vanilla extract
- 1½ cups chopped toasted pecans

PRALINE SUNDAE TOPPING
- 1½ cups packed light brown sugar
- ⅔ cup light corn syrup
- ¼ cup unsalted butter
- 1 (5-oz.) can evaporated milk
- 1 cup chopped toasted pecans
- ¼ tsp. kosher salt

1. Prepare the Ice Cream: Bring 1½ cups water to a simmer in bottom pan of a double boiler over medium. Combine milk, cream, brown sugar, salt, eggs, and remaining 1½ cups water in top of double boiler, and cook, whisking constantly, until sugar dissolves, about 15 minutes. Continue to cook, stirring often, until mixture thickens and thinly coats the back of a wooden spoon, about 15 minutes. Add butter and vanilla, and cook, stirring constantly, until butter melts, about 2 minutes. Transfer to a medium bowl; cover and chill until cold, about 2 hours.

2. Pour chilled mixture into the frozen freezer bowl of a 1½-quart electric ice-cream maker, add chopped pecans, and proceed according to manufacturer's instructions. (Instructions and time may vary.) Transfer Ice Cream to a freezer-safe container; cover and freeze until firm, about 1 hour.

3. Prepare the Praline Sundae Topping: Combine sugar, corn syrup, and butter in a medium saucepan over medium. Bring to a boil, and cook, stirring constantly, 2 minutes. Remove from heat, and cool slightly, about 15 minutes.

4. Whisk in evaporated milk until smooth. Stir in pecans and salt. Cool to room temperature, about 20 minutes.

5. Transfer topping to an airtight container, and chill until thickened, about 30 minutes. Serve over Ice Cream.

Double-Chocolate Pecan Pie

ACTIVE 20 MIN. - TOTAL 5 HOURS, 20 MIN.

SERVES 12

CHOCOLATE CRUST

1 ½ cups all-purpose flour, plus more for surface

2 Tbsp. granulated sugar

2 Tbsp. unsweetened cocoa

¼ tsp. table salt

½ cup cold salted butter, cubed

4-5 Tbsp. ice-cold water

FILLING

1 ⅓ cups dark chocolate chips, divided

3 large eggs

¼ cup plus 2 Tbsp. salted butter, melted

¾ cup dark corn syrup

½ cup packed light brown sugar

¼ cup granulated sugar

1 Tbsp. all-purpose flour

1 Tbsp. vanilla extract

½ tsp. table salt

1 cup chopped toasted pecans

¾ cup pecan halves (not toasted)

1. Prepare the Chocolate Crust: Pulse flour, sugar, cocoa, and salt in a food processor until combined, 3 or 4 times. Add cold butter, and pulse until mixture resembles small peas, 8 to 10 times. Add 4 tablespoons of the water, 1 at a time, and pulse just until moist clumps form and mixture begins to form a ball, 8 to 10 times. (If necessary, add up to 1 tablespoon more ice-cold water, and pulse until desired consistency is reached.) Gather dough into a ball, and flatten into a disk. Wrap in plastic wrap, and chill until firm, about 1 hour.

2. Preheat oven to 325°F. Roll dough into a 12-inch circle (about ⅛ inch thick) on a lightly floured surface. Fit into a 9-inch pie plate; fold edges under, and crimp.

3. Prepare the Filling: Sprinkle 1 cup of the chocolate chips evenly over bottom of piecrust. Whisk eggs in a large bowl until frothy. Add melted butter, and whisk until fully incorporated. Whisk in syrup, sugars, flour, vanilla, and salt. Stir in chopped toasted pecans. Pour mixture over chocolate chips in piecrust. Arrange pecan halves evenly over mixture.

4. Bake in preheated oven until set around edges and slightly wobbly in center, 55 minutes to 1 hour, tenting with aluminum foil after 35 to 40 minutes.

Cool completely before slicing, about 3 hours.

5. Place remaining ⅓ cup chocolate chips in a microwavable bowl, and microwave on MEDIUM (50% power) until melted and smooth, 1 minute to 1 minute and 30 seconds, stirring every 30 seconds. Drizzle over pie.

Butter Pecan Layer Cake with Browned Butter Frosting

ACTIVE 45 MIN. - TOTAL 1 HOUR, 45 MIN.

SERVES 12

Shortening

1 ½ cups finely chopped pecans, divided

1 cup plus 1 ½ Tbsp. salted butter, softened, divided

2 cups granulated sugar

5 large eggs, separated

1 Tbsp. vanilla extract

2 cups all-purpose flour, plus more for pans

1 tsp. baking soda

¼ tsp. table salt

1 cup whole buttermilk

Browned Butter Frosting (recipe follows)

1. Grease (with shortening) and flour 3 (9-inch) round cake pans; line with parchment paper, and grease parchment.

2. Preheat oven to 350°F. Cook 1 cup of the pecans and 1 ½ tablespoons of the butter in a small skillet over medium, stirring, until toasted, 6 to 8 minutes. Spread pecans on wax paper; cool about 10 minutes.

3. Meanwhile, beat remaining 1 cup butter with a heavy-duty stand mixer on medium speed until creamy; gradually add sugar, beating until light and fluffy. Add egg yolks, 1 at a time, beating just until blended after each addition. Stir in vanilla.

4. Stir together flour, baking soda, and salt; add to butter mixture alternately with buttermilk, beginning and ending with flour mixture. Beat at low speed until blended after each addition. Stir in cooled butter-toasted pecans.

5. Beat egg whites on medium speed until stiff peaks form; fold one-third of egg whites into batter. Gently fold in remaining beaten egg whites just until blended. Pour into prepared pans.

6. Bake in preheated oven until a wooden pick inserted in center comes

out clean, 20 to 22 minutes. Cool in pans on wire racks 10 minutes. Remove from pans, and cool completely on wire racks, about 20 minutes.

7. Meanwhile, spread remaining ½ cup finely chopped pecans on a baking sheet and bake at 350°F until toasted, about 5 minutes.

8. Spread Browned Butter Frosting between layers and on top and sides of cake. Gently press toasted pecans around bottom of cake about 1 inch up the sides.

Browned Butter Frosting

ACTIVE 25 MIN. - TOTAL 1 HOUR, 25 MIN.

MAKES ABOUT 4 ½ CUPS

Cook 1 ½ cups salted butter in a medium-size heavy saucepan over medium, stirring occasionally, until butter is fragrant and milk solids turn golden brown, 10 to 12 minutes. Remove pan from heat, and immediately pour butter into a small bowl. Cover and chill until butter is cool and almost firm, about 1 hour, stirring every 15 minutes. (If butter becomes solid, it will soften again once you begin beating it.) Beat browned butter with a heavy-duty electric stand mixer fitted with the paddle attachment on medium speed until smooth and fluffy, about 3 minutes. Gradually add 6 cups powdered sugar alternately with ⅓ cup whole milk, beginning and ending with sugar. Beat on low speed until well blended after each addition. Beat in 1 ½ tsp. vanilla extract. Use immediately.

Pumpkin-Spice Bundt with Brown Sugar Icing and Candied Pecans

ACTIVE 40 MIN. - TOTAL 2 HOURS, 40 MIN.

SERVES 12

1 cup salted butter, softened

1 cup granulated sugar

1 cup packed light brown sugar

4 large eggs

1 ½ cups canned pumpkin

2 tsp. vanilla extract

3 cups all-purpose flour, plus more for pan

1 Tbsp. baking powder

1 ½ tsp. pumpkin pie spice

½ tsp. baking soda

½ tsp. table salt

1 cup whole buttermilk
1 cup chopped toasted pecans
  Shortening
  Candied Pecans (recipe follows)
  Brown Sugar Icing (recipe follows)

1. Preheat oven to 350°F. Beat butter with a heavy-duty electric stand mixer on medium speed until creamy. Gradually add sugars, and beat until fluffy. Add eggs, 1 at a time, beating just until blended. Add pumpkin and vanilla, beating just until blended.

2. Stir together flour, baking powder, pumpkin pie spice, baking soda, and salt. Add to butter mixture alternately with buttermilk, beginning and ending with flour mixture. Beat at low speed just until blended after each addition. Stir in chopped pecans. Spoon batter into a greased (with shortening) and floured 12-cup Bundt pan.

3. Bake in preheated oven until a wooden pick inserted in center comes out clean, 50 to 60 minutes. Cool in pan on a wire rack 10 minutes; remove from pan, and cool completely on a wire rack, about 1 hour. While cake bakes, prepare Candied Pecans.

4. Prepare Brown Sugar Icing, and spoon over top of cake, allowing it to drip down sides. Top with Candied Pecans while icing is still soft.

Candied Pecans
ACTIVE 10 MIN. - TOTAL 30 MIN.
MAKES 1 CUP

Stir together ¼ cup granulated sugar, ¼ tsp. pumpkin pie spice, and a pinch of table salt in a heavy saucepan over medium. Add 1 cup roughly chopped pecans, and cook, stirring constantly, until sugar melts and coats pecans, 7 to 8 minutes. (Sugar will appear grainy before it melts and coats pecans.) Spread on lightly greased (with cooking spray) wax paper, and cool 20 minutes.

Brown Sugar Icing
ACTIVE 15 MIN. - TOTAL 15 MIN.
MAKES ABOUT 1 ⅓ CUPS

Bring 1 cup packed light brown sugar, ⅓ cup heavy cream, and ¼ cup salted butter to a boil in a 1-quart saucepan over medium, stirring often. Boil, stirring often, 1 minute; remove from heat. Gradually whisk in 1 cup powdered sugar and 1 tsp. vanilla extract until smooth. Use immediately.

Toasted Coconut-Pecan Cupcakes with Coconut-Cream Cheese Frosting
ACTIVE 20 MIN. - TOTAL 1 HOUR, 10 MIN.
MAKES 2 ½ DOZEN

1 cup salted butter, softened
2 cups granulated sugar
5 large eggs, separated
2 tsp. vanilla extract
¼ tsp. coconut extract
2 cups all-purpose flour
2 tsp. baking powder
¼ tsp. table salt
1 cup well-shaken canned coconut milk
1 cup sweetened flaked coconut, toasted
1 ⅓ cups finely chopped toasted pecans, divided
  Coconut-Cream Cheese Frosting (recipe follows)

1. Preheat oven to 350°F. Beat butter with a heavy-duty stand mixer on medium speed until fluffy; gradually add sugar, beating until well blended. Add egg yolks, 1 at a time, beating just until blended. Add extracts; beat until blended.

2. Stir together flour, baking powder, and salt in a bowl; add to butter mixture alternately with coconut milk, beginning and ending with flour mixture. Beat at low speed just until blended after each addition. Stir in coconut and 1 cup of the pecans.

3. Beat egg whites on high speed until stiff peaks form; fold one-third of egg whites into batter. Gently fold in remaining beaten egg whites just until combined. Place 30 paper baking cups in 3 (12-cup) muffin pans; spoon batter into cups, filling two-thirds full.

4. Bake in preheated oven until a wooden pick inserted in centers comes out clean, 18 to 20 minutes. Remove from pans to wire racks; cool completely, 30 minutes.

5. Spread Coconut-Cream Cheese Frosting onto cupcakes, and sprinkle with remaining ⅓ cup toasted pecans.

Coconut-Cream Cheese Frosting
ACTIVE 10 MIN. - TOTAL 10 MIN.
MAKES 4 CUPS

Beat 1 (8-oz.) pkg. cream cheese, softened, and ½ cup salted butter, softened, with an electric mixer on medium speed until creamy; add 3 Tbsp. whole milk and 1 tsp. vanilla extract, beating well. Gradually add 1 (16-oz.) pkg. powdered sugar, sifted, beating until smooth. Stir in 1 (7-oz.) pkg. sweetened flaked coconut.

Mini Pecan Monkey Bread Loaves
ACTIVE 20 MIN. - TOTAL 1 HOUR, 45 MIN.
SERVES 12

1 (1-lb., 9-oz.) pkg. frozen yeast roll dough (24 count)
½ cup granulated sugar
½ cup packed light brown sugar
2 tsp. ground cinnamon
¼ tsp. ground ginger
1 ¼ cups chopped toasted pecans
½ cup salted butter, melted
  Caramel Topping (recipe follows)

1. Thaw roll dough according to package directions; cut rolls in half. Stir together sugars, cinnamon, and ginger in a small bowl. Coat 2 (6-cavity) mini fluted tube cake pans with cooking spray. Sprinkle 1 tablespoon pecans in the bottom of each cavity.

2. Coat each roll half in melted butter; dredge in sugar mixture. Place 4 coated roll halves on pecans in each cavity, and top each with 1 teaspoon of the remaining sugar mixture. Drizzle with any remaining melted butter. (Discard any leftover sugar mixture.) Sprinkle remaining ½ cup pecans over loaves. Spoon Caramel Topping over loaves.

3. Cover each pan with plastic wrap, and let rise until doubled in size, about 1 hour.

4. Preheat oven to 325°F. Bake until golden brown and done, 20 to 25 minutes. Let stand in pans on a wire rack 5 minutes. Invert loaves onto a platter, and spoon any remaining topping from pans onto loaves. Serve warm.

Caramel Topping
ACTIVE 10 MIN. - TOTAL 10 MIN.
MAKES ABOUT 1 CUP

Bring ¾ cup packed light brown sugar, 6 Tbsp. salted butter, and ¼ cup heavy cream to a boil in a small saucepan over medium, stirring constantly; boil, stirring constantly, 1 minute. Remove from heat, and stir in 1 tsp. vanilla extract. Stir constantly 3 minutes; use immediately.

PUMPKIN-SPICE BUNDT

Candied pecans and a rich, buttery icing turn a simple pumpkin Bundt cake into a grand finale dessert. For the smoothest texture and most impressive presentation, make sure the icing is still warm when you spoon it over the cake (recipe, page 257).

TOASTED COCONUT-PECAN CUPCAKES WITH COCONUT-CREAM CHEESE FROSTING

Coconut and pecans are a match made in Southern dessert heaven, so these cupcakes are divine. Coconut extract and coconut milk (be sure to shake the can) make the pecan-filled cake taste and smell sensational.

BUTTER PECAN LAYER CAKE WITH BROWNED BUTTER FROSTING

Nutty Browned Butter Frosting meets tender pecan cake in this showstopping three-layer dessert. When browning the butter for the frosting, pour the butter into a bowl as soon as it turns golden brown, or it will continue to cook and get too dark (recipe, page 257).

FUDGY FLOURLESS CHOCOLATE-PECAN COOKIES

Believe it or not, these chewy, brownie-like cookies are gluten free. Try not to eat them all in one sitting–our Test Kitchen found them especially hard to resist.

ACTIVE 15 MIN. - TOTAL 45 MIN.

MAKES ABOUT 20

- 3 cups powdered sugar
- ⅔ cup unsweetened cocoa
- ¼ tsp. table salt
- 3 large egg whites, at room temperature
- 2 tsp. vanilla extract
- 1 (4-oz.) semisweet chocolate bar, chopped
- 1 cup chopped toasted pecans

1. Preheat oven to 350°F. Sift together powdered sugar, cocoa, and salt in a large bowl.

2. Whisk egg whites until frothy. Stir egg whites and vanilla into powdered sugar mixture. (Batter will be very thick.) Stir in chopped chocolate and pecans until well combined.

3. Drop cookies 3 inches apart using a 1½-inch cookie scoop (about 2 tablespoons) on a parchment paper-lined baking sheet lightly greased with cooking spray.

4. Bake in preheated oven until tops are shiny and cracked, 8 to 10 minutes. Cool on baking sheet 5 minutes; transfer to wire racks, and cool completely, about 15 minutes.

Baked Shells
and Greens,
page 268

Weeknight Wonders

Seven satisfying suppers—all ready in
30 minutes or less—to help make the busy
back-to-school season run like clockwork

CRISP BITS OF BACON
GIVE THIS NUTRITIOUS
STEW A RICHER AND
DEEPER FLAVOR

Quick Chicken and Barley Stew

Cool fall nights call for warm, comforting suppers. This chicken stew is filled with good-for-you vegetables and whole grains.

ACTIVE 15 MIN. - TOTAL 30 MIN.
SERVES 4

- 3 bacon slices
- 1 Tbsp. olive oil
- 1 cup chopped yellow onion (about 1 medium onion)
- 1 cup ¼-inch-thick diagonally cut carrots (about 2 medium carrots)
- 1 cup ¼-inch-thick diagonally cut celery (about 3 stalks)
- 1 Tbsp. garlic cloves, minced (about 3 garlic cloves)
- 1 tsp. kosher salt
- ½ tsp. black pepper
- 4 (6-oz.) boneless, skinless chicken breasts
- 4 cups low-sodium chicken broth
- 1 cup uncooked quick-cooking barley
- 1 (8-oz.) pkg. baby spinach
- 2 Tbsp. chopped fresh flat-leaf parsley

1. Cook bacon in a large Dutch oven over medium until crisp, about 6 minutes, turning once. Transfer bacon to a plate lined with paper towels, reserving drippings in Dutch oven. Crumble bacon, and set aside.

2. Add olive oil to drippings in Dutch oven; increase heat to medium-high. Add yellow onion, carrots, and celery; cook, stirring occasionally, until tender, about 3 to 4 minutes. Stir in garlic, kosher salt, and pepper, and cook until fragrant, about 1 minute.

3. Add chicken and broth to Dutch oven. Cook on medium-high until broth begins to boil, about 2 to 3 minutes. Reduce heat to medium-low. Stir in barley, and cook until chicken is cooked through and a thermometer inserted in the thickest portion reads 165°F, about 8 to 10 minutes more. Remove chicken, shred into large pieces, and return to Dutch oven. Add spinach, and stir until wilted, about 1 minute. Stir in parsley; top each serving with crumbled bacon.

Nutritional information (per serving):
Calories: 469 - Protein: 51g - Carbs: 41g - Fiber: 7g - Fat: 12g

Burrito Bowls

Charred corn, seasoned black beans, creamy avocado, tangy pico de gallo, cilantro-lime rice—every bite of this burrito in a bowl is a delicious surprise.

ACTIVE 10 MIN. - TOTAL 10 MIN.
SERVES 4

- 1 (15-oz.) can unsalted black beans, drained and rinsed
- ¼ cup water
- ½ tsp. chili powder
- ¼ tsp. ground cumin
- ½ tsp. kosher salt, divided
- 1 Tbsp. olive oil
- 1 cup fresh corn kernels (from 2 ears)
- 1 Tbsp. fresh lime juice (from 1 lime), divided

- 1 (8.8-oz.) pouch microwavable brown rice
- ¼ cup chopped fresh cilantro, divided
- 4 cups finely chopped romaine lettuce hearts (from about 1 heart)
- 4 oz. queso blanco, crumbled (about 1 cup)
- 2 ripe avocados, sliced
- ½ cup pico de gallo
- 4 Tbsp. light sour cream

1. Combine beans, water, chili powder, cumin, and ¼ teaspoon of the salt in a small saucepan, and cook over medium until beans are hot, about 3 to 4 minutes. Remove from heat, and cover to keep warm.

2. Heat oil in a medium-size cast-iron skillet over medium-high. Add corn, and cook, stirring occasionally, until slightly charred, about 5 minutes. Sprinkle with 1½ teaspoons of the lime juice and remaining ¼ teaspoon salt. Set aside.

3. Cook brown rice according to package instructions, and transfer to a medium bowl. Stir in 2 tablespoons of the cilantro and remaining 1½ teaspoons lime juice.

4. Divide warm beans, corn, rice, lettuce, cheese, and avocado among 4 bowls. Top with pico de gallo, sour cream, and remaining 2 tablespoons cilantro.

Nutritional information (per serving):
Calories: 470 - Protein: 17g - Carbs: 51g - Fiber: 13g - Fat: 25g

Roasted Tomato Macaroni and Cheese

Mac and cheese is always a winner with the kids, but the addition of roasted tomatoes will delight grown-ups too. For the smoothest, creamiest results, we let the white sauce cool slightly before whisking in the shredded cheeses.

ACTIVE 20 MIN. - TOTAL 1 HOUR
SERVES 6

- 8 oz. uncooked elbow macaroni
- 4 plum tomatoes (about 1 lb.), cut into ¼-inch-thick slices
- 1 Tbsp. olive oil
- 1 tsp. chopped fresh oregano
- ¼ tsp. black pepper
- 1¼ tsp. kosher salt, divided
- 1 Tbsp. unsalted butter
- 2 Tbsp. all-purpose flour
- ½ tsp. dry mustard
- 1½ cups 2% reduced-fat milk
- 4 oz. Monterey Jack cheese, shredded (about 1 cup)
- 3 oz. sharp Cheddar cheese, shredded (about ¾ cup)
- 2 oz. fontina cheese, shredded (about ½ cup)
- 1 oz. Parmesan cheese, grated (about ⅓ cup)

1. Cook pasta according to package directions. Drain and set aside.

2. Preheat oven to 450°F. Place tomato slices on a wire rack on a baking sheet. Brush on oil, and sprinkle with oregano, pepper, and ¼ teaspoon of the salt. Bake in preheated oven until slightly charred, about 18 to 20 minutes.

3. Meanwhile, melt butter in a medium saucepan over medium until melted, about 1 minute. Whisk in flour, and cook, whisking constantly, until the mixture takes on a slightly nutty color and smell, about 2 to 3 minutes. Whisk in dry mustard. Slowly whisk in milk, whisking constantly, and continue to cook until slightly thickened, about 4 to 5 minutes. Remove from heat, and cool slightly, about 3 minutes. Slowly whisk in Monterey Jack, Cheddar, fontina, and remaining 1 teaspoon salt; whisk constantly to combine and melt cheeses, about 2 minutes. Stir in pasta.

4. Spoon pasta mixture into a lightly greased 11- x 7-inch (2-quart) baking dish, and top with tomato slices. Sprinkle with Parmesan cheese. Bake at 450°F until bubbly and tomatoes are charred and aromatic, about 10 minutes. Serve immediately.

Nutritional information (per serving):
Calories: 411 - Protein: 19g - Carbs: 36g - Fiber: 2g - Fat: 21g

MICROWAVABLE RICE COOKS IN MINUTES TO COMPLETE THIS EASY, FLAVORFUL MEAL.

Sheet Pan Shrimp and Vegetables with Rice

Roasted lemon, garlic, and thyme give this shrimp dinner a heavenly taste and aroma; cooking it on one baking sheet makes assembly and cleanup a breeze.

ACTIVE 10 MIN. - TOTAL 25 MIN.
SERVES 4

- 2 Tbsp. olive oil
- 1 Tbsp. minced garlic (about 3 garlic cloves)
- ¼ tsp. crushed red pepper
- 1½ tsp. fresh thyme leaves, divided
- 1 lb. raw medium shrimp, peeled and deveined
- 1 pt. grape tomatoes
- 1 medium zucchini (about 5 oz.), cut diagonally into ½-inch slices (about 1 cup)
- 1 medium-size yellow squash (about 5 oz.), cut diagonally into ½-inch slices (about 1 cup)
- 1 lemon, cut into quarters
- 1 tsp. kosher salt
- ½ tsp. black pepper
- 2 (8.5-oz.) pouches microwavable basmati rice

1. Preheat broiler with oven rack 6 inches from heat.

2. Stir together olive oil, garlic, crushed red pepper, and ¾ teaspoon of the thyme in a small bowl. Place shrimp and tomatoes in 2 separate bowls. Combine zucchini and yellow squash in a third bowl. Toss each with one-third of oil mixture.

3. Heat a rimmed baking sheet in the oven, 2 minutes. Add zucchini, squash, and lemon (flesh side up) to hot baking sheet, and bake until squash begins to soften, about 5 minutes. Add tomatoes, and bake until tomatoes begin to burst, about 5 minutes. Stir in shrimp; bake until shrimp are cooked through and zucchini is tender and lightly browned, about 5 minutes. Remove from oven, and sprinkle with salt and pepper. Squeeze juice from roasted lemon over vegetables; stir to combine.

4. Cook rice according to package directions. Divide rice, shrimp, and vegetables among 4 plates. Top evenly with remaining ¾ teaspoon thyme.

Nutritional information (per serving):
Calories: 371 - Protein: 22g - Carbs: 48g - Fiber: 3g - Fat: 11g

CANDIED PECANS
ADD SWEETNESS
AND CRUNCH TO
THIS SIMPLE SALAD.

Kale and Sweet Potato Salad with Chicken

Can't convince the kids that kale is a delicious green? Use chopped romaine hearts or spinach for a good substitute.

ACTIVE 30 MIN. - TOTAL 30 MIN.
SERVES 4

- 2 Tbsp. fresh lemon juice (from 1 lemon)
- 1 tsp. Dijon mustard
- ½ tsp. honey
- 1 tsp. kosher salt, divided
- 6 Tbsp. olive oil, divided
- 1½ cups cubed sweet potato (from 1 [8-oz.] sweet potato)
- 1 tsp. finely chopped fresh rosemary, divided
- ½ tsp. black pepper, divided
- 4 (5-oz.) boneless, skin-on chicken breasts
- 1 tsp. salted butter
- 1 tsp. light brown sugar
- ¼ cup chopped pecans, toasted
- 8 oz. kale leaves, thinly sliced (about 7 cups loosely packed)

1. Whisk together lemon juice, mustard, honey, and ½ teaspoon of the salt until combined. While whisking, slowly drizzle in 4 tablespoons of the oil to emulsify. Set aside.

2. Preheat oven to 425°F. Toss together sweet potatoes and 1 tablespoon of the oil, ½ teaspoon of the rosemary, and ¼ teaspoon each of the salt and pepper. Spread in a single layer on 1 end of a large rimmed baking sheet.

3. Rub chicken with remaining 1 tablespoon oil, and place on other end of baking sheet, skin side up. Sprinkle with remaining ½ teaspoon rosemary, ¼ teaspoon salt, and ¼ teaspoon pepper.

4. Roast in preheated oven until sweet potatoes are tender (stirring potatoes once halfway through) and chicken is golden brown and a thermometer inserted in thickest portion registers 165°F, about 20 minutes. Let sweet potatoes and chicken cool.

5. Meanwhile, melt butter in a small skillet over medium. Add sugar, and cook, stirring constantly, until dissolved, about 1 minute. Add pecans, and cook, stirring, until sugar mixture no longer sticks to the pan and instead coats the pecans. Remove from heat. Spread pecans in a single layer on parchment paper; cool completely, 10 minutes.

6. Cut chicken into ½-inch slices. Combine kale and sweet potatoes in a large bowl; drizzle with half of the dressing, and toss gently to coat. Divide mixture among 4 plates; top with sliced chicken and candied pecans. Drizzle with remaining dressing.

Nutritional information (per serving):
Calories: 487 - Protein: 31g - Carbs: 15g -
Fiber: 2g - Fat 34g

Baked Shells and Greens

Give your go-to lasagna the week off, and try this hearty, meaty baked pasta that's easier to make and also a crowd-pleaser.

ACTIVE 15 MIN. - TOTAL 30 MIN.
SERVES 5

- 8 oz. uncooked medium shell pasta
- 1 Tbsp. olive oil
- 1 cup chopped white onion (from 1 large onion)
- 1 Tbsp. minced garlic (about 2 garlic cloves)
- 1 lb. ground turkey
- 1 bunch Swiss chard, stems removed, chopped (about 10 oz. chopped leaves)
- ¾ tsp. kosher salt
- ½ tsp. black pepper
- 1 (24-oz.) jar lower-sodium marinara sauce
- ½ cup small fresh basil leaves, divided
- 1 (8-oz.) pkg. preshredded whole-milk mozzarella cheese

1. Preheat oven to 350°F. Cook shell pasta according to package directions; drain and cover to keep warm.

2. While pasta cooks, heat olive oil in a large skillet over medium. Add onion, and cook, stirring often, until translucent, about 3 minutes. Add minced garlic, and cook, stirring constantly, until fragrant, about 30 seconds. Add ground turkey, and cook, stirring often, until turkey is browned and cooked through, about 5 minutes. Working in batches, add chopped Swiss chard and cook, stirring constantly, until wilted, about 2 minutes. Sprinkle mixture with salt and pepper. Stir in marinara sauce, and bring mixture to a boil. Remove from heat, and add ¼ cup of the chopped fresh basil. Stir to combine.

3. Stir together pasta and marinara mixture in a lightly greased 13- x 9-inch baking dish until combined. Top mixture with shredded mozzarella, and bake in preheated oven until cheese is melted, about 5 to 7 minutes. Sprinkle with remaining ¼ cup fresh basil leaves, and serve hot.

Nutritional information (per serving):
Calories: 449 - Protein: 31g - Carbs: 41g - Fiber: 4g - Fat: 18g

BLACK-EYED PEAS TAKE THE PLACE OF CHICKPEAS IN THIS NEW SOUTHERN SPIN ON FALAFEL.

Black-Eyed Pea Fritter Sandwiches with Slaw

Tuck the crunchy red cabbage slaw into the pita bread, or serve it as a side salad.

ACTIVE 25 MIN. - TOTAL 25 MIN.
SERVES 6

- 2 (16-oz.) cans black-eyed peas, drained and rinsed
- 1 medium-size red bell pepper
- 1 cup finely chopped yellow onion (from 1 medium onion)
- 2 large eggs, lightly beaten
- ½ cup all-purpose flour
- 1¼ tsp. kosher salt, divided
- ½ tsp. black pepper, divided
- 2 cups shredded red cabbage
- ½ cup julienne carrots
- 2 Tbsp. fresh lemon juice
- 1 Tbsp. honey
- 1 Tbsp. white wine vinegar
- 6 Tbsp. olive oil, divided
- ¾ cup plain low-fat yogurt
- 1 tsp. Dijon mustard
- 3 (2-oz.) whole-wheat pita rounds, halved
- ½ cup chopped fresh cilantro

1. Roughly mash black-eyed peas using a potato masher in a large bowl. Thinly slice half of the red bell pepper, and set aside. Finely chop remaining half of bell pepper. Add finely chopped bell pepper, yellow onion, and eggs to peas; stir, using a fork, to combine. Add flour, ¾ teaspoon of the salt, and ¼ teaspoon of the black pepper, and stir with fork until a loose dough is formed. Chill until ready to use.

2. Combine sliced bell pepper, cabbage, and carrots in a large bowl. Whisk together lemon juice, honey, white wine vinegar, 4 tablespoons of the olive oil, ¼ teaspoon of the salt, and ⅛ teaspoon of the black pepper in a small bowl; pour over cabbage mixture, and toss to coat. Chill 15 minutes or until ready to serve (up to 30 minutes).

3. Whisk together yogurt, Dijon mustard, remaining ¼ teaspoon kosher salt and ⅛ teaspoon black pepper to combine. Set aside.

4. Heat remaining 2 tablespoons oil in a large nonstick skillet over medium-high. Working in 2 batches, drop ¼-cup portions of fritter dough in hot oil and press into patties using the back of a spoon. Cook until browned, about 2 minutes. Turn and brown other side, 1 to 2 minutes more. Place fritters on a plate until ready to serve. Fill each pita half with 2 fritters. Top each evenly with slaw, yogurt sauce, and cilantro.

Nutritional information (per serving):
Calories: 353 - Protein: 17g - Carbs: 55g - Fiber: 9g - Fat: 18g

PAN-FRIED OKRA
HAS LESS FAT
THAN DEEP-FRIED.
RECIPE, PAGE 271

Easy Okra

Three new spins on this signature Southern veggie

LOVE OKRA. As I write this, a tiny silver okra pendant hangs on a necklace around my neck. This simple little pod is my talisman, a reminder of my "Southernness" and my calling as a Southern chef and food writer.

This garden gem is integral to many of the rich, thick, and spicy gumbos of Louisiana. A pan of stewed okra and tomatoes screams summer from Texas to the Carolinas. Sizzling-hot fried okra has been scooped from black cast-iron skillets across the Deep South for many generations. Pickled okra, once a way to preserve the vegetable at the end of the season, now routinely bobs in martini glasses. As Southern cooking continues to evolve, that's just the beginning.

If we're talking okra, we must acknowledge the elephant in the room: the slime. My top tips for minimizing okra's naturally mucilaginous texture? Add tomato, lemon juice, vinegar, or some other acid when cooking. Also, cook it quickly over high heat, and don't overcrowd the pan. The three delicious recipes that follow focus on this Southern jewel and these slime-busting tricks.

CHICKPEAS
AND MIDDLE
EASTERN SPICES
LIVEN UP OKRA
AND TOMATOES.

Okra and Chickpeas in Fresh Tomato Sauce

Serve this colorful medley as a side or a boldly flavored vegetarian main dish.

ACTIVE 15 MIN. · TOTAL 30 MIN.
SERVES 6

- 2 Tbsp. extra-virgin olive oil, plus more for serving
- 1 medium-size yellow onion, chopped (about 1 ¾ cups)
- 2 garlic cloves, very finely chopped
- 5 garden-ripe tomatoes, cored and chopped (about 4 cups)
- 1 Tbsp. ground cumin
- 1 Tbsp. harissa (or Sriracha chili sauce)
- 1 tsp. lemon zest, plus 1 Tbsp. fresh juice (from 1 lemon)
- 1 lb. fresh okra, stems trimmed, cut into ½-inch-thick slices
- 1 ½ tsp. kosher salt, divided
- ¾ tsp. black pepper, divided
- 1 (15.5-oz.) can chickpeas, drained and rinsed
- ¼ cup chopped fresh flat-leaf parsley

1. Heat oil in a large skillet over medium-low. Add yellow onion, and cook, stirring often, until soft and translucent, about 6 minutes. Add garlic and cook, stirring often, until fragrant, 45 to 60 seconds. Add tomatoes, cumin, harissa, lemon zest, and lemon juice, and cook, stirring once or twice, until tomatoes start to break down, about 5 minutes.

2. Add okra, 1 teaspoon of the kosher salt, and ½ teaspoon of the black pepper. Reduce heat to low, and cover skillet. Cook, stirring occasionally, until okra is just tender, about 10 minutes.

3. Add chickpeas, and stir to combine. Cover and cook just until chickpeas are heated through, about 3 minutes. Stir in chopped parsley and remaining ½ teaspoon salt and ¼ teaspoon pepper. Serve immediately.

Grilled Creole Chicken and Okra

ACTIVE 30 MIN. - TOTAL 45 MIN.

SERVES 4

- 1½ lb. boneless, skinless chicken thighs, cut into 2-inch pieces
- 12 oz. smoked andouille sausage, cut into 1-inch-thick pieces
- 1 pt. grape tomatoes
- 12 oz. finger-size fresh okra, stems trimmed (about 4 cups)
- 1 large sweet onion (about 12 oz.), cut into ¼-inch-thick rings
- 1 medium-size red bell pepper, cut into 1-inch squares
- 1 medium-size poblano chile or green bell pepper, cut into 1-inch squares
- ¼ cup pure olive oil
- 1 Tbsp. Creole or Cajun seasoning, divided
- 12 (10-inch) metal skewers
- ¼ cup ketchup, warmed
- 4 scallions, white and pale green parts only, chopped
  Hot sauce (optional)

1. Prepare a charcoal fire using about 6 pounds of charcoal briquettes; let burn until coals are completely covered with a thin coating of light gray ash, 20 to 30 minutes. Spread the coals evenly over grill bottom; place grate on grill, and heat until hot. (It is hot when you can hold your hand 5 inches above the grill surface for no longer than 3 or 4 seconds.) Or preheat a gas grill to high (450°F to 550°F).

2. Combine chicken, sausage, tomatoes, okra, onion, bell pepper, and poblano in a large bowl. Add oil and 2 teaspoons of the Creole seasoning, and toss to coat. Thread chicken, sausage, tomatoes, and okra, separately, onto 10-inch metal skewers. Thread bell pepper and poblano onto a 10-inch skewer. (You will end up with a skewer of chicken, a skewer of sausage, etc. The onions will go directly on the grill. You can use a metal grilling basket instead of skewers for the vegetables.)

3. Place chicken on grate over hottest part of grill; arrange sausage over slightly cooler heat. Arrange onions and the skewered vegetables at the edges of the grill. Grill, uncovered, turning once or twice, until chicken juices run clear and chicken is done, the sausage is heated through, and the vegetables are tender and slightly charred, 8 to 10 minutes. Remove meat and vegetables from skewers, and transfer with onion to a large bowl.

4. Add ketchup and scallions to grilled mixture in bowl, and toss together. Immediately cover tightly with plastic wrap or aluminum foil, and let stand until vegetables are slightly wilted, about 5 minutes. Remove plastic wrap from bowl. Stir to combine; sprinkle with remaining 1 teaspoon Creole seasoning and, if desired, hot sauce.

Pan-Fried Okra with Cornmeal

Using two medium skillets gives the okra plenty of room to cook up extra crispy. Or if you prefer, you can make all of the okra in a single large skillet.

ACTIVE 10 MIN. - TOTAL 28 MIN.

SERVES 4

- 6 Tbsp. canola oil, divided
- 2 lb. fresh okra, stems trimmed, cut into ½-inch pieces
- 1½ tsp. coarse sea salt
- 1 tsp. black pepper
- ⅔ cup fine yellow cornmeal
- ⅛ tsp. cayenne pepper

Place 1½ tablespoons of the canola oil in each of 2 medium-size nonstick skillets, and heat over medium-high. Divide okra between skillets, and stir to coat. Cover and cook, stirring occasionally, until bright green, about 10 minutes. Sprinkle okra in each skillet with ¾ teaspoon salt and ½ teaspoon black pepper. Divide yellow cornmeal and cayenne pepper evenly between skillets; stir to coat. Drizzle 1½ tablespoons oil over mixture in each skillet, and cook, uncovered, stirring occasionally, until okra is tender and browned, about 6 minutes.

SERVE GRILLED CREOLE CHICKEN AND OKRA OVER STEAMED RICE, AND ADD HOT SAUCE FOR AN EXTRA KICK.

The Scoop on Cobbler

Welcome fall with this hot, bubbling, old-fashioned apple dessert

COBBLER MAY BE one of the homiest-looking desserts, but it's actually a delicate balancing act between the tender topping and cooked fruit. Overdo it on the filling, and you're digging into a soupy pie; add too much topping, and you're eating biscuits with fruit sauce. But get the ratio just right, and it's pure comfort in a bowl.

How you decide to top a cobbler is a matter of personal preference. Some cooks choose a chewy layer of piecrust, others like craggy drop biscuits, and some opt for a thin and cakelike batter that bakes up around the fruit. (Just don't use streusel— that's a crisp, folks.) While we would never turn down a bowl of any of these cobblers, our Test Kitchen prefers the look and taste of tender, flaky biscuits that are made with a round cutter.

The second key to mastering this classic is to cook the fruit before the crust is added, which prevents "al dente" apples and infuses the fruit with cinnamon, lemon, and brown sugar.

While we love summer cobblers made with peaches or berries, fall might be our favorite time of year for this cozy dessert. A fresh crop of apples is in season, the weather is cool enough to turn on the oven, and there aren't many desserts that taste better topped with a dollop of vanilla ice cream— our third secret to a great apple cobbler.

EASY AS 1-2-3

①
SUGAR
Light brown sugar is a perfect match for apples and cinnamon; it's more complex than granulated sugar but not as intense as dark brown sugar.

②
FLOUR
White Lily self-rising soft wheat flour is our Test Kitchen's go-to for the lightest, most tender biscuits. We use all-purpose flour to thicken the filling.

③
LEMON ZEST AND JUICE
A little fresh lemon brightens the sweetness of the apples.

For Single Servings

Preheat oven and prepare apple filling as directed in Step 1. Prepare biscuit dough as directed in Step 2. Proceed with Step 3, omitting baking dish and dividing filling evenly among 8 lightly greased 8-oz. ramekins. Place ramekins on a baking sheet; bake in preheated oven 10 minutes. Proceed with Step 4, reducing total number of biscuits to 8. Proceed with Step 5, placing 1 biscuit on top of hot filling in each ramekin. Brush each with melted butter, and sprinkle with sugar. Bake and cool as directed. Top servings with ice cream.

Classic Apple Cobbler

ACTIVE 1 HOUR • TOTAL 2 HOURS, 10 MIN., INCLUDING 30 MIN. COOLING

SERVES 6

- 2 ½ lb. Granny Smith apples (about 5 large), peeled and cut into ½-inch-thick wedges
- 2 ½ lb. Braeburn apples (about 5 large), peeled and cut into ½-inch-thick wedges
- 1 ¼ cups firmly packed light brown sugar
- 4 Tbsp. all-purpose flour
- 6 Tbsp. salted butter, divided
- 2 cups self-rising soft wheat flour (such as White Lily)
- 3 Tbsp. granulated sugar, divided
- ½ cup cold salted butter, cut into small cubes
- 1 tsp. lemon zest, plus 2 Tbsp. fresh juice (from 1 lemon)
- ¾ tsp. ground cinnamon
- ½ tsp. table salt
- ¾ - 1 cup cold heavy cream, divided
  Vanilla ice cream

1. Preheat oven to 425°F. Toss together apples, brown sugar, and all-purpose flour in a large bowl. Melt 4 tablespoons of the butter in a large skillet over medium-high. Add apple mixture, and cook, stirring often, until apples are tender and syrup thickens, 20 to 25 minutes.

2. Meanwhile, stir together self-rising flour and 2 tablespoons of the granulated sugar in a large bowl. Cut ½ cup cold butter cubes into self-rising flour mixture with a pastry blender or fork until mixture is crumbly and resembles small peas; freeze 10 minutes.

3. Remove apples from heat; stir in lemon zest and juice, cinnamon, and salt. Spoon apple mixture into a lightly greased 8-inch square (2-quart) baking dish. Bake in preheated oven 15 minutes, placing a baking sheet on oven rack directly below dish to catch any drips.

4. Meanwhile, make a well in center of flour mixture. Add ¾ cup cream; stir just until dough comes together, adding additional cream up to 1 cup, 1 tablespoon at a time, if needed. Turn dough out onto a lightly floured surface, and knead lightly 3 or 4 times. Roll or pat dough to ¾- to 1-inch thickness. Cut with a 2 ½-inch round cutter; reroll scraps once, and repeat process to make 9 biscuits.

5. Place biscuits on top of hot apple mixture in baking dish. Melt remaining 2 tablespoons butter, and brush over biscuits. Sprinkle biscuits with remaining 1 tablespoon granulated sugar. Return cobbler to oven, and bake until biscuits are golden and done, 15 to 17 minutes. Cool 30 minutes; top servings with ice cream.

Fried Nuts, Three Ways

ACTIVE 10 MIN. - TOTAL 40 MIN.
SERVES 8

Bring 10 cups **water** and 2 Tbsp. **kosher salt** to a boil in a large pot over high. Add 2 cups **nuts,** and cook until slightly softened, 30 to 45 seconds. Drain nuts, and spread on paper towels; cool 2 minutes. Meanwhile, pour **canola oil** to a depth of 1 ½ inches into a Dutch oven. Heat over medium-high to 325°F. Toss together nuts and ⅓ cup **powdered sugar** in a bowl; stir until nuts are evenly coated with sugar and almost all excess sugar is melted. Carefully add coated nuts to hot oil; fry until lightly golden, about 3 minutes. Using a spider skimmer or large slotted spoon, remove nuts to paper towels; drain briefly, about 10 seconds. Transfer hot nuts to a medium bowl, and toss with **spice mixture** (recipes follow). Cool 30 minutes.

HOT-AND-SWEET PEANUTS

NUTS: 2 cups raw, shelled **peanuts**

SPICE MIXTURE: Combine 2 Tbsp. **light brown sugar,** 1 tsp. **cayenne pepper,** and ½ tsp. each **chili powder** and **kosher salt.**

FIVE-SPICE PECANS

NUTS: 2 cups **pecan** halves

SPICE MIXTURE: Combine 2 tsp. **kosher salt,** 1 tsp. **orange zest,** and ¾ tsp. **Chinese five-spice powder.**

ROSEMARY ALMONDS

NUTS: 2 cups whole blanched **almonds**

SPICE MIXTURE: Combine 2 Tbsp. fresh **rosemary** leaves and 2 tsp. **kosher salt** in a spice grinder; pulse until powdery, 15 times.

Five-Spice Pecans

Rosemary Almonds

Hot-and-Sweet Peanuts

Fancy Fried Nuts

Surprisingly simple ways to spice up peanuts, pecans, and almonds

October

TRUE GRITS

The life cycle of each bag of Jim Barkley's
extraordinary artisan grits can be measured
in footsteps—from corn row to gristmill to cloth sack

To become a maker and purveyor of artisan grits, one needs dried corn, a mill, and a plan. Passion for good grits doesn't hurt either.

In fact, that's where Jim Barkley started, and then the rest followed. At Barkley's Mill on Southern Cross Farm in Weaverville, North Carolina, what began as a lark to make grits to give as holiday gifts has now grown into a burgeoning specialty-foods company that sells heirloom grits to upscale restaurants.

Much like the wooden waterwheel chugging round on the mill at the front edge of their farm and estate, Barkley and his family took a few turns on their way to milling premium grits. After dabbling in raising cattle and a couple of crops, Southern Cross Farm found its true north when the Barkleys questioned the type of corn, an often overlooked component in commercial grits. Their answer turned out to be an heirloom selection called Hickory King Dent corn.

Just as table grapes differ from vineyard grapes, fresh table corn is unlike corn destined to be dried and milled. Some of the old-timers living in the Blue Ridge Mountains dreamily recalled a corn selection called Hickory King Dent that dates back to the late 1800s and was praised for its robust flavor and texture when dried. One afternoon a few years ago, Barkley and his friends tasted dried-on-the-cob kernels, which they loosened with the sides of their thumbs and tumbled onto a wooden table in the corncrib. When the nibbling and vetting were done, their clear preference was for the chunky Hickory King Dent kernels, nearly the size of Scrabble tiles, off-white with a dark dot of germ that's visible in unbleached whole-grain grits.

Jim Barkley grows a prized selection of heirloom corn at his North Carolina farm.

And with that, Southern Cross Farm started growing Hickory King Dent. The stalks can reach a height of 16 feet, but each one bears only a couple of ears, which sport only eight rows of kernels. Like most heirloom vegetables, this open-pollinated and non-GMO corn is prized for its flavor, not its profusion and convenience.

Each kernel of corn that passes through Barkley's Mill is harvested, selected, and sorted by hand. It's slow going, taking four men eight hours to work through 50 bushels of ears. Barkley avers that repeated close inspection and hand-holding matters, even though it results in a quarter of the corn being culled for not meeting their standards. Perfect kernels move on to their mill—and not just any mill.

Barkley purchased two vintage (1919 and 1923) Williams Stone Burr Gristmills, which are now refurbished and mounted side by side in his pristine millhouse. To power the wheels, belts, and pulleys that ferry the corn from the bins to the grindstones, water burbles downhill from the same millpond that also irrigates the fields.

The beauty of these old machines is more than stone-deep: Grinding between vertical stones keeps the corn from overheating during the milling process, protecting the integrity of the whole grain. The freshly ground grits are scooped by hand into cloth sacks, tied closed, and chilled, which is how whole-grain grits should be stored. It's difficult to find more expensive grits, but the Barkleys believe that eaters who value corn grits that taste like corn will pay to partake.

—SHERI CASTLE

Cheesy Grits-and-Ale Soup

ACTIVE 50 MIN. - TOTAL 50 MIN.

SERVES 6

2	Tbsp. salted butter
½	large sweet onion, finely chopped
1	celery stalk, finely chopped
2	garlic cloves, minced
4	cups whole milk
1	(12-oz.) bottle brown ale
1 ½	cups reduced-sodium chicken broth
1 ½	tsp. kosher salt
¾	cup uncooked stone-ground grits
12	oz. extra-sharp Cheddar cheese, grated (about 3 cups)
2	tsp. cornstarch
½	tsp. cayenne pepper
2	tsp. Dijon mustard
1	tsp. Worcestershire sauce
	Thinly sliced scallions
	Garlicky Pumpernickel Croutons (recipe follows)

1. Melt butter in a Dutch oven over medium; add onion, celery, and garlic, and cook, stirring constantly, until softened, about 5 minutes. Stir in milk, ale, broth, and salt. Bring to a gentle simmer, and whisk in grits. Reduce heat to low; cook, whisking often, until grits are tender and thickened, about 25 minutes. (Liquid should barely bubble.)

2. Toss together cheese, cornstarch, and cayenne pepper in a bowl. Add cheese mixture to soup, ½ cup at a time, whisking until melted after each addition. Stir in mustard and Worcestershire sauce; add salt to taste. Top servings with scallions and Garlicky Pumpernickel Croutons.

Garlicky Pumpernickel Croutons

ACTIVE 10 MIN. - TOTAL 20 MIN.

MAKES 3 CUPS

Preheat oven to 400°F. Microwave 2 Tbsp. salted butter and 1 large minced garlic clove in a microwave-safe bowl on HIGH until butter is melted, about 30 seconds. Spread 3 cups torn pumpernickel bread on a baking sheet. Drizzle with butter mixture; toss to coat. Bake in preheated oven 8 to 10 minutes. Sprinkle with ½ tsp. kosher salt and ¼ tsp. black pepper.

Clockwise from top left: Chicken Chili Pot Pie with a cheesy grits crust; a view of Southern Cross Farm; rustic Italian-Style Grits and Greens with pulled pork and mushrooms; Hickory King Dent heirloom corn kernels

Buttermilk Stone–Ground Grits

Buttermilk adds a subtle, creamy tang to the grits. Enjoy them plain, or try one of our fun stir-ins or toppers.

ACTIVE 30 MIN. · TOTAL 30 MIN.
SERVES 4

Bring 4 cups water, 1 cup whole milk, and 1¼ tsp. kosher salt to a boil in a medium saucepan over medium-high. Gradually whisk in 1 cup uncooked stone-ground grits; return to a boil. Reduce heat to medium-low, and simmer, stirring occasionally, until creamy and thickened, 25 to 30 minutes. Remove from heat, and stir in ¾ cup whole buttermilk and 2 Tbsp. unsalted butter. Cover and keep warm until ready to serve.

STIR-INS AND TOPPERS

1 Spiced Pumpkin

Stir 1 cup canned pumpkin, 2 tsp. pure maple syrup, ¾ tsp. black pepper, and ½ tsp. pumpkin pie spice into warm grits. Sprinkle servings with spiced pecans.

2 Hatch Chile Breakfast Bowl

Stir 2 (4-oz.) cans diced hot Hatch green chiles, drained, and 8 oz. Monterey Jack cheese, shredded (about 2 cups), into warm grits. Top each serving with a fried egg, pico de gallo, and fresh cilantro leaves.

3 Pear-Granola

Peel and dice 2 large pears. Melt 2 Tbsp. unsalted butter in a small skillet over medium. Add pears, and cook until softened, about 5 minutes. Stir 4 to 5 Tbsp. light brown sugar and ½ tsp. ground cinnamon into warm grits. Top servings with cooked pears and your favorite crunchy granola.

4 Caramelized Onion and Pancetta

Cook 4 oz. diced pancetta in a large skillet over medium, stirring often, until browned and crisp. (You will have about ½ cup cooked pancetta.) Remove with a slotted spoon, reserving 2 Tbsp. drippings in skillet. Chop 2 medium-size sweet onions. Cook in reserved drippings over medium-high, stirring constantly until caramelized, 15 to 20 minutes. Stir in 1 ½ Tbsp. minced fresh sage. Stir onions and pancetta into warm grits. Sprinkle servings with crumbled blue cheese.

5 Country Ham and Shrimp

Stir 3 oz. Parmesan cheese, grated (about ¾ cup), into warm grits. Toss 1 lb. peeled and deveined raw medium-size shrimp with ¾ tsp. Creole seasoning. Cook ½ cup chopped country ham in 2 Tbsp. unsalted butter, melted in a small skillet over medium-high, stirring constantly, just until beginning to brown, about 3 minutes. Stir in shrimp and 2 garlic cloves, minced; cook, stirring constantly, 2 minutes. Stir in ½ cup sliced scallions, ¼ cup chicken stock, and ¼ cup dry white wine, and cook until shrimp just turn pink and liquid is reduced by about half, about 2 minutes. Serve shrimp mixture over warm grits.

6 Roasted Tomato and Garlic

Halve 1 ½ (10-oz.) containers grape tomatoes. Toss together tomatoes, 1 Tbsp. olive oil, ½ tsp. kosher salt, and ½ tsp. black pepper on an aluminum foil-lined baking sheet. Bake at 400°F until browned, about 30 minutes. Stir tomatoes, ¼ cup chopped fresh basil, and 2 garlic cloves, finely grated, into warm grits. Sprinkle servings with crumbled feta cheese.

7 Pimiento Cheese and Brisket

Stir 8 oz. Cheddar cheese, grated (about 2 cups), 1 (4-oz.) jar diced pimientos, drained, 3 scallions, thinly sliced, and ¾ tsp. Worcestershire sauce into warm grits. Top servings with sliced brisket and a drizzle of your favorite barbecue sauce.

8 Smoked Gouda and Andouille

Cook 8 oz. chopped andouille sausage in a large skillet over medium until lightly browned, about 4 minutes; drain on paper towels. Stir cooked sausage into warm grits. Add 8 oz. smoked Gouda cheese, shredded (about 2 cups), 2 Tbsp. chopped fresh flat-leaf parsley, and 1 Tbsp. hot sauce. Stir until Gouda cheese is melted and smooth.

9 Blackberry-Yogurt Grits

Omit buttermilk in grits. Stir ¾ cup plain Greek yogurt and 2 ½ Tbsp. honey into warm grits. Top servings with blackberry jam, fresh blackberries, toasted almonds, and a drizzle of honey.

10 Fresh Corn and Chèvre

Stir 2 cups fresh corn kernels (about 4 ears) into grits during last 5 minutes of cooking. Stir 4 oz. chèvre (goat cheese), crumbled (about ½ cup), and ⅓ cup chopped fresh chives into warm grits just before serving.

Chicken Chili Pot Pie

This hearty and comforting chicken chili is made with poblano chiles and butternut squash. You can make individual servings in 10-ounce ramekins or one large pot pie using a 3-quart baking dish. Either way, everyone will love the puffed, cheesy cilantro-grits crust.

ACTIVE 45 MIN. - TOTAL 2 HOURS, 10 MIN.
SERVES 6

- 1 ½ lb. ground dark meat chicken
- 2 poblano chiles, seeded and chopped
- 1 medium-size yellow onion, chopped
- 2 garlic cloves, minced
- 2 Tbsp. tomato paste
- 2 Tbsp. chili powder
- 2 tsp. ground cumin
- 1 (15-oz.) can black beans, drained and rinsed
- 1 (14.5-oz.) can diced tomatoes, drained
- ½ cup chicken stock
- ½ small butternut squash, peeled and cubed (about 2 cups)
- 3 tsp. kosher salt, divided
- 1 tsp. black pepper, divided
- 3 ½ cups water
- 1 cup uncooked yellow stone-ground grits
- 8 oz. extra-sharp Cheddar cheese, shredded (about 2 cups)
- ¾ cup chopped fresh cilantro, plus more cilantro leaves for garnish
- 3 large eggs, lightly beaten

1. Cook chicken, poblano chiles, onion, and garlic in a Dutch oven over medium-high until meat crumbles and is no longer pink, 10 to 12 minutes. Stir in tomato paste, chili powder, and cumin, and cook, stirring constantly, 1 minute. Stir in black beans, tomatoes, and chicken stock; bring to a boil. Reduce heat to medium-low, and simmer, stirring occasionally, 20 minutes.

2. Stir in squash, and cook until squash is just beginning to soften, about 5 minutes. Stir in 1 teaspoon of the salt and ½ teaspoon of the black pepper. Transfer chili to 6 lightly greased 10 oz. ramekins (or a 3-quart baking dish).

3. Preheat oven to 400°F. Bring water and 1 teaspoon of the salt to a boil in a large saucepan over high; whisk in grits, and cook, stirring often, until tender and thickened, about 25 minutes. Remove from heat, and whisk in cheese and cilantro. Stir in remaining 1 teaspoon salt and ½ teaspoon black pepper. Gradually stir about one-fourth of grits mixture into eggs; add egg mixture to remaining hot grits mixture, stirring constantly. Spoon hot grits mixture over chili.

4. Bake in preheated oven until crust is set and golden, 22 to 25 minutes for ramekins or 30 to 35 minutes for baking dish. Let stand 10 minutes. Garnish with cilantro leaves, if desired.

Italian-Style Grits and Greens

To serve this make-ahead meal family style, spread the Parmesan grits and greens on a wooden board or oversize platter placed in the center of your table. Top with pulled pork and garlicky sautéed mushrooms. Use your slow cooker to keep the grits warm until you're ready to serve. The pork can be made up to two days ahead and reheated in a skillet.

ACTIVE 30 MIN. - TOTAL 13 HOURS, INCLUDING 8 HOURS CHILLING
SERVES 6

- 9 garlic cloves
- 1 (3- to 3 ½-lb.) boneless pork shoulder roast (Boston butt)
- 1 Tbsp. granulated sugar
- 2 tsp. Italian seasoning
- 3 ½ tsp. kosher salt, divided
- 2 tsp. black pepper, divided
- 4 ½ cups water
- 1 ½ cups uncooked stone-ground grits
- ½ cup heavy cream
- 2 oz. Parmesan cheese, grated (about ½ cup), plus more for garnish
- 3 Tbsp. olive oil, divided
- 1 bunch curly kale, chopped
- 12 oz. assorted mushrooms, roughly chopped
- 1 large shallot, chopped
- 1 cup chicken stock
- 3 Tbsp. finely chopped fresh flat-leaf parsley
- Crushed red pepper

1. Mince 1 garlic clove, and set aside. Halve remaining 8 cloves. Make 16 small, deep cuts in roast, and insert garlic halves. Stir together granulated sugar, Italian seasoning, 2 teaspoons of the salt, and 1 ½ teaspoons of the black pepper. Place pork in a large bowl; rub with sugar mixture. Cover and chill 8 to 24 hours.

2. Preheat oven to 325°F. Place pork on a rack in a roasting pan, and bake in preheated oven until meat shreds easily with a fork, 4 to 4 ½ hours.

3. Meanwhile, stir together water and grits in a lightly greased 3- to 4-quart slow cooker. Let stand 2 minutes, allowing grits to settle to bottom; tilt slow cooker slightly, and skim off solids using a fine wire-mesh strainer. Cover and cook on HIGH until grits are tender and thickened, 2 ½ to 3 hours, stirring every 45 minutes. Add cream and grated Parmesan, and whisk until cheese is melted. Stir in 1 teaspoon of the salt and ¼ teaspoon of the pepper. Cover and keep warm.

4. Remove pork from oven; let stand 15 minutes. Shred pork with 2 forks. Heat 1 tablespoon of the oil in a large skillet over medium-high. Add kale, and cook, stirring constantly, until wilted and tender, about 3 minutes. Stir kale into grits. Wipe skillet clean.

5. Heat remaining 2 tablespoons oil in skillet over medium-high; add mushrooms and shallot, and cook, stirring constantly, until golden, 5 to 7 minutes. Add minced garlic, and cook 1 minute.

6. Add chicken stock and shredded pork, stirring and scraping to loosen browned bits from bottom of skillet. Cook until pork is thoroughly heated, about 3 minutes. Sprinkle with chopped fresh parsley and remaining ½ teaspoon salt and ¼ teaspoon black pepper. Spread warm grits on a large wooden board or warm piece of marble. Top with pork mixture. Garnish with crushed red pepper and additional Parmesan, if desired.

Bacon-and-Chive Grit Fries with Smoky Hot Ketchup

ACTIVE 30 MIN. - TOTAL 5 HOURS, 10 MIN., INCLUDING 4 HOURS, 15 MIN. CHILLING
SERVES 6

- 1 cup uncooked quick-cooking grits
- 2 cups whole milk
- 2 cups chicken stock
- 1 tsp. kosher salt
- 4 oz. fontina cheese, shredded (about 1 cup)
- ½ cup cooked and finely crumbled bacon (about 8 slices)
- ½ cup thinly sliced fresh chives
- ½ tsp. black pepper
- 1 ½ cups all-purpose flour
- 2 large eggs
- ¼ cup water
- 3 cups panko (Japanese-style breadcrumbs)
- Peanut oil

Smoky Hot Ketchup (recipe follows)

1. Prepare grits according to package directions, using milk, stock, and salt. Remove from heat; let stand 5 minutes. Add cheese, bacon, chives, and pepper, and stir until cheese is melted. Spoon mixture into a lightly greased 9-inch square pan; chill 4 to 24 hours. Invert grits onto a large cutting board. Cut into ¾-inch-thick, 4-inch-long strips.

2. Place flour in a shallow dish. Whisk together eggs and water in a second shallow dish. Place panko in a third shallow dish. Dredge grit fries in flour; dip in egg wash, and roll in panko, pressing gently to adhere. Place grit fries in freezer for 15 minutes.

3. Pour oil to a depth of 1 inch in a large, heavy skillet; heat over medium-high to 350°F. Fry grit fries, in batches, in hot oil until golden brown, 3 to 4 minutes. Drain on paper towels, and sprinkle with additional salt and pepper to taste. Place on a wire rack in a rimmed baking sheet, and keep warm in a 225°F oven up to 30 minutes, if desired. Serve warm with Smoky Hot Ketchup.

Smoky Hot Ketchup

MAKES 1 CUP

Stir together 1 cup ketchup, 1 Tbsp. hot sauce (such as Tabasco), and ¾ tsp. smoked paprika in a small bowl. Chill until ready to serve.

LET'S HAVE SUPPER

FOR SOUTHERNERS, A SUPPER CLUB IS MORE THAN A SHARED MEAL—IT'S A LIFELONG TIE THAT BINDS

BACON BOW TIE CRACKERS.
page 286

THE MENU

BACON BOW TIE CRACKERS

BRUSSELS SPROUT-AND-LEEK SLAW
with Bacon and Pecans

EASY EVERYTHING DINNER ROLLS

ROASTED BEET-AND-CITRUS SALAD
with Honey-Orange Vinaigrette

BRAISED COLA-AND-BOURBON
BRISKET

RUSTIC MASHED POTATOES
with Whole-Grain Mustard

SALTED CARAMEL BANANA PUDDING

BRUSSELS SPROUT-AND-LEEK SLAW
WITH BACON AND PECANS, *page 286*

A DINNER PARTY brings a group of people together over a meal, but it is just a one-off event. A potluck asks attendees to contribute food or drink, but the menu is lucky or not, as is the guest list. A cooking co-op shares the meal-prep duties, but participants do not always eat together. A supper club is a little bit of each of these, but it goes further, deeper, and longer.

Supper clubs gather regularly and remain intact for years, sometimes even decades. Members take their participation very seriously, sticking together despite life's inevitable interruptions and other challenges. The mix of participants—including their personalities and proclivities—is not indiscriminate. Everyone in the group must get along and have compatible expectations on how the supper club will operate.

There are no fixed rules for supper clubs, but there is surprising consistency on certain points. Members take turns as congenial host and charming guests. The host usually selects and prepares the entrée, the others provide sides and desserts, and those with the least interest or skill in cooking (or the busiest schedules of late) bring the beverages.

The menu is carefully orchestrated and often built around a chosen theme, which can be a type of cuisine, an occasion, or a curiosity to learn something new and different. No supper club meal should be mistaken for a humdrum dinner at home. However, if the host hits a snag at the last minute, everyone will go out or order in rather than cancel.

Food matters to supper clubs, but abiding friendship and consistent fellowship matter most. These close-knit cooks and eaters may get together around a table with one another more often than they do with their extended families. It's as though each member swears an amiable allegiance to just show up, time and again, carrying a bowl or a bottle and a readiness to share.

—SHERI CASTLE

Bacon Bow Tie Crackers

ACTIVE 10 MIN. - TOTAL 1 HOUR, 45 MIN.
SERVES 8

  8   thin bacon slices (about 6 oz.)

 24 rectangle-shaped buttery crackers
      (such as Club or Captain's
      Wafers)

1. Preheat oven to 250°F. Cut each bacon slice crosswise into thirds (to make a total of 24 pieces). Wrap 1 bacon piece around narrow center of each cracker without overlapping ends. Arrange in a single layer, seam side down, on a lightly greased wire rack set in a rimmed baking sheet.

2. Bake in preheated oven until bacon is crisp and center edges have pulled in to resemble a bow tie, about 1 hour and 30 minutes. Cool on wire rack 5 minutes before serving.

Brussels Sprout-and-Leek Slaw with Bacon and Pecans

ACTIVE 30 MIN. - TOTAL 45 MIN.
SERVES 8

  6   thick-cut bacon slices, diced
      (about 6 oz.)

  1   large leek, thinly sliced (about
      2 cups)

  1   lb. fresh Brussels sprouts,
      trimmed and shredded (about
      8 cups)

 ⅓   cup olive oil

 ¼   cup apple cider vinegar

  2   Tbsp. honey

 ½   tsp. kosher salt

 ¼   tsp. black pepper

 ½   cup chopped toasted pecans

  2   Tbsp. thinly sliced fresh chives

1. Cook bacon in a large, heavy skillet over medium until crisp, about 15 minutes. Transfer to a plate lined with paper towels. Reserve 1 tablespoon of the drippings in skillet; transfer 2 tablespoons of the drippings to a small bowl. Dice bacon, and set aside.

2. Add leeks to skillet, and cook, stirring often, 3 minutes. Combine leeks and Brussels sprouts in a large bowl.

3. Add olive oil, apple cider vinegar, honey, salt, and pepper to reserved

ROASTED BEET-AND-CITRUS SALAD WITH HONEY-ORANGE VINAIGRETTE

EASY EVERYTHING DINNER ROLLS

2 tablespoons of drippings, and whisk to combine. Add to Brussels sprouts and leeks; toss to coat. Stir in chopped pecans, chives, and diced bacon. Serve immediately.

Easy Everything Dinner Rolls

To make your own everything bagel seasoning mix for this recipe, combine 2 tablespoons sesame seeds, 1 tablespoon poppy seeds, 1 tablespoon dried minced onion, 2 teaspoons dried minced garlic, and 1 teaspoon coarse salt in a small bowl.

ACTIVE 10 MIN. - TOTAL 3 HOURS, 25 MIN.
MAKES 12

  1   large egg

 ½   cup everything bagel seasoning
      mix

 12 frozen, unbaked yeast dinner rolls
      (such as Rhodes or Bridgford)
      Olive oil, for drizzling

1. Whisk egg in a small bowl. Spread seasoning mix on a plate. Dip top and sides of each frozen roll in egg, and dip top of each roll in seasoning. Place in a single layer, seasoning side up, on a 9-inch baking pan lightly coated with cooking spray. Cover with plastic wrap lightly coated with cooking spray. Thaw,

let rise, and bake according to package directions.

2. Drizzle hot rolls lightly with oil; break rolls apart, and serve warm.

Roasted Beet-and-Citrus Salad with Honey-Orange Vinaigrette

ACTIVE 20 MIN. - TOTAL 2 HOURS, 5 MIN.
SERVES 8

  1   bunch red baby beets (about 1½ lb.)

  1   bunch yellow baby beets
      (about 1½ lb.)

  1   (24-oz.) jar refrigerated citrus
      salad, drained (such as
      Del Monte)

  3   Tbsp. white balsamic vinegar or
      rice wine vinegar

  2   Tbsp. floral honey (such as
      wildflower honey)

  1   Tbsp. orange zest (from 2 small
      oranges)

  1   tsp. kosher salt, divided

 ½   tsp. black pepper, divided

 ⅓   cup olive oil

  1   Tbsp. fresh thyme leaves

1. Preheat oven to 350°F. Scrub beets, and trim greens to 1 inch. Wrap red beets in a single layer in an aluminum foil pouch, closing it tightly. Wrap yellow beets in a second foil pouch. Bake in

RUSTIC MASHED POTATOES WITH WHOLE-GRAIN MUSTARD

BRAISED COLA-AND-BOURBON BRISKET

preheated oven until tender, about 1 hour and 15 minutes. Uncover and cool completely, about 30 minutes.

2. Rub beets to remove skins; slice into ¼-inch-thick rounds. Arrange on a serving platter. Arrange citrus segments on beets.

3. Whisk together vinegar, honey, zest, ½ teaspoon of the salt, and ¼ teaspoon of the pepper in a small bowl. Add the oil in a slow, steady stream, whisking continuously, until emulsified. Drizzle vinaigrette over beets and citrus. Sprinkle with thyme and remaining ½ teaspoon salt and ¼ teaspoon pepper. Serve at room temperature.

Braised Cola-and-Bourbon Brisket

ACTIVE 20 MIN. · TOTAL 3 HOURS, 50 MIN.
SERVES 8

- 1 (4 ½- to 5-lb.) first cut (flat) beef brisket, at room temperature
- 1 Tbsp. plus ½ tsp. kosher salt, divided
- 1 ½ tsp. plus ¼ tsp. black pepper, divided
- 2 Tbsp. vegetable oil
- 1 (14-oz.) bottle balsamic vinegar ketchup (such as Heinz)
- 1 (12-oz.) bottle cane-sweetened cola (such as Coca-Cola)
- 1 ½ cups lower-sodium chicken broth
- 1 (1-oz.) envelope dry onion soup and dip mix
- 1 Tbsp. herbes de Provence

- 6 medium carrots, halved and cut into 4-inch lengths
- 4 medium parsnips, halved and cut into 4-inch lengths
- 1 large yellow onion, finely chopped
- 2 Tbsp. bourbon
- 2 Tbsp. fresh thyme leaves

1. Preheat oven to 325°F. Sprinkle both sides of brisket with 1 tablespoon of the salt and 1 ½ teaspoons of the pepper. Heat oil in a Dutch oven over medium-high. Add brisket, and cook until deeply browned, 5 to 6 minutes on each side. Transfer brisket to a plate.

2. Stir together balsamic vinegar ketchup, cola, chicken broth, onion soup mix, and herbes de Provence in a large bowl. Pour slowly into Dutch oven, and stir and scrape to loosen browned bits from bottom of Dutch oven. Return brisket and any juices to Dutch oven. Bring to a boil over medium-high, and cover with foil followed by a tight-fitting lid. Transfer Dutch oven to preheated oven.

3. Bake 2 hours. Turn brisket over. Tuck in carrots and parsnips, and sprinkle onion into liquid around edge of brisket. Replace foil and lid, and continue baking until brisket is fork-tender, about 1 hour.

4. Use a slotted spoon to transfer brisket, carrots, and parsnips to a serving platter. Cover with foil to keep warm. Puree cooking liquid in Dutch oven with an immersion blender to make gravy. Simmer gravy over medium until heated through. Stir in bourbon, and

sprinkle with remaining ½ teaspoon salt and ¼ teaspoon pepper.

5. Slice brisket. Spoon some of the hot gravy over brisket and vegetables, and sprinkle with thyme. Serve remaining gravy in serving dish on table.

Rustic Mashed Potatoes with Whole-Grain Mustard

ACTIVE 20 MIN. · TOTAL 45 MIN.
SERVES 8

- 3 lb. Yukon Gold potatoes, unpeeled, cut into 2-inch chunks
- 1 Tbsp. plus 2 ½ tsp. kosher salt, divided
- 1 cup whole milk, warmed
- ¼ cup salted butter, at room temperature
- 3 Tbsp. whole-grain mustard
- ½ tsp. black pepper

1. Place potatoes and 1 tablespoon of the salt in a large saucepan; cover potatoes with cold water, about 6 cups. Bring to a boil over high, and reduce heat to medium. Partially cover pan, and simmer until potatoes are just tender enough to pierce with a fork, about 20 minutes. Drain well, and return to warm pan. Let stand 5 minutes.

2. Mash potatoes with a handheld potato masher or a large fork. Stir in warm milk, butter, and mustard. Stir in pepper and remaining 2 ½ teaspoons salt. Serve immediately.

Salted Caramel Banana Pudding

ACTIVE 20 MIN. · TOTAL 1 HOUR, 50 MIN.

SERVES 8

SHORTCUT SALTED CARAMEL
- ¼ cup salted butter
- ¼ cup packed light brown sugar
- ¾ cup dulce de leche
- ½ cup heavy cream
- 1 tsp. kosher salt

CUSTARD
- ¾ cup granulated sugar
- ⅓ cup all-purpose flour
- ¼ tsp. kosher salt
- 2 cups whole milk
- 4 large egg yolks
- 1 Tbsp. salted butter
- 1 tsp. pure vanilla extract

WHIPPED CREAM
- 1 cup heavy cream
- ¼ cup powdered sugar

ADDITIONAL INGREDIENTS
- 28 crisp gourmet cookies (such as Lotus Biscoff)
- 4 small, ripe, firm bananas, cut into thin rounds (about 4 cups)

1. Prepare the Shortcut Salted Caramel: Melt butter and light brown sugar in a small saucepan over medium, stirring occasionally. Stir in dulce de leche. Bring to a boil, stirring constantly, until smooth, about 2 minutes. Remove from heat, and stir in cream and salt. Cool 10 minutes.

2. Prepare the Custard: Whisk together granulated sugar, flour, and salt in a large, heavy saucepan. Whisking constantly, add whole milk in a slow, steady stream. Whisk in egg yolks. Cook over medium-high, stirring continuously with a rubber spatula, until it bubbles around the edges and coats the spatula, 8 to 10 minutes. Remove from heat, add butter, and stir until it melts. Stir in vanilla extract. Press plastic wrap directly on surface to prevent a skin from forming, and cool completely, about 1 hour.

3. Prepare the Whipped Cream: Beat heavy cream with an electric mixer on medium-high speed until foamy; gradually add powdered sugar, beating until soft peaks form.

4. Assemble the pudding: Cover bottom of a 2-quart baking dish or serving bowl with 14 cookies, breaking them as needed. Drizzle with half of the Shortcut Salted Caramel; top with half of the sliced bananas and half of the Custard. Repeat layers with remaining cookies, caramel, bananas, and Custard. Spread Whipped Cream on top, and chill 30 minutes before serving.

---

7 SECRETS TO SUPPER CLUB SUCCESS

NO. 1
Show up, time after time.
The key to a cohesive club is to remain committed and participate regularly.

NO. 2
Agree upon (and then meet) expectations.
Every club needs its own house rules on how elaborate or casual the meals and decor will be.

NO. 3
Don't overdo it or under-deliver on your menu.
Showing off causes intimidation. Slacking off causes resentment. (When necessary, invoke the fourth rule.)

NO. 4
Don't cancel. Life happens.
Rather than skip or cancel the supper when things take a turn for the crazy, order in dinner and use paper plates.

NO. 5
Embrace the themed meal.
Themes can provide a focal point for the menu so cooks can be creative without going rogue.

NO. 6
Choose members wisely.
It's necessary to make sure that everyone in the core group gets along and gets the idea. This is an opportunity to handpick your own second family. The "who" is always more important than the "what."

NO. 7
Have fun, and relax.
A supper club should feel like a respite from a hectic life, not an onerous task to check off the to-do list.

SALTED CARAMEL
BANANA PUDDING

Chicken, Sweet Potato, and Corn Slow-Cooker Chowder, *page 291*

Soup's On!

Seven delicious ways to warm up weeknights this fall

Roasted Tomato-Eggplant Soup with Garlic Croutons

Roasted Tomato-Eggplant Soup with Garlic Croutons

Tomato soup gets a flavorful new twist: Roasted eggplant adds creaminess, and caramelized onions and carrots add sweetness.

ACTIVE 40 MIN. - TOTAL 1 HOUR, 20 MIN.
SERVES 6

- 3 lb. vine-ripe red tomatoes, quartered
- 1 (1-lb.) eggplant, peeled and cut into ¼-inch slices
- 1 lb. carrots, peeled and cut into ¾-inch pieces
- 1 medium-size sweet onion, peeled and cut into ¼-inch wedges
- 10 garlic cloves
- ¼ cup olive oil
- 1 tsp. black pepper
- 1 Tbsp. kosher salt, divided
- 8 cups vegetable broth
- 1½ cups half-and-half
- 1 Tbsp. red wine vinegar
   Garlic Croutons (recipe follows)
- 3 oz. feta cheese, crumbled (about ¾ cup)
   Fresh basil leaves

1. Preheat oven to 400°F. Lightly spray 2 rimmed baking sheets with cooking spray; arrange tomatoes, eggplant, carrots, onion, and garlic cloves in a single layer on baking sheets. Drizzle olive oil evenly over vegetables; sprinkle with pepper and 1½ teaspoons of the salt. Roast in preheated oven until tender and lightly browned, about 40 minutes, rotating baking sheets halfway through.

2. Scrape vegetables and cooking juices into a large Dutch oven. Stir in vegetable broth, half-and-half, and remaining 1½ teaspoons salt. Bring to a boil over medium-high. Remove from heat. Puree soup with an immersion blender. Stir in vinegar.

3. Ladle about 2 cups soup into each of 6 bowls, top each with ¼ cup Garlic Croutons, and 2 tablespoons feta. Sprinkle with basil.

Garlic Croutons

ACTIVE 25 MIN. - TOTAL 25 MIN.
MAKES 5½ CUPS

Preheat oven to 400°F. Heat ¼ cup olive oil and 4 garlic cloves in a small saucepan over medium-high. Cook, swirling saucepan often, until garlic turns golden brown, 4 to 5 minutes. Remove from heat, mash garlic gently with a fork, and cool about 5 minutes. Pour oil through a fine wire-mesh strainer; discard solids. Cut 1 (10-oz.) French baguette into ½-inch cubes, and place in a medium bowl; drizzle with oil, and sprinkle with 2 Tbsp. chopped fresh flat-leaf parsley, ½ tsp. kosher salt, and ¼ tsp. black pepper. Toss to coat. Place in a single layer on a rimmed baking sheet. Bake in preheated oven 7 to 9 minutes. Let cool slightly, about 2 minutes.

Chicken, Sweet Potato, and Corn Slow-Cooker Chowder

Great for a game-day get-together, this hearty and creamy soup feeds a crowd with little hands-on time required.

ACTIVE 25 MIN. - TOTAL 4 HOURS, 55 MIN.
SERVES 10

- 8 cups chicken broth
- 1½ lb. sweet potatoes, peeled and cut into ¼-inch pieces (about 4½ cups)
- 2 (1-lb.) bone-in, skinless chicken breasts
- 2 cups fresh corn kernels (from 4 ears)
- 2 cups chopped yellow onion (from 2 onions)
- 1¼ cups chopped red bell pepper (from 1 large bell pepper)
- 1¼ cups chopped yellow bell pepper (from 1 large bell pepper)
- 1 cup chopped celery (from 3 stalks)
- 2 tsp. kosher salt
- 1 tsp. black pepper
- 1 cup heavy cream
- 5 Tbsp. cornstarch
- ¼ cup chopped fresh flat-leaf parsley
   Hot sauce
   Finely chopped chives

1. Combine first 10 ingredients in a 6-quart slow cooker. Cover and cook on HIGH until chicken and sweet potatoes are tender, about 4 hours. Remove chicken from slow cooker. Coarsely shred, discarding bones; set aside.

2. Whisk together cream and cornstarch in a bowl until smooth; stir into soup. Cover and cook until slightly thickened, about 30 minutes. Stir in chicken and parsley. Top with hot sauce and chives.

White Bean,
Fennel, and Italian
Sausage Soup with
Parmesan Toasts

White Bean, Fennel, and Italian Sausage Soup with Parmesan Toasts

Pantry staples and a few fresh ingredients combine to make a comforting soup that's ready to eat in less than an hour. Serve with a glass of your favorite red wine and a couple of our crunchy Parmesan Toasts for dunking.

ACTIVE 45 MIN. - TOTAL 45 MIN.
SERVES 8

- 1 lb. mild Italian sausage, casings removed
- 2 cups thinly sliced yellow onion (from 1 medium)
- 1 cup thinly sliced celery (from about 3 stalks)
- 1 cup thinly sliced fennel (from 1 small fennel bulb)
- 3 garlic cloves, chopped (about 1 Tbsp.)
- ½ tsp. kosher salt
- ½ tsp. crushed red pepper
- 1 tsp. black pepper, divided
- ¼ cup dry white wine
- 6 cups chicken stock
- 2 (15-oz.) cans cannellini beans, drained and rinsed
- 1 (14.5-oz.) can fire-roasted diced tomatoes, undrained
- 16 (¼-inch) French baguette slices (from 1 large baguette)
- 1 Tbsp. olive oil
- 1 oz. Parmigiano-Reggiano cheese, grated (about ¼ cup)
  Chopped fresh rosemary

1. Heat a large Dutch oven over medium-high. Add sausage, and cook, stirring to crumble, until no longer pink, 6 to 8 minutes. Drain, leaving 1 tablespoon of drippings with sausage in Dutch oven. Add onion, celery, fennel, garlic, salt, red pepper, and ½ teaspoon of the black pepper. Cook, stirring often, until vegetables have softened, about 5 minutes. Add white wine, and scrape any browned bits from the bottom of the Dutch oven. Stir in chicken stock, beans, and tomatoes; bring to a boil. Reduce heat to medium-low, and simmer 10 minutes.

2. Preheat broiler with oven rack 6 inches from heat. Place baguette slices on a rimmed baking sheet, and brush 1 side of each piece with olive oil. Sprinkle evenly with cheese and remaining ½ teaspoon pepper. Broil until cheese is melted and beginning to brown, 1 to 2 minutes. Remove from oven.

3. Ladle 1 ½ cups soup into each of 8 bowls; sprinkle with chopped rosemary, and serve with toasts.

Sausage Minestrone

Sausage and vegetables freeze well and taste even better the next day after the flavors have had time to meld. If you're planning to enjoy the soup later, prepare the pasta separately so it doesn't turn mushy.

ACTIVE 25 MIN. - TOTAL 14 HOURS, 55 MIN., INCLUDING 8 HOURS SOAKING
SERVES 5

- ¾ cup dried navy beans (about 5 oz.)
- ¾ cup dried butter beans or baby limas (about 5 oz.)
- 8 oz. smoked sausage (such as Conecuh), cut into ¼-inch slices
- 1 cup chopped yellow onion (from 1 onion)
- 1 Tbsp. chopped garlic (about 3 garlic cloves)
- 6 cups chicken stock
- 1 cup chopped carrots (from 3 carrots)
- 1 cup chopped celery (from 3 stalks)
- 1 cup fresh corn kernels (from 2 ears)
- ¾ tsp. kosher salt
- ½ tsp. black pepper
- 3 cups thinly sliced collard greens (from 1 bunch)
- 1 cup uncooked large elbow macaroni

1. Place dried beans in a large bowl, and cover with 3 to 4 inches of water. Soak beans 8 hours or overnight. Drain and place in a 6-quart slow cooker.

2. Heat a large nonstick skillet over medium-high. Add sausage slices; cook until lightly browned, about 6 minutes. Using tongs, add sausage to slow cooker. Add onion and garlic to skillet; cook over medium-high, stirring often, until onions are slightly softened, 4 to 5 minutes. Transfer to slow cooker.

3. Add chicken stock, carrots, celery, corn, salt, and pepper to slow cooker; stir to combine. Cover and cook on HIGH until beans are tender, about 6 hours. Stir in collard greens and pasta; cover and cook until collards and pasta are tender, about 30 minutes. Serve immediately.

Sausage
Minestrone

Smoked Chicken, Squash, and Rice Soup

Smoked chicken, which you can pick up from your favorite barbecue restaurant, gives this soup a nice depth of flavor. Lime juice, avocado, and cilantro add a Latin accent.

ACTIVE 30 MIN. · TOTAL 45 MIN.
SERVES 6

- 2 Tbsp. olive oil
- 1 ½ cups chopped zucchini (from 1 zucchini)
- 1 ½ cups chopped yellow squash (from 2 squash)
- 1 cup chopped white onion (from 1 onion)
- 2 tsp. ground coriander
- 1 tsp. kosher salt
- ½ tsp. black pepper
- 6 cups chicken stock
- 2 cups cooked long-grain white rice
- 1 tsp. lime zest, plus 2 Tbsp. fresh juice (from 1 lime)
- 12 oz. smoked chicken, shredded
- ½ cup chopped fresh cilantro
- 2 small ripe avocados, sliced
  Cilantro leaves

Heat oil in a large Dutch oven over medium-high. Add next 6 ingredients; cook, stirring often, until onions are softened, about 6 minutes. Add chicken stock, rice, lime zest, and lime juice. Bring to a boil, and reduce heat to medium-low. Cover and simmer until squash pieces are tender, about 10 minutes. Stir in chicken and chopped cilantro. Ladle into bowls; top with avocado, and, if desired, garnish with cilantro leaves.

Creamy Potato-and-Ham Hock Slow-Cooker Soup

The potatoes absorb the rich, smoky flavor of the ham hocks in this one-pot soup. Serve with crusty bread, a salad, and hot sauce on the side for an easy meal both kids and adults will love.

ACTIVE 45 MIN. · TOTAL 4 HOURS, 45 MIN.
SERVES 8

- 4 ½ lb. russet potatoes, chopped (about 10 cups)
- 2 lb. smoked ham hocks (about 3 ham hocks)
- 2 cups chopped yellow onion (from 1 medium onion)
- 1 cup chopped celery (from 3 stalks)
- 2 Tbsp. minced garlic cloves (about 4 garlic cloves)
- 2 Tbsp. chopped fresh thyme
- 2 ½ tsp. kosher salt
- 1 tsp. black pepper
- 5 cups chicken broth
- 1 cup heavy cream
  Chopped fresh chives
  Hot sauce

1. Place potatoes, ham hocks, onion, celery, garlic, thyme, salt, and pepper in a 7-quart slow cooker; add broth, and stir to combine. Cover and cook on HIGH until potatoes are tender, 4 hours. Remove ham hocks, and place on a plate to cool 15 minutes.

2. Puree soup in slow cooker with an immersion blender until it's creamy but whole pieces of potato are still visible. Add cream, and stir. Once ham hocks are cool enough to handle, remove all meat and chop; discard fat and bone. Add meat to soup, and stir to combine.

3. Ladle soup in bowls; top with chopped chives and a dash of hot sauce.

Southern Wedding Soup

We gave this Italian-American classic our own spin with fresh greens and pork-and-beef meatballs. If you can't find ditalini pasta, any small shape (like orzo or elbow macaroni) will work just as well.

ACTIVE 30 MIN. - TOTAL 45 MIN.
SERVES 8

MEATBALLS
- 1 lb. ground sirloin
- 1 lb. ground pork
- 1 cup finely chopped yellow onion (from 1 onion)
- ½ cup Italian-seasoned breadcrumbs
- 2 oz. Parmesan cheese, grated (about ½ cup)
- ¼ cup chopped fresh flat-leaf parsley
- 1 Tbsp. Worcestershire sauce
- 2 tsp. kosher salt
- 2 large eggs, lightly beaten

SOUP
- 1 Tbsp. olive oil
- 1 cup chopped yellow onion (from 1 small onion)
- 1 cup chopped celery (from 3 medium stalks)
- 1 Tbsp. sliced garlic cloves (from 2 large garlic cloves)
- 1 tsp. kosher salt
- 10 cups chicken stock
- ¼ cup jarred refrigerated basil pesto sauce
- 1 cup uncooked ditalini pasta (about 4 ½ oz.)
- 1 (5-oz.) pkg. baby kale
  Shaved Parmesan cheese

1. Prepare the Meatballs: Preheat oven to 400°F. Combine first 9 ingredients in a medium bowl. Mix gently with hands until incorporated. Line a rimmed baking sheet with parchment paper. Using a tablespoon, form mixture into balls, and place on baking sheet. Bake in preheated oven until cooked through and lightly browned, about 10 minutes. Remove Meatballs from oven; cover to keep warm.

2. Prepare the Soup: Heat olive oil in a large Dutch oven over medium-high. Add onion, celery, garlic, and salt; cook until onions have softened, 5 to 6 minutes. Stir in chicken stock and pesto. Reduce heat to medium; simmer until celery is tender, about 10 minutes.

3. Increase heat to medium-high. Bring to a boil, and add pasta; cook until al dente, about 5 minutes. Reduce heat to medium-low, and stir in kale; cook until wilted, about 2 minutes.

4. Place 4 Meatballs and 1 ½ cups Soup in each of 8 bowls. Top with shaved Parmesan.

Pressure-Cooker Beef-and-Bean Chili

While the beef bones in the recipe are optional, they give the chili a greater depth of flavor. Most meat departments sell bones, or you can add a meaty piece of beef with the bone still attached.

ACTIVE 20 MIN. - TOTAL 55 MIN.
SERVES 6

- 2 Tbsp. canola oil
- 1 lb. beef stew meat
- 1½ cups chopped white onion
- 1 cup chopped poblano chile
- 2 Tbsp. tomato paste
- 2 Tbsp. unsweetened cocoa
- 1 Tbsp. chili powder
- 1¼ tsp. kosher salt
- ¾ tsp. black pepper
- ½ tsp. granulated sugar
- 2 cups beef broth
- 2 (14.5-oz.) cans fire-roasted diced tomatoes
- 1 (16-oz.) can light red kidney beans
- 12 oz. beef bones (optional)

  TOPPINGS
  Shredded sharp Cheddar cheese
  Sour cream
  Fresh cilantro leaves
- 1 small jalapeño chile, thinly sliced

1. Heat oil in a programmable pressure cooker (such as Instant Pot) set on sauté or in a heavy-bottomed pressure cooker over medium-high. Add beef to pot, and cook, stirring once, until browned, about 10 minutes. Remove beef from pot. Add onion and poblano chile to pot, and cook, stirring occasionally, until starting to soften, about 3 minutes. Add tomato paste, cocoa, chili powder, salt, pepper, and sugar; cook, stirring often, until fragrant, about 2 minutes. Add broth, tomatoes, beans, browned beef, and, if desired, beef bones to pot; bring to a boil. Cover pot with lid, and bring to full pressure according to manufacturer's directions. Reduce heat to normal or medium, and maintain high pressure for 30 minutes. Remove from heat, if needed, and release steam according to manufacturer's directions. Discard beef bones, if using.

2. Serve chili with cheese, sour cream, cilantro, and jalapeño slices for topping.

Pressure-Cooker Chili

Win over the weekend crowd with a dish that's easy to make and just as comforting as ever

What Can I Bring?

BY **ELIZABETH HEISKELL**

WHEN A FRIEND invites you to a party, it's the first thing you ask. And most times, the host will say: "I already have it all taken care of." But that does not mean you should arrive empty-handed. In my new book, I answer that enduring question for any occasion life serves up. Here, I share two easy, crowd-pleasing recipes that guarantee you'll be invited back again and again.

GET THE BOOK!
What Can I Bring? Southern Food for Any Occasion Life Serves Up will be on sale October 17.

ENTERTAINING **EXPERT** AND *TODAY SHOW* CONTRIBUTOR ELIZABETH HEISKELL

Crack Crackers

I've been known to eat so many of these crackers that my tongue goes white and swollen from too much salt. If this happens to you, ask someone to hide the bag. Your accomplice should know there's a good chance they'll be awoken in the middle of the night by a cracker addict demanding to know where the Cheddar cheese treasure has been hidden.

ACTIVE 5 MIN. - TOTAL 1 HOUR, 5 MIN.
SERVES 24

Preheat oven to 300°F. Whisk together ⅓ cup olive oil, 1 (1-oz.) package ranch dressing mix, 1 Tbsp. dried dill, and 1 Tbsp. garlic powder in a small bowl. Drizzle over 2 (16-oz.) packages bite-size Cheddar cheese crackers (such as Cheez-It) in a large bowl. Toss to coat. Divide between 2 large rimmed baking sheets, and spread in an even layer. Bake 30 minutes or until lightly toasted, stirring every 10 minutes. Cool on pans 30 minutes. Store in large ziplock plastic bags or in airtight containers.

GREAT BAKE SALE,
TAILGATE, OR
AFTER-DINNER
TREATS

Fudge Cake

When my mother talks about this fudgy dessert, her eyes glaze over. The cake was sold at the Lowry Motor Court restaurant in Greenville, Mississippi. Mama said they displayed it by the register under a glass dome, and each perfectly square slice was neatly wrapped in wax paper.

ACTIVE 15 MIN. - TOTAL 2 HOURS, 10 MIN.
SERVES 16

- 1 **cup unsalted butter**
- 4 **(1-oz.) squares semisweet baking chocolate, finely chopped**
- 1¾ **cups granulated sugar**
- 4 **large eggs**
- 1 **cup all-purpose flour, sifted**
  Dash of kosher salt
- 1 **cup chopped toasted pecans**
- 1 **teaspoon vanilla extract**
  Powdered sugar

1. Preheat oven to 300°F. Place butter and chocolate in a large microwave-safe bowl. Microwave on HIGH until completely melted, about 1 minute, stirring every 20 seconds. Add granulated sugar, and stir until well combined. Cool 10 minutes. Add eggs, 1 at a time, and stir until blended after each addition. Fold in all-purpose flour and salt. Stir in chopped toasted pecans and vanilla extract.

2. Coat a 9-inch square pan with cooking spray. Line bottom and sides of pan with parchment paper, allowing 4 to 5 inches to extend over sides. Coat parchment paper with cooking spray. Pour cake mixture into prepared pan.

3. Bake in preheated oven until a wooden pick inserted in center comes out clean, 45 to 50 minutes. Cool in pan on a wire rack 30 minutes. Lift cake from pan, using parchment paper sides as handles, and cool completely, about 30 minutes. Cut into squares, and dust with powdered sugar before serving.

Hot Potatoes

Two flavorful ways
to top a simple spud in
under 30 minutes

Basic "Baked" Potato

ACTIVE 5 MIN. - TOTAL 15 MIN.
SERVES 1

Scrub 1 (8-oz.) russet potato; pierce potato all over with a fork. Place in a medium-size microwavable bowl, and rub potato with ¼ tsp. olive oil. Micro-wave on HIGH until mostly tender, about 5 minutes. Flip potato, and microwave on HIGH until fully tender, about 2 to 3 more minutes. Let stand 5 minutes before serving or using in another recipe.

Spanakopita "Baked" Potato

ACTIVE 20 MIN. - TOTAL 20 MIN.
SERVES 1

Preheat broiler with oven rack 6 inches from heat. Thinly slice 2 small garlic cloves, and chop 2 cups firmly packed baby spinach. Cook garlic in ½ tsp. olive oil in a skillet over medium, stirring often, until softened and lightly golden, about 2 to 3 minutes. Add spinach, and cook, stirring occasionally, until wilted, about 1 minute. Remove spinach mixture from heat, and set aside. Cut 1 Basic "Baked" Potato in half, and scoop out pulp into a bowl, leaving ¼-inch-thick shells. Mash pulp with 1 ½ Tbsp. warm whole milk, 2 ½ tsp. olive oil, ¼ tsp. kosher salt, and ⅛ tsp. black pepper until mostly smooth. Fold in spinach mixture. Spoon into shells, and place on a baking sheet. Top evenly with 2 Tbsp. feta cheese. Broil until lightly browned and warmed through, 2 to 3 minutes. Sprinkle evenly with 1 tsp. chopped fresh dill and ¼ tsp. lemon zest.

Nutritional information (per serving):
Calories: 401 - Protein: 11g - Carbs: 47g - Fiber: 5g - Fat: 21g

Pizza "Baked" Potato

ACTIVE 20 MIN. - TOTAL 20 MIN.
SERVES 1

Preheat broiler with oven rack 6 inches from heat. Cook 1 ½ oz. ground hot Italian sausage in a skillet over medium until browned, 2 to 3 minutes. Transfer to a bowl; reserve drippings in skillet. Add ¼ cup each finely chopped bell pepper and yellow onion to skillet; cook until softened, 5 minutes. Add 1 tsp. each no-salt-added tomato paste and minced garlic; cook 30 seconds. Add ⅓ cup no-salt-added pureed tomatoes, 3 Tbsp. water, ½ tsp. chopped fresh oregano, and sausage. Bring to a simmer; cook until slightly thickened, 3 minutes. Cut 1 Basic "Baked" Potato in half; scoop out pulp into a bowl, leaving ¼-inch-thick shells. Mash pulp with 1 ½ Tbsp. warm whole milk, 2 tsp. melted butter, and ¼ tsp. kosher salt. Fold in half of tomato mixture. Spoon into shells; place on a baking sheet. Top with remaining tomato mixture and 1 oz. shredded part-skim mozzarella cheese. Broil 1 to 2 minutes. Top with fresh oregano.

Nutritional information (per serving):
Calories: 483 - Protein: 22g - Carbs: 60g - Fiber: 6g - Fat: 19g

Homemade Oatmeal Pies

Make over an old-fashioned childhood favorite with a surprising salty-sweet caramel filling

Oatmeal-Caramel Cream Pies

ACTIVE 20 MIN. - TOTAL 1 HOUR
SERVES 24

- 1 cup salted butter, softened
- ¾ cup granulated sugar
- ¾ cup firmly packed light brown sugar
- 2 large eggs
- 2 tsp. vanilla extract
- 1½ cups all-purpose flour
- 1 tsp. baking soda
- ½ tsp. table salt
- ½ tsp. ground cinnamon
- 3 cups uncooked regular rolled oats
- 1 cup chopped toasted pecans
- Salted Caramel Buttercream (recipe follows)

1. Preheat oven to 350°F. Beat butter and sugars with a heavy-duty stand mixer on medium speed until creamy, about 2 minutes; add eggs and vanilla, and beat until just combined. Whisk together flour, baking soda, salt, and cinnamon in a small bowl; gradually add to butter mixture, beating on low speed just until combined, about 10 seconds. Stir in oats and pecans.

2. Using a 1½-inch cookie scoop, drop spoonfuls of dough 3 inches apart on parchment paper-lined baking sheets. (Or use your hands to shape dough into 2-inch balls.) Bake in preheated oven until golden but still soft in center, 9 to 10 minutes. Cool 1 minute on baking sheets; remove cookies to wire racks, and cool completely, about 20 minutes.

3. Pipe or spread about 1½ tablespoons Salted Caramel Buttercream on 1 flat side of half of cooled cookies; top with remaining cookies, flat side down, pressing gently.

Salted Caramel Buttercream

ACTIVE 10 MIN. - TOTAL 40 MIN.
MAKES ABOUT 3 CUPS

Microwave 16 caramel candies (such as Kraft) and 1 Tbsp. heavy cream in a microwave-safe bowl on HIGH until mixture is smooth and melted, about 1 minute, stirring at 3-second intervals. Stir in 1 additional Tbsp. cream. Cool at room temperature until lukewarm, about 30 minutes. Beat ½ cup softened salted butter and 3 oz. softened cream cheese with an electric mixer on medium speed until creamy; add 2 tsp. vanilla extract and ½ tsp. kosher salt; beat until combined. Gradually add 1 (16-oz.) pkg. powdered sugar alternately with caramel mixture, beating on low speed until blended after each addition. Add 1 Tbsp. cream, 1 tsp. at a time, to reach desired consistency, if needed.

KNOW-HOW

Secrets to Slow–Cooker Soups

Give it space. Fill the slow cooker no more than half to two-thirds full so there's extra room for the liquid to bubble and simmer.

Thaw frozen ingredients first. This will ensure they don't alter the overall cook time and temperature.

Add herbs at the end. Long cook times and delicate ingredients, like fresh herbs, don't mix.

KITCHEN TRICKS

4 Tasty Soup Toppers

Add a little crunch or a dollop of cream for a burst of unexpected flavor

1. FLASH-FRIED HERBS
Fry fresh, thoroughly dried herb leaves (such as sage, parsley, or basil) in ¼ inch of hot canola oil until they crisp up, about 30 seconds. Transfer to a paper towel-lined plate, and sprinkle with salt while the herbs are still hot.

2. CRISPY CHICKPEAS
Heat oven to 400°F. Drain, rinse, and dry 1 (15-oz.) can chickpeas. Place chickpeas on a rimmed baking sheet; use your hands to coat evenly with 1 Tbsp. olive oil. Sprinkle with salt. Roast 25 to 30 minutes or until golden and crisp.

3. SPICY SOUR CREAM
Combine 1 cup sour cream; 1 to 2 Tbsp. Sriracha chili sauce, chipotle paste, or adobo sauce from canned chipotle peppers; 1 tsp. fresh lime juice; and 1 tsp. salt in a small bowl. Chill sour cream until ready to use.

4. BUTTERY CRACKER CRUMBS
Melt 4 Tbsp. unsalted butter in a saucepan. Add 1 cup roughly crushed saltine crackers and 1 tsp. seasoned salt, and cook until the crackers are evenly coated and golden brown, about 2 minutes.

November

OLD-SCHOOL
GREEN BEAN
CASSEROLE
page 308

THE NEW
SOUTHERN
SIDEBOARD

CANDIED YAMS
page 307

ANGEL BISCUITS
page 308

CRANBERRY SALAD
page 307

When we started planning this year's Thanksgiving feast, it was all those delicious and flavorful sides that really had the Test Kitchen talking. So we cooked up nine classics that everyone expects, each with two variations: one for folks who want to put a slight spin on tradition and the other for holiday hosts excited to try something different. Create a menu by mixing and matching your favorites, or make them all. Just like guests around our table, there's always room for one more memorable addition.

CAN'T-SAY-NO
DRESSING

Many argue that this is the best part of the feast, so we're serving our go-to recipe along with two adventurous ways to shake it up.

THE CLASSIC

Cornbread Dressing

A great Southern-style dressing starts with cornbread that's baked in a skillet for a crisp, golden crust. Our simple recipe can be made up to a month ahead if stored in the freezer. For best results, prepare the cornbread up to two days in advance so it can dry out completely.

ACTIVE 40 MIN. - TOTAL 3 HOURS
SERVES 15

CORNBREAD
2 cups self-rising white cornmeal mix
1 tsp. granulated sugar (optional)
2 large eggs
2 cups whole buttermilk
3 Tbsp. salted butter

DRESSING
½ cup salted butter
3 cups chopped sweet onion (from 2 large onions)
2 cups chopped celery (from 6 stalks)
2 Tbsp. chopped fresh sage
1 tsp. chopped fresh thyme
6 large eggs
1 (14-oz.) pkg. herb-seasoned stuffing mix (such as Pepperidge Farm)
10 cups chicken broth
2 tsp. black pepper
1 tsp. kosher salt

1. Prepare the Cornbread: Preheat oven to 425°F. Combine self-rising cornmeal mix and, if desired, sugar in a large bowl. Stir together eggs and buttermilk in a medium bowl; add to cornmeal mixture, stirring just until moistened.

CORNBREAD DRESSING

2. Heat salted butter in a 10-inch cast-iron skillet in preheated oven 5 minutes. Stir melted butter into batter. Pour batter into hot skillet.

3. Bake in preheated oven until Cornbread is golden, about 25 minutes; cool in skillet 20 minutes. Remove from skillet to a wire rack, and cool completely, 20 to 30 more minutes. Crumble Cornbread. Freeze in a large heavy-duty ziplock plastic bag up to 1 month, if desired. Thaw in refrigerator.

4. Prepare the Dressing: Preheat oven to 350°F. Melt butter in a large skillet over medium-high; add onion and celery, and cook, stirring often, until tender, 10 to 12 minutes. Add sage and thyme, and cook, stirring often, 1 minute.

5. Stir together eggs in a very large bowl; stir in crumbled Cornbread, onion mixture, stuffing mix, chicken broth, black pepper, and kosher salt until blended.

6. Spoon mixture into 2 lightly greased 13- x 9-inch (3-quart) baking dishes. Cover and freeze up to 3 months, if desired; thaw in refrigerator 24 hours. (Uncover and let stand at room temperature 30 minutes before baking.)

7. Bake, uncovered, in preheated oven until lightly browned and cooked through, 1 hour to 1 hour and 15 minutes.

MAKE IT AHEAD: All three dressing options can be made a day in advance. Let the cooked dressing cool to room temperature, and then store, covered, in the refrigerator. Reheat before serving.

MAMA'S WITH A TWIST

Pecan-Herb Cornbread Dressing

Prepare recipe as directed, increasing fresh thyme to 2 tsp. and adding 2 tsp. chopped fresh rosemary with herbs in Step 4. Stir 1 ½ cups chopped toasted pecans and ½ cup chopped fresh flat-leaf parsley into Cornbread mixture in Step 5; proceed as directed. Garnish with additional chopped parsley.

DELICIOUSLY DIFFERENT

Cornbread Dressing with Smoked Sausage and Apples

Cook 12 oz. chopped smoked sausage in a large skillet until cooked through; transfer to a paper towel to drain; wipe skillet clean. Prepare recipe as directed, adding 2 large unpeeled Braeburn or Fuji apples, chopped (about 9 oz.), to onion mixture during the last 5 minutes of cook time in Step 4 before adding herbs. Stir sausage into Cornbread mixture in Step 5; proceed as directed.

Herbed Breadcrumb-Topped Macaroni and Cheese

Roasted Broccoli Macaroni and Cheese

Best-Ever Macaroni and Cheese

BRING ON THE MAC AND CHEESE

Everyone's beloved comfort food deserves a spot on the holiday table—especially this version. Our secret is the cubes of Cheddar cheese that melt as the pasta bakes, creating pockets of rich, gooey goodness in every bite.

THE CLASSIC

Best-Ever Macaroni and Cheese

ACTIVE 25 MIN. - TOTAL 1 HOUR, 10 MIN.
SERVES 10

- 16 oz. uncooked large elbow macaroni, large shells, or cavatappi pasta
- 6 Tbsp. salted butter
- ⅓ cup grated yellow onion
- 2 tsp. dry mustard
- 1 tsp. kosher salt
- ¼ tsp. black pepper
- ⅛ tsp. freshly grated nutmeg
- ⅛ tsp. cayenne pepper
- 6 Tbsp. all-purpose flour
- 3 ½ cups milk
- 1 ¾ cups heavy cream
- 2 tsp. Worcestershire sauce
- 4 oz. extra-sharp yellow Cheddar cheese, shredded (about 1 cup), plus 4 oz. diced (about 1 cup), divided
- 4 oz. sharp white Cheddar cheese, shredded (about 1 cup), plus 4 oz. diced (about 1 cup), divided

1. Preheat oven to 350°F. Prepare pasta according to package directions for al dente.

2. Melt butter in a large saucepan over medium. Add next 6 ingredients; cook, stirring, 30 seconds. Add flour, and cook, stirring, until golden, 2 minutes. Gradually whisk in milk and cream. Bring to a boil, whisking occasionally. Reduce heat to medium-low; simmer, whisking, until slightly thickened, 5 minutes. Stir in Worcestershire sauce. Remove from heat; stir in ¾ cup each of shredded Cheddar cheeses until melted. (Reserve remaining ¼ cup each of shredded cheeses.) Stir in pasta and diced cheeses; pour into a lightly greased 13- x 9-inch (3-quart) baking dish.

3. Bake on a rimmed baking sheet in preheated oven until bubbly and golden, 30 minutes. Remove from oven; increase oven temperature to broil. Sprinkle with reserved shredded cheeses; broil 6 inches from heat until cheeses are melted and golden, about 2 minutes. Remove from oven; cool slightly on a wire rack, about 15 minutes.

MAKE IT AHEAD: Prepare through Step 2 up to 1 day in advance; cover and refrigerate. Bring to room temperature before proceeding with Step 3.

DELICIOUSLY DIFFERENT

Roasted Broccoli Macaroni and Cheese

Preheat oven to 450°F. Toss together 6 cups broccoli florets (24 oz.), 1 tsp. minced garlic, 1 Tbsp. extra-virgin olive oil, 1 tsp. kosher salt, and ½ tsp. black pepper in a large bowl. Spread mixture in 1 layer on a rimmed baking sheet; bake in preheated oven until lightly browned, 20 minutes. Prepare recipe as directed, stirring broccoli into cheese sauce with pasta and diced cheeses before baking.

MAMA'S WITH A TWIST

Herbed Breadcrumb-Topped Macaroni and Cheese

Prepare as directed using entire amount of cheeses through Step 2. Stir together ½ cup panko (Japanese-style bread-crumbs), 2 Tbsp. melted salted butter, 1 tsp. chopped fresh sage, and ½ tsp. each chopped fresh thyme and rosemary; sprinkle over casserole before baking. Bake until topping is golden brown. Omit broiling.

IT'S ALL ABOUT MASHED POTATOES

Plain potatoes can stand on their own when they're prepared our way—with buttermilk and crème fraîche.

THE CLASSIC

Buttermilk Mashed Potatoes

ACTIVE 15 MIN. - TOTAL 40 MIN.
SERVES 6

- 3 lb. russet potatoes, peeled and roughly chopped
- ½ cup whole buttermilk
- 1 cup salted butter, softened
- 8 oz. crème fraîche
- 1½ tsp. kosher salt
- ½ tsp. ground white pepper

1. Place potatoes in a large Dutch oven with cold water to cover by 2 inches. Bring to a boil over medium-high. Boil until tender, 25 minutes. Drain; return potatoes to Dutch oven over medium. Cook, stirring once, until potatoes dry out slightly, 50 seconds.

2. Place buttermilk and softened butter in a microwavable glass bowl; microwave on HIGH until warm, 30 to 60 seconds. Add warm buttermilk mixture, crème fraîche, salt, and white pepper to potatoes; mash with a potato masher.

MAKE IT AHEAD: Prepare 1 day ahead; cover and refrigerate. Reheat before serving.

MAMA'S WITH A TWIST

Mashed Potatoes with Bacon and Crispy Scallions

Prepare recipe as directed; keep potatoes warm. Cook 4 bacon slices in a medium skillet over medium-high until crisp. Drain on paper towels, reserving drippings in skillet. Crumble bacon. Cook 1 cup sliced scallions in hot drippings until lightly browned and crispy, 3 to 4 minutes. Transfer to paper towels to drain. Top warm potatoes with scallions and bacon.

DELICIOUSLY DIFFERENT

Rustic Mashed Red Potatoes with Parmesan

Omit crème fraîche. Substitute 3 lb. small, unpeeled red potatoes, roughly chopped, for russet potatoes. Prepare recipe as directed, adding 4 oz. herbed cream cheese (about ½ cup) and 4 oz. Parmesan cheese, shredded (about 1 cup), to potatoes before coarsely mashing. Top with ¼ cup chopped fresh chives.

THE LAST WORD ON COLLARD GREENS

A Southern Thanksgiving spread isn't complete without slow-cooked greens.

THE CLASSIC

Slow-Cooker Collard Greens with Ham Hocks

ACTIVE 15 MIN. - TOTAL 9 HOURS, 15 MIN.
SERVES 12

- 2 smoked ham hocks (1 ¼ lb. total)
- 2 (14-oz.) cans chicken broth
- 2 (1-lb.) pkg. prewashed chopped fresh collard greens
- ½ cup chopped sweet onion (from 1 onion)
- 2 Tbsp. light brown sugar
- 2 Tbsp. apple cider vinegar
- 2 tsp. kosher salt
- 1 tsp. crushed red pepper
- ½ tsp. black pepper

Combine all ingredients in a 6-quart oval slow cooker. Cover and cook on LOW 9 hours. Carefully remove ham hocks and all bits of bone before stirring greens after cooking. Cool ham hocks, and thoroughly remove all fat and bone; return meat to slow cooker. Stir into greens, and serve.

MAKE IT AHEAD: You can make the collard greens up to 2 days in advance. Refrigerate them in the slow-cooker insert. Allow the insert to stand at room temperature for 30 minutes before returning it to the slow cooker to reheat the greens. (Immediately heating a chilled insert could cause it to crack.)

MAMA'S WITH A TWIST

Garlicky Collard Greens with Confetti Chowchow

Prepare recipe as directed, stirring 2 Tbsp. minced garlic (about 4 garlic cloves) into collard green mixture in slow cooker before cooking. Meanwhile, prepare the Confetti Chowchow: Place 1 cup each finely chopped sweet onion (2 ½ oz.), red bell pepper (6 oz.), and yellow bell pepper (6 oz.) in a small saucepan. Add 1 seeded and finely chopped large jalapeño chile (¼ cup) and ½ cup each water, distilled white vinegar, and fresh lemon juice (from 4 lemons). Then add ¼ cup granulated sugar and 1 teaspoon kosher salt. Bring to a boil over medium-high, stirring to dissolve sugar. Remove from heat, and let stand until cool and vegetables are slightly softened, about 30 minutes. Serve Confetti Chowchow over collard greens.

DELICIOUSLY DIFFERENT

Vegetarian Slow-Cooker Collard Greens

Omit ham hocks and substitute vegetable broth for the chicken broth. Prepare recipe as directed, stirring 1 Tbsp. smoked paprika and 1 (14.5-oz.) can fire-roasted diced tomatoes, drained, into collard green mixture in slow cooker before cooking. Serve with Confetti Chowchow, if desired.

GOTTA TRY THESE CANDIED YAMS

Lightly spiced with cinnamon, nutmeg, and vanilla, these baked sweet potatoes turn out perfectly caramelized and tender.

THE CLASSIC

Candied Yams

ACTIVE 20 MIN. - TOTAL 1 HOUR, 25 MIN.
SERVES 12

- 4 lb. sweet potatoes, peeled and cut into ½-inch-thick rounds
- ½ cup salted butter
- ¾ cup granulated sugar
- ¾ cup packed light brown sugar
- ¼ cup heavy cream
- 1 Tbsp. vanilla extract
- 1 tsp. ground cinnamon
- 1 tsp. kosher salt
- ¼ tsp. ground nutmeg

1. Preheat oven to 350°F. Layer sweet potato slices in a lightly greased 13- x 9-inch baking dish.

2. Melt butter in a small saucepan over medium. Add sugars, stirring until well combined. Stir in cream; cook, stirring often, just until mixture comes to a simmer, 5 to 7 minutes. Remove from heat; stir in vanilla extract, cinnamon, salt, and nutmeg.

3. Pour sugar mixture evenly over sweet potatoes, and cover with lightly greased aluminum foil. Bake, covered, in preheated oven, about 40 minutes. Uncover and gently stir potato mixture. Bake, uncovered, until potatoes are tender, 25 to 30 more minutes. Transfer potatoes to a serving bowl with a slotted spoon; pour syrup over potatoes. Serve immediately.

MAKE IT AHEAD: Assemble up to 3 days in advance. Make the recipe through Step 3, store it covered in the refrigerator, and reheat before serving on Thanksgiving Day.

MAMA'S WITH A TWIST

Candied Yams with Rosemary and Orange Zest

Omit vanilla extract, ground cinnamon, and ground nutmeg. Prepare recipe as directed, stirring 1 Tbsp. orange zest and 1 ½ tsp. chopped fresh rosemary in with salt after removing from heat in Step 2. Proceed as directed, and garnish with small fresh rosemary sprigs and orange zest.

DELICIOUSLY DIFFERENT

Spicy Candied Yams with Toasted Pecans

Omit vanilla extract and nutmeg. Prepare recipe as directed, stirring 2 Tbsp. seeded, minced jalapeño chile (from 1 small jalapeño chile) into melted butter in Step 2, and cook 1 minute. Proceed as directed, stirring 1 tsp. ground cumin in with ground cinnamon and kosher salt and sprinkling plated sweet potatoes with 1 cup roughly chopped toasted pecans just before serving.

THE REAL-DEAL CRANBERRY SALAD

Give the canned stuff the year off, and whip up this sweet side instead.

THE CLASSIC

Cranberry Salad

ACTIVE 25 MIN. - TOTAL 4 HOURS, 55 MIN.
SERVES 12

- 4 cups fresh or frozen cranberries (14 oz.)
- ¾ cup packed light brown sugar
- ½ cup fresh orange juice (from 2 oranges)
- 1 cup peeled and chopped Bartlett pears (about 2 small pears)
- 1 cup chopped fresh pineapple (from 1 pineapple)
- ½ cup thinly sliced celery (from 2 stalks)
- ½ cup chopped toasted pecans

Bring cranberries, brown sugar, and orange juice to a boil in a large saucepan over medium-high, stirring often. Reduce heat to medium-low, and simmer, stirring occasionally, until cranberries pop and mixture thickens, 12 to 15 minutes. Remove from heat, and cool to room temperature, about 30 minutes. Stir in Bartlett pears, pineapple, celery, and pecans. Transfer to a serving bowl; cover and chill salad 4 to 24 hours.

MAKE IT AHEAD: The cranberry salads can be made 3 days in advance. Cover and store in the refrigerator.

MAMA'S WITH A TWIST

Spiked Cranberry-Orange Salad

Prepare recipe as directed, substituting 1 cup clementine segments (from 4 clementines) for Bartlett pears and ½ cup chopped toasted walnuts for pecans. Stir in 2 Tbsp. orange liqueur and 1 Tbsp. orange zest (from 1 orange) with clementines, chopped pineapple, sliced celery, and walnuts. Proceed as directed.

DELICIOUSLY DIFFERENT

Cranberry-Apple-Ginger Salad

Omit Bartlett pears and pecans. Prepare recipe as directed, substituting ½ cup apple cider for fresh orange juice and stirring 1 Tbsp. minced fresh ginger (from 1 [½-inch] piece of ginger) and 1 tsp. black pepper into cranberry mixture before cooking. Stir in 1 peeled and chopped Fuji apple (about 9 oz.) with pineapple and celery. Proceed as directed.

NEXT-LEVEL GREEN BEAN CASSEROLE

Our homemade mushroom cream sauce and crispy fried shallots will make you wonder why this casserole isn't served year-round.

THE CLASSIC

Old-School Green Bean Casserole

ACTIVE 20 MIN. - TOTAL 50 MIN.

SERVES 10

- 3 (15-oz.) pkg. frozen French-cut green beans, thawed and well drained
- ½ cup salted butter, divided
- 1 (8-oz.) pkg. sliced fresh cremini mushrooms, roughly chopped
- 1 large shallot, chopped
- 6 Tbsp. all-purpose flour
- 4 cups whole milk
- 4 oz. Parmesan cheese, shredded (about 1 ½ cups)
- 2 tsp. kosher salt
- ½ tsp. black pepper
- 1 (8-oz.) can diced water chestnuts, drained
- 1 cup crispy fried onions or shallots (about 2 oz.)

1. Preheat oven to 350°F. Squeeze green beans lightly in hands to remove water.

2. Heat 2 tablespoons of the butter in a Dutch oven over medium-high. Add mushrooms and shallot, and cook, stirring often, until mixture is deeply browned and caramelized, 8 to 10 minutes. Transfer mixture to a plate, and without wiping out Dutch oven, add remaining 6 tablespoons butter to Dutch oven. Melt butter over medium-high; whisk in flour, and cook, whisking constantly, 1 minute. Gradually add milk, whisking until smooth. Cook, whisking, until thickened and bubbly, about 4 minutes. Remove from heat, and whisk in Parmesan cheese, kosher salt, and black pepper until melted and smooth. Stir in green beans, mushroom mixture, and water chestnuts; spoon into a lightly greased 13- x 9-inch (3-quart) baking dish.

3. Bake in preheated oven until bubbly around edges, 15 minutes. Remove from oven; top with fried onions or shallots. Return to oven; bake until topping is golden brown, 15 minutes.

MAKE IT AHEAD: Prepare recipe through Step 2 up to 3 days in advance; cover and refrigerate. On the day of, add toppings and bake; add 10 minutes to the initial bake time if using a refrigerated casserole.

DELICIOUSLY DIFFERENT

Bacon-Brussels Sprout-Green Bean Casserole

Substitute 1 lb. trimmed and quartered fresh Brussels sprouts for 1 pkg. green beans. Cook 6 bacon slices in a Dutch oven over medium until crisp, 6 to 8 minutes. Drain bacon on paper towels, reserving drippings in Dutch oven. Crumble bacon; set aside. Cook Brussels sprouts and green beans in reserved drippings just until tender and lightly browned, 8 to 10 minutes. Remove vegetables from Dutch oven. Prepare recipe as directed without wiping out Dutch oven, stirring Brussels sprouts and green beans into cream sauce with mushroom mixture and water chestnuts at the end of Step 2. Top with bacon and fried onions or shallots after 15 minutes of baking in Step 3.

MAMA'S WITH A TWIST

Lemon-Almond Green Bean Casserole

Omit mushrooms and fried onions or shallots. Stir together 1 cup panko (Japanese-style breadcrumbs), 1 cup untoasted sliced almonds, ½ tsp. kosher salt, and 2 Tbsp. melted salted butter. Prepare as directed, whisking 1 Tbsp. fresh lemon juice into cream sauce and stirring ½ cup toasted sliced almonds into green bean mixture in Step 2. Top casserole with panko mixture; bake 30 minutes at 350°F.

JUST ONE MORE BISCUIT

Our Angel Biscuits are a light and flaky cross between a buttermilk biscuit and a Parker House roll.

THE CLASSIC

Angel Biscuits

ACTIVE 20 MIN. - TOTAL 2 HOURS, 40 MIN.

MAKES ABOUT 3 ½ DOZEN

- ½ cup warm water (100°F to 110°F)
- 1 (¼-oz.) pkg. active dry yeast (2 ¼ tsp.)
- 1 tsp. plus 3 Tbsp. granulated sugar, divided
- 5 cups all-purpose flour
- 1 Tbsp. baking powder
- 1 ½ tsp. table salt
- 1 tsp. baking soda
- ½ cup cold salted butter, cubed
- ½ cup cold shortening, cubed
- 2 cups whole buttermilk
- 6 Tbsp. salted butter, melted and divided

1. Stir together warm water, yeast, and 1 teaspoon of the sugar in a small bowl. Let stand 5 minutes.

2. Stir together flour, baking powder, salt, baking soda, and remaining 3 tablespoons sugar in a large bowl; cut cold butter and cold shortening into flour mixture with a pastry blender or 2 forks until crumbly. Add yeast mixture and buttermilk to flour mixture, stirring just until dry ingredients are moistened. Cover bowl with plastic wrap; chill at least 2 hours or up to 5 days.

3. Preheat oven to 400°F. Turn dough out onto a lightly floured surface, and knead 3 or 4 times. Gently roll into a ½-inch-thick circle, and fold in half; repeat. Gently roll to ½-inch thickness; cut with a 2-inch round cutter. Reroll remaining scraps, and cut with cutter. Place rounds with sides touching in a 12-inch cast-iron skillet or on a parchment paper-lined baking sheet. (If using a 12-inch skillet, place remaining biscuits in a 10-inch skillet or on a baking sheet.)

Brush biscuits with 3 tablespoons of the melted butter.

4. Bake in preheated oven until golden, 15 to 20 minutes. Brush with remaining 3 tablespoons melted butter, and serve.

MAKE IT AHEAD: The dough can be made 1 week in advance; store in the refrigerator.

DELICIOUSLY DIFFERENT

Parmesan-Herb Angel Biscuits

Prepare recipe as directed, reducing sugar in Step 2 to 1 Tbsp. and stirring 3 oz. Parmesan cheese, grated (about ¾ cup); 1 Tbsp. chopped fresh thyme; and 1½ tsp. chopped fresh rosemary into flour mixture. Sprinkle biscuits with 1 oz. Parmesan cheese, grated (about ¼ cup), before baking.

MAMA'S WITH A TWIST

Cornmeal Angel Biscuits

Prepare recipe as directed, substituting 1 cup plain yellow cornmeal for 1 cup all-purpose flour.

MAKE ROOM FOR
CORN
PUDDING

Every spoonful of this creamy, not-too-sweet side dish explodes with corn.

THE CLASSIC

Savory Corn Pudding

ACTIVE 25 MIN. - TOTAL 1 HOUR, 10 MIN.
SERVES 12

- 3   Tbsp. all-purpose flour
- 2   Tbsp. granulated sugar
- 2   tsp. baking powder
- 2   tsp. kosher salt
- 6   large eggs
- 2   cups heavy cream
- ½   cup salted butter, melted and cooled
- 2   Tbsp. canola oil
- 6   cups fresh corn kernels (from 8 ears)
- ½   cup chopped sweet onion (from 1 onion)
- 2   Tbsp. chopped fresh thyme, divided

1. Preheat oven to 350°F. Stir together flour, sugar, baking powder, and salt in a small bowl until blended. Whisk together eggs, cream, and melted butter in a medium bowl until blended.

2. Heat canola oil in a large skillet over medium-high. Add corn and onion, and cook, stirring often, until onion is softened, about 5 minutes. Stir in 1 Tbsp. thyme. Remove from heat, and let cool slightly, about 5 minutes. Stir flour mixture and corn mixture into egg mixture. Spoon into a 13- x 9-inch (3-quart) baking dish, and bake in preheated oven until set and golden brown, about 40 minutes. Let stand 5 minutes before serving. Sprinkle with remaining 1 Tbsp. thyme.

MAKE IT AHEAD: Bake as directed, let cool, and then cover and chill up to 2 days. Reheat covered with foil.

SAVORY CORN PUDDING

MAMA'S WITH A TWIST

Three-Cheese Corn Pudding

Omit chopped fresh thyme. Prepare casserole recipe as directed, stirring 3 oz. each shredded white Cheddar, sharp yellow Cheddar, and Parmesan cheeses (about ¾ cup each) and ¼ cup chopped fresh flat-leaf parsley into cooled corn mixture in Step 2. Bake casserole as directed.

DELICIOUSLY DIFFERENT

Green Chile-Corn Pudding

Omit chopped fresh thyme. Prepare recipe as directed, cooking 1 cup seeded, chopped poblano chile (from 1 medium chile) with corn and onion in Step 2. Stir 1 (8-oz.) pkg. shredded Mexican cheese blend (2 cups); 1 (5-oz.) can mild diced green chiles, drained; and ¼ cup chopped fresh cilantro into corn mixture before baking. Garnish with additional torn cilantro.

LOST PIES OF THE SOUTH

by **NANCIE MCDERMOTT**

This Thanksgiving, we're inviting you on a little road trip, an imaginary excursion through 10 Southern states, each one with a particular pie worthy of your holiday table. You won't need a map, a seat belt, or car keys for this journey—just an appetite to try something different. These pies, each with a distinct provenance, are full of stories and flavors that are unique to the states from which they came. Feeling adventurous? Bake a streusel-topped persimmon pie inspired by the tangy fruit that grows wild throughout North Carolina. Then try a transparent pie, which is as beloved in some corners of the Bluegrass State as a glass of well-aged bourbon. Or treat yourself to a smooth pumpkin pie made with cushaw squash, an old-time favorite of Cajun and Creole cooks in Louisiana. Wherever you call home, these delicious desserts will give you even more reasons to be thankful.

MOLASSES
WHIPPED CREAM

*recipe,
page 321*

Sliced Sweet Potato Pie

As an accomplished research scientist and educator at Alabama's Tuskegee Institute in the early 20th century, George Washington Carver featured a recipe for Sliced Potato Pie in an agricultural bulletin about sweet potatoes, which encouraged African-American farmers to cultivate the root vegetable as a cash crop and nutritional powerhouse. This double-crust, old-fashioned pie may look ordinary on the outside, but when it's sliced, the inside reveals vibrant orange layers of sweet potatoes flecked with spices and sweetened with sugar and sorghum syrup. We love the simplicity of the classic custard-style sweet potato pie, but on a special occasion like Thanksgiving—a day filled with memory and meaning—this handsome antique version is well worth the time it takes to prepare. For an extra-special touch, we suggest topping each slice with a dollop of whipped cream flavored with molasses and vanilla. Every bite of this dessert tastes like autumn and reminds us what a generous genius Carver was.

recipe,
page 321

CARAMEL
SAUCE

Arkansas Black Apple Pie

ARKANSAS First cultivated in Benton County, Arkansas, in 1870, the Arkansas Black apple is a distinctive heirloom that ripens to a deep red on the tree but transforms to a nearly black hue after a few weeks in storage. Fragrant, tart, and tasty out of hand as well as in baked goods, it also thrives in parts of Georgia, Texas, Tennessee, West Virginia, and beyond the South in Pennsylvania and California. The Arkansas Black keeps for months and ripens after it's picked, improving in flavor and texture over time.

No wonder it's been a favorite of home cooks for generations and continues to be sought out by knowledgeable pastry chefs today. Be on the lookout for this member of the Winesap apple family at farmers' markets and local produce stands. If Arkansas Blacks are not available in your area, Granny Smith apples will make a fine substitute. Though this pie is delicious on its own, it tastes even better served warm with a scoop of vanilla ice cream and a generous drizzle of our homemade Caramel Sauce spiked with apple brandy.

recipe,
page 322

BROWN SUGAR-
BOURBON
WHIPPED CREAM

Peanut Pie

GEORGIA Sure, Georgia has a bounty of gorgeous, plump peaches available by the bushel basket, certain to sweeten the sting of summer's heat. But when it comes to signature, sustaining agricultural contributions to the state's economy, it's really peanuts for the win. Around half of the nation's entire crop of this legume hails from South Georgia soil, and the state shines as the birthplace of President Jimmy Carter–who was also a successful peanut farmer. Runner peanuts, the most common type grown in Georgia, are prized for making rich and creamy peanut butter, which we put to good use in this irresistible dessert. The crunchy, cookie-like peanut butter crust is a perfect partner for the gooey filling spiked with sorghum syrup for a nice farmhouse flavor. A layer of cocktail peanuts delivers a salty note that contrasts nicely with the sweetness underneath. And because we can't leave well enough alone, we topped each slice with a spoonful of Brown Sugar-Bourbon Whipped Cream for a fine, fancy finish.

WHIPPED CRÈME FRAÎCHE AND SUGARED CRANBERRIES

recipe, page 323

Transparent Pie

KENTUCKY We know all about bluegrass music, bourbon, burgoo, and a little horse race known as the Derby, but the state of Kentucky has another sweet reason to brag. It's home to transparent pie, a memorable dessert with a filling made from a few key ingredients: butter, sugar, eggs, flour, vanilla, and a splash of milk or cream. The filling, which is encased in a golden, flaky crust, has the eggy richness of a chess pie but without the cornmeal or vinegar. Magee's Bakery in Maysville, Kentucky, has served up the Bluegrass State's signature confection for decades. Theirs is so good that Kentucky native George Clooney brought his bride by the bakery to sample his favorite pie while on a trip home in 2015. We've kept our version of the classic simple while offering two beautiful holiday embellishments: Sugared Cranberries and Whipped Crème Fraîche. The cranberries bring a glorious pop of color and flavor, and clouds of Whipped Crème Fraîche temper this pie's signature sweetness with a welcome tang.

recipe.
page 323

VANILLA
BEAN
CUSTARD
SAUCE

Cushaw Pie

LOUISIANA A large crookneck winter squash, the cushaw *(Cucurbita mixta)* is a keeper wherever it grows, from its ancient origins in Mesoamerica all the way up into what is now the Southern and Southwestern United States. Graced with a variegated green-striped exterior and golden, naturally sweet flesh, cushaws easily reach 10 pounds. *The Picayune's Creole Cook Book,* first published in 1901, includes a recipe for Pumpkin Pie or *Tarte de Citrouille* with this note: "Use the delicate cashaws *[sic]* for this pie."

Over a century later, you can still spot cushaws at some New Orleans farmers' markets and in home gardens, but concern for their future has led to their inclusion on the *Ark of Taste,* a catalog of foods that are facing extinction. If you're lucky enough to get your hands on a cushaw, roast and puree it to make this distinctive dessert. (Or you can substitute plain canned pumpkin puree for the filling.) Either way, top each slice with our smooth and rich Vanilla Bean Custard Sauce and a few candied pecans.

PECAN
STREUSEL

*recipe,
page 324*

Persimmon Pie

Thriving along the perimeter of North Carolina's corn and tobacco fields, wherever forests meet furrows, tall, spindly persimmon trees lose their leaves in the fall, around the time their fruit turns ripe. Out come all the creatures, from birds and squirrels to opossums and human beings, competing for the flame-colored crop. Frost makes the fruit sweeter, as does the messy work of processing the pulp through a sieve to remove seeds and stems. Thankfully, you can order frozen persimmon puree online (we recommend La Vigne Organics; *lavignefruits.com*) or use the fine domesticated persimmon selections that are available at most grocery stores and farmers' markets nowadays. Both the soft, pointy Hachiya and the firm, tomato-shaped Fuyu can be pureed to make the flavorful filling for this dessert. Make your own crumbly pecan-studded streusel to crown the center of this pie, providing an extra autumnal note to the silky-smooth, gently spiced filling.

Grapefruit Chess Pie

SOUTH CAROLINA Beyond the city of Charleston's sparkling waterfront and colorful buildings is a quieter kind of beauty that most people never get a chance to see. Hidden from public view is an exotic world of backyard citrus trees planted by optimistic residents who hoped the Lowcountry climate might be hospitable enough to let the trees bear fruit. That it has done, and Charleston natives (and brothers) Matt and Ted Lee write about this "unheralded food asset" in their cookbook, *The Lee Bros.*

Charleston Kitchen (2013). Scattered here and there behind older homes around the city, trees bear kumquats, lemons, limes, oranges, and grapefruit—a secret spread-out orchard. Inspired by a neighbor's harvest, the resourceful duo made a creamy, custardy version of Grapefruit Chess Pie. Our take on the Lees' recipe includes Ruby Red grapefruit and a whimsical crust featuring leaf shapes. Thanksgiving declares the arrival of winter, but this lovely dessert reminds us it won't be all snow and ice: It's citrus season too.

*recipe,
page 325*

Over the Moon Chocolate Pie

TENNESSEE   Behold: A nontraditional pie for your holiday table inspired by a sweet confection born in 1917 in Chattanooga. One hundred years later, MoonPie treats are still made there daily and cherished as a lunch box dessert, as a convenience store snack, and (in miniature form) as a prized throw in Mobile, Alabama's annual Mardi Gras parades. The MoonPie is wonderful, famous, and worthy of such adoration, but technically, it's not a pie. Made from two round graham crackers pressed together with marshmallow filling and dipped in chocolate, it's more of a sandwich cookie. So we stepped in to fill the gap between the name and the thing. Our Over the Moon Chocolate Pie is made with a graham cracker crust, has a rich chocolate filling with a touch of Tennessee whiskey (another nod to its birthplace), and is finished off with light clouds of marshmallowy meringue. It's a salute, an homage, an expression of thankfulness for an old-timey Southern snack that continues to endure through generations.

recite,
page 326

Double-Decker Pecan Cheesecake Pie

TEXAS Texas and pecans go back a long way. Native to 152 counties in the Lone Star State, pecan trees have thrived along rivers and streams here for thousands of years. Texans love their old groves of native pecans almost like family, going so far as to designate the beloved icon as the state tree of Texas in 1919. And nearly a century later, a determined group of elementary school students had pecan pie declared the official pie of Texas in 2013. Early historical references to pecan pie include a 1914 *Christian Science Monitor* recipe for Texas Pecan Pie. This recipe predates today's standard corn syrup–based version, calling instead for a simple egg custard filling with chopped nuts on top. Our double-decker confection brings together the two delicious desserts by pairing a layer of creamy cheesecake with a chess-style brown sugar filling. The result is a layered dessert sure to inspire second (or third) helpings and a repeat appearance at next year's gathering.

recipe, page 326

BRANDY WHIPPED CREAM

Caramel Tart

VIRGINIA Rich in history and blessed with fertile soil and a generous climate, the Old Dominion state has an abundance of food-centric reasons for gratitude. First among them is Virginia's status as the birthplace of Edna Lewis, renowned chef, cookbook author, and lifelong champion of the food of the South. In her memoir, *The Taste of Country Cooking,* Lewis shares recipes and stories of her childhood in the rural community of Freetown, founded in lush Central Virginia with the help of her grandfather following

emancipation. Her book, divided into seasons and by occasions, brims with recipes for elegant feasts, picnic spreads, and holiday gatherings. In it, Lewis shares a recipe for Caramel Pie with an admonition: "This is a very haunting dessert, so rich and sweet one could easily overindulge. It's great after a heavy meal, to be served as tiny tarts or in very slender wedges." We agree with Lewis' note about "slender wedges" but couldn't resist dressing up our version with a flourish: whipped cream boosted with a little brandy.

Single-Crust Pie Pastry

ACTIVE 10 MIN. - TOTAL 2 HOURS, 10 MIN.

MAKES 1 CHILLED DOUGH DISK

- 1½ cups all-purpose flour
- ½ tsp. table salt
- 6 Tbsp. cold unsalted butter, cubed
- 2 Tbsp. cold shortening, cubed
- 3 to 4 Tbsp. ice water

1. Pulse flour and salt in a food processor until combined, 3 to 4 times. Add cubed butter and shortening, and pulse until mixture resembles small peas, 4 or 5 times. Sprinkle 3 tablespoons ice water over top of mixture. Pulse 4 times. Add up to 1 more tablespoon of water, 1 teaspoon at a time, pulsing after each addition until dough just begins to clump together.

2. Turn dough out onto a lightly floured work surface; knead until dough comes together, 2 or 3 times. Shape and flatten dough into a disk. Wrap in plastic wrap, and chill 2 hours or up to 2 days.

Double-Crust Pie Pastry

ACTIVE 10 MIN. - TOTAL 2 HOURS, 10 MIN.

MAKES 2 CHILLED DOUGH DISKS

- 3 cups all-purpose flour
- 1 tsp. table salt
- ¾ cup cold unsalted butter, cubed
- ¼ cup cold shortening, cubed
- 4 to 6 Tbsp. ice water

1. Pulse flour and salt in a food processor until combined, 3 or 4 times. Add cubed butter and shortening, and pulse until mixture resembles small peas, 4 or 5 times. Sprinkle 4 tablespoons ice water over top of mixture. Pulse 4 times. Add up to 2 more tablespoons of water, 1 tablespoon at a time, pulsing after each addition until dough just begins to clump together.

2. Turn dough out onto a lightly floured work surface; gently knead until dough comes together, 2 or 3 times. Divide dough in half. Shape and flatten each half into a disk. Wrap each disk in plastic wrap. Chill 2 hours or up to 2 days.

Sliced Sweet Potato Pie with Molasses Whipped Cream

ACTIVE 1 HOUR - TOTAL 6 HOURS, 30 MIN.

SERVES 8

CRUST
Double-Crust Pie Pastry (at left)

SWEET POTATO FILLING

- 3 lb. sweet potatoes (about 6 medium-size sweet potatoes, about 2 inches in diameter)
- 1¼ cups granulated sugar
- 2 Tbsp. all-purpose flour
- ¼ tsp. ground allspice
- ½ tsp. ground ginger
- ½ tsp. ground nutmeg
- ¼ tsp. ground cloves
- ¼ cup sorghum syrup or molasses or pure cane syrup or honey
- ⅓ cup cold unsalted butter, chopped into small pieces

EGG WASH

- 1 large egg
- 1 Tbsp. water
- 2 Tbsp. granulated sugar (optional)

ADDITIONAL INGREDIENT
Molasses Whipped Cream (recipe follows)

1. Prepare the Crust: Unwrap chilled pie dough disks from Double-Crust Pie Pastry, and place on a lightly floured surface. Let stand at room temperature until slightly softened, about 5 minutes. Sprinkle each disk with flour. Roll 1 disk into a 12-inch circle. Carefully fit dough circle into a 9-inch deep-dish glass pie plate, leaving a 1½-inch overhang. Refrigerate until ready to use. Roll remaining disk into a 10-inch circle, and refrigerate until ready to use.

2. Prepare the Sweet Potato Filling: Place whole, unpeeled sweet potatoes in a large pot with water to cover by 2 inches. Bring to a rolling boil over high. Reduce heat to medium, maintaining a gentle boil. Cook until sweet potatoes are just tender enough to be sliced, but not so tender that they fall apart, 25 to 35 minutes. (Remove any smaller sweet potatoes as they are done, allowing larger ones to cook until they reach the ideal texture.)

3. Stir together sugar, flour, allspice, ginger, nutmeg, and cloves in a small bowl.

4. Drain sweet potatoes, and transfer to a platter to cool. Peel potatoes; trim and discard any fibers. Cut potatoes crosswise into ¼-inch-thick rounds. (You will need about 4 cups to generously fill piecrust.) Gently toss sweet potatoes with sugar-spice mixture.

5. Preheat oven to 350°F. Cover bottom of piecrust in pie plate with a layer of Sweet Potato Filling; continue to layer to fill piecrust. Add additional filling to center, building it up a little higher than outer edges. Sprinkle all remaining sugar-spice mixture in bowl over top of pie; drizzle with sorghum syrup, and dot with butter pieces.

6. Carefully place 10-inch dough circle over filling. Fold edges of bottom crust up and over edges of top crust, and press firmly to seal. Using the tines of a fork, press dough around piecrust edge to make a decorative design. Using a sharp knife, cut 8 slits in top piecrust for steam to escape.

7. Prepare the Egg Wash: Stir together egg and water in a small bowl. Using a pastry brush, brush egg mixture evenly over piecrust. Sprinkle sugar over crust, if desired. Place pie on a baking sheet.

8. Bake in preheated oven until crust is browned, filling is bubbly, and sweet potatoes are tender all the way through, about 1 hour.

9. Transfer pie to a wire rack, and cool to room temperature, about 4 hours. Serve Molasses Whipped Cream with pie.

Molasses Whipped Cream

ACTIVE 5 MIN. - TOTAL 5 MIN.

MAKES ABOUT 2 ¼ CUPS

- 1 cup cold whipping cream or heavy cream
- 2 Tbsp. molasses (not blackstrap), pure cane syrup, or sorghum syrup
- ½ tsp. vanilla extract

Using chilled beaters and a large chilled bowl, beat cream with an electric mixer on high speed until thickened, 2 minutes. Add molasses, and beat until stiff peaks form, 2 minutes. Add vanilla extract; beat 1 minute. Cover and chill until ready to serve.

Arkansas Black Apple Pie with Caramel Sauce

ACTIVE 1 HOUR, 40 MIN. - TOTAL 7 HOURS

SERVES 8

APPLE FILLING

- 5 to 6 Arkansas Black or Granny Smith apples (about 3 ½ lb.), peeled and thinly sliced
- 1 Tbsp. fresh lemon juice (from 1 lemon) or apple cider vinegar
- 1 cup granulated sugar

¼ cup all-purpose flour

1 tsp. ground cinnamon

½ tsp. freshly grated or ground nutmeg

¼ tsp. ground allspice

¼ tsp. kosher salt

CRUST
Double-Crust Pie Pastry (page 321)

2 Tbsp. cold unsalted butter, diced

EGG WASH

1 large egg

1 Tbsp. water

2 Tbsp. granulated sugar (optional)

ADDITIONAL INGREDIENTS
Caramel Sauce (recipe follows)

Ice cream (optional)

1. Prepare the Apple Filling: Place apples and fresh lemon juice in a large bowl; toss well to coat. Stir together granulated sugar, flour, ground cinnamon, freshly grated nutmeg, ground allspice, and kosher salt in a bowl; add to apple mixture, and toss well to combine.

2. Prepare the Crust: Preheat oven to 425°F. Unwrap 1 chilled pie dough disk from Double-Crust Pie Pastry, and place on a lightly floured surface. Let stand at room temperature until slightly softened, about 5 minutes. Sprinkle dough with flour, and roll into a 12-inch circle. Carefully fit dough circle into a 9-inch deep-dish glass pie plate, leaving a 1-inch overhang. Spoon filling into prepared crust, packing lightly to fill crust. Smooth out filling until even. (Do not mound in center.) Sprinkle diced butter over apples.

3. Unwrap remaining chilled pie dough disk, and place on a lightly floured surface. Let stand at room temperature until slightly softened, about 5 minutes. Sprinkle dough with flour, and roll into a 12-inch circle. Cut dough round into 10 (¾-inch-wide) strips. Arrange strips in a lattice design over filling; trim strips to be even with the bottom crust's 1-inch overhang. Fold dough edges under, and crimp. Place pie on a rimmed baking sheet.

4. Prepare the Egg Wash: Stir together large egg and water in a small bowl. Using a pastry brush, brush egg mixture evenly over piecrust. Sprinkle granulated sugar over piecrust, if desired.

5. Bake in preheated oven 15 minutes. Reduce oven temperature to 350°F. Loosely cover pie with aluminum foil. Bake at 350°F until crust is golden

brown, apples are tender, and juices are bubbly, 1 hour to 1 hour and 10 minutes, removing foil for the last 10 minutes of baking to finish browning crust. Transfer pie to a wire rack, and cool completely, about 3 hours. Serve pie with Caramel Sauce and, if desired, ice cream.

Caramel Sauce

ACTIVE 40 MIN. - TOTAL 55 MIN.

MAKES ABOUT 1 ½ CUPS

1 ½ cups granulated sugar

3 Tbsp. water

¾ cup heavy cream

½ tsp. vanilla extract

¼ tsp. kosher salt

1 to 2 Tbsp. (½ to 1 oz.) apple brandy (such as Calvados) (optional)

1. Using a long-handled wooden or heatproof metal spoon, stir together sugar and 3 tablespoons water in a deep, heavy 10-inch skillet or medium-size enameled cast-iron saucepan over medium. Cook, stirring occasionally, until sugar is mostly dissolved. Increase heat to medium-high, and bring mixture to a boil, stirring constantly. Cook, stirring, until mixture turns into a clear syrup. Continue to cook, stirring constantly, until mixture dries out, turning sandy and crumbly, and then begins to melt again. Cook, stirring often, until melted mixture darkens to an amber color, 8 to 10 minutes. Remove pan from heat.

2. Carefully pour in heavy cream, stirring constantly. (Caramel will bubble up, boil vigorously, and steam profusely.) Stir constantly until boiling gradually subsides. Return pan to medium-high; cook, stirring until mixture is smooth. Remove pan from heat; stir in vanilla extract, kosher salt, and, if desired, apple brandy. Let Caramel Sauce stand until room temperature, 15 to 20 minutes.

3. Transfer room-temperature Caramel Sauce to a jar or container with an airtight lid. Keep refrigerated up to 2 weeks. Warm over low heat before using.

Georgia Peanut Pie with Peanut Butter Crust and Brown Sugar–Bourbon Whipped Cream

ACTIVE 30 MIN. - TOTAL 5 HOURS, 30 MIN.

SERVES 8

PEANUT BUTTER CRUST

1 ¼ cups all-purpose flour

¼ cup cocktail peanuts or dry-roasted salted peanuts

2 tsp. light brown sugar

½ tsp. kosher salt

5 Tbsp. cold unsalted butter, cubed

2 Tbsp. creamy peanut butter

1 Tbsp. cold shortening, cubed

4 to 6 Tbsp. ice water

PEANUT BUTTER FILLING

1 ¼ cups packed light or dark brown sugar

1 Tbsp. all-purpose flour

¼ tsp. kosher salt

½ cup unsalted butter, melted

3 large eggs

⅓ cup evaporated milk or half-and-half

⅓ cup sorghum syrup, pure cane syrup, or dark corn syrup

½ tsp. vanilla extract

½ cup creamy peanut butter

1 ½ cups cocktail peanuts or dry-roasted salted peanuts

BROWN SUGAR-BOURBON WHIPPED CREAM

1 cup cold whipping cream or heavy cream

2 Tbsp. light brown sugar

1 Tbsp. (½ oz.) bourbon

½ tsp. vanilla extract

1. Prepare the Peanut Butter Crust: Combine flour, peanuts, brown sugar, and salt in bowl of a food processor; process until peanuts are ground and mixture is combined. Add butter, peanut butter, and shortening, and pulse until mixture resembles small peas, 10 to 12 times. Sprinkle 4 tablespoons ice water over top of mixture. Pulse 4 times. Add up to 2 more tablespoons of water, 1 tablespoon at a time, pulsing after each addition until dough just begins to clump together. Remove dough from processor; shape and flatten into a disk. Wrap disk in plastic wrap, and chill 2 hours or up to 2 days.

2. Preheat oven to 375°F. Place chilled dough disk on a lightly floured piece of parchment paper. Sprinkle dough with flour. Top with another piece of parchment paper. Roll dough into a 13-inch circle. Remove and discard top sheet of parchment. Starting at 1 edge of dough, wrap dough around rolling pin, separating dough from bottom sheet of parchment as you roll. Discard bottom sheet of parchment. Place rolling pin wrapped with dough over a 9-inch (1 ½-inch-deep) glass pie plate. Unroll dough, and gently press it into pie plate. Trim dough, leaving ½-inch overhang; fold edges under, and crimp.

3. Prepare Peanut Butter Filling: Stir together brown sugar, flour, and kosher salt in a large bowl. Stir in melted butter. Whisk eggs well in a medium bowl; whisk in milk, sorghum, and vanilla. Add peanut butter; whisk until blended. Add dry ingredients, stirring until blended. Spoon filling into prepared piecrust. Sprinkle peanuts over top, and place pie on a rimmed baking sheet.

4. Bake in preheated oven 10 minutes. Reduce oven temperature to 350°F, and bake until puffed and golden brown and until center is set, 45 to 55 minutes, shielding edges with aluminum foil to prevent overbrowning, if necessary. Transfer pie to a wire rack, and cool completely, about 2 hours.

5. Prepare the Brown Sugar-Bourbon Whipped Cream: Using chilled beaters and a large chilled bowl, beat whipping cream with an electric mixer on high speed until thickened, about 2 minutes. Add sugar, and beat until stiff peaks form, about 2 minutes. Add bourbon and vanilla, and beat until well combined. Cover and chill until ready to serve.

Transparent Pie with Whipped Crème Fraîche and Sugared Cranberries

ACTIVE 40 MIN. - TOTAL 11 HOURS, 20 MIN.
SERVES 8

SUGARED CRANBERRIES
1 ½ cups water
2 ¾ cups granulated sugar, divided
2 cups fresh cranberries (about 8 oz.)
CRUST
Single-Crust Pie Pastry (page 321)
FILLING
1 ½ cups granulated sugar
4 tsp. all-purpose flour
⅛ tsp. kosher salt
6 Tbsp. unsalted butter, melted
3 large eggs
½ cup half-and-half or evaporated milk
½ tsp. vanilla extract
WHIPPED CRÈME FRAÎCHE
2 (8-oz.) containers crème fraîche
6 Tbsp. granulated sugar
1 tsp. vanilla extract

1. Prepare the Sugared Cranberries: Stir together 1 ½ cups water and 1 ¾ cups of the sugar in a medium saucepan. Place over medium, and bring to a simmer, stirring often until sugar dissolves. Continue simmering sugar syrup, without letting it boil, until it thickens slightly, 8 to 10 minutes. Remove from heat, and cool until warm, about 5 minutes. (If cranberries are combined with the sugar syrup when it is too hot, they may burst from the heat.)

2. Combine fresh cranberries and warm sugar syrup in a large bowl. Cool to room temperature, stirring occasionally. Cover bowl, and chill 8 hours or overnight.

3. Sprinkle a rimmed baking sheet with ½ cup of the sugar. Pour chilled cranberry mixture through a wire-mesh strainer over a bowl. (Reserve cranberry syrup in bowl for another use.) Spread cranberries in a single layer on sugar on baking sheet. Sprinkle with remaining ½ cup sugar. Gently shake baking sheet, making sure cranberries are evenly coated with sugar. Let stand, uncovered, until cranberries are dry and crisp, about 2 hours. Shake off any excess sugar on cranberries, and place in an airtight container. Store at room temperature for up to 2 days.

4. Prepare the Crust: Preheat oven to 375°F. Unwrap chilled pie dough disk from Single-Crust Pie Pastry, and place on a lightly floured surface. Let stand at room temperature until slightly softened, about 5 minutes. Sprinkle dough with flour, and roll into a 12-inch circle. Carefully fit dough circle into a 9-inch glass pie plate; fold edges under, and crimp. Line pastry with parchment paper, and fill with pie weights or dried beans.

5. Bake in preheated oven 15 minutes. Transfer crust to a wire rack; remove pie weights and parchment, and let crust cool, about 30 minutes. Increase oven temperature to 400°F.

6. Prepare the Filling: Whisk together sugar, flour, and salt in a large bowl. Add melted butter to flour mixture, stirring with a fork until mixture is combined and resembles damp sand.

7. Whisk eggs in a medium bowl until well beaten. Add half-and-half and vanilla, and whisk until well combined. Pour egg mixture over sugar-butter mixture, and whisk to combine into a smooth, thick, creamy yellow filling. Pour into prepared piecrust.

8. Bake at 400°F for 5 minutes. Reduce oven temperature to 375°F. Bake until edges puff up and center is fairly firm, wiggling only slightly when you gently nudge pie plate, about 35 minutes. Transfer pie to a wire rack, and cool to room temperature, about 2 hours.

9. Prepare the Whipped Crème Fraîche: Beat crème fraîche in a large bowl with an electric mixer on medium-high speed until soft and lightened in texture, about 2 minutes. Add sugar and vanilla, and beat until smooth, fluffy, and well combined, about 2 minutes. Cover and chill until ready to serve. Top pie with Whipped Crème Fraîche and Sugared Cranberries.

Cushaw Pie with Vanilla Bean Custard Sauce

ACTIVE 45 MIN. - TOTAL 8 HOURS
SERVES 8

VANILLA BEAN CUSTARD SAUCE
5 large egg yolks
½ cup granulated sugar
Pinch of kosher salt
½ vanilla bean pod
2 cups half-and-half
CRUST
Double-Crust Pie Pastry (page 321)
CUSHAW FILLING
¾ cup granulated sugar
½ tsp. ground ginger
½ tsp. kosher salt
¼ tsp. ground nutmeg
2 cups roasted cushaw puree (or other winter squash such as Candy Roaster, butternut squash, kabocha squash, or canned pumpkin)
¾ cup heavy cream, evaporated milk, or half-and-half
¼ cup honey or pure maple syrup
2 large eggs, well beaten
Chopped candied pecans (optional)

1. Prepare the Vanilla Bean Custard Sauce: Whisk together egg yolks, granulated sugar, and kosher salt in a medium bowl until very smooth. Set aside.

2. Split vanilla bean open lengthwise, and scrape out seeds into a medium saucepan. Add half-and-half, and cook over medium, whisking vigorously, to disperse seeds into milk and until small bubbles form around edges of pan and

mixture is very hot but not quite boiling. Remove from heat.

3. Whisking constantly, gradually pour ¼ cup hot half-and-half mixture into egg yolk mixture. Continue whisking hot half-and-half mixture into egg yolk mixture, ¼ cup at a time, until completely combined. Transfer mixture to saucepan, and place over low heat.

4. Cook, whisking constantly, until custard thickens enough to coat the back of a spoon and your finger leaves a clear line when drawn through the custard, 20 to 25 minutes. (Do not allow it to boil, or it will curdle.) Immediately remove from heat, and quickly pour through a fine wire-mesh strainer over a medium bowl. Discard solids in strainer.

5. Let custard cool 10 minutes, stirring occasionally. Place plastic wrap directly on the custard (to prevent a film from forming). Refrigerate until very cold, at least 4 hours or overnight. (It will thicken as it chills.)

6. Prepare the Crust: Preheat oven to 375°F. Unwrap chilled pie dough disks from Double-Crust Pie Pastry, and place on a lightly floured surface. Let stand at room temperature until slightly softened, about 5 minutes. Sprinkle each disk with flour, and roll into 12-inch circles. Carefully fit 1 dough circle into a 9-inch deep-dish glass pie plate; fold edges under, and press to flatten.

7. Cut the remaining disk into ¼-inch strips. Braid the strips, 3 at a time. Using a pastry brush, brush a little water around the entire edge of the bottom crust. Gently press the braided strips to the moistened edge to adhere. Line pastry with parchment paper, and fill with pie weights or dried beans.

8. Bake in preheated oven 15 minutes. Transfer to a wire rack, and remove pie weights and parchment. Cool 30 minutes. Increase oven temperature to 450°F.

9. Prepare the Cushaw Filling: Stir together sugar, ginger, kosher salt, and nutmeg in a small bowl. Whisk together roasted cushaw puree, heavy cream, honey, and eggs in a medium bowl until thickened and smooth. Stir in sugar-spice mixture until incorporated. Pour filling into prepared piecrust.

10. Bake at 450°F for 10 minutes. Reduce oven temperature to 325°F. Bake until edges puff up and center is almost firm, wiggling only slightly in center when you gently nudge pie plate, about 30 minutes. Transfer to a wire rack, and cool to room temperature, about 2 hours. Sprinkle with chopped candied pecans, if desired. Serve with Vanilla Bean Custard Sauce.

Persimmon Pie with Pecan Streusel

ACTIVE 50 MIN. - TOTAL 6 HOURS, 45 MIN.
SERVES 8

PECAN STREUSEL
¼ cup plus 2 Tbsp. all-purpose flour
2 Tbsp. packed light brown sugar
2 Tbsp. granulated sugar
¼ tsp. ground cinnamon
  Pinch of freshly grated or ground nutmeg
  Pinch of kosher salt
¼ cup unsalted butter, softened to room temperature and cut into 4 pieces
2 Tbsp. plus 2 tsp. roughly chopped pecans

CRUST
Single-Crust Pie Pastry (page 321)

PERSIMMON FILLING
3 cups persimmon puree (such as La Vigne Organics)
1 cup granulated sugar
2 Tbsp. all-purpose flour
1 tsp. ground cinnamon
½ tsp. ground nutmeg
½ tsp. kosher salt
3 Tbsp. unsalted butter, melted
¾ cup evaporated milk
3 large eggs, well beaten

1. Prepare the Pecan Streusel: Whisk together flour, sugars, cinnamon, nutmeg, and salt in a bowl. Using your fingers, rub butter into dry ingredients until mixture is crumbly and forms large, moist clumps. Add pecans, and work into clumps until incorporated. Refrigerate until mixture is very cold and firm, 1 to 2 hours. (Or cover bowl, and refrigerate up to 2 days.)

2. Prepare the Crust: Preheat oven to 375°F. Unwrap chilled pie dough disk from Single-Crust Pie Pastry, and place on a lightly floured surface. Let stand at room temperature until slightly softened, about 5 minutes. Sprinkle dough with flour, and roll into a 12-inch circle. Carefully fit dough circle into a 9-inch deep-dish glass pie plate, leaving a ½-inch overhang. Fold edges under.

3. Prepare the Persimmon Filling: Place persimmon puree in a large saucepan over medium-high; bring to a boil. Reduce heat to medium-low, and simmer, stirring often, until reduced to 2 cups, about 30 minutes. Pour puree on a rimmed baking sheet to quickly cool, about 10 minutes, stirring occasionally.

4. Stir together sugar, flour, cinnamon, nutmeg, and kosher salt in a small bowl until well combined. Add melted butter to sugar mixture, stirring with a fork until mixture is evenly combined and resembles damp sand.

5. Stir together evaporated milk and eggs in a medium bowl. Add sugar-butter mixture, and stir until mixture is smooth and creamy. Add persimmon puree, and stir until well combined.

6. Pour filling into piecrust. Bake in preheated oven until filling is partially set (has lost its initial liquid texture and overall shiny surface), 25 to 30 minutes.

7. Remove pie from oven. Reduce oven temperature to 350°F. Using your fingers, break cold Pecan Streusel into small clumps, and sprinkle over center of pie. Return pie to oven, and bake until pie filling is firm, puffed up, and set, 25 to 30 minutes. Transfer pie to a wire rack, and cool to room temperature, about 3 hours.

Grapefruit Chess Pie

ACTIVE 1 HOUR - TOTAL 5 HOURS, 20 MIN.
SERVES 8

CRUST
Double-Crust Pie Pastry (page 321)
2 Tbsp. granulated sugar

FILLING
2 large Ruby Red grapefruit
¾ tsp. kosher salt
2 large eggs
1 large egg white
½ cup heavy cream, at room temperature
¼ cup unsalted butter, melted
1 cup granulated sugar
3 Tbsp. all-purpose flour
2 Tbsp. fine yellow cornmeal
  Sweetened whipped cream

1. Prepare the Crust: Preheat oven to 375°F. Unwrap chilled pie dough disks from Double-Crust Pie Pastry, and place on a lightly floured surface. Let stand at room temperature until slightly softened, about 5 minutes. Sprinkle

dough disks with flour. Roll 1 disk into a 12-inch circle, and carefully fit into a 9-inch deep-dish glass pie plate. Trim dough to cover flat rim of pie plate. Set aside in refrigerator.

2. Roll remaining dough disk to ¼-inch thickness. Use a 1-inch leaf-shaped cutter or a paring knife to cut out, free-form, 35 to 40 leaves from pie dough piece. Use back edge of paring knife to score lines in dough leaves to resemble veins.

3. Brush dough leaves with water, and attach to piecrust edge; gently pressing to adhere. Sprinkle with sugar. Chill 30 minutes.

4. Cut a square of parchment paper large enough to completely cover pie plate. Crumble parchment, and crush into a tight ball. (This helps soften its texture so it will fit over the unbaked piecrust evenly.) Open ball of crushed parchment sheet, and flatten out. Carefully line pastry with parchment, covering inner pastry well and shielding dough leaves without touching them. Fill with pie weights or dried beans.

5. Bake piecrust in preheated oven 15 minutes. Remove piecrust from oven, and carefully remove pie weights and parchment paper. Return to oven, and bake until mostly dry and golden, about 10 minutes, loosely covering dough leaves with aluminum foil or parchment paper to prevent overbrowning. Transfer crust to a wire rack, and cool 30 minutes.

6. Prepare the Filling: Reduce oven temperature to 300°F. Finely grate 1 grapefruit to yield 2 teaspoons zest; set aside.

7. Slice off stem end and base of each grapefruit, exposing juicy pulp inside. Place 1 grapefruit on a cutting board with flat base down. Cut off a 2-inch-wide strip of peel and white pith, slicing deeply along the curved side to expose juicy pulp inside. Cut another strip from opposite side of fruit, and continue, alternating sides, completely exposing fruit. Discard peel and pith.

8. Working over a shallow bowl to catch the juice, remove grapefruit segments from pith using a small, sharp knife. Hold fruit in 1 hand and a small knife in the other, slicing along inside wall of 1 segment from outside to center. Slice other side to release juicy segment, and place in a bowl. Continue around the fruit, squeezing core over bowl to capture all the juice. Gently strain segments into bowl, reserving segments and juice separately. You will need 1 cup grapefruit segments and ½ cup grapefruit juice. Stir grapefruit zest and salt into grapefruit juice. Reserve any extra segments or juice for another use.

9. Whisk together eggs and egg white in a large bowl until light, creamy, and smooth. Whisk in cream and melted butter. Stir together sugar, flour, and cornmeal in a medium bowl. Add to egg mixture, in 3 batches, whisking well after each addition. Add grapefruit juice mixture; stir until well combined, smooth, and creamy.

10. Carefully spoon filling into prepared piecrust. Arrange grapefruit segments on filling, placing gently so they float on top. Place pie on a rimmed baking sheet. Loosely cover dough leaves with aluminum foil to avoid overbrowning.

11. Bake at 300°F until top is browned and pie filling is set, about 50 minutes, removing foil for last 5 to 10 minutes of baking. Transfer pie to a wire rack, and cool completely, about 2 hours. Serve with sweetened whipped cream.

Over the Moon Chocolate Pie
ACTIVE 50 MIN. - TOTAL 9 HOURS, 55 MIN.
SERVES 8

GRAHAM CRACKER CRUST
1½ cups graham cracker crumbs
½ cup unsalted butter, melted
⅓ cup granulated sugar
MARSHMALLOW LAYER
1½ cups miniature marshmallows
CHOCOLATE FILLING
12 oz. semisweet chocolate chips
10 oz. milk chocolate chips
1 cup heavy cream
1 Tbsp. unsalted butter
¼ tsp. kosher salt
1 tsp. vanilla extract
2 Tbsp. (1 oz.) Tennessee whiskey (optional)
MARSHMALLOW MERINGUE
2 large egg whites
1 cup granulated sugar
¼ cup light corn syrup
¼ tsp. cream of tartar
¼ tsp. kosher salt
1 tsp. vanilla bean paste or vanilla extract

1. Prepare the Graham Cracker Crust: Preheat oven to 350°F. Place graham cracker crumbs, melted butter, and granulated sugar in a medium bowl. Stir until mixture is well combined and resembles damp sand. Press on bottom and up sides of a 9-inch deep-dish glass pie plate.

2. Bake in preheated oven until crust is firm, dry, and lightly browned, about 10 minutes. Transfer to a wire rack, and cool to room temperature, about 20 minutes.

3. Prepare the Marshmallow Layer: Spread marshmallows in an even layer on bottom of baked Graham Cracker Crust. Return crust to preheated oven, and bake just until marshmallows begin to melt, about 3 minutes. (Do not let marshmallows turn brown or crisp.) Remove from oven, and spread melted marshmallows into an even layer using a small offset spatula or the back of a teaspoon. Cool to room temperature, about 20 minutes.

4. Prepare the Chocolate Filling: Combine chocolate chips in a large bowl. Bring cream to a simmer in a medium saucepan over medium-high. Cook until cream is very hot and bubbles start to form around edges of pan. Remove from heat, and immediately pour over chocolate chips. Let stand 1 minute. Add butter and salt, and whisk until chocolate is completely melted and mixture is smooth. Gently whisk in vanilla, and, if desired, whiskey. Cool to room temperature, 15 to 20 minutes. (Filling should be thickened but still pourable.)

5. Spoon Chocolate Filling over melted marshmallow in piecrust, and spread in an even layer. Loosely cover pie with plastic wrap, and let stand at room temperature 8 hours or overnight. (No need to refrigerate the pie. It is best left at room temperature.)

6. Prepare the Marshmallow Meringue: Fill a medium saucepan one-third full of water, and bring it to a simmer over medium-high. Reduce heat to low, maintaining a simmer.

7. Whisk together egg whites, sugar, light corn syrup, cream of tartar, and salt in a large heatproof bowl. Set bowl over saucepan of simmering water. (Or use a double boiler instead of saucepan and heatproof bowl.) Cook, whisking constantly, until sugar completely dissolves. Remove bowl from heat.

8. Beat mixture with an electric mixer on medium speed until mixture begins to thicken, scraping down sides of bowl often to maintain a smooth texture, 3 to 4 minutes.

9. Increase mixer speed to high, and continue beating and scraping down sides as mixture thickens and becomes smooth and shiny. Continue beating until mixture becomes a glossy meringue that holds its shape, clings to a spoon, forms curly peaks, and leaves tracks from beaters in surface, 5 to 10 minutes.

10. Add vanilla bean paste. Beat on high speed, scraping down sides of bowl often, until meringue starts to lose its glossy shine and develops a sheen, 1 to 2 minutes.

11. Spoon Marshmallow Meringue over top of pie. (Use meringue within 2 to 3 hours for fluffiest texture, or cover and refrigerate for up to 3 days. Meringue will lose some of its puffiness and loft but will remain beautiful, usable, and delicious.)

Double-Decker Pecan Cheesecake Pie

ACTIVE 20 MIN. - TOTAL 4 HOURS, 20 MIN.
SERVES 8

CRUST
Single-Crust Pie Pastry (page 321)
CREAM CHEESE FILLING
1 (8-oz.) pkg. cream cheese, at room temperature
1 large egg
1 tsp. vanilla bean paste
½ tsp. kosher salt
⅓ cup granulated sugar
BROWN SUGAR FILLING
2 large eggs
½ cup packed light brown sugar
½ cup dark or light corn syrup
1 to 2 Tbsp. (½ to 1 oz.) Tennessee whiskey
1 tsp. vanilla bean paste or vanilla extract
ADDITIONAL INGREDIENTS
½ cup chopped pecans
1¼ cups pecan halves

1. Prepare the Crust: Preheat oven to 375°F. Unwrap chilled pie dough disk from Single-Crust Pie Pastry, and place on a lightly floured surface. Let stand at room temperature until slightly softened, about 5 minutes. Sprinkle dough with flour, and roll into a 12-inch circle. Carefully fit dough circle into a 9-inch deep-dish glass pie plate; fold

edges under, and crimp. Line pastry with parchment paper, and fill with pie weights or dried beans.

2. Bake in preheated oven 15 minutes. Transfer piecrust to a wire rack, and remove pie weights and parchment. Let crust cool 30 minutes.

3. Prepare the Cream Cheese Filling: Beat cream cheese, egg, vanilla bean paste, and salt in a medium bowl with an electric mixer on medium speed until light and fluffy, 1 to 2 minutes. Add sugar, and beat until filling is smooth and fluffy, about 2 minutes. Spoon filling into prepared piecrust.

4. Prepare the Brown Sugar Filling: Whisk eggs until bright yellow and well combined. Add brown sugar, corn syrup, Tennessee whiskey, and vanilla bean paste, and whisk together until thickened and smooth.

5. Sprinkle chopped pecans over Cream Cheese Filling in piecrust. Gently spoon Brown Sugar Filling over chopped pecans. Arrange pecan halves over Brown Sugar Filling. Place pie on a baking sheet. Bake at 375°F for 10 minutes. Reduce oven temperature to 350°F, and bake until filling is puffed up and set and crust is golden brown, 40 to 45 minutes. Transfer pie to a wire rack, and cool completely, 2 to 3 hours.

Caramel Tart with Brandy Whipped Cream

ACTIVE 40 MIN. - TOTAL 6 HOURS, 25 MIN.
SERVES 12

TART CRUST
1¼ cups all-purpose flour
⅓ cup granulated sugar
½ tsp. table salt
½ cup cold unsalted butter
1 large egg yolk
2 to 3 Tbsp. ice water
CARAMEL FILLING
1½ cups packed light brown sugar
1 Tbsp. all-purpose flour
⅛ tsp. kosher salt
½ cup whole milk, at room temperature
2 Tbsp. dark corn syrup or sorghum syrup or pure maple syrup
1 Tbsp. unsalted butter, melted
1 tsp. vanilla extract
1 large egg, separated
BRANDY WHIPPED CREAM
1 pt. cold whipping cream or heavy cream

¼ cup granulated sugar
2 Tbsp. (1 oz.) brandy
½ tsp. vanilla extract

1. Prepare the Tart Crust: Combine flour, granulated sugar, and salt in bowl of a food processor. Pulse until well combined, 5 to 7 times. Add butter, and pulse just until mixture resembles coarse sand, 5 to 7 times.

2. Add egg yolk and 2 tablespoons ice water, and pulse until mixture comes together and forms a ball, adding remaining 1 tablespoon ice water, 1 teaspoon at a time, if necessary. Shape and flatten dough into a disk. Wrap in plastic wrap, and chill 1 hour or up to 2 days.

3. Grease (with butter) a 9-inch fluted tart pan with removable bottom. Unwrap chilled dough disk, and place on a lightly floured surface. Let stand at room temperature until slightly softened, about 5 minutes. Sprinkle dough with flour, and roll into a 10-inch circle. Gently drape dough circle over prepared tart pan; place in pan. Press dough on bottom and up sides of pan. Cover and chill 30 minutes or up to 2 days.

4. Prepare the Caramel Filling: Preheat oven to 350°F. Stir together brown sugar, flour, and salt in a large bowl.

5. Whisk together whole milk, dark corn syrup, melted butter, vanilla extract, and egg yolk in a bowl, and pour over brown sugar mixture. Stir until well combined.

6. Whisk egg white in a medium bowl until thick and creamy and holds soft peaks. Fold beaten egg white into corn syrup mixture until incorporated and mixture becomes caramel colored and smooth. Spoon Caramel Filling into prepared Tart Crust. Place pan on a rimmed baking sheet.

7. Bake in preheated oven until center is set and filling is puffed and golden brown, 45 to 50 minutes. Transfer to a wire rack, and cool completely, about 3 hours.

8. Prepare the Brandy Whipped Cream: Using chilled beaters and a large chilled bowl, beat cold whipping cream with an electric mixer on high speed until thickened, about 2 minutes. Add sugar, and beat until stiff peaks form, about 2 minutes. Stir in brandy and vanilla extract. Top servings with Brandy Whipped Cream.

COLLARD
GREEN CREOLE
DIRTY RICE
page 328

TRADE KALE FOR
COLLARDS

These leafy greens are healthy,
delicious, in season, and in style

by **VIRGINIA WILLIS**

DO YOU REMEMBER just a few years ago when kale became the hot new thing? Suddenly, bunches of glamorous greens with sophisticated, international names (like Lacinato, Red Russian, Siberian, and Smooth German) started gracing supermarket shelves. Farmers' markets didn't miss out on the craze either and offered colorful bundles of Scarlet and Dwarf Blue kale—with equally precious prices. Restaurant menus featured the vegetable in the form of snacks, salads, smoothies, and soups. Kale was sexy; kale was on the catwalk; kale was the beauty queen of brassicas.

But according to a 2014 study of the nutritional density of powerhouse fruits and vegetables conducted by the Centers for Disease Control and Prevention, it turns out it's a case of style over substance in this situation. Kale, the supermodel of superfoods, came in at number 15, while collard greens—kale's country cousin—ranked 10th. Kale was a full five spots below collards; it didn't even make it into the top 10.

Why haven't collard greens gotten kale's celebrity treatment? Down South, we know that collards are good and good for you. Heirloom selections like Georgia Southern and Alabama Blue certainly don't sound exotic, but they are the stars of country cooking. However, in the rest of America, collards are misunderstood, thought to be the domain of poor Southerners, and they're prepared only in one way: drowned in pork fat and cooked beyond recognition into a form of army green pabulum. We are partially to blame for that misconception. As Southerners moved away from their native region or improved their financial situations, many left behind down-home cooking styles too. And while I love old-school collard greens (especially with a wedge of skillet cornbread), there are so many more ways to enjoy them. Anything kale can do, collards can do too.

TURKEY-AND-COLLARD GREEN STEW

simmer, stirring occasionally, until greens are tender, about 45 minutes. Add shredded turkey, and cook until heated through, about 5 minutes. Stir in salt and pepper. Spoon stew over hot cooked rice, and serve with hot sauce.

Collard Green Creole Dirty Rice

ACTIVE 20 MIN. - TOTAL 40 MIN.
SERVES 6

- 1 Tbsp. canola oil
- 1 medium-size yellow onion, chopped (about 2 cups)
- 1 celery stalk, chopped (about ½ cup)
- 1 poblano chile, seeded and chopped
- 3 garlic cloves, minced (about 2 tsp.)
- 4 oz. chicken sausage (such as andouille or Italian), casings removed, finely chopped
- 1 cup uncooked long-grain white rice
- 1 Tbsp. chopped fresh thyme
- 2 tsp. smoked paprika
- ¼ tsp. cayenne pepper or more to taste
- 2 cups chicken stock
- 8 oz. collard greens, stems trimmed, large ribs removed, and finely chopped
- 1 tsp. coarse kosher salt
- 1 tsp. black pepper
- 2 scallions, trimmed and thinly sliced
  Hot sauce

1. Heat oil in a large skillet over medium. Add onion, celery, and poblano, and cook, stirring often, until onion is translucent, about 5 minutes. Add garlic; cook, stirring constantly, until fragrant, about 1 minute. Add sausage; cook, stirring with a wooden spoon, until sausage crumbles and is no longer pink, about 3 minutes. Add rice, thyme, paprika, and cayenne; cook, stirring constantly, until fragrant, about 1 minute. Stir in stock, collard greens, salt, and black pepper. Bring to a boil; cover and reduce heat to low. Simmer until rice is tender, about 18 minutes.

2. Remove from heat, and let stand, covered, 5 minutes. Add scallions, and fluff with a fork to combine. Serve warm with hot sauce.

Turkey-and-Collard Green Stew

ACTIVE 25 MIN. - TOTAL 1 HOUR, 15 MIN.
SERVES 10

- 3 Tbsp. canola oil or bacon drippings, divided
- ½ lb. chaurice, fresh Mexican chorizo, or hot Italian pork sausage, casings removed
- 3 Tbsp. all-purpose flour
- 1 medium-size sweet onion, chopped (about 2 cups)
- 1 medium-size red bell pepper, chopped (about 1 cup)
- 1 celery stalk, chopped (about ½ cup)
- 3 garlic cloves, minced (about 2 tsp.)
- 1 qt. unsalted chicken stock or reduced-fat, low-sodium chicken broth
- 1½ lb. collard greens, stems trimmed, large ribs removed, and roughly chopped
- 8 oz. shredded roasted turkey
- 1 tsp. coarse kosher salt
- ½ tsp. black pepper
- 5 cups hot cooked rice
  Hot sauce

1. Heat 1 tablespoon of the oil in a large, heavy-bottomed saucepan over medium. Add sausage, and cook, stirring often with a wooden spoon, until sausage crumbles and is cooked through, about 5 minutes. Using a slotted spoon, transfer sausage to a plate lined with paper towels to drain, reserving drippings in saucepan.

2. Stir in flour and remaining 2 tablespoons oil with a wooden spoon, and cook, stirring constantly, until mixture turns deep golden brown, about 10 minutes. Add onion, bell pepper, and celery, and cook, stirring often, until onion is translucent, about 4 minutes. Add garlic, and cook, stirring often, until fragrant, 1 minute. Add stock, stirring with a wooden spoon to loosen any browned bits from bottom of pan. Bring to a boil.

3. Stir in collard greens and cooked sausage; reduce heat to low, and

Sweet Potato-and-Collard Green Gratin

ACTIVE 30 MIN. - TOTAL 1 HOUR, 45 MIN.

SERVES 8 TO 10

- ½ tsp. freshly grated nutmeg
  Pinch of ground allspice
- 2 tsp. coarse sea salt, divided
- 2 tsp. black pepper, divided
- 1 Tbsp. olive oil, plus more for greasing dish
- 8 oz. collard greens, stems trimmed, large ribs removed, and roughly chopped
- 2 garlic cloves, minced (about 2 tsp.)
- 2 Tbsp. unsalted butter
- 2 Tbsp. all-purpose flour
- 1½ cups 2% reduced-fat milk, warmed (about 120°F)
- 4 oz. Parmigiano-Reggiano cheese, grated (about ½ cup), divided
- 3 Tbsp. panko (Japanese-style breadcrumbs), divided
- 3 lb. sweet potatoes, peeled and cut into ¼-inch-thick slices (about 4 medium potatoes)

2 Tbsp. melted unsalted butter

1. Preheat oven to 400°F. Combine nutmeg, allspice, and 1 teaspoon each of the salt and pepper in a bowl; set aside.

2. Heat 1 tablespoon of the oil in a large skillet over medium-high. Add collard greens, and cook, stirring often, until bright green, about 2 minutes. Add garlic, and cook, stirring constantly, until fragrant, about 1 minute. Season with ¼ teaspoon each of the salt and pepper.

3. Melt 2 tablespoons butter in a small, heavy-bottomed saucepan over medium. Whisk in flour; cook, whisking constantly, until mixture bubbles and flour is cooked but not browned, about 2 minutes. Whisk in warm milk; bring to a boil, whisking occasionally. Reduce heat to low, and cook, whisking occasionally, until sauce thickens, about 2 minutes. Add ¼ cup of the cheese, stirring until melted. Season with ½ teaspoon each of the salt and pepper. Remove white sauce from heat.

4. Sprinkle 1 tablespoon of the panko on bottom of a 2-quart baking dish lightly greased with olive oil. Layer half of the sweet potatoes evenly over breadcrumbs; season with remaining ¼ teaspoon each salt and pepper. Spoon collard green mixture over sweet potatoes; sprinkle with half of nutmeg mixture. Top with remaining sweet potatoes; sprinkle with remaining nutmeg mixture.

5. Pour white sauce over sweet potatoes, and cover dish with a piece of parchment paper. Bake in preheated oven until sweet potatoes are soft when pierced with the tip of a knife, about 40 minutes. Meanwhile, combine 2 tablespoons melted butter and remaining 2 tablespoons panko and ¼ cup cheese. Reduce oven temperature to 375°F. Remove dish from oven, discard parchment, and sprinkle panko mixture evenly over potatoes. Bake, uncovered, until golden brown, about 25 more minutes. Transfer to a wire rack; let stand 10 minutes before serving.

THANKSGIVING EDITION

For our best-ever turkey recipe, go to *southernliving.com/turkey*.

KITCHEN TRICKS

Secrets to Crispy, Golden Turkey

▶ START WITH DRY SKIN
Moisture is the enemy of a crisp exterior. Use paper towels to thoroughly pat the outside of the turkey dry before it goes into the oven. Or simply air-dry it, uncovered, in the refrigerator one day in advance.

▶ ADD SOME FAT
After patting the exterior dry, fully coat the turkey with an even layer of oil or butter. Oil (which does not contain water) will yield the crispiest skin, but butter will give it more flavor.

▶ KEEP IT UNCOVERED
Tenting the cooked poultry with aluminum foil traps heat and creates steam, which will soften that perfect skin. Cool the turkey as is in the pan—it will still be warm by the time it hits the serving platter.

GREAT DEBATE

Dry Brine vs. Wet Brine

Test Kitchen pros face off over the best way to brine a bird

"Dry-brining with a mix of salt and sugar draws the natural moisture of the bird to the surface for the crispiest skin and most flavorful meat you've ever had. It's much less messy too."

MARK DRISKILL

"Wet-brining is the best way to lock in moisture. The long soak breaks down the turkey's protein fibers, allowing it to absorb the seasoned water, which adds more flavor and tenderizes the meat. This method requires extra time and fridge space (or a cooler), but the results are well worth it."

PAIGE GRANDJEAN

CROWD-PLEASERS

Two Turkeys Are Better than One

Are you prepared for hungry holiday guests? Rather than hunting for a supersize bird big enough for everyone, buy two that weigh 12 pounds or less, and cook them at the same time in separate pans (if oven space allows). Two smaller turkeys will cook more evenly and quickly than a single giant one. Bonus: extra drumsticks!

SEASONAL STAPLES

Ingredients for Great Gravy

1. WONDRA FLOUR
This finely ground flour will dissolve instantly in hot liquid for consistently silky-smooth, lump-free results.

2. LOW-SODIUM CHICKEN STOCK
Using reduced-sodium chicken stock allows you to control the seasoning better.

3. HEAVY CREAM
Finish the gravy by stirring in 1 to 2 tablespoons of heavy cream, which will add extra richness.

INSTANT UPGRADES

Better-Tasting Dressing

Even if you've served the same recipe for generations, four tiny tweaks will take this traditional holiday dish to the next level

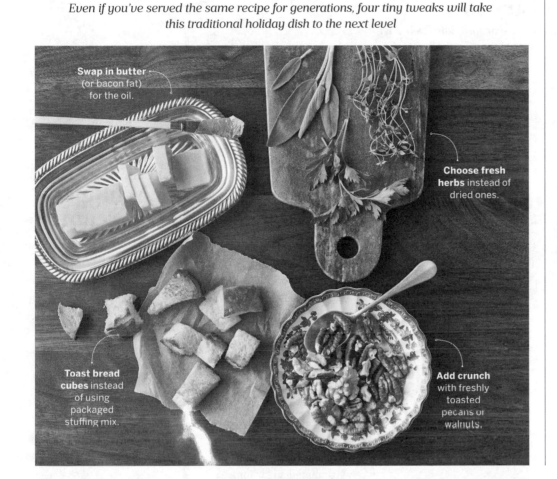

Swap in butter (or bacon fat) for the oil.

Choose fresh herbs instead of dried ones.

Toast bread cubes instead of using packaged stuffing mix.

Add crunch with freshly toasted pecans or walnuts.

"The key to Southern-style dressing is savory corn-bread that's been properly dried. Bake it one to two days ahead, and let it cool. Wrap it in plastic wrap, and store it on your countertop until you're ready to make the dressing. Air-drying creates a better texture than oven-toasting."

—Robby Melvin
Test Kitchen Director

ALMOST HOMEMADE

Fast & Fancy Frozen Rolls

Tasty bread toppers that will rise to your most festive occasions

1

PARKER HOUSE
Brush frozen rolls with melted butter. Sprinkle tops with black pepper, flaky salt, and sesame seeds. Then bake as directed.

2

CLOVERLEAF
Brush frozen rolls with melted honey butter. Sprinkle tops with flaky salt and chopped rosemary leaves. Then bake as directed.

3

YEAST
Brush frozen rolls with olive oil. Sprinkle tops with grated Parmesan cheese, onion flakes, and fresh thyme leaves. Then bake as directed.

MADE WITH LOVE

Pie Baking Tips from Our Pastry Pro

Test Kitchen baker extraordinaire Deb Wise shares her tips for mastering these classics

Pumpkin

WHISK THE SPICES into the plain pumpkin puree; they will be incorporated more evenly in the filling.

WATCH THE PIE carefully at the end of the baking time. Remove it from the oven when the center (about a 3-inch circle) is still wobbly like gelatin. As the pie cools, it will firm up but remain creamy and silky.

ADD AN EXTRA EGG to the pumpkin filling for softer, more custard-like results.

ENSURE A CRISP CRUST by baking the pie on a rack in the lower third of the oven.

Apple

SLICE THE APPLES evenly so they will bake in the same amount of time.

AVOID THE GAP between the top crust and the filling by partially cooking apples in a skillet before you add them to the pie. Uncooked apples will shrink during baking.

COOL THE FILLING before pouring it into the bottom crust. This will keep the butter firm, which makes for a flakier crust.

Pecan

DON'T OVERTOAST the pecans. Spread the nuts in a single layer on a baking sheet, and toast at 350°F for 5 to 6 minutes or until just fragrant.

CHOP PECANS instead of using whole nuts, which will make it tricky to cut clean slices of pie.

USE LIGHT CORN SYRUP and granulated sugar for a rich, buttery taste, or mix dark corn syrup with packed brown sugar to achieve a deeper caramel flavor.

REMOVE THE PIE from the oven when a knife inserted in the center comes out with a clear coating of the filling that is not grainy or lumpy. The filling will firm up as it cools.

KNOW-HOW

The Right Way to Make Whipped Cream

▶ You can choose between heavy cream and whipping cream. Heavy cream has a higher fat content, which makes sturdier whipped cream. Whipping cream beats up a bit silkier and lighter.

▶ Whipped cream comes together much faster if everything is cold. Start with chilled cream, and pop the mixing bowl and beaters (or whisk) in the freezer for 15 minutes.

▶ Use powdered sugar or superfine granulated sugar for the smoothest texture.

ADD EXTRA FLAVOR

Start with 2 cups whipped cream, and then gently fold in 1 tablespoon of any of these ingredients.

1. Finely minced crystallized ginger
2. Ground cinnamon
3. Fresh orange zest
4. Almond extract

December

HOMEMADE
for the
Holidays

No gift is more appreciated than one
that has been made from scratch—
especially when it tastes as good as it looks

The Craft Cocktail

Pineapple Margarita Mix

When poured into a glass flip-top bottle, this tangy cocktail mixer makes a fantastic hostess gift, especially when you include a batch of homemade Lime Sea Salt and a bottle of tequila.

ACTIVE 10 MIN. - TOTAL 10 MIN.

MAKES 2 ½ CUPS MIX

Add 1 cup pineapple juice and 2 Tbsp. granulated sugar to a 16-ounce glass bottle with a tight-fitting lid. Cover with lid; shake vigorously until sugar dissolves, 1 minute. Add ¾ cup orange liqueur (such as Cointreau or Grand Marnier) and ¾ cup fresh lime juice. Cover with lid; shake until well combined. Give as a gift with a bottle of tequila and Lime Sea Salt. The mix can be refrigerated up to 3 days; shake before serving.

Lime Sea Salt

ACTIVE 20 MIN. - TOTAL 20 MIN.

MAKES 1 CUP

Line a rimmed baking sheet with parchment paper. Spread 1 ½ Tbsp. fresh lime zest across prepared baking sheet. Bake at 150°F (or lowest temperature) until zest is fragrant and dry but not browned, 10 minutes. Remove from oven; cool on baking sheet set on a wire rack. Combine 1 cup coarse sea salt and cooled zest. Store in an airtight container up to 6 months.

The Candy— with a Kick

Fudgy Pecan Bourbon Balls

These decadent little candies are a cross between bourbon balls and chocolate truffles. Nestle each candy in a mini baking cup, and package them in cardboard jewelry boxes wrapped with festive wrapping paper.

ACTIVE 30 MIN. - TOTAL 4 HOURS
MAKES ABOUT 2 DOZEN

- 8 oz. 60% cacao dark chocolate, cut into ½-inch pieces
- ½ cup heavy cream
- ¼ cup (2 oz.) bourbon
- ¾ cup pecan halves, finely chopped

1. Place chocolate in a medium bowl. Bring the cream and bourbon just to a simmer in a saucepan over medium. Remove from heat, and pour over chocolate. Let stand 1 minute, and then stir vigorously until cream and chocolate are thoroughly blended. Let mixture cool 15 minutes. Cover with plastic wrap, and chill until firm, about 2 hours. (If you cannot make the truffles immediately, the mixture will keep, covered, in the fridge for up to 1 week.)

2. Place chopped pecans in a shallow plate. Line a baking sheet with parchment paper.

3. Working quickly and using a small warmed teaspoon (dipped into hot water and then dried), scoop chilled chocolate mixture by 2 teaspoon portions, and shape each into a ball. Place each ball on chopped pecans. Once the plate is filled, wash hands, and roll balls in pecans to completely cover. Transfer balls to a parchment paper-lined baking sheet. Repeat with remaining chocolate mixture and pecans.

4. Chill balls until firm, about 1 hour. (Or freeze until firm, about 10 minutes.) Enjoy them now, gift them, or store them in an airtight container in the fridge for up to 1 week.

The Cool Condiment

Hot Honey

Delicious drizzled over biscuits or fried chicken or whisked into a vinaigrette, this chile-infused honey will make a welcome addition to anyone's pantry.

ACTIVE 5 MIN. - TOTAL 30 MIN.
MAKES 4 CUPS

Combine 8 red Fresno chiles, sliced in half and seeded, 8 dried chiles (such as Thai, red Fresno, or jalapeño), crushed, and 4 cups light honey (such as clover) in a small saucepan. Bring to a simmer over medium-high, and simmer until infused, 4 to 5 minutes. Remove from heat, and cool 10 minutes. Pour honey through a fine wire-mesh strainer into a bowl; discard chiles. Divide honey evenly among 4 (½-pint) jars, and gift. For the longest shelf life, store in the fridge for up to 4 weeks but bring to room temperature before use. The honey will keep a couple weeks stored at room temperature.

Scones

Sweet Potato-Cranberry Scones with Molasses-Orange Butter

ACTIVE 15 MIN. - TOTAL 1 HOUR

MAKES 8 SCONES

- 3 cups all-purpose flour
- 5 Tbsp. maple sugar
- 4 tsp. baking powder
- ½ tsp. sea salt
- ½ cup unsalted butter, diced
- 2 large eggs, separated
- ¾ cup dried cranberries
- ¾ cup half-and-half
- 1 cup mashed roasted sweet potato (from 1 [8-oz.] potato), at room temperature
- 1 tsp. orange zest (from 1 orange)
- ½ cup Molasses-Orange Butter (recipe follows)

1. Preheat oven to 375°F. Line a baking sheet with parchment paper, and lightly coat with cooking spray.

2. Stir together flour, maple sugar, baking powder, and salt in a large bowl. Add butter, and, using your fingertips, blend quickly and lightly into flour. (Don't let it melt on your fingers.)

3. Add egg yolks, and stir until just combined. Stir in cranberries.

4. Whisk together half-and-half, sweet potato, and orange zest in a separate bowl until well combined. Gradually add wet ingredients to dry ingredients, and stir gently just until dough holds together without crumbling. Add additional milk or flour, if needed.

5. Transfer dough to center of prepared baking sheet, and, using parchment paper or oiled hands, shape dough into an 8-inch round. Slice round into 8 large wedges, pulling them apart slightly as you cut.

6. Lightly beat egg whites until barely foamy. Brush tops of scones with egg whites.

7. Bake scones in preheated oven until lightly browned, 22 to 24 minutes. Cool on baking sheet on wire rack 20 minutes before serving with Molasses-Orange Butter. Store scones in an airtight container at room temperature for up to 3 days.

Molasses-Orange Butter

ACTIVE 5 MIN. · TOTAL 5 MIN.

MAKES ½ CUP

Whisk together ½ cup unsalted butter, at room temperature, ½ tsp. molasses, ½ tsp. orange zest plus 2 tsp. orange juice (from 1 orange), ⅛ tsp. sea salt in a bowl until well combined. Taste and add more sea salt, if desired. Store in refrigerator for up to 1 week.

The Single-Serve Treat

Mexican Hot Chocolate Mug Cake

These mini cake mixes make adorable gifts when packaged in 12-ounce microwavable mugs. Attach a gift tag with baking instructions (below).

ACTIVE 10 MIN. - TOTAL 15 MIN.

MAKES 1 CAKE MIX

For each cake, combine ¼ cup all-purpose flour, 3 Tbsp. granulated sugar, ⅛ tsp. kosher salt, 2 Tbsp. each of unsweetened cocoa, chopped toasted pecans, and bittersweet chocolate chips, and ¼ tsp. each of baking powder and cinnamon in a small food-safe gift bag. Place 3 Tbsp. mini marshmallows in a separate bag. Place both bags inside a 12-ounce microwavable mug.

To prepare each cake, stir ¼ cup whole milk, 3 tablespoons canola oil, and ½ teaspoon vanilla extract into the dry ingredients in mug. Microwave on HIGH until cake rises and is cooked through, 60 to 90 seconds. Remove from microwave, and sprinkle marshmallows on top. Microwave on HIGH for 5 more seconds. Serve immediately.

Create Your Own Carryall

These scones look great and travel well when tucked in a bowl wrapped up in a large (30 inches or more) kitchen towel or pretty fabric.

1. Transfer the butter into a small glass jar with a lid. Spread the kitchen towel out on a surface with the patterned side facing down. Place the bowl in the center of the towel.

2. Fold up the two opposite corners of the towel and tuck them into the center of the bowl. Arrange the scones and jar of butter inside the bowl.

3. Grab the two opposite corners of the towel, pull them up over the bowl, and tie into a handle.

MAMA'S MYSTERY FRUITCAKE

by Cassandra King

I N THE SMALL FARMING COMMUNITY where I grew up, everyone celebrated Christmas in much the same way. We put up a tree then hung it with lights, ornaments, and tinsel. Our houses were decorated inside and out with holly, magnolia leaves, and wreaths of cedar. We sang carols in church and posed as angels, wise men, or shepherds. We exchanged gifts with friends and kin. Santa Claus came down the chimney with a sack of toys. And on Christmas Day, families gathered for a feast of traditional dishes that seldom varied from year to year.

It's the feast that I remember most fondly, not the stockings or dolls or bikes. The King family took turns hosting the Christmas dinner and bringing their signature dishes: Aunt Collie Ruth's chicken and dressing, Cousin Helen's dumplings, Jell-O salad from Aunt Rosalyn, Uncle Rex's homemade rolls. But it was my mother who created the biggest stir. Her fruitcakes, one light and the other dark, were always eagerly anticipated and sometimes even applauded. What made them so special that a single taste could convert the most avid fruitcake hater? It would be years before I would know.

My mother's fruitcake preparation began several weeks before Christmas. In a ritual worthy of a Truman Capote tale, Mother began with the pecans that grew on our farm. My sisters and I had to pick them up, but everyone helped with the cracking, sitting together after supper. Daddy was appointed to chop the nuts in perfectly sized pieces for the cakes; Mother chopped up dates and the candied fruit, cherries, and pineapple. Her preference was for currants over raisins but as a lesser ingredient. She turned up her nose at citron, which she swore was the reason fruitcakes got a bad rap.

Mother baked the dark cakes and then the white ones in tube pans. The main difference was the dark cake called for brown sugar and spices—allspice and mace—while the lighter cake had no spices and used white sugar. I remember the batter of each being so thick that she mixed it by hand. The cakes always turned out picture-perfect, heavy and dense with pecans, dates, and other fruits. A teetotaler herself, Mother sent Daddy to the liquor store for their best whiskey, some of which went into the cake batter. She sprinkled whiskey over each cake then wrapped them tightly in booze-saturated cheesecloth. Finally, the cakes were stored in airtight crockery to mature for weeks. Mother checked on them and occasionally sprinkled a bit more whiskey over the cheesecloth to keep the cakes nice and moist.

When I grew up and had my own family, my own Christmas traditions, I didn't try to duplicate Mother's fruitcakes because she gave us one each year. After she died, no fruitcake I ever had was as good as hers. My kids refused to even try one, so the desserts disappeared from my repertoire. Several years later, in a different household and a different time, I had married a man who was writing his own cookbook. I shared my stories with him, of growing up on a farm and raising the food we ate (farm-to-table before it was cool).

When I told about my mother's fruitcakes, he got excited. "Unlike most people, I actually love fruitcake," he said. "Let's make one this year."

Alas, it wasn't the success I'd hoped for. I'd found Mother's old cookbook from her women's club but approached it skeptically. Obviously, she'd modified it to suit her tastes by changing a lot of the ingredients. Oh, the cake my husband and I made turned out beautifully, but it wasn't Mother's. After a couple more failed attempts, I finally modified her recipe to suit our palates. I substituted dried fruit for the candied stuff and used brandy instead of whiskey for soaking the fruit, mixing into the batter, and dousing the cheesecloth. That one, we declared a success. No, it wasn't Mother's, but we liked it. I made an extra one to take to the Christmas dinner that the King family (what was left of us) was having at the farm. My father was in his nineties; who knew how many more Christmas dinners he'd have?

I told Daddy I had a surprise dessert, so after dinner, I brought out my beautiful fruitcake. After unwrapping the cheesecloth, I placed it on Mother's crystal serving plate, surrounded it with holly leaves, then brought it in to much fanfare. My sister had dished up ambrosia, a medley of fresh oranges, pineapple, and pecans, that Mother used to make. When I placed the pedestaled cake in the middle of the table, my father's face lit up. "You made your mama's white fruitcake!" he cried. "Ah . . . sort of," I hedged. Using Mother's ornate silver knife, I cut generous pieces for everyone and placed them on the dessert plates, next to the ambrosia. I saw Daddy eyeing his suspiciously.

"Just try it, Daddy," I said. "It's not Mother's, okay? But it's still good."

I could tell by his frown that he wasn't quite in agreement, though he gamely took a bite. "Your mama made the best fruitcake in these parts," he said. "She was famous for them. Even folks who didn't like fruitcake liked hers."

My husband caught my eye and winked, and my sisters hid their smiles. We'd all known Daddy wasn't likely to appreciate my efforts, though he'd be too polite to say so. I turned to him rather defensively. "You need to know that I tried everything to duplicate Mother's fruitcake, Daddy, but I finally gave up. Obviously she had a magic touch that I lack."

He stared at me for a minute and then surprised all of us by throwing back his head to laugh, and saying, "Ha! She had a secret ingredient, all right, but she never knew it."

"What on earth?" I gasped.

Daddy laughed so hard he slapped his knee. "It was me. Every time your mama wasn't looking, I'd sneak into the closet and pour more whiskey over those cakes. That's how come everybody liked them so much. She would've killed me if she'd known."

It took a minute to sink in, then we looked around the table at each other and howled with laughter. Between giggles, I said, "Do y'all remember Aunt Collie Ruth saying she'd go to her grave before she ever let a drop of whiskey cross her lips?"

"Maybe so," Daddy said, "but she always had two pieces of your mama's fruitcake."

I glared at him. "You should've told me! All this time, I've been trying to figure out Mother's secret."

Daddy shrugged it off. "You never asked me. You girls always thought your mama was the only one who knew anything about cooking. I'm not a bad cook myself."

"Light" Fruitcake

ACTIVE 35 MIN. - TOTAL 4 HOURS, 40 MIN., PLUS 24 HOURS REST TIME

SERVES 16 TO 20

- 3 cups chopped mixed dried fruit (such as cherries, apricots, dates, prunes, and apples)
- 1 cup chopped dried pineapple
- ½ cup currants
- ¼ cup finely chopped crystallized ginger (or more to taste)
- 1 cup brandy or bourbon
- 1 cup unsalted butter
- 1½ cups granulated sugar
- 5 large eggs
- 1 Tbsp. vanilla extract
- 3 cups all-purpose flour
- 1 tsp. baking powder
- 1 tsp. salt
- 2 cups pecans, chopped
  Cheesecloth

1. Combine the mixed dried fruit (including pineapple and currants) and crystallized ginger in a large bowl. Stir together with 1 cup brandy or bourbon; cover and set aside the mixture 2 hours to infuse the dried fruit.

2. Preheat the oven to 325°F. Grease a tube pan with cooking spray. Meanwhile, beat butter and sugar in a large bowl. Add eggs, 1 egg at a time, beating just until blended after each addition. Stir in the vanilla. In a separate large bowl, whisk together the flour, baking powder, and salt. Using a large wooden spoon or spatula, stir the flour mixture into the butter mixture until thoroughly combined (do not beat with mixer).

3. Stir in the soaked fruit mixture and chopped pecans. (Mixture will be thick.)

4. Scrape the mixture into the prepared tube pan, smoothing the top with a spatula. Bake 1 hour and 10 minutes or until a wooden pick inserted into the center of the fruitcake comes out clean. Cool 15 minutes before removing from pan. Cool completely on a wire rack, about 45 minutes.

5. Soak a layer of cheesecloth in enough brandy or bourbon to thoroughly moisten (about ½ cup). Wrap the fruitcake in the cheesecloth, then wrap it in foil. Set aside for at least 24 hours before serving to allow the flavors to mellow.

Cheers TO THE Holidays!

TOAST THE HOLIDAY SEASON WITH A MENU
OF TASTY **APPETIZERS** AND CROWD-PLEASING **PUNCHES**

*Blue Cheese-and-Pecan
Stuffed Cherry Peppers*

A Cocktail Party for 10

The Guest List: **YOUR BEST FRIENDS** / *The Look:* **FANCY AND FUN**
The Menu: **FINGER FOODS AND FESTIVE LIBATIONS**

Blue Cheese-and-Pecan Stuffed Cherry Peppers / Prosciutto-and-Manchego Cheese Straws (6)
Crispy Pork Meatballs (6) / Garlic Butter-Roasted Shrimp Cocktail (1) / Spinach and Artichoke Bites (2)
Spiced Orange Bourbon Punch (3) / Cranberry Sangria Punch (4) / DIY Deviled Egg Bar (5) / Fizzy Cider Punch

THE RECIPES

These sophisticated-looking appetizers and cocktails are surprisingly easy to prepare

Blue Cheese-and-Pecan Stuffed Cherry Peppers

Yellow and red pickled cherry peppers (or Peppadew peppers) are sold in jars and at olive bars in upscale grocery stores. Look for peppers with the stems and seeds removed.

ACTIVE 20 MIN. - TOTAL 20 MIN.
SERVES 20

- 4 oz. cream cheese, softened
- 2 ⅓ oz. crumbled blue cheese (about 6 Tbsp.)
- 6 Tbsp. heavy cream
- ½ cup plus 2 Tbsp. finely chopped toasted pecans, divided
- 3 (16-oz.) jars cherry peppers, drained (50 to 60 cherry peppers)
- 2 Tbsp. thinly sliced fresh chives

Place cream cheese, blue cheese, and heavy cream in a medium bowl. Beat with an electric mixer on medium-high speed until well blended and light and fluffy. Stir in ½ cup finely chopped pecans. Spoon mixture into a piping bag fitted with a ¾-inch-wide tip, and pipe about 1 tablespoon mixture into open end of each pepper. Place peppers on a platter, and sprinkle with remaining 2 tablespoons pecans. Sprinkle chives evenly over stuffed peppers. Serve immediately, or chill until ready to serve.

Prosciutto-and-Manchego Cheese Straws

It's not a party without cheese straws, and these are extra fancy for the holidays with the addition of nutty Manchego cheese and salty prosciutto. Defrost the puff pastry sheets in the refrigerator instead of on the countertop and they won't be as sticky and tricky to handle. And don't worry about getting perfect twists; the finished product should look a bit rustic.

ACTIVE 20 MIN. - TOTAL 35 MIN.
SERVES 20

- 2 (14-oz.) pkg. frozen puff pastry sheets, thawed
- 1 large egg, lightly beaten
- 6 oz. Manchego cheese, shredded (about 1½ cups)
- 8 to 10 prosciutto or serrano ham slices (about 5 oz.)
- 1 Tbsp. minced fresh thyme

1. Preheat oven to 375°F. Line 2 baking sheets with parchment paper.

2. Unfold 1 sheet of puff pastry on a lightly floured work surface, and roll out to a 10- x 16-inch rectangle. Brush pastry surface edge to edge with a small amount of beaten egg. Sprinkle evenly with ¾ cup of the shredded cheese, and lay half of the prosciutto slices across lower half of pastry (along 10-inch side), overlapping slices slightly. Fold top portion of pastry over prosciutto with ends of pastry meeting to form an 8- x 10-inch rectangle. Repeat with second puff pastry sheet.

3. Cut each pastry rectangle into 20 (½- x 8-inch) strips. Working with 1 strip at a time, use both hands to twist and form a spiral stick; place on prepared baking sheets, pressing ends onto parchment to adhere. Brush each twist with remaining egg wash, and sprinkle with thyme.

4. Bake in preheated oven until strips are puffed and golden brown, 15 to 17 minutes.

Crispy Pork Meatballs

Flavored with soy sauce, ginger, and garlic, and served with spicy mayonnaise and pickled cucumbers, these meatballs will steal the show at any gathering. Cook the meatballs after the other ingredients are ready, so you can assemble the skewers quickly and serve them hot.

ACTIVE 30 MIN. - TOTAL 1 HOUR
SERVES 10

PICKLED CUCUMBERS
- 4 to 5 Persian cucumbers
- ½ cup seasoned rice vinegar
- 2 tsp. granulated sugar
- ½ tsp. kosher salt

SAUCE
- ½ cup mayonnaise
- 1 Tbsp. Sriracha chili sauce
- 1 tsp. mirin
- 1 tsp. soy sauce

MEATBALLS
- 1¼ lb. ground pork
- 2 Tbsp. minced fresh scallions (from 1 scallion)
- 1 Tbsp. minced fresh garlic (from 3 garlic cloves)
- 1 Tbsp. minced fresh ginger
- 1 Tbsp. soy sauce
- 1 Tbsp. fish sauce
- 1 Tbsp. mirin
- 1 Tbsp. seasoned rice vinegar
- 1 cup panko (Japanese-style breadcrumbs)
- 1 cup canola oil

ADDITIONAL INGREDIENTS
- 40 (3-inch) wooden picks
- 40 fresh basil leaves

1. Prepare the Pickled Cucumbers: Very thinly slice cucumbers lengthwise with a mandoline or a sharp knife, making 40 slices. Stir together vinegar, sugar, and salt in a small bowl until sugar is dissolved. Add cucumber slices, and toss to coat. Let stand 20 minutes; drain. Chill until ready to assemble meatball bites.

2. Prepare the Sauce: Combine all Sauce ingredients in a small bowl, and stir to blend. Set aside.

3. Prepare the Meatballs: Combine pork, scallions, garlic, ginger, soy sauce, fish sauce, mirin, and vinegar in a large bowl; mix gently with hands until incorporated, and form into 40 meatballs (1 tablespoon each). Spread panko in a shallow dish. Roll meatballs in panko to coat, and place on a baking sheet lined with parchment paper.

4. Heat oil in a large skillet over medium-high. Cook meatballs, in batches, until cooked through and panko is crispy, turning often to brown evenly, 4 to 5 minutes. Transfer to a baking sheet lined with paper towels, and cover with aluminum foil to keep warm.

5. To assemble: Spread Sauce on bottom of a large serving platter. Fold 1 Pickled Cucumber slice and skewer with a wooden pick; add 1 basil leaf and 1 Meatball. Repeat with remaining ingredients. Place picks, meatball side down, into Sauce. Serve immediately.

Garlic Butter-Roasted Shrimp Cocktail

Swap out your usual chilled shrimp cocktail for tender roasted shrimp cooked in lemon garlic butter served with a spicy homemade cocktail sauce. Serve on a big platter with wooden picks, or spoon a bit of cocktail sauce in small cups and place a few shrimp in each cup.

ACTIVE 20 MIN. - TOTAL 25 MIN.
SERVES 8 TO 10

- ⅔ cup ketchup
- ⅓ cup chili sauce
- 3 Tbsp. grated fresh horseradish
- 1 tsp. lemon zest, plus 1 Tbsp. fresh juice (from 1 lemon)
- ½ tsp. Old Bay seasoning
- ½ tsp. hot pepper sauce (such as Tabasco)
- ½ cup (4 oz.) salted butter
- 4 garlic cloves, minced
- 1 lemon, cut in ¼-inch-thick slices
- ¼ tsp. crushed red pepper
- 2 lb. large peeled, deveined raw shrimp, tail on
- 2 Tbsp. chopped fresh flat-leaf parsley

- ½ tsp. kosher salt
- ¼ tsp. black pepper

1. Stir together ketchup, chili sauce, horseradish, lemon zest, lemon juice, Old Bay, and hot pepper sauce in a medium bowl; chill until ready to use.

2. Preheat oven to 450°F. Place butter, garlic, lemon slices, and crushed red pepper in the center of a rimmed baking sheet. Place baking sheet in oven, and heat until butter melts and garlic is fragrant, about 5 minutes. Add shrimp, and toss in butter mixture; spread in a single layer. Roast in preheated oven until shrimp turn pink and are just cooked through, 4 to 5 minutes. Transfer shrimp and pan juices to a large platter. Squeeze juice from roasted lemon slices over shrimp; sprinkle with parsley, salt, and pepper. Serve with chilled cocktail sauce.

Spinach and Artichoke Bites

We took the flavors of a classic spinach-artichoke dip and made it easier to eat while holding a cocktail. If you want to add a peppery bite to the filling, substitute arugula for the spinach leaves.

ACTIVE 25 MIN. - TOTAL 40 MIN.
SERVES 16

- 3 cups packed spinach leaves (about 3 oz.)
- 1 (9.9-oz.) jar marinated artichoke hearts, drained
- 4 oz. Gruyère cheese, shredded (about 1 cup)
- 2 oz. cream cheese
- 2 (8-oz.) cans refrigerated crescent rolls
- 1 large egg, lightly beaten

1. Combine spinach, drained artichoke hearts, shredded Gruyère, and cream cheese in a food processor, and pulse until smooth, about 5 times, stopping to scrape down sides as needed.

2. Preheat oven to 375°F. Line 2 baking sheets with parchment paper. Separate crescent roll dough triangles where perforated. Cut each triangle in half from tip to base, creating 2 triangles out of each. Gently pat and stretch the wide end of each triangle to make it a bit wider. Spoon about ½ tablespoon of filling on wide end of each triangle. Roll from widest part of triangle, pinching

sides slightly, toward tip, enclosing filling; curve slightly to create a crescent. Place on prepared baking sheets, about 1 inch apart.

3. Lightly brush beaten egg over surface of each crescent. Bake in preheated oven until golden brown, about 12 minutes, rotating pans halfway through bake time.

Spiced Orange Bourbon Punch

Loaded with the traditional Christmas flavors of citrus and spice, this nicely balanced punch will be a hit with bourbon lovers. If you prefer, you can substitute ginger ale for ginger beer, but make sure to use fresh-squeezed orange juice; it makes a big difference.

ACTIVE 10 MIN. - TOTAL 50 MIN.
SERVES 16

SPICED SIMPLE SYRUP
- 2 cinnamon sticks
- 2 whole star anise
- 2 whole cloves
- 3 whole allspice
- 1 cup granulated sugar
- 1 cup water

PUNCH
- 3 cups fresh orange juice (from 9 oranges)
- 1 cup (8 oz.) bourbon
- 1 (12-oz.) bottle ginger beer (such as Ginger People)
- 1 (12-oz.) bottle carbonated mineral water (such as Topo Chico)
- 1 navel orange, thinly sliced
- Freshly grated nutmeg (optional)

1. Prepare the Spiced Simple Syrup: Combine cinnamon sticks, star anise, cloves, allspice, sugar, and water in a small saucepan over medium-high, stirring until sugar is dissolved. Bring to a boil, and remove from heat; let cool to room temperature, about 40 minutes. Pour through a fine wire-mesh strainer, discarding solids. Chill syrup until ready to use. Syrup can be stored in refrigerator in an airtight container up to 2 weeks.

2. Prepare the Punch: Place ¾ cup of Spiced Simple Syrup in a pitcher. Add orange juice, bourbon, ginger beer, and carbonated water, and stir to combine. Serve over ice with an orange slice. Garnish with a sprinkle of nutmeg, if desired.

Cranberry Sangria Punch

This ruby-red punch is a staff favorite, but it comes with a warning: It goes down so easy, you're likely to overdo it. Make the punch up to one day ahead, and add the Champagne right before serving.

ACTIVE 20 MIN. - TOTAL 40 MIN.
SERVES 10

- 2 cups frozen or fresh cranberries
- 1 cup granulated sugar
- 1 cup water
- 1 (750-milliliter) bottle sangria, chilled
- ¼ cup (2 oz.) Campari
- 1 large navel orange, thinly sliced
- 1 large Granny Smith apple, thinly sliced
- 1 (750-milliliter) bottle brut Champagne, chilled

1. Combine cranberries, sugar, and water in a medium saucepan over medium-high, and bring to a boil, stirring often until sugar dissolves and berries just begin to pop, about 3 to 4 minutes. Remove from heat, and cool 30 minutes.

2. Stir together sangria, Campari, and cooled cranberries with pan juices in a large pitcher or a small punch bowl. Add orange and apple slices. Just before serving, add Champagne.

3. Serve over ice in punch glasses or old-fashioned glasses with a few pieces of fruit in each glass.

DIY Deviled Egg Bar

Add extra flair to your usual deviled egg platter with an array of fun toppings. Boil and peel the eggs a day in advance, or purchase precooked eggs at the grocery store to save time.

ACTIVE 30 MIN. - TOTAL 30 MIN.
SERVES 10

- 30 large hard-cooked eggs, peeled and chilled
- ¾ cup mayonnaise
- 1 Tbsp. fresh lemon juice (from 1 lemon)
- ¼ tsp. table salt
- ¼ tsp. black pepper
- 1 tsp. paprika

Fizzy Cider Punch

Cut eggs in half lengthwise, and transfer yolks to a medium bowl, keeping whites intact. Add mayonnaise, lemon juice, salt, and pepper to bowl; stir with a fork until very smooth. Place yolk mixture in a piping bag fitted with a ¾-inch-wide tip, and pipe into wells of egg whites (about 1 tablespoon per egg half). Place on a platter; sprinkle with paprika. Serve with desired toppings (below).

Pickled Okra and Pimientos

Thinly slice pickled okra crosswise. Wedge a slice in deviled eggs; sprinkle with finely chopped pimientos.

Capers and Smoked Paprika

Chop drained capers, and place on top of deviled eggs; sprinkle with a dash of smoked paprika.

Pickled Red Onions, Bacon, and Chives

Whisk together ½ cup red wine vinegar, ¼ cup granulated sugar, and 1 tsp. table salt in a small bowl. Finely chop a small red onion, and soak in vinegar mixture 30 minutes. Drain and pat dry. Top deviled eggs with pickled red onions, crispy bacon crumbles, and chopped chives.

Fizzy Cider Punch

This effervescent punch is perfect for holidays down South, where the weather is more likely to be sunny and warm than snowy and cold. Add the Prosecco right before you are ready to serve the punch to keep it bubbly.

ACTIVE 5 MIN. - TOTAL 5 MIN.
SERVES 10

- 1 medium Granny Smith apple
- 1 medium Honeycrisp apple
- 4 cups apple cider, chilled
- 1½ cups (12 oz.) brandy, chilled
- 1 (750-milliliter) bottle Prosecco, chilled

1. Using a mandoline or a knife, slice apples into very thin round slices, with peel and core intact. Cut slices in half to create half moons, and place in a large pitcher or small punchbowl. Stir in apple cider and brandy; chill.

2. Add Prosecco just before serving. Serve over ice in punch glasses or old-fashioned glasses with a few apple slices in each glass.

Christmas Eve
WITH ALL THE TRIMMINGS

*THIS ELEGANT **SIT-DOWN DINNER** IS EVERYTHING YOU WANT
IN A HOLIDAY MEAL—AND IT'S EASY ON THE COOK TOO*

A Christmas Eve Feast for Eight

The Guest List: **CLOSE FAMILY** / *The Look:* **ALL-OUT ELEGANCE**
The Menu: **BEEF TENDERLOIN AND SEASONAL SIDES**

Stuffed Beef Tenderloin with Burgundy-Mushroom Sauce (1) / Cider-Glazed Carrots with Walnuts (1)
Buttermilk Fantail Rolls (1) / Herbed Potato Stacks (2) / Sautéed Green Beans with
Pearl Onions (4) / Beet, Fennel, and Apple Salad (3)

THE RECIPES

Bright, fresh vegetables and a sumptuous tenderloin make a memorable holiday meal

Stuffed Beef Tenderloin with Burgundy-Mushroom Sauce

Everyone will 'ooh' and 'aah' over these tender spirals of beef filled with creamy spinach and leeks and topped with a decadent mushroom sauce.

SERVES 8

ACTIVE 55 MIN. - TOTAL 1 HOUR, 45 MIN.

BEEF

- 3 (10-oz.) pkg. frozen chopped spinach, thawed
- 3 Tbsp. unsalted butter
- 2 medium leeks, thinly sliced
- 1 garlic clove, minced (about 1 tsp.)
- 3 Tbsp. all-purpose flour
- 1 cup heavy cream
- 1 oz. Parmigiano-Reggiano cheese, grated (about ¼ cup)
- 2 tsp. fresh lemon juice (from 1 lemon)
- ¼ tsp. grated whole nutmeg
- 2 tsp. kosher salt, divided
- 1 tsp. black pepper, divided
- 1 (4-lb.) beef tenderloin, trimmed
- 1 Tbsp. extra-virgin olive oil

SAUCE

- 2 Tbsp. unsalted butter, divided
- 1 Tbsp. olive oil
- 2 (8-oz.) pkg. cremini mushrooms, quartered
- 1 medium shallot, minced
- ½ cup dry red wine (such as Burgundy)
- 1 cup beef broth
- 1 Tbsp. Dijon mustard
- ½ tsp. chopped fresh rosemary
- ½ tsp. kosher salt
- ¼ tsp. black pepper

1. Prepare the Beef: Preheat oven to 350°F. Drain spinach well; press between paper towels to remove excess moisture. Melt butter in a medium-size straight-sided saucepan over medium. Add leeks and garlic, and cook, stirring occasionally, until softened, about 4 minutes. Add flour, and cook, whisking constantly, 3 minutes; whisk in cream until smooth. Add spinach, and cook, stirring occasionally, until mixture is very thick, about 5 minutes. Stir in cheese, lemon juice, nutmeg, 1 teaspoon of the salt, and ½ teaspoon of the pepper. Remove from heat, and let cool 10 minutes.

2. Meanwhile, using a sharp knife, make a horizontal cut through center of beef, cutting to, but not through, other side. (The cut should be within ½ inch of other side.) Open top cut piece, as you would a book, and lay flat. Place beef between 2 sheets of plastic wrap. Using flat side of a meat mallet or back of a small heavy skillet, pound beef to ½-inch thickness and about a 13-inch square. Spread leek-spinach mixture evenly over beef, leaving a ½-inch border around edges. Roll up beef, and tie with kitchen twine, securing at 2-inch intervals. Brush evenly with olive oil; sprinkle with remaining 1 teaspoon salt and ½ teaspoon pepper.

3. Place beef on a wire rack set over a rimmed baking pan. Bake in preheated oven 30 minutes. Increase oven temperature to 450°F (do not remove beef from oven). Bake until a meat thermometer registers 125°F, about 20 minutes. Remove from heat, and let stand 30 minutes before slicing.

4. Prepare the Sauce: While beef rests, melt 1 tablespoon of the butter with olive oil in a large skillet over medium-high. Add mushrooms, and cook, stirring once or twice, until lightly browned, 5 to 6 minutes. Add shallot; cook, stirring constantly, until tender, 1 to 2 minutes. Stir in wine; cook, stirring constantly, 2 minutes. Stir in broth; reduce heat to medium, and simmer, stirring constantly, 5 minutes. Stir in mustard, rosemary, salt, and pepper, and cook 1 minute. Remove from heat, and stir in remaining 1 tablespoon butter until combined. Serve sauce with beef.

Beet, Fennel, and Apple Salad

This sophisticated first course sets the tone for the rest of the meal. Red and white striped candy cane beets make this bright and crunchy salad look extra festive but you can substitute red or golden beets.

SERVES 6

ACTIVE 10 MIN. - TOTAL 55 MIN.

- 2 medium-size candy cane beets (about 4 to 6 oz. each)
- 1 small fennel bulb, trimmed (about 5 oz.), halved lengthwise and cored
- 1 medium-size Granny Smith apple (about 8 oz.), halved and cored
- 4 cups firmly packed arugula (about 5 oz.)
- ¼ cup firmly packed fresh flat-leaf parsley leaves
- ¼ cup firmly packed fresh mint leaves
- ¼ cup extra-virgin olive oil
- 2 Tbsp. white wine vinegar
- 1 tsp. orange zest plus 1 Tbsp. fresh juice (from 1 orange)
- ¾ tsp. kosher salt
- ½ tsp. honey
- ¼ tsp. black pepper

1. Place beets in a medium saucepan with cold water to cover. Bring to a boil over high; reduce heat to low, and simmer until beets are tender, 35 to 40 minutes. Drain and let stand until cool enough to handle, about 15 minutes. Peel beets, and cut into wedges.

2. While beets are cooling, use a mandoline or sharp knife to cut fennel bulb and apple into very thin slices. Place in a large bowl with beet wedges, arugula, parsley, and mint.

3. Whisk together oil, vinegar, zest, juice, salt, honey, and pepper in a small bowl. Drizzle vinaigrette over beet mixture, and toss to coat. Serve immediately.

Cider-Glazed Carrots with Walnuts

A few pantry staples—apple cider vinegar, dry mustard, and paprika—turn simple glazed carrots into something special.

SERVES 6

ACTIVE 15 MIN. - TOTAL 25 MIN.

- 2½ lb. medium carrots, peeled and cut into 2-inch diagonal pieces (about 9 cups)
- ¼ cup packed light brown sugar

3 Tbsp. apple cider vinegar
2 Tbsp. unsalted butter
1 tsp. kosher salt
½ tsp. dry mustard
½ tsp. paprika
½ cup toasted walnut pieces
1 Tbsp. chopped fresh flat-leaf parsley

1. Place carrots in a large saucepan with water to cover, and bring to a boil over high. Reduce heat to low, and simmer until tender, 3 to 5 minutes. Drain and set aside.

2. Combine brown sugar, cider vinegar, butter, salt, dry mustard, and paprika in a large nonstick skillet over low; cook, stirring often, until butter melts. Increase heat to medium-high, and bring to a boil. Reduce heat to medium; add carrots. Cook, stirring constantly, until carrots are glazed and sauce is syrupy, 3 to 4 minutes. Remove from heat. Stir in walnuts; sprinkle with chopped parsley, and toss to combine. Serve immediately.

Herbed Potato Stacks

Potatoes are not usually the prettiest dish on the table, but this year will be an exception.

SERVES 6

ACTIVE 10 MIN. - TOTAL 1 HOUR, 10 MIN.

4 large russet potatoes (about 2 ¾ lb.), peeled
3 Tbsp. unsalted butter, melted
2 Tbsp. olive oil
1 tsp. chopped fresh thyme, plus whole leaves for garnish
1 tsp. chopped fresh rosemary
1 ½ tsp. kosher salt
½ tsp. black pepper
Flaky sea salt (such as Maldon)

1. Preheat oven to 375°F. Coat a 12-cup muffin pan with cooking spray. Cut potatoes into 1/16-inch-thick slices using a mandoline or sharp knife.

2. Whisk together butter, olive oil, chopped thyme, chopped rosemary, kosher salt, and pepper in a large bowl. Add potato slices, and toss until evenly coated.

3. Working quickly, layer potato slices into stacks in muffin cups, filling each cup to the top. Bake in preheated oven until edges and tops are golden brown and centers are tender, 45 to 55 minutes. Remove from oven, and let potato stacks stand in pan 3 to 5 minutes. Carefully remove potato stacks from pan; sprinkle with sea salt, and, if desired, garnish with thyme leaves. Serve immediately.

Buttermilk Fantail Rolls

These dinner rolls take a bit of time to make but the buttery, flaky layers are more than worth it.

SERVES 12

ACTIVE 45 MIN. - TOTAL 10 HOURS, 15 MIN.

½ cup warm water (105°F to 110°F)
2 (¼-oz.) envelopes active dry yeast
6 Tbsp. plus 1 tsp. granulated sugar, divided
2 large eggs, lightly beaten
1 cup whole buttermilk, at room temperature
1 ¼ tsp. kosher salt
½ cup plus 2 Tbsp. unsalted butter, melted and divided
3 ¾ to 4 cups all-purpose flour, divided
¼ cup unsalted butter, softened and divided
Flaky sea salt (such as Maldon)

1. Combine warm water, yeast, and 1 teaspoon of the sugar in a 1-cup liquid measuring cup; let stand until foamy, about 5 minutes.

2. Stir together eggs, buttermilk, kosher salt, ½ cup of the melted butter, and remaining 6 tablespoons sugar in a medium bowl. Add yeast mixture and 3 ½ cups of the flour; stir until a dough forms. Sprinkle a work surface with ¼ cup of the flour; turn dough out onto floured surface, and knead until smooth and slightly elastic, about 4 minutes, adding up to an additional ¼ cup flour if needed. Place dough in a lightly greased bowl; turn to grease top; cover with plastic wrap, and chill 8 to 24 hours.

3. Coat 2 (12-cup) muffin pans with cooking spray. Punch chilled dough down, and turn out onto a lightly floured surface. Divide dough in half. Roll 1 dough half into a 16- x 12-inch rectangle (about ¼ inch thick). Brush top with 2 tablespoons of the softened butter. Starting from a 12-inch side, cut dough into 6 (2-inch-wide) strips. Cut dough strips crosswise into quarters. (You will have 24 [4- x 2-inch] dough pieces.)

4. Stack 3 dough pieces together, buttered side up. Top with a fourth piece, buttered side down. Repeat with remaining 20 dough pieces, making 6 stacks. Cut each stack in half crosswise, making a total of 12 stacks of 2-inch squares. Place 1 stack on its side, layers facing up, in each muffin cup. Cover loosely with plastic wrap. Repeat process with remaining dough half, 2 tablespoons softened butter, and muffin pan. Let rolls rise in a warm (80°F to 85°F) place, free from drafts, until doubled in size, about 1 hour.

5. Preheat oven to 375°F. Bake rolls until golden brown, 12 to 15 minutes. Brush rolls with remaining 2 tablespoons melted butter, and sprinkle with desired amount of sea salt.

Sautéed Green Beans with Pearl Onions

We upgraded this classic holiday side dish with a tangy balsamic glaze and sweet caramelized onions.

SERVES 8

ACTIVE 10 MIN. - TOTAL 20 MIN.

1 lb. fresh green beans, trimmed
1 ½ Tbsp. unsalted butter, divided
1 ½ cups frozen pearl onions (about 7 oz.), thawed and patted dry with a paper towel
1 garlic clove, minced (about 1 tsp.)
⅓ cup balsamic vinegar
1 Tbsp. granulated sugar
½ tsp. kosher salt
¼ tsp. black pepper

1. Cook beans in boiling water to cover in a large saucepan until tender-crisp, 3 to 4 minutes. Plunge beans into ice water to stop the cooking process; drain well.

2. Heat 1 tablespoon of the butter in a large nonstick skillet over medium. Add onions; cook, stirring often, until lightly caramelized and tender, about 10 minutes. Add garlic, and cook, stirring constantly, until fragrant, about 1 minute. Add balsamic vinegar and sugar, and cook until reduced to a light syrup consistency, 3 to 4 minutes. Add beans, salt, pepper, and remaining ½ tablespoon butter, and toss to coat. Serve immediately.

Festival OF Bites

BREAK OUT THE MENORAH AND YOUR CAST-IRON SKILLET. IT'S TIME FOR A **HANUKKAH CELEBRATION** *WITH A FESTIVE MENU FROM CHEF TODD GINSBERG OF ATLANTA RESTAURANT, THE GENERAL MUIR*

A Hanukkah Dinner for 12

The Guest List: **FRIENDS AND FAMILY** / *The Look:* **COZY AND CLASSIC**
The Menu: **TOP-YOUR-OWN LATKES AND APPLE FRITTER SUNDAES**

Potato Latkes (3) / Tahini, Yogurt, and Roasted Red Peppers (3) / Herbed Sour Cream and
Smoked Salmon (3) / Warm Apple Compote and Aged Cheddar (3) / Young Lettuces and Shaved
Winter Vegetables with Walnut Vinaigrette (1)/ Apple Fritters with Salted Caramel Sauce (2)

THE RECIPES

Serve the latkes and toppings family-style for a fun, informal meal

Potato Latkes

These latkes fry up crisp and golden with deliciously frizzled, lacy edges. The key, Ginsberg says, is enough clarified butter in the pan at all times. "If you do not hear sizzling, there's not enough fat," he says.

ACTIVE 30 MIN. - TOTAL 30 MIN.
SERVES 12

- 6 large russet potatoes, peeled and grated (about 5 lb.)
- ½ yellow onion, grated (about ¾ cup)
- 2 large eggs
- ½ cup all-purpose flour
- 1 tsp. kosher salt
- ⅔ cup Clarified Butter (recipe follows)
- ½ tsp. black pepper

1. Rinse grated potatoes in a colander with hot water. (Hot water will act as a blanch to prevent discoloration.) Drain and squeeze the potatoes to remove as much excess liquid as possible.

2. Place potatoes, onion, and eggs in a bowl, and stir to combine. Stir together flour and salt in a small bowl until combined; gradually add to potato mixture, stirring until combined.

3. Heat Clarified Butter on an electric griddle or in a large skillet over medium-high. Drop 6 to 8 loosely packed ¼ cupfuls of potato mixture into hot butter; press lightly with a spatula to flatten into 3-inch rounds.

4. Reduce temperature to medium, and cook until golden, 3 to 4 minutes per side. Place on a plate lined with paper towels. Sprinkle with pepper; serve warm.

Clarified Butter

ACTIVE 5 MIN. - TOTAL 5 MIN.
MAKES 2/3 CUP

Melt 1 cup unsalted butter in a small saucepan over medium-high; bring to a boil. (The water content of the butter will look foamy and begin to evaporate.) Reduce heat to medium-low, and simmer until solids sink to the bottom of the saucepan, about 5 minutes. Pour the butter through a fine wire-mesh strainer lined with cheesecloth or a coffee filter, and discard the solids.

Warm Apple Compote and Aged Cheddar Topping

ACTIVE 20 MIN. - TOTAL 20 MIN.
SERVES 12

- 2 Tbsp. unsalted butter
- 1 lb. small Pink Lady, Honeycrisp, or Arkansas Black apples, ½ inch diced
- 2 Tbsp. turbinado sugar or light brown sugar
- 1 Tbsp. fresh lemon juice (from 1 lemon)
-    Potato Latkes (recipe at left)
- 4 oz. aged Cheddar cheese (not too sharp), shaved (about 2 cups)
-    Pinch of kosher salt

Melt butter in a heavy-bottomed saucepan over medium-high. Stir in diced apples, sugar, and lemon juice, and bring to a boil. Reduce heat to low, and cook, stirring often, until apples cook down and sauce thickens, about 15 minutes. Top Potato Latkes with compote, Cheddar shavings, and sprinkle with salt.

Herbed Sour Cream and Smoked Salmon Topping

ACTIVE 10 MIN. - TOTAL 20 MIN.
SERVES 12

- 1 tsp. baking soda
- 1¼ tsp. kosher salt, divided
- ½ bunch each of fresh chives, tarragon, and parsley
- 1 cup sour cream or crème fraîche
- ¼ tsp. black pepper
- 1 tsp. olive oil
- 1 tsp. fleur de sel
- 8 oz. smoked salmon

1. Bring a large pot of water to a boil. Prepare an ice bath.

2. Add baking soda and 1 teaspoon of the salt to boiling water. Add herbs, and cook until very soft, 3 to 5 minutes. (A parsley leaf rubbed between 2 fingers should disintegrate.) Using a slotted spoon, remove herbs, and immediately plunge into ice bath; let stand until cold.

3. Remove herbs from ice bath, and let excess water drip off. Place in a blender or food processor, and process until very smooth. Pour through a wire-mesh strainer into a bowl to strain off excess liquid. Discard liquid.

4. Stir together blended herbs, sour cream, pepper, and remaining ¼ teaspoon salt in a bowl until combined. Drizzle with olive oil, and sprinkle with fleur de sel. Serve with smoked salmon.

Tahini, Yogurt, and Roasted Red Pepper Topping

ACTIVE 10 MIN. - TOTAL 1 HOUR, 10 MIN.
SERVES 12

- 2 medium-size red bell peppers
- 1 Tbsp. canola oil
- ¼ cup tahini (sesame paste) (such as Soom)
- 1 tsp. fresh lemon juice (from 1 lemon)
- ½ tsp. kosher salt
- ½ tsp. ground cumin
- 4 to 6 Tbsp. water
- 1 cup plain whole-milk yogurt or Greek yogurt

HOW TO COOK LATKES FOR A CROWD

Latkes can be made ahead and reheated, especially when cooked on a griddle instead of deep-fried (which can make them soggy). Cook the latkes up to 4 hours ahead of time and do not refrigerate them. A half-hour before serving, crisp up the latkes on the griddle, then transfer to a baking sheet with a thin layer of clarified butter on the bottom. Place the latkes in a 400°F oven 3 to 5 minutes. Serve immediately.

1 tsp. olive oil

¼ tsp. black pepper

Potato Latkes (page 351)

2 Tbsp. chopped fresh flat-leaf parsley

1. Preheat oven to 450°F. Lightly coat peppers with canola oil, and place on a baking sheet lined with aluminum foil. Roast in preheated oven until browned, 25 to 30 minutes. Remove from oven, and wrap peppers with plastic wrap; let steam 30 minutes to 1 hour. Peel and seed peppers, discarding peel and seeds. Cut into strips, and chop; set aside.

2. Whisk together tahini, lemon juice, salt, cumin, and 4 tablespoons of the water in a medium bowl until smooth and creamy. If needed, stir in remaining 2 tablespoons water to thin sauce.

3. Stir together yogurt, olive oil, and black pepper in a bowl. Top each latke with 1 tablespoon yogurt mixture, 2 teaspoons chopped bell pepper, and a drizzle of tahini sauce (about 1 teaspoon). Sprinkle with chopped parsley.

Young Lettuces and Shaved Winter Vegetables with Walnut Vinaigrette

This light and fresh salad adds color to the table and balances out the richness of the rest of the menu.

ACTIVE 10 MIN. - TOTAL 10 MIN.

SERVES 12

2 Tbsp. walnut oil

2 Tbsp. grapeseed oil

2 Tbsp. balsamic vinegar

½ tsp. kosher salt

½ tsp. black pepper

3- to 4-oz. carrots, peeled, thinly sliced

3 (2-oz.) radishes, thinly sliced

2 (4-oz.) baby turnips, halved and thinly sliced

1 (5- to 6-oz.) kohlrabi, peeled, halved, and thinly sliced

4 (3- to 4-oz.) bunches young lettuces, torn

Whisk together walnut oil, grapeseed oil, vinegar, salt, and pepper together in a small bowl. Combine vegetables and lettuces in a large bowl; drizzle with dressing, and toss to coat.

Apple Fritters with Salted Caramel Sauce

Filled with a spiced apple compote, dipped in a vanilla glaze, and topped with a luscious caramel sauce, these over-the-top fritters take a bit of time to assemble, but are oh-so worth it.

ACTIVE 1 HOUR - TOTAL 2 HOURS, 30 MIN.

SERVES 16

DOUGH

2 Tbsp. cold unsalted butter

4 cups all-purpose flour

1 ½ cups whole milk, room temperature

⅓ cup granulated sugar

1 Tbsp. instant yeast

1 tsp. kosher salt

2 large eggs

Vegetable oil

APPLE FILLING

¼ cup unsalted butter

1 tsp. vanilla extract

7 small Granny Smith apples, peeled and diced (about 18 oz.)

¼ cup granulated sugar

½ tsp. ground cinnamon

1 cup apple cider

¼ cup apple cider vinegar

GLAZE

1 ½ cups powdered sugar

¼ cup whole milk

½ tsp. vanilla extract

SALTED CARAMEL SAUCE

1 cup heavy cream

½ tsp. flaky sea salt (such as Maldon)

1 cup granulated sugar

2 Tbsp. light corn syrup

1½ Tbsp. water

⅛ tsp. cream of tartar

1 ½ Tbsp. sour cream

Vanilla or rum raisin ice cream

1. Prepare the Dough: Chill a bowl and dough hook attachment of a heavy-duty electric stand mixer before beginning. Cut cold butter into cubes, and set aside at room temperature. Add flour, milk, sugar, yeast, salt, and eggs to chilled bowl, and stir until combined. Beat on low speed with hook 30 minutes. Add butter, a few pieces at a time, and beat until incorporated, about 5 minutes.

2. Place dough on a lightly floured surface, and shape into a 14- x 10-inch rectangle. Fold in thirds, top to bottom, (as you would a letter) then in thirds, left to right. Press out any trapped air. Grease top of dough with vegetable oil, cover, and let stand in a warm (80°F to 85°F) place until doubled in size, 45 minutes to 1 hour. Fold dough in thirds again, top to bottom, and left to right. Chill 1 hour before rolling and shaping.

3. Prepare the Filling: Melt butter in a saucepan over medium. Add vanilla, and bring to a boil. Add diced apples, and stir to coat. Add sugar and cinnamon, and cook, stirring often, 5 minutes. Increase heat to medium-high. Add cider and vinegar, and cook, stirring occasionally, until liquid is mostly evaporated, 10 to 15 minutes. Spread mixture on a baking sheet to cool.

4. Line a baking sheet with parchment paper, and grease paper with vegetable oil. Place chilled dough on a lightly floured surface, and roll into a 12- x 7-inch rectangle. Spread apples on dough, leaving a ½-inch border. Fold dough in thirds, as you would a letter. Repeat folding once. Roll into a 12- x 7-inch rectangle once more. Cut into 16 squares. Gently place squares on baking sheet.

5. Preheat deep fryer to 350°F (or pour oil to a depth of 3 inches in a Dutch oven over medium). Cook fritters, in batches, in hot oil until deep golden brown, 2 to 3 minutes per side. Place on a plate lined with paper towels.

6. Prepare the Glaze: Whisk together powdered sugar, milk, and vanilla in a bowl until smooth. Dip fritters into glaze. Place on a wire rack to cool and set.

7. Prepare the Salted Caramel Sauce: Combine cream and salt in a saucepan over medium-high; heat just until bubbles form around edges. (Do not boil.) Remove from heat, and set aside. Combine sugar, corn syrup, and water in a separate saucepan, and cook over high, until sugar is dissolved, swirling pan occasionally. Sprinkle cream of tartar around edges of sugar mixture, and remove from heat. Gradually add cream mixture to sugar mixture, whisking constantly until smooth. Add sour cream, whisking constantly until smooth. Serve fritters warm with Salted Caramel Sauce and ice cream.

Pancake Bake with
Cinnamon Streusel

A MERRY
Make-Ahead
BRUNCH

HERE'S A CHRISTMAS GIFT: *THIS DELICIOUS MEAL WON'T STEAL*
ANY TIME AWAY FROM FAMILY ON DECEMBER 25

Christmas Brunch for 10

The Guest List: **THE WHOLE GANG** / *The Look:* **COMFORTABLE AND CHEERY**
The Menu: **A "HELP-YOURSELF" BUFFET OF SWEET AND SAVORY DISHES**

Pancake Bake with Cinnamon Streusel / Sausage-and-Cheese Grits Quiche (1)
Country Ham Hash (1) / Sweet-and-Spicy Sheet Pan Bacon (2) / Citrus Salad with Granola (2)
Christmas Sunrise (3) / Romaine with Creamy Olive Dressing (4)

THE RECIPES

With a little planning, this entire brunch menu can be made or prepped in advance

Pancake Bake with Cinnamon Streusel

Don't spend Christmas morning flipping pancakes. Instead, make them in advance and turn them into a bread pudding-like casserole topped with sweet streusel.

ACTIVE 45 MIN. - TOTAL 9 HOURS, 40 MIN., INCLUDING 8 HOURS CHILLING

SERVES 10

PANCAKES

- 2 ²/₃ cups (about 11 ³/₈ oz.) all-purpose flour
- 1 Tbsp. granulated sugar
- 2 tsp. baking powder
- 1 ½ tsp. baking soda
- 1 ½ tsp. kosher salt
- 3 cups whole buttermilk
- 3 large eggs
- 6 Tbsp. unsalted butter, melted

CASSEROLE AND STREUSEL

- 6 large eggs
- 1 ½ cups heavy cream
- 1 cup whole milk
- ¼ cup granulated sugar
- 1 tsp. vanilla extract
- ½ cup all-purpose flour
- 1 cup roughly chopped pecans
- ¼ cup packed light brown sugar
- ¾ tsp. ground cinnamon
- ¼ tsp. kosher salt
- ¼ cup cold unsalted butter, cubed
- Pure maple syrup

1. Prepare the Pancakes: Stir together flour, sugar, baking powder, baking soda, and salt in a large bowl. Whisk together buttermilk and eggs in a medium bowl; gradually stir buttermilk mixture into flour mixture. Gently stir in butter. (Batter will be lumpy.) Let stand 5 minutes.

2. Pour about ¼ cup batter for each pancake onto a hot (350°F) buttered griddle.

3. Cook until tops are covered with bubbles and edges look dry, about 3 minutes. Turn and cook until golden brown, about 3 more minutes. (You should make about 30 pancakes.)

4. Prepare the Casserole and Streusel: Cut each pancake in half. Lightly grease a 13- x 9-inch baking dish with cooking spray. Arrange pancake halves, cut sides down and overlapping slightly, in 3 rows starting at 1 long end of prepared baking dish.

5. Whisk together eggs, cream, milk, granulated sugar, and vanilla in a large bowl. Slowly pour egg mixture over pancakes; cover casserole with plastic wrap, and refrigerate at least 8 hours or overnight.

6. Preheat oven to 350°F. Combine flour, pecans, brown sugar, cinnamon, and salt in a medium bowl; cut butter into flour mixture with a pastry blender (or use your fingers) until mixture is crumbly.

7. Uncover casserole, and sprinkle flour mixture evenly over casserole, and bake, uncovered, in preheated oven until center is set, 50 to 55 minutes. Let stand 5 minutes before serving. Drizzle each serving with syrup.

Sausage-and-Cheese Grits Quiche

The traditional sausage-and-egg casserole gets a holiday makeover when cooked in a springform pan instead of a baking dish.

ACTIVE 30 MIN. - TOTAL 10 HOURS, 30 MIN., INCLUDING 8 HOURS CHILLING

SERVES 10

- 3 cups whole milk
- ¼ cup unsalted butter
- ¾ cup uncooked regular grits
- 1 tsp. kosher salt, divided
- ½ tsp. black pepper, divided
- 4 oz. sharp Cheddar cheese, shredded (about 1 cup)
- 4 oz. processed cheese (such as Velveeta), cubed
- 8 oz. mild ground pork breakfast sausage
- 6 large eggs
- 1 cup heavy cream
- 1 Tbsp. Dijon mustard
- ¼ cup thinly sliced scallions (from 2 scallions)
- 1 oz. Parmesan cheese, grated (about ¼ cup)
- 2 Tbsp. finely chopped fresh chives

1. Bring milk and butter to a simmer in a large saucepan over medium-high, stirring occasionally, 5 to 7 minutes. Stir in grits, ½ teaspoon salt, and ¼ teaspoon pepper, and cook, stirring often, until grits are tender and mixture is thickened, about 15 minutes. Remove from heat, and stir in Cheddar and processed cheese until smooth. Pour grits mixture into a lightly greased 9-inch springform pan. Let cool to room temperature, about 30 minutes. Cover loosely with aluminum foil, and chill 8 to 24 hours.

2. Meanwhile, cook sausage in a large nonstick skillet over medium-high, breaking sausage into small pieces with a wooden spoon, until browned, 6 to 8 minutes. Transfer to a plate lined with paper towels to drain well. Let cool to room temperature, about 10 minutes. Transfer to an airtight container, and chill 8 to 24 hours.

3. Preheat oven to 325°F. Place springform pan on a rimmed baking sheet lined with aluminum foil. Whisk together eggs, cream, Dijon, and remaining ½ teaspoon salt and ¼ teaspoon pepper in a large bowl. Fold in scallions and cooked sausage. Pour evenly over grits mixture in prepared pan. Bake in preheated oven until just set, about 1 hour and 10 minutes. Sprinkle with Parmesan cheese, and let stand 20 minutes.

4. Run a sharp knife around edges of pan, and remove outer ring. Sprinkle quiche with chives just before serving.

Country Ham Hash

Savory country ham adds toothsome texture to this hash and pairs well with the red onion, garlic, and bell peppers.

ACTIVE 40 MIN. - TOTAL 40 MIN.

SERVES 6

- 8 oz. sliced country ham
- 3 Tbsp. unsalted butter
- 1 ½ lb. russet potatoes, peeled and cut into ½-inch pieces
- 1 cup chopped red onion (from 1 medium onion)

1 cup chopped red or orange bell
    pepper (from 1 medium bell pepper)
1 tsp. chopped garlic (from 1 large
    garlic clove)
½ tsp. black pepper
¼ tsp. kosher salt
1 Tbsp. chopped fresh rosemary

1. Cook ham in a large skillet over medium, turning occasionally, until golden brown, about 10 minutes. Transfer to a plate lined with paper towels.

2. Return skillet to medium-high, and melt butter in skillet. Add potatoes, onion, and bell pepper, spreading in an even layer. Cover and cook until potatoes soften, about 8 minutes. Uncover and stir in garlic, pepper, and salt. Cook, uncovered, without stirring, 2 minutes. Stir and continue cooking in 2-minute intervals, stirring after each interval, until potatoes are golden, about 15 minutes total.

3. Chop cooked ham, and stir into potato mixture. Cook, stirring occasionally, until lightly browned, 2 to 3 minutes. Sprinkle with rosemary, and serve immediately.

Christmas Sunrise

ACTIVE 10 MIN. - TOTAL 4 HOURS, 10 MIN.
SERVES 8

1 ½ cups granulated sugar
¾ cup water
1 ½ cups cranberry juice cocktail
    (such as Ocean Spray)
¼ cup (2 oz.) grenadine
4 cups tangerine juice
2 cups chilled lime-flavored sparkling
    water, club soda, or Prosecco
Thin tangerine slices

1. Cook sugar and water in a small saucepan over medium-high, stirring occasionally, until sugar dissolves and mixture comes to a boil, 2 to 3 minutes. Boil, stirring occasionally, 2 minutes. Remove syrup from heat, and let cool about 30 minutes. Stir together cooled syrup, cranberry juice, and grenadine until incorporated. Cover and refrigerate until well chilled, 4 hours or overnight.

2. Fill 8 tall 12-ounce glasses with ice cubes, and pour ⅓ cup cranberry syrup mixture into each glass. Slowly pour about ½ cup tangerine juice over the back side of a spoon into each glass.

Do not stir. Slowly pour ¼ cup chilled sparkling water into each glass. Garnish with tangerine slices.

Citrus Salad with Granola

Make the coconut and pecan granola up to three days ahead, then assemble the fruit salad and yogurt the morning of your brunch.

ACTIVE 20 MIN. - TOTAL 1 HOUR, 35 MIN.
SERVES 8

GRANOLA
1 cup demerara sugar
¾ cup water
½ cup honey
4 cups uncooked old-fashioned
    regular rolled oats
2 cups roughly chopped pecans
2 cups unsweetened flaked dried
    coconut
½ tsp. kosher salt
2 tsp. vanilla extract
¼ cup canola oil
CITRUS SALAD
2 Tbsp. vanilla bean paste
6 cups plain whole-milk Greek yogurt
2 Ruby Red grapefruit, sectioned
    (about 1 cup)
2 blood oranges or Cara Cara
    oranges, sectioned (about ¾ cup)

1. Prepare the Granola: Preheat oven to 350°F. Cook sugar, water, and honey in a small saucepan over medium-high, stirring occasionally, until sugar dissolves and mixture comes to a simmer, about 4 minutes. Remove syrup from heat, and let cool slightly, about 20 minutes.

2. Stir together oats, pecans, coconut, and salt in a large bowl. Whisk vanilla and oil into cooled syrup, and drizzle syrup mixture evenly over oat mixture. Stir until evenly coated.

3. Line 2 rimmed baking sheets with aluminum foil, and lightly grease foil. Divide oat mixture evenly between 2 prepared baking sheets. Bake in preheated oven, rotating baking sheets and stirring halfway through baking time, until golden brown, about 25 minutes. Transfer baking sheets to wire racks to cool completely, about 30 minutes. Break granola into pieces. Store at room temperature in an airtight container.

4. Prepare the Citrus Salad: Stir vanilla bean paste into yogurt, and divide

yogurt mixture among 8 (1-pint) mason jars or tall glasses. Top each with granola and citrus sections.

Sweet-and-Spicy Sheet Pan Bacon

Prepare the bacon in advance so it can absorb all the flavors from the brown sugar-cayenne pepper rub.

ACTIVE 15 MIN. - TOTAL 9 HOURS, INCLUDING
8 HOURS CHILLING
SERVES 10

Combine ½ cup packed light brown sugar, 2 tsp. black pepper, 1 tsp. kosher salt, and ½ tsp. cayenne pepper in a small bowl. Place a lightly greased rack in each of 2 aluminum foil-lined 18- x 13-inch sheet pans, and arrange 24 oz. thick-cut bacon slices in a single layer on each rack. Sprinkle bacon evenly on both sides with spice mixture (about 1 unpacked tsp. per side), and rub gently to coat. Cover pans loosely with foil, and refrigerate 8 to 24 hours. Uncover bacon, and bake at 375°F, rotating pans halfway through baking time, until deep golden brown and crisp around the edges, about 40 minutes. Let cool on racks in pans about 5 minutes. Transfer to a serving platter.

Romaine with Creamy Olive Dressing

A simple, fresh salad is always a welcome addition to a brunch menu.

ACTIVE 15 MIN. - TOTAL 15 MIN.
SERVES 8

¾ cup mayonnaise
1 Tbsp. liquid from 1 (8-oz.) jar
    green pimiento-stuffed olives
1 Tbsp. fresh lemon juice (from
    ½ lemon)
½ tsp. black pepper
⅓ cup chopped pimiento-stuffed
    green olives (from 1 [8-oz.] jar)
2 Tbsp. chopped fresh flat-leaf parsley
4 heads baby romaine lettuce,
    halved vertically

Whisk together mayonnaise, olive liquid, lemon juice, and pepper in a medium bowl. Stir in chopped olives and parsley. Place romaine halves on a serving platter, and drizzle with mayonnaise mixture. Serve immediately.

THE Sweetest Tradition

IT'S NOT CHRISTMAS WITHOUT OUR ANNUAL **WHITE CAKE**. AND THIS ONE IS A STUNNER: THREE LAYERS OF THE BEST VANILLA CAKE YOU'VE EVER HAD COVERED IN TANGY CREAM CHEESE FROSTING AND TRIMMED WITH SPARKLING EDIBLE ORNAMENTS. YOU WON'T FIND A PRETTIER—OR MORE DELICIOUS—CENTERPIECE FOR YOUR HOLIDAY TABLE THAN THIS ONE.

THE RECIPES

This luscious confection will be the star of the Christmas feast

Snowy Vanilla Cake with Cake Ball Ornaments

SERVES 12

ACTIVE 15 MIN. - TOTAL 1 HOUR, 15 MIN.

- 2 ¼   cups granulated sugar
- 1 ¼   cups salted butter, softened
- 7   large egg whites, at room temperature
- 3 ½   cups cake flour, plus more for pans
- 4   tsp. baking powder
- ½   tsp. table salt
- 1   cup water
- 2   tsp. vanilla extract
-    Shortening
-    Cream Cheese Buttercream (recipe follows)
-    Cake Ball Ornaments (recipe follows)

1. Preheat oven to 350°F. Beat sugar and butter at medium speed with a heavy-duty stand mixer until fluffy, 3 to 5 minutes. Gradually add egg whites, one-third at a time, beating well after each addition.

2. Sift together cake flour, baking powder, and salt; gradually add to butter mixture alternately with water, beginning and ending with flour mixture. Stir in vanilla. Divide batter evenly among 3 greased (with shortening) and floured 9-inch round cake pans.

3. Bake in preheated oven until a wooden pick inserted in center comes out clean, 19 to 21 minutes. Cool in pans on wire racks 10 minutes; remove from pans to wire racks, and cool completely, about 30 minutes. Spread Cream Cheese Buttercream between layers and on top and sides of cake. Attach Cake Ball Ornaments to top of cake.

Cream Cheese Buttercream

MAKES 2 ¾ CUPS

ACTIVE 10 MIN. - TOTAL 10 MIN.

- 1   (8-oz.) pkg. cream cheese, softened
- 1   cup salted butter, softened
- 2   (16-oz.) pkg. powdered sugar
- 2   Tbsp. whole milk
- 2   tsp. vanilla extract
- ¼   tsp. table salt

Beat cream cheese and butter in a large bowl with an electric mixer on medium speed until smooth. Gradually add powdered sugar, milk, vanilla, and salt, and beat until blended and smooth. Increase speed to medium-high, and beat until light and fluffy.

Cake Ball Ornaments

MAKES 20 CAKE BALLS

ACTIVE 1 HOUR, 55 MIN. - TOTAL 8 HOURS, 25 MIN.

- 4   oz. white fondant (about the size of a tennis ball)
- 1   cup powdered sugar
- 1 ½   Tbsp. meringue powder
- 1 to 2   Tbsp. water
-    Bronze, gold, red, green, and white edible luster spray
- 1   pkg. vanilla cake mix (such as Pillsbury Traditional Vanilla Cake Mix (do not use a "super-moist" type)
- 1   cup ready-to-spread cream cheese frosting
- 1 ½   lb. vanilla candy coating disks (such as Wilton Candy Melts)
- 20   (4-inch) skewers
- 1   (6-inch-thick) piece of sturdy plastic foam (such as Styrofoam)
-    Gold, red, green, and white edible luster dust
-    White, gold, and silver nonpareils (optional)

1. Make tops of ornaments by forming 20 pea-sized balls from fondant. Lightly press each ball into the shape of a drum. Score sides vertically with a sharp knife; set aside to dry.

2. Form 20 pearl-sized balls from fondant. Using a wooden skewer, poke a hole into middle of each ball, and gently shape into a slightly larger donut-shaped circle. Let fondant pieces dry completely, about 1 hour.

3. Place powdered sugar, meringue powder, and 1 tablespoon of the water in a small bowl, and beat with an electric mixer on low speed until combined. Increase speed to high, and beat until white and fluffy, adding, if needed, up to 1 tablespoon water, 1 teaspoon at a time, and beating until smooth and thick. Transfer icing to a piping bag with #2 decorating tip.

4. Attach edge of 1 donut-shaped fondant piece to the flat side of each drum-shaped piece with a small dot of icing; spray with bronze edible luster spray. Let dry completely, about 30 minutes.

5. Prepare cake mix according to package directions for 2 (8-inch) round pans; let cool completely on a wire rack. Crumble cake with fingers into fine crumbs in a large bowl. Add cream cheese frosting; stir until mixture is the consistency of cookie dough. Shape mixture into 20 (1-inch) balls, and place on a parchment paper-lined baking sheet. Cover and chill until firm, about 2 hours or up to 2 days. Reserve any remaining cake mixture for another use.

6. Place candy coating in a medium-size microwavable bowl (or 4-cup glass measuring cup), and microwave until melted, about 1 minute and 30 seconds, stirring at 30-second intervals.

7. Dip ½ inch of blunt end of 1 skewer in melted candy coating; insert dipped end of skewer about three-quarters through 1 chilled cake ball. (Do not insert all the way through.) Place on parchment paper-lined baking sheet. Repeat with remaining skewers and cake balls. Chill 30 minutes.

8. Dip chilled cake balls in melted candy coating, twirling and lightly tapping skewers on lip of bowl to create a smooth coating around cake balls. Stick skewers upright in the plastic foam; let cake balls stand at room temperature until hardened, about 20 minutes. Decorate balls with assorted colors of edible luster spray and edible luster dust. Let dry completely, about 30 minutes.

9. Pipe royal icing onto colored cake balls in decorative patterns. Add nonpareils, if desired. Let dry 1 hour. Carefully remove skewers from cake balls, if desired. Attach Cake Ball Ornaments to top of cake, securing with icing or wooden picks.

Christmas

WITH THE
Test Kitchen

GET IN THE SPIRIT WITH A FRESH BATCH OF FESTIVE **HOLIDAY TREATS**
FROM THREE OF SOUTHERN LIVING'S VERY BEST BAKERS

Gingerbread Latte Cake with Vanilla Whipped Cream Frosting

Sea Salt–Caramel Cake

Eggnog Spice Cake with Bourbon Custard Filling and Eggnog Buttercream

CAKES WITH
PAM LOLLEY

When Pam Lolley bakes a layer cake, the entire Test Kitchen lines up for a slice. Your family will have the same reaction to her latest creations inspired by the flavors of the holiday season.

Sea Salt–Caramel Cake

We love these tender cake layers, but the caramel frosting steals the show.

ACTIVE 45 MIN. - TOTAL 2 HOURS
SERVES 16

CAKE LAYERS
- 1 cup salted butter, softened
- 2 cups granulated sugar
- 3 large eggs
- 2 ½ cups all-purpose flour, plus more for dusting pans
- ½ tsp. table salt
- ½ tsp. baking soda
- 1 ½ cups whole buttermilk
- 1 Tbsp. vanilla extract
  Shortening

CARAMEL FROSTING
- 1 cup unsalted butter
- 1 cup packed light brown sugar
- 1 cup packed dark brown sugar
- ½ cup heavy cream
- 4 cups (about 1 lb.) powdered sugar, sifted
- 2 tsp. vanilla extract
- ½ tsp. fine sea salt
  Flaky sea salt (such as Maldon) (optional)

1. Prepare the Cake Layers: Preheat oven to 350°F. Beat butter with a heavy-duty electric stand mixer on medium speed until creamy. Gradually add granulated sugar, beating until light and fluffy. Add eggs, 1 at a time, beating just until blended after each addition. Whisk together flour, salt, and baking soda in a medium bowl. Add flour mixture to butter mixture alternately with buttermilk, beginning and ending with flour mixture, beating on low speed until blended after each addition. Stir in vanilla.

2. Pour batter into 3 greased (with shortening) and floured 8-inch round cake pans. Bake in preheated oven until a wooden pick inserted in center of cakes comes out clean, 22 to 24 minutes. Cool in pans on wire racks 10 minutes. Transfer cake layers from pans to wire racks, and cool completely, about 1 hour.

3. Prepare the Caramel Frosting: Bring butter and both brown sugars to a boil in a 3 ½-quart saucepan over medium, whisking constantly. Whisk in cream, and return to a boil. Remove from heat. Pour mixture into the bowl of a heavy-duty electric stand mixer fitted with the whisk attachment. With mixer running on medium speed, gradually add powdered sugar, vanilla, and fine sea salt. Beat until thickened and spreadable, 8 to 10 minutes. (If you overbeat frosting and it becomes too thick to spread, beat in 1 to 2 teaspoons hot water.)

4. Assemble the Cake: Spread frosting between layers and on top and sides of cake. If desired, sprinkle top of cake with flaky sea salt.

Gingerbread Latte Cake with Vanilla Whipped Cream Frosting

If the holiday season officially starts after your first gingerbread latte, this is the cake of your coffee-loving dreams.

ACTIVE 30 MIN. - TOTAL 2 HOURS
SERVES 16

CAKE
- 3 ¾ cups all-purpose flour, plus more for dusting pans
- ½ cup chopped crystallized ginger
- 2 tsp. baking powder
- 1 tsp. baking soda
- 1 tsp. table salt
- 1 tsp. ground cinnamon
- ¼ tsp. ground ginger
- ¼ tsp. ground nutmeg
- 1 cup salted butter, softened
- 1 ½ cups packed light brown sugar
- 3 large eggs, separated
- 1 ½ cups hot strong brewed coffee
- ½ cup molasses
  Shortening

ESPRESSO SIMPLE SYRUP

¾ cup hot very strong brewed coffee

½ cup granulated sugar

VANILLA WHIPPED CREAM FROSTING

3 cups heavy cream

1½ tsp. vanilla bean paste

½ cup granulated sugar

Finely crushed gingersnap cookies

1. Prepare the Cake: Preheat oven to 350°F. Process flour, crystallized ginger, baking powder, baking soda, salt, cinnamon, ground ginger, and nutmeg in a food processor until crystallized ginger is finely ground, about 1 minute. Set aside.

2. Beat butter with a heavy-duty electric stand mixer on medium speed until creamy. Gradually add brown sugar, beating until light and fluffy. Add egg yolks, 1 at a time, beating just until blended after each addition. Stir together coffee and molasses in a glass measuring cup. Add flour mixture to butter mixture alternately with coffee mixture, beginning and ending with flour mixture, beating on low speed just until blended after each addition.

3. Place egg whites in a bowl. Beat with an electric mixer on high speed until stiff peaks form. Gently fold egg whites, in thirds, into batter, folding just until incorporated after each addition.

4. Spoon batter into 3 greased (with shortening) and floured 9-inch round cake pans. Bake in preheated oven until a wooden pick inserted in center of cakes comes out clean, 19 to 22 minutes.

5. Meanwhile, prepare the Espresso Simple Syrup: Bring coffee and granulated sugar to a boil in a small saucepan over medium-high. Boil, stirring occasionally, until reduced to about ½ cup, 5 to 6 minutes.

6. Remove cake layers from oven, and cool in pans on wire racks 10 minutes. Transfer cake layers from pans to wire racks, and brush evenly with warm Espresso Simple Syrup. Cool completely, about 1 hour.

7. Prepare the Vanilla Whipped Cream Frosting: While cakes cool, beat cream and vanilla bean paste with an electric mixer on medium speed until foamy, 1 to 2 minutes. Gradually add granulated sugar, beating until stiff peaks form, about 2 minutes. (Do not overbeat.)

8. Assemble the Cake: Spread frosting between layers and on top and sides of cake. Gently press crushed gingersnaps around the bottom of the cake, forming a 2-inch cuff.

Eggnog Spice Cake with Bourbon Custard Filling and Eggnog Buttercream

This towering four-layer cake is everything you want in a glass of eggnog—it's ultra creamy, slightly boozy, and topped with fresh nutmeg.

ACTIVE 45 MIN. - TOTAL 6 HOURS

SERVES 16

FILLING

½ cup granulated sugar

¼ cup cornstarch

¼ tsp. table salt

2 cups half-and-half

4 large egg yolks

3 Tbsp. salted butter

2 Tbsp. bourbon

CAKE LAYERS

1 cup salted butter, softened

2 cups granulated sugar

4 large eggs

3¼ cups all-purpose flour, plus more for dusting pans

2½ tsp. baking powder

¾ tsp. table salt

½ tsp. ground cinnamon

¼ tsp. ground nutmeg

¾ cup whole milk

½ cup refrigerated eggnog

1 tsp. vanilla extract

Shortening

BUTTERCREAM

1 cup salted butter, softened

1 tsp. vanilla extract

1 (2-lb.) pkg. powdered sugar, divided

¼ cup refrigerated eggnog

½ to ¾ cup heavy cream, divided

Grated fresh nutmeg (optional)

1. Prepare the Filling: Whisk together granulated sugar, cornstarch, and salt in a heavy saucepan. Whisk together half-and-half and egg yolks in a glass bowl. Gradually whisk half-and-half mixture into sugar mixture. Cook over medium, whisking constantly, until mixture starts to bubble, 7 to 8 minutes.

Cook, whisking constantly, 1 minute; remove from heat. Whisk in butter and bourbon. Transfer to a medium bowl. Place plastic wrap directly on warm Filling to prevent a film from forming. Let stand 30 minutes; chill 4 to 24 hours.

2. Prepare the Cake Layers: Preheat oven to 350°F. Beat butter with a heavy-duty electric stand mixer on medium speed until creamy. Gradually add granulated sugar, beating until light and fluffy. Add eggs, 1 at a time, beating just until blended after each addition. Stir together flour, baking powder, salt, cinnamon, and nutmeg in a large bowl. Stir together milk and eggnog in a glass measuring cup. Add flour mixture to butter mixture alternately with milk mixture, beginning and ending with flour mixture, beating on low speed just until blended after each addition. Stir in vanilla.

3. Divide batter evenly among 4 greased (with shortening) and floured 9-inch round cake pans. Bake in preheated oven until a wooden pick inserted in center of cakes comes out clean, 16 to 19 minutes. Cool in pans on wire racks 10 minutes. Transfer cakes from pans to wire racks, and cool completely, about 1 hour.

4. Prepare the Buttercream: Beat butter with a heavy-duty electric stand mixer on medium speed until creamy. Gradually add vanilla and 1 cup of the powdered sugar. Stir together eggnog and ½ cup of the cream in a small bowl. Gradually add remaining powdered sugar to butter mixture alternately with eggnog mixture, beating on low speed until blended after each addition. Beat on high speed until smooth and fluffy. Beat in up to ¼ cup cream, 1 tablespoon at a time, if necessary, to reach desired consistency.

5. Assemble the Cake: Place 1 cup of the Buttercream in a large piping bag. Place 1 cake layer on a serving platter; pipe a ½-inch-thick ring of frosting on the very outer edge of the cake. Spread ⅓ cup of the Filling inside the ring. Repeat procedure with 2 cake layers. Top with fourth cake layer. Spread top and sides of cake with a very thin layer of Buttercream. Chill 30 minutes.

6. Place remaining Buttercream in a large piping bag fitted with a 1M large star tip. Pipe 1½-inch-wide tight zigzags up sides of the cake, starting at the base each time and making sure each zigzag touches the one beside it. If desired, sprinkle cake with nutmeg.

Snowy Tree Cookies

To make these adorable 3-D trees, you'll need star-shaped cookie cutters in six different sizes.

ACTIVE 30 MIN. - TOTAL 3 HOURS, 50 MIN.
MAKES 1 DOZEN

- 1 cup unsalted butter, softened
- 1½ cups powdered sugar, divided
- 1 large egg yolk
- 1 tsp. vanilla extract
- ½ tsp. green food coloring gel, plus more if necessary to reach desired shade of green
- 2½ cups all-purpose flour
- 1 Tbsp. plus 1 to 2 tsp. whole milk, divided

1. Beat butter with a heavy-duty electric stand mixer on medium speed until creamy. Gradually add ¾ cup of the powdered sugar, beating until light and fluffy, about 2 minutes. Reduce speed to medium-low; add egg yolk, and beat just until blended. Add vanilla and food coloring gel; beat just until combined. Gradually add flour, beating until blended, about 1 minute.

2. Turn dough out onto a clean work surface. Divide dough in half, and pat each half into a 5-inch-wide disk. Wrap each dough disk in plastic wrap; chill 2 hours or up to 5 days.

3. Unwrap 1 dough disk, and place on a lightly floured surface. Roll dough to about ³/₁₆-inch thickness (between ⅛ inch and ¼ inch thick). Repeat with second dough disk. Using each of 6

star-shaped cutters (1 inch, 1¼ inches, 1½ inches, 2 inches, 2¼ inches, and 2½ inches), cut 12 cookies of each size from dough. Place cookies on parchment paper-lined baking sheets, grouping cookies of same size together. Chill cookies 30 minutes to 1 hour.

4. Preheat oven to 325°F. Bake cookies in batches in preheated oven until edges are very light golden and centers are pale, 8 to 10 minutes for smaller cookies and 10 to 12 minutes for larger cookies. Cool cookies on baking sheets 2 minutes. Transfer cookies to wire racks to cool completely, about 20 minutes.

5. Stir together remaining ¾ cup powdered sugar and 1 tablespoon of the milk in a small bowl, adding up to 2 teaspoons more milk, ½ teaspoon at a time, until icing reaches desired consistency. Place icing in a piping bag or large ziplock plastic freezer bag with 1 corner cut to form a piping tip. Pipe icing in thin, decorative lines on edges of cooled cookies. Working with 1 cookie tree at a time, pipe a small amount of icing in the center of each cookie, and layer cookies in stacks of 6, with the largest cookie on bottom and smallest on top. Let stand until icing dries, about 10 minutes.

Red-Velvet Santa-Hat Meringues

Kids will love eating and decorating these crisp, chocolaty cookies.

ACTIVE 15 MIN. - TOTAL 2 HOURS, 15 MIN.
MAKES 4 DOZEN

- 4 large egg whites, at room temperature
- 1 tsp. red food coloring gel, plus more if necessary to reach desired shade of red
- ¼ tsp. cream of tartar
- ½ cup granulated sugar
- ½ cup powdered sugar
- 1 Tbsp. unsweetened cocoa
- 4 oz. white chocolate baking bar, finely chopped
- ½ cup white nonpareils
- 24 miniature marshmallows, halved crosswise

1. Preheat oven to 225°F. Line 2 rimmed baking sheets with parchment paper.

2. Place egg whites in a clean, dry bowl. Beat with an electric mixer on medium-high speed until foamy. Add food coloring

gel and cream of tartar. Increase speed to high, and beat until mixture forms soft peaks. Gradually add granulated sugar, beating until whites are stiff and shiny.

3. Sift together powdered sugar and cocoa in a separate bowl. Sprinkle one-third of powdered sugar mixture on egg white mixture; gently fold until thoroughly incorporated. Repeat procedure 2 times with remaining powdered sugar mixture. Transfer mixture to a large piping bag or large ziplock plastic freezer bag with 1 corner cut about ½ inch to form a piping tip.

4. Pipe meringues onto prepared baking sheets, forming small "santa hats" by piping a 1½-inch-wide round, and swirling and lifting up bag. Bake in preheated oven until meringues are firm and dry, about 1 hour and 30 minutes. Turn off oven, and let meringues stand in oven with door closed 20 minutes.

5. Remove meringues from oven, and cool completely on baking sheets on wire racks, about 20 minutes. Gently peel meringues off parchment.

6. Place chopped white chocolate in a small microwavable bowl. Microwave on MEDIUM until melted and smooth, about 1 minute and 30 seconds, stirring every 30 seconds.

7. Place nonpareils in a shallow plate or bowl. Dip bottoms of meringues in melted white chocolate, and dip in nonpareils. Place on parchment paper, and let stand until set, about 30 minutes. Dip cut halves of marshmallows in melted white chocolate, and place on tips of hats. Let stand until set, about 15 minutes. Store in an airtight container at room temperature.

Light Bulb Sugar Cookies

Made with sorghum syrup, ginger, vanilla, and ground cardamom, these cookies are a delicious change of pace from your usual sugar cookies.

ACTIVE 25 MIN. - TOTAL 5 HOURS
MAKES 5 DOZEN

COOKIES
- 1 cup unsalted butter, softened
- ¼ cup granulated sugar
- ¼ cup packed light brown sugar
- 1 Tbsp. grated fresh ginger
- 1 Tbsp. sorghum syrup

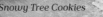

Snowy Tree Cookies

Red-Velvet Santa-Hat Meringues

Light Bulb Sugar Cookies

¼ tsp. vanilla extract

2 ¼ cups all-purpose flour

¼ tsp. table salt

¼ tsp. ground cardamom

ROYAL ICING

3 ¾ cups powdered sugar

3 large pasteurized egg whites

½ tsp. cream of tartar

Pinch of kosher salt

ADDITIONAL INGREDIENTS
Food coloring gels in desired colors

Assorted candy sprinkles

Edible gold luster dust

Decorative string or ribbon

1. Prepare the Cookies: Beat butter with a heavy-duty electric stand mixer on medium speed until creamy. Gradually add granulated sugar and brown sugar, beating until light and fluffy, about 2 minutes. Add ginger, sorghum, and vanilla; beat until combined. Stir together flour, salt, and cardamom in a small bowl. Gradually add flour mixture to butter mixture, beating on low speed until well blended.

2. Turn dough out onto a clean work surface. Divide dough in half, and pat each half into a ½-inch-thick disk. Wrap each dough disk in plastic wrap, chill 2 hours.

3. Preheat oven to 300°F. Unwrap 1 dough disk, and place on a lightly floured surface. Roll dough to about ³⁄₁₆-inch thickness (between ⅛ inch and ¼ inch thick). Using a 3 ½-inch light-bulb-shaped cutter, cut shapes from dough, rerolling scraps once. Using a straw or metal piping tip, cut a small hole toward bottom of each light bulb for stringing cookies together. Place cookies on a parchment paper-lined baking sheet, leaving 2 inches between cookies. Repeat with second dough disk, rerolling scraps once. Freeze cookies 15 minutes.

4. Bake cookies, in batches, in preheated oven until light golden on edges and centers are set, 14 to 16 minutes. Cool cookies on baking sheets 2 minutes. Transfer cookies to wire racks to cool completely, about 20 minutes.

5. Prepare the Royal Icing: Combine all Royal Icing ingredients in the bowl of a

heavy-duty electric stand mixer fitted with the whisk attachment. Beat on medium speed until thick and glossy, about 3 minutes.

6. Divide icing into small bowls, and stir in desired amounts of food coloring gel. (If not using icing immediately, cover with plastic wrap.) Transfer 1 color of icing to a piping bag, and pipe a small line of icing around edges of cookies to create a border. Thin remaining icing with a couple drops of water. Using a wooden pick, paintbrush, or offset spatula, cover cookies with thinned icing to piped border. Repeat with other colors and remaining cookies as desired.

7. Decorate cookies with sprinkles, and brush bases of light bulbs with luster dust. Let stand until icing is dry, about 2 hours. String cookies on decorative string or ribbon.

Cranberry Pull-Apart Bread with Orange-Cream Cheese Icing

Best-Ever Sticky Buns

Spicy Sausage-and-Cheddar Kolaches

BREADS WITH
PAIGE GRANDJEAN

Paige Grandjean is a new addition to the Test Kitchen but she's already established herself as one of the best bread bakers on staff. Paige has a special way with yeast and flour and is always dreaming up new recipes, like these three breads tailor-made for Christmas morning breakfast.

Spicy Sausage-and-Cheddar Kolaches

Kolaches are a hit in Texas, and we think they deserve a wider following. Our savory take on this Czech pastry is filled with smoky Conecuh sausage and sharp Cheddar.

ACTIVE 40 MIN. - TOTAL 3 HOURS
MAKES 20 TO 22

- 1 cup whole milk
- ¾ cup salted butter, divided
- ½ cup warm water (100°F to 110°F)
- 1 (¼-oz.) envelope active dry yeast
- ⅓ cup plus 1 tsp. granulated sugar, divided
- 2 large eggs, beaten
- ¾ tsp. table salt
- 5 ¼ to 6 cups bread flour, divided, plus more for dusting
- 1 ¼ lb. Conecuh sausage or spicy smoked sausage
- 4 oz. sharp Cheddar cheese, shredded (about 1 cup)

1. Combine milk and ½ cup of the butter in a small saucepan. Cook over medium-low, stirring occasionally, until butter melts, about 5 minutes. Transfer mixture to a medium bowl, and cool slightly to 100°F to 110°F, about 10 minutes.

2. Stir together warm water, yeast, and 1 teaspoon of the sugar in a small bowl. Let stand until foamy, about 5 minutes.

3. Combine eggs, salt, and remaining ⅓ cup sugar in the bowl of a heavy-duty electric stand mixer fitted with a dough hook attachment. Beat on medium-low speed just until combined. Stir in milk mixture and yeast mixture. Gradually add 4 ½ cups of the bread flour, beating just until incorporated. With mixer on low speed, gradually add up to ¾ cup more flour, ¼ cup at a time, just until dough pulls away from sides of bowl.

4. Turn dough out onto a lightly floured work surface. Knead until smooth and elastic, about 10 minutes, adding up to ¾ cup flour, in very small amounts, if necessary, to keep dough workable. Place dough in a lightly greased bowl, turning to coat all sides. Cover and let stand in a warm place until dough doubles in size, about 1 hour.

5. Cut sausage into 20 to 22 (2-inch-long) straight pieces, reserving curved pieces for another use. Divide dough into 20 to 22 (2-ounce) balls (a little larger than a golf ball). Roll each ball into a 4-inch-wide circle on a lightly floured surface. (Keep remaining dough balls covered while working.) Place about 1 tablespoon of the cheese on lower third of each dough circle, and top with 1 sausage piece. Fold dough over filling, folding in sides; pinch to seal. Place kolaches, seam side down, on 2 baking sheets lined with parchment paper, leaving 1 inch between kolaches. Keep kolaches covered while working. Cover kolaches loosely with plastic wrap, and let stand in a warm place until dough doubles in size, about 45 minutes.

6. Preheat oven to 375°F. Microwave remaining ¼ cup butter in a small microwavable bowl on HIGH until melted, about 45 seconds. Brush kolaches with half of melted butter. Bake kolaches in preheated oven until golden brown, 14 to 16 minutes. Brush kolaches with remaining melted butter, and serve hot.

Cranberry Pull-Apart Bread with Orange-Cream Cheese Icing

If you're bringing this to a Christmas brunch, reserve the icing and drizzle it over the bread just before serving.

ACTIVE 40 MIN. - TOTAL 3 HOURS, 15 MIN.
MAKES 2 LOAVES

BREAD
- ¼ cup warm water (100°F to 110°F)

1   (¼-oz.) envelope active dry yeast

¾   cup plus 1 tsp. granulated sugar, divided

½   cup unsalted butter, softened

1   tsp. table salt

2   large eggs

1   cup whole milk

4 ½ to 5 cups bread flour, divided, plus more for dusting

1 ½   cups frozen cranberries (about 5 ½ oz.), thawed and coarsely chopped

1   Tbsp. orange zest (from 1 orange)

ICING

6   Tbsp. cream cheese, softened

2   Tbsp. unsalted butter, softened

⅛   tsp. table salt

2 ¼   cups (about 9 oz.) powdered sugar

1   tsp. vanilla extract

2   Tbsp. fresh orange juice, divided (from 1 orange)

1. Prepare the Bread: Stir together water, yeast, and 1 teaspoon of the granulated sugar in a small bowl. Let stand until foamy, about 5 minutes.

2. Beat butter with a heavy-duty electric stand mixer on medium speed until creamy, about 1 minute. Add salt and ½ cup of the sugar; beat until light and fluffy, about 3 minutes. Add eggs, 1 at a time, beating well after each addition. Stir in milk and yeast mixture. Gradually add 4 ½ cups of the bread flour, beating on medium-low just until combined.

3. Turn dough out onto a lightly floured work surface. Knead until smooth and elastic, about 5 minutes, adding up to ½ cup flour, in very small amounts, if necessary to keep dough workable. Place dough in a lightly greased bowl, turning to coat all sides. Cover and let stand in a warm place until dough doubles in size, about 1 hour and 30 minutes.

4. Combine cranberries, orange zest, and remaining ¼ cup sugar in a medium bowl. Set aside.

5. Turn dough out onto a lightly floured work surface. Divide dough in half. Roll 1 dough half into a 16- x 10-inch rectangle, and cut into 8 (5- x 4-inch) rectangles. Spoon about 1 tablespoon of the cranberry mixture on each rectangle. Fold rectangles in half over filling so that short sides meet, and stand, cut side up and fold side down, in a lightly greased 8- x 4-inch loaf pan. Repeat with second dough half, remaining cranberry mixture, and a second loaf pan. Cover pans loosely with plastic wrap, and let stand in a

warm (80°°F to 85°F) place, free from drafts, until dough doubles in size, about 1 hour.

6. Preheat oven to 350°F. Remove and discard plastic wrap. Bake bread in preheated oven until golden brown and a wooden skewer inserted in center of bread comes out clean, about 30 minutes, shielding with aluminum foil after 20 minutes to prevent excess browning, if necessary.

7. Cool bread in pans 10 minutes. Transfer bread from pans to wire rack to cool slightly, at least 10 minutes.

8. Prepare the Icing: While bread cools, beat cream cheese, butter, and salt with an electric mixer on medium speed until creamy. Gradually add powdered sugar, beating until combined. Stir in vanilla and 1 tablespoon of the orange juice. Stir in up to 1 more tablespoon orange juice, 1 teaspoon at a time, until icing is smooth and creamy.

9. Brush bread lightly with icing, and serve with remaining icing for dipping.

Best-Ever Sticky Buns

These ooey-gooey pecan-topped rolls truly live up to their name.

SERVES 12

ACTIVE 40 MIN. - TOTAL 9 HOURS, 50 MIN., INCLUDING 8 HOURS CHILLING

DOUGH

1   (8-oz.) container sour cream

6   Tbsp. salted butter, plus more for greasing pan

1   tsp. table salt

⅓   cup plus 1 tsp. granulated sugar, divided

⅓   cup warm water (100°F to 110°F)

1   (¼-oz.) pkg. active dry yeast

2   large eggs, beaten

3 ¾ to 4 ½ cups bread flour, divided, plus more for dusting

FILLING

1   cup packed dark brown sugar

2   tsp. ground cinnamon

TOPPING

½   cup packed dark brown sugar

6   Tbsp. salted butter, melted

¼   cup granulated sugar

¼   cup light corn syrup

2   Tbsp. heavy cream

¼   tsp. table salt

ADDITIONAL INGREDIENT

1   cup toasted pecans, coarsely chopped

1. Prepare the Dough: Combine sour cream, butter, salt, and ⅓ cup of the granulated sugar in a small saucepan. Cook over medium-low, stirring occasionally, just until butter melts, about 4 minutes. Remove from heat, and cool to 100°F to 110°F.

2. Stir together warm water, yeast, and remaining 1 teaspoon granulated sugar in a small bowl. Let stand until foamy, about 5 minutes.

3. Combine sour cream mixture, yeast mixture, and eggs in the bowl of a heavy-duty electric stand mixer fitted with a dough hook attachment. With mixer on medium-low speed, gradually add 3 ¾ cups of the flour, beating until a soft dough forms and pulls away from sides, but still adheres to bottom of bowl.

4. Turn dough out onto a lightly floured surface. Knead until smooth and elastic, about 10 minutes, adding up to ¾ cup flour, in very small amounts, if necessary, to keep the dough workable. (Dough should be tacky, but not sticky.) Place dough in a lightly greased bowl, turning to coat all sides. Cover and chill overnight.

5. Turn dough out onto a lightly floured work surface. Roll dough into a 16- x 20-inch rectangle.

6. Prepare the Filling: Stir together brown sugar and cinnamon in a small bowl.

7. Sprinkle Filling evenly over dough rectangle, pressing gently to adhere, leaving a 1-inch border on both long sides. Starting at 1 long side, roll up dough, jelly-roll style. Using a piece of unflavored dental floss, cut off and discard 1 inch from each end of roll. Cut roll crosswise into 12 (1 ½-inch-wide) pieces.

8. Prepare the Topping: Stir together all Topping ingredients in a small bowl.

9. Assemble the Sticky Buns: Pour Topping into a lightly greased 13- x 9-inch metal baking pan. Spread to coat bottom of pan evenly. Sprinkle evenly with pecans. Place rolls, cut side down, in baking pan with sides touching. Cover with plastic wrap, and let stand in a warm (80°F to 85°F) place, free from drafts, until rolls double in size, 45 minutes to 1 hour.

10. Preheat oven to 375°F. Remove and discard plastic wrap from buns. Bake in preheated oven until golden brown, 20 to 22 minutes. Cool in pan 5 minutes. Carefully invert buns onto a serving platter. Serve warm.

COOKING ⓈⓁ SCHOOL

TIPS AND TRICKS FROM THE SOUTH'S MOST TRUSTED KITCHEN

Secrets to Stuffed Beef Tenderloin

Four steps for mastering this showstopping main dish
(Stuffed Beef Tenderloin with Burgundy-Mushroom Sauce, page 347)

"Beef is sold by grade: prime, choice, and select. Prime has the best marbling and is the priciest, but choice is also a good option for holiday meals."

—Robby Melvin
Test Kitchen Director

Holiday Essentials for a Merry Feast

SALTED BUTTER
For serving with the bread basket.

FOOD STORAGE CONTAINERS
For packaging leftovers fast and efficiently.

TABLE SALT AND FINELY GROUND BLACK PEPPER
For filling seasonal shakers.

EXTRA ICE
For chilling bottles and beverages when you run out of refrigerator space.

Parchment Paper Is a Cook's Best Friend

It's nonstick, heat- and water-resistant, and not just for baking

[1] Line baking sheets when roasting vegetables in the oven.

[2] Doubles as a cooling rack for fried foods like latkes.

[3] Cover a dish to prevent splatters when reheating in the microwave or oven.

Step 1
Using a sharp knife, cut horizontally through the center of the beef, cutting to, but not through, the other side. Open flat, as you would a book.

Step 2
Place the beef between 2 sheets of plastic wrap; pound to an even ½-inch thickness (about 13 inches square) using a meat mallet or small heavy skillet.

Step 3
Spread the filling evenly over the beef, leaving a ½-inch border around the edges. Roll up the beef like a jelly roll.

Step 4
Using kitchen twine, secure at 2-inch intervals. Brush all sides of the beef evenly with olive oil; sprinkle with salt and pepper.

Fill a Piping Bag Like a Pro

1

Fit a piping bag with an icing tip. Place the empty bag tip-side down in a glass about 3 inches shorter than the top of the bag.

2

Using a rubber spatula, scrape the icing into the bag, filling it about one half to two-thirds full. Fold up the top of the bag and remove it from the glass.

3

Twist the top of the bag where the icing ends, pushing the icing down into the bag to release trapped air. Close the bag with a twist tie or rubber band.

> "Make a double or triple batch of your favorite cookie dough, then freeze it so you can have freshly baked cookies throughout the entire holiday season with much less work."
>
> **—Deb Wise**
> Test Kitchen Professional

Baking Tools That Hit the Sweet Spot

Before whipping up the holiday confections, add these three helpers to your list

[1]
GIR ULTIMATE SPATULA
Why we love it:
This silicone spatula feels great to hold and the angled tip scrapes up every last bit of batter from a bowl. Bonus: It can be used for high heat cooking too. $12.95; gir.co

[2]
19-INCH FRENCH ROLLING PIN
Why we love it:
A tapered, handle-less wooden pin is easy to clean and rolls out dough for pies and cookies like a dream. $22.50; whetstone-woodenware.com

[3]
OXO GOOD GRIPS OFFSET ICING SPATULA
Why we love it:
Once you've frosted a cake or cupcake with this sturdy yet flexible offset spatula, you'll never use a butter knife again. $9.99; amazon.com

OUR MOST DECADENT CHEESECAKES

For over half a century, cooks have looked with confidence to the pages of *Southern Living* for delicious tried-and-true recipes that have been tested to perfection. Since the beginning, cheesecakes have been a clear reader favorite, sure to satisfy a sweet tooth of all ages. A tasty and versatile dessert, the cheesecake has a long history that dates back thousands of years to humble beginnings in ancient Greece. In much more recent history, *Southern Living* has made a meaningful mark on the dessert's legacy by perfecting classic recipes and developing delectable variations. From old-fashioned classics such as *New York Cheesecake* and *Vanilla Cheesecake with Cherry Topping* to new twists on Southern favorites such as *Pecan-Cheesecake Pie* and *Salted Caramel Black Bottom Cheesecake*, we bring you 24 decadent cheesecake recipes from The South's Most Trusted Kitchen. This tempting feature on the legendary cheesecake is our delicious bonus to you, our beloved and dedicated readers. We invite you to share these tasty recipes with your loved ones, and we thank you for making *Southern Living* the South's most iconic lifestyle brand.

New York Cheesecake

Although cakes made from various cheeses were first crafted in ancient Greece and Rome, the cheesecake we all know and love wasn't created until much later. Many New Yorkers claim to have created the original recipe, and by the early 1900s, every restaurant seemed to have its own version. But Arnold Reuben of the legendary Turf Restaurant on 49th and Broadway is officially credited with being the one to introduce to Manhattanites in 1929 what is now known as New York cheesecake.

ACTIVE 45 MIN. - TOTAL 11 HOURS, 15 MIN.

SERVES 16

CRUST

- 3 oz. all-purpose flour (about ²⁄₃ cup)
- 3 Tbsp. granulated sugar
- 2 Tbsp. chilled butter, cut into small pieces
- 1 Tbsp. ice water

FILLING

- 4 cups fat-free cottage cheese
- 2 cups granulated sugar
- 2 (8-oz.) pkg. ¹⁄₃-less-fat cream cheese, softened
- 1.1 oz. all-purpose flour (about ¼ cup)
- ½ cup fat-free sour cream
- 1 Tbsp. lemon zest
- 1 Tbsp. vanilla extract
- ¼ tsp. table salt
- 5 large eggs

1. Prepare the Crust: Preheat oven to 400°F. Weigh or lightly spoon 3 ounces flour into a dry measuring cup; level with a knife. Pulse flour and 3 tablespoons sugar in a food processor 2 times or until combined. Add butter; pulse 6 times or until mixture resembles coarse meal. With processor on, slowly pour ice water through food chute, processing just until blended (do not allow dough to form a ball).

2. Firmly press mixture into bottom of a 9-inch springform pan coated with cooking spray. Bake at 400°F for 10 minutes or until lightly browned; cool on a wire rack.

3. Reduce oven temperature to 325°F.

4. Prepare the Filling: Strain cottage cheese through a cheesecloth-lined strainer for 10 minutes; discard liquid. Process cottage cheese in food processor until smooth.

5. Beat 2 cups sugar and cream cheese in a large bowl with a mixer at medium speed until smooth. Weigh or lightly spoon 1.1 ounces flour into a dry measuring cup; level with a knife. Add flour, sour cream, and next 4 ingredients to cream cheese mixture; beat well. Add cottage cheese, stirring until well blended. Pour mixture into prepared crust.

6. Bake at 325°F for 1 hour and 30 minutes or until almost set. Turn off oven. Cool cheesecake in oven, with door closed, 1 hour. Remove cheesecake from oven; run a knife around outside edge. Cool to room temperature. Cover and chill at least 8 hours.

Note: You can also make the cheesecake in a 10- x 2 ½-inch springform pan. Bake at 300°F for 1 hour and 30 minutes or until almost set. Turn off oven. Cool cheesecake in closed oven 30 minutes.

Baby Bananas Foster Cheesecakes

Perfect for a holiday pickup dessert, these one-bite cheesecakes deliver all the goodness of traditional Bananas Foster.

ACTIVE 24 MIN. - TOTAL 5 HOURS, 12 MIN.

MAKES 3 DOZEN

CRUST

- ¾ cup cinnamon graham cracker crumbs (about 4 sheets)
- ¼ cup finely chopped pecans
- ¼ cup butter, melted

FILLING

- 1 (8-oz.) pkg. cream cheese, softened
- ⅓ cup packed light brown sugar
- 2 large eggs
- 2 Tbsp. sour cream
- 2 Tbsp. dark rum, divided
- ½ tsp. ground cinnamon
- 3 medium bananas

TOPPING

- ½ cup caramel topping

1. Prepare the Crust: Preheat oven to 325°F. Stir together graham cracker crumbs, pecans, and butter in a bowl. Press crumb mixture into bottom of 3 (12-cup) miniature muffin pans. Bake at 325°F for 8 minutes; let cool.

2. Prepare the Filling: Beat cream cheese with a mixer at medium speed until creamy. Gradually add brown sugar, beating just until blended. Add eggs, 1 at a time, beating just until yellow disappears after each addition. Stir in sour cream, 1 tablespoon of the rum, and cinnamon.

3. Mash 1 banana; add mashed banana to cream cheese mixture, beating at low speed just until blended. Spoon cream cheese batter into prepared crust in pans, filling full.

4. Bake at 325°F for 18 minutes or until set. Remove cheesecakes from oven; cool completely in pans on a wire rack, about 15 minutes. Cover and chill 4 hours.

5. Prepare the Topping: Heat caramel topping in a saucepan over low 2 to 3 minutes. Remove from heat; add remaining 1 tablespoon rum. Slice remaining 2 bananas into 36 slices, about ¼ inch thick; add to caramel sauce, stirring to coat.

6. Remove cheesecakes from pans. Place 1 caramel-coated banana slice on each cheesecake. Arrange cheesecakes on a serving platter.

Lemon Bar Cheesecake

ACTIVE 40 MIN. - TOTAL 22 HOURS, 45 MIN.

SERVES 10 TO 12

CRUST
- 8 ½ oz. all-purpose flour (about 2 cups)
- ½ cup powdered sugar
- ¼ tsp. table salt
- 4 oz. cold butter, cubed
- 2 large egg yolks
- 1 to 2 Tbsp. ice-cold water

FILLING
- 4 (8-oz.) pkg. cream cheese, softened
- 1 cup granulated sugar
- 4 large eggs
- 2 tsp. vanilla extract
- 2 cups Quick and Easy Lemon Curd, divided (recipe follows)
- Candied Lemon Slices (optional) (recipe follows)

1. Prepare the Crust: Pulse first 3 ingredients in a food processor 3 or 4 times or just until blended. Add butter, and pulse 5 or 6 times or until crumbly. Whisk together egg yolks and 1 tablespoon ice-cold water in a small bowl; add to butter mixture, and process until dough forms a ball and pulls away from sides of bowl, adding remaining 1 tablespoon ice-cold water, 1 teaspoon at a time, if necessary. Shape dough into a disk; wrap in plastic wrap. Chill 4 to 24 hours.

2. Roll dough into a 14-inch circle on a lightly floured surface. Fit dough into a lightly greased 9-inch dark springform pan, gently pressing on bottom and up sides of pan; trim and discard excess dough. Chill 30 minutes.

3. Meanwhile, preheat oven to 325°F. Prepare the Filling: Beat cream cheese with a mixer at medium speed 3 minutes or until smooth. Gradually add granulated sugar, beating until blended. Add eggs, 1 at a time, beating just until yellow disappears after each addition. Beat in vanilla. Pour two-thirds of cheesecake batter (about 4 cups) into prepared crust; dollop 1 cup lemon curd over batter in pan, and gently swirl with a knife. Spoon remaining batter into pan.

4. Bake at 325°F for 1 hour to 1 hour and 10 minutes or just until center is set. Turn off oven. Let cheesecake stand in oven, with door closed, 15 minutes. Remove from oven, and gently run a knife around outer edge of cheesecake

to loosen from sides of pan. (Do not remove sides of pan.) Cool completely in pan on a wire rack, about 1 hour. Cover and chill 8 to 24 hours.

5. Remove sides of pan, and transfer cheesecake to a serving platter. Spoon remaining 1 cup lemon curd over cheesecake, and, if desired, top with Candied Lemon Slices.

Quick and Easy Lemon Curd

MAKES 2 CUPS

Grate zest from 6 **lemons** to equal 2 tablespoons. Cut lemons in half; squeeze juice into a measuring cup to equal 1 cup. Beat ½ cup softened **butter** and 2 cups **sugar** with a mixer at medium speed until blended. Add 4 large **eggs,** 1 at a time, beating just until blended after each addition. Gradually add **lemon juice** to butter mixture, beating at low speed just until blended after each addition; stir in zest. (Mixture will look curdled.) Transfer to a 3-qt. microwave-safe bowl. Microwave at

HIGH 5 minutes, stirring at 30-second intervals, 1 to 2 more minutes or until mixture thickens, coats the back of a spoon, and starts to mound slightly when stirred. Place plastic wrap directly on warm curd (to prevent a film from forming), and chill 4 hours or until firm. Store in an airtight container in refrigerator up to 2 weeks.

Candied Lemon Slices

Cut 2 small **lemons** into ⅛-inch-thick rounds; discard seeds. Stir together 1 cup **sugar,** 2 tablespoons fresh **lemon juice,** and ¾ cup **water** in a large skillet over medium until sugar is dissolved. Add **lemon slices,** and simmer gently, keeping slices in a single layer and turning occasionally, 14 to 16 minutes or until slightly translucent and rinds are softened. Remove from heat. Place slices in a single layer in a wax paper-lined jelly-roll pan, using tongs. Cool completely, about 1 hour. Cover and chill 2 hours to 2 days. Reserve syrup for another use.

Baklava Cheesecake

Purchase prepared baklava from a local Greek restaurant, or, if you have time, make your own. It's the hidden surprise in each slice of this decadent dessert.

ACTIVE 18 MIN. - TOTAL 11 HOURS, 50 MIN.
SERVES 10

CRUST
- 1 ½ cups walnut halves
- 1 cup granulated sugar, divided
- 2 Tbsp. unsalted butter, melted

FILLING
- 2 ½ (8-oz.) pkg. cream cheese, softened
- 1 (8-oz.) pkg. mascarpone cheese, softened
- 3 large eggs
- 1 tsp. almond extract
- ¼ tsp. table salt
- 5 (3-oz.) pieces baklava

ADDITIONAL INGREDIENT
- 12 walnut halves
- Honey Syrup (recipe follows)

1. Prepare the Crust: Preheat oven to 350°F. Pulse 1 ½ cups walnuts and ¼ cup of the sugar in a food processor 4 or 5 times or until walnuts are finely ground. Add butter; pulse until mixture resembles coarse sand. Press mixture firmly on bottom of a lightly greased 9-inch springform pan. Bake 12 to 14 minutes or until lightly browned. Cool on a wire rack.

2. Reduce oven temperature to 300°F. Prepare the Filling: Beat cream cheese, mascarpone, and remaining ¾ cup sugar with a mixer at medium speed until blended. Add eggs, 1 at a time, beating just until blended after each addition. Add almond extract and salt, beating at low speed just until blended.

3. Cut each baklava piece into 2 small triangles, about 2 x 3 inches. Arrange baklava pieces in a ring over baked crust, with pointed end of each piece pointing toward center and wide ends around outside edge of pan. Pour batter over baklava into baked crust.

4. Bake at 300°F for 1 hour and 20 minutes or until center is almost set. Remove from oven; gently run a knife around edge of cheesecake to loosen from sides of pan. Cool completely on a wire rack, about 2 hours. Cover and chill 8 hours. Remove sides of pan. Top with walnut halves. Drizzle with Honey Syrup.

Honey Syrup

Combine ½ cup **honey,** 2 teaspoons **orange blossom water,** and ½ teaspoon **orange zest** in a small saucepan. Bring to a boil over medium-high. Remove from heat; cool completely.

Vanilla Cheesecake with Cherry Topping

You can make both the cheesecake and the topping up to three days ahead and store them separately in the refrigerator. Or chill the cooled cheesecake in the pan for two hours, then wrap in heavy-duty plastic wrap and freeze for up to two months. Thaw the cheesecake in the refrigerator.

ACTIVE 30 MIN. - TOTAL 11 HOURS, 15 MIN.
SERVES 16

CRUST
- ¾ cup graham cracker crumbs
- ¼ cup granulated sugar
- 2 Tbsp. butter, melted
- 2 tsp. water

FILLING
- 3 (8-oz.) pkg. fat-free cream cheese, softened
- 2 (8-oz.) pkg. ⅓-less-fat cream cheese, softened
- 1 cup granulated sugar
- 3 Tbsp. all-purpose flour
- ¼ tsp. table salt
- 1 (8-oz.) container fat-free sour cream
- 4 large eggs
- 2 tsp. vanilla extract
- 1 vanilla bean, split lengthwise

TOPPING
- ⅔ cup tawny port or other sweet red wine
- ½ cup granulated sugar
- 2 (10-oz.) bags frozen pitted dark sweet cherries
- 2 Tbsp. fresh lemon juice
- 4 tsp. cornstarch
- 4 tsp. water

1. Prepare the Crust: Preheat oven to 400°F. Combine first 3 ingredients, tossing with a fork. Add 2 teaspoons water; toss with a fork until moist and crumbly. Gently press mixture into bottom and 1 ½ inches up sides of a 9-inch springform pan coated with cooking spray. Bake at 400°F for 5 minutes; cool on a wire rack.

2. Reduce oven temperature to 325°F. Prepare the Filling: Beat cheeses with a mixer at high speed until smooth. Combine 1 cup sugar, flour, and salt, stirring with a whisk. Add to cheese mixture; beat well. Add sour cream; beat well. Add eggs, 1 at a time, beating well after each addition. Stir in vanilla. Scrape seeds from vanilla bean; stir seeds into cheese mixture, reserving bean halves.

3. Pour cheese mixture into prepared pan; bake at 325°F for 1 hour and 15 minutes or until cheesecake center barely moves when pan is touched. Remove cheesecake from oven; run a knife around outside edge. Cool to room temperature. Cover and chill at least 8 hours.

4. Prepare the Topping: Combine port, ½ cup sugar, cherries, and reserved vanilla bean halves in a large saucepan; bring to a boil. Cook 5 minutes or until cherries are thawed and mixture is syrupy. Remove vanilla bean halves; discard.

5. Combine juice, cornstarch, and 4 teaspoons water, stirring with a whisk until well blended. Stir cornstarch mixture into cherry mixture; bring to a boil. Reduce heat; simmer 3 minutes or until mixture is slightly thick and shiny. Remove from heat; cool to room temperature. Cover and chill. Serve over cheesecake.

Blueberry Mini Cheesecakes

ACTIVE 30 MIN. - TOTAL 10 HOURS, 43 MIN.
MAKES 5 MINI CHEESECAKES

CRUST
- 2 cups toasted slivered almonds
- 1 ½ cups granulated sugar, divided
- 3 Tbsp. butter, melted
- 4 Tbsp. all-purpose flour, divided

FILLING
- 3 (8-oz.) pkg. cream cheese, softened
- ½ tsp. table salt
- 4 large eggs
- 1 (8-oz.) container sour cream
- 1 tsp. vanilla extract
- 1 Tbsp. lemon zest
- 1 ½ cups fresh blueberries

TOPPING
- 1 cup whipping cream
- 2 tsp. granulated sugar
- 2 Tbsp. sour cream
- Garnishes: blueberries, lemon zest curls

1. Prepare the Crust: Preheat oven to 350°F. Pulse almonds in a food processor 5 or 6 times or until finely ground. Combine ground almonds, ¼ cup of the sugar, 3 tablespoons butter, and 1 tablespoon of the flour in a small bowl. Press mixture onto bottom and halfway up sides of 5 lightly greased 4 ½-inch springform pans. Bake crusts at 350°F for 8 minutes. Let cool on a wire rack. Reduce heat to 300°F.

2. Prepare the Filling: Beat cream cheese with a mixer at medium speed until smooth. Combine remaining 1 ¼ cups sugar, 3 tablespoons flour, and ½ teaspoon salt. Add to cream cheese, beating until blended. Add eggs, 1 at a time, beating well after each addition. Add 1 (8-ounce) container sour cream, vanilla, and lemon zest, beating just until blended. Gently stir in blueberries. Spoon about 1 ½ cups batter into each prepared crust. (Pans will be almost full. Batter will reach about ¼ inch from tops of pans.) Place on a baking sheet.

3. Bake at 300°F for 35 to 40 minutes or until almost set. Turn off oven. Let cheesecakes stand in oven, with door partially open, 30 minutes. Remove cheesecakes from oven; gently run a knife around edges of cheesecakes to loosen from sides of pans. Cool in pans on a wire rack until completely cool, about 30 minutes. Cover and chill 8 hours. Remove sides of pans.

4. Prepare the Topping: Beat whipping cream at high speed until foamy; gradually add 2 teaspoons sugar, beating until stiff peaks form. Fold in 2 tablespoons sour cream. Spread over cheesecakes. Garnish, if desired.

Note: To prepare cheesecakes using frozen blueberries, toss frozen berries with 2 tablespoons all-purpose flour and 1 tablespoon sugar. Proceed with recipe as directed.

Blueberry Cheesecake: Prepare recipe as directed through Step 1, pressing mixture onto bottom and 1 ½ inches up sides of a lightly greased 9-inch springform pan. Proceed with recipe as directed through Step 2, pouring batter into prepared pan. Proceed with recipe as directed, increasing bake time to 1 hour and 10 minutes or until almost set.

Pecan-Cheesecake Pie

ACTIVE 15 MIN. - TOTAL 2 HOURS, 10 MIN.

SERVES 8

CRUST
- ½ (14.1-oz.) pkg. refrigerated piecrusts

FILLING
- 1 (8-oz.) pkg. cream cheese, softened
- 4 large eggs
- ¾ cup granulated sugar, divided
- 2 tsp. vanilla extract, divided
- ¼ tsp. table salt

TOPPING
- 1 ¼ cups chopped pecans
- 1 cup light corn syrup

1. Prepare the Crust: Preheat oven to 350°F. Fit piecrust into a 9-inch pie plate according to package directions. Fold edges under, and crimp.

2. Prepare the Filling: Beat cream cheese, 1 egg, ½ cup sugar, 1 teaspoon vanilla, and salt with a mixer at medium speed until smooth. Pour cream cheese mixture into piecrust; sprinkle evenly with chopped pecans.

3. Prepare the Topping: Whisk together corn syrup and remaining 3 eggs, ¼ cup sugar, and 1 teaspoon vanilla; pour mixture over pecans. Place pie on a baking sheet.

4. Bake at 350°F on lowest oven rack 50 to 55 minutes or until pie is set. Cool on a wire rack 1 hour or until completely cool. Serve immediately, or cover and chill up to 2 days.

Cranberry Swirl Cheesecake

We wanted that thick, almost showstopping texture, plus lots of tang, like a New York cheesecake. The garnet swirl of fruit makes it very elegant. If the cranberry mixture gets too thick, add a tablespoon of water and whirl it around in the food processor.

ACTIVE 38 MIN. - TOTAL 10 HOURS, 53 MIN.

SERVES 12

CRUST
- 4 oz. chocolate graham crackers
- 3 Tbsp. canola oil

TOPPING
- 1½ cups fresh cranberries
- ½ cup granulated sugar
- ¼ cup Chambord (raspberry liqueur)
- 3 Tbsp. water

FILLING
- 1 cup granulated sugar
- 2 (8-oz.) pkg. ⅓-less-fat cream cheese, softened
- 4 oz. fat-free cream cheese, softened
- 1 cup plain fat-free Greek yogurt
- 2 tsp. vanilla extract
- ⅛ tsp. table salt
- 3 large eggs
- 2 large egg whites

1. Prepare the Crust: Preheat oven to 375°F. Wrap outside bottom and sides of a 9-inch springform pan tightly with a double layer of heavy-duty foil. Lightly spray inside bottom and sides of pan with cooking spray.

2. Process crackers in a food processor until finely ground. Drizzle with oil; pulse until combined. Press mixture into bottom and ½ inch up sides of prepared pan. Bake at 375°F for 8 minutes; cool on a wire rack. Reduce oven temperature to 325°F.

3. Prepare the Topping: Place cranberries, sugar, liqueur, and 3 tablespoons water in a saucepan; bring to a boil. Cook 8 minutes or until cranberries pop and mixture is syrupy. Cool 20 minutes. Process mixture in a food processor 1 minute or until smooth.

4. Prepare the Filling: Combine 1 cup sugar and cheeses in a large bowl; beat with a mixer at medium speed until smooth. Beat in yogurt, vanilla, and salt. Add 3 eggs, 1 at a time, beating well after each addition.

5. Place 2 egg whites in a medium bowl; beat with a mixer at high speed until soft peaks form, using clean, dry beaters. Fold beaten egg whites into cream cheese mixture. Pour filling into crust. Spoon cranberry mixture over filling; gently swirl with a knife. Place springform pan in a 13- x 9-inch metal baking pan. Add hot water to pan to a depth of 2 inches. Bake at 325°F for 50 minutes or until center of cheesecake barely moves when pan is touched.

6. Turn off oven. Cool cheesecake in closed oven 30 minutes. Remove cheesecake from oven. Run a knife around outside edge. Cool on a wire rack. Cover and chill 8 hours.

CRANBERRY SWIRL CHEESECAKE

Hazelnut Layered Cheesecake

Using low-fat and fat-free cream cheeses to lighten a cheesecake isn't new, but adding a little flour and baking powder helps lighten the texture, making it creamy and smooth. Toasting the hazelnut meal really boosts its flavor in the cake layer. Instead of buying hazelnut meal, you can toast whole nuts, let them cool completely, and process in a food processor until finely ground. If you prefer, you can skip brushing the cake with the Frangelico liqueur.

ACTIVE 1 HOUR - TOTAL 13 HOURS, 11 MIN.

SERVES 14

CAKE
- 2.25 ounces hazelnut meal (about ½ cup)
- ½ cup granulated sugar
- 2 Tbsp. unsalted butter, softened
- 2 Tbsp. canola oil
- 2 large egg whites (reserve yolks for cheesecake)
- 1.5 oz. all-purpose flour (about ⅓ cup)
- 2 tsp. cornstarch
- ½ tsp. baking powder
- ¼ tsp. table salt
- 1 Tbsp. hazelnut liqueur (such as Frangelico) (optional)

CHEESECAKE
- 12 oz. ⅓-less-fat cream cheese
- 4 oz. fat-free cream cheese
- ¾ cup granulated sugar
- 3 large eggs
- 2 large egg yolks (reserved from cake)
- 2 Tbsp. all-purpose flour
- 1 tsp. vanilla extract
- 1 tsp. ground cinnamon
- ½ tsp. ground ginger
- ½ tsp. ground allspice
- ½ tsp. baking powder
- ¼ tsp. table salt
- ¼ tsp. ground cloves
- 1 cup canned pumpkin

BRITTLE
- ⅓ cup granulated sugar
- 1 Tbsp. water
- 3 Tbsp. hazelnuts, roasted and coarsely chopped
- 1 cup frozen fat-free whipped topping, thawed

1. Prepare the Cake: Preheat oven to 350°F. Sprinkle hazelnut meal evenly on a rimmed baking sheet. Bake at 350°F for 4 to 5 minutes or until lightly browned, stirring after 3 minutes. Cool completely, about 20 minutes.

2. Combine sugar, butter, and oil in a large bowl; beat with a mixer at medium speed until well combined, about 3 minutes. Add egg whites; beat 1 minute. Weigh or lightly spoon flour into a dry measuring cup; level with a knife. Combine flour, toasted hazelnut meal, cornstarch, baking powder, and salt in a bowl; stir with a whisk. Add flour mixture to sugar mixture; beat at low speed 1 minute or until just combined.

3. Spoon batter into a 9-inch springform pan coated with baking spray; smooth top. Bake at 350°F for 13 minutes or until a wooden pick inserted in center comes out clean. Brush top of hot cake with hazelnut liqueur, if desired. Cool completely in pan on a wire rack (do not remove or loosen sides of springform pan).

4. Reduce oven temperature to 325°F.

5. While cake cools, prepare the Cheesecake: Place cream cheeses in a large bowl; beat at medium speed 2 minutes or until smooth. Add sugar and next 10 ingredients; beat at low speed 2 minutes or until well combined. Add pumpkin; beat at low speed until combined. Pour cheesecake batter over top of cooled hazelnut cake.

6. Bake at 325°F for 50 minutes or until cheesecake center barely moves when pan is touched. Remove cheesecake from oven. Run a knife around outside edge. Cool completely on a wire rack. Cover and chill 8 hours or overnight.

7. Prepare the Brittle: Place sugar and 1 tablespoon water in a small heavy saucepan over medium; cook until sugar dissolves, stirring occasionally. Continue cooking about 2 minutes or until golden (do not stir).

8. While sugar mixture cooks, sprinkle chopped hazelnuts over a 14- x 2-inch area on parchment paper lightly coated with cooking spray. Drizzle caramelized sugar over nuts. Cool 10 minutes or until firm; break into 14 pieces. To serve, cut cheesecake into wedges, dollop each wedge with whipped topping, and top with Brittle.

Layered Peppermint Cheesecake

ACTIVE 1 HOUR, 10 MIN. - TOTAL
8 HOURS. 30 MIN.

SERVES 10 TO 12

PEPPERMINT CHEESECAKE LAYERS

- 3 (8-oz.) pkg. cream cheese, softened
- ½ cup granulated sugar
- 2 Tbsp. unsalted butter, softened
- 3 large eggs
- 1 Tbsp. all-purpose flour
- 1 ½ cups sour cream
- 2 tsp. vanilla extract
- ¼ tsp. peppermint extract
- ⅔ cup crushed hard peppermint candies

SOUR CREAM CAKE LAYERS

- 1 (18.25-oz.) pkg. white cake mix
- 2 large eggs
- 1 (8-oz.) container sour cream
- ⅓ cup vegetable oil
- ½ cup water

WHITE CHOCOLATE MOUSSE FROSTING

- ⅔ cup granulated sugar
- ¼ cup water
- 1 cup white chocolate chips
- 2 cups whipping cream
- 2 tsp. vanilla extract

Garnish: assorted peppermint candies

1. Prepare the Peppermint Cheesecake Layers: Preheat oven to 325°F. Line bottom and sides of 2 (8-inch) round cake pans with aluminum foil, allowing 2 to 3 inches to extend over sides; lightly grease foil. Beat cream cheese, ½ cup sugar, and 2 tablespoons butter with a mixer at medium speed 1 to 2 minutes or until creamy and smooth. Add 3 eggs, 1 at a time, beating until blended after each addition. Add flour and next 3 ingredients, beating until blended. Fold in crushed candies. Pour batter into prepared pans. Place cake pans in a large baking pan; add hot water to baking pan to a depth of 1 inch.

2. Bake at 325°F for 25 minutes or until set. Remove from oven to wire racks; cool completely in pans, about 1 hour. Cover cheesecakes (do not remove from pans), and freeze 4 to 6 hours or until frozen solid. Lift frozen cheesecakes from pans, using foil sides as handles. Gently remove foil from cheesecakes. Wrap in plastic wrap, and return to freezer until ready to assemble cake.

3. Preheat oven to 350°F. Prepare the Sour Cream Cake Layers: Beat cake mix, next 3 ingredients, and ½ cup water with a mixer at low speed 30 seconds or just until moistened; beat at medium speed 2 minutes. Spoon batter into 3 greased and floured 8-inch round cake pans.

4. Bake at 350°F for 15 to 20 minutes or until a wooden pick inserted in center comes out clean. Cool in pans on wire racks 10 minutes; remove from pans to wire racks, and cool completely, about 1 hour.

5. Prepare White Chocolate Mousse Frosting: Cook ⅔ cup sugar and ¼ cup water in a small saucepan over medium-low, stirring often, 3 to 4 minutes or until sugar is dissolved. Add chips; cook, stirring constantly, 2 to 3 minutes or until chocolate is melted and smooth, stirring at 30-second intervals. Remove from heat. Cool to room temperature, about 30 minutes, whisking occasionally.

6. Beat cream and 2 teaspoons vanilla with a mixer at high speed 1 to 2 minutes or until soft peaks form. Gradually fold white chocolate mixture into whipped cream mixture, folding until mixture reaches spreading consistency.

7. Assemble the cake: Place 1 cake layer on a cake stand or plate. Top with 1 frozen cheesecake layer. Top with second cake layer and remaining cheesecake layer. Top with remaining cake layer. Spread top and sides of cake with frosting. Chill until ready to serve. Garnish with candies.

Salted Caramel Black Bottom Cheesecake

Sweet, salty, chocolaty, gooey—what's not to love about this showstopping cheesecake?

ACTIVE 33 MIN. - TOTAL 12 HOURS, 18 MIN.
SERVES 12

CRUST
- 5 cups mini-pretzel twists
- 3 Tbsp. granulated sugar
- ¾ cup butter, melted

FILLING
- 1 cup semisweet chocolate chips
- ½ cup whipping cream
- ¾ cup caramel sauce
- 1 tsp. coarse sea salt
- 2 (8-oz.) pkg. cream cheese, softened
- 1 cup granulated sugar
- 2 (8-oz.) containers mascarpone cheese, softened
- 4 large eggs
- 2 Tbsp. all-purpose flour
- 1½ tsp. vanilla extract

TOPPING
- Star-shaped cookie cutters
- 4 (2-oz.) chocolate candy coating squares
- Coarse sea salt or sea salt flakes
- White sparkling sugar

1. Prepare the Crust: Preheat oven to 325°F. Process pretzels and 3 tablespoons granulated sugar in a food processor until pretzels are coarsely crushed. With processor running, pour butter through food chute; process until pretzels are finely crushed. Press mixture on bottom and 1 inch up sides of a 9-inch springform pan.
2. Prepare the Filling: Microwave chocolate chips and whipping cream in a small microwave-safe bowl at HIGH 1 minute or until melted; stir until smooth. Spread chocolate mixture over crust. Freeze 10 minutes.
3. Stir together caramel sauce and 1 teaspoon salt. Beat cream cheese and 1 cup granulated sugar with a mixer at medium speed until creamy. Add mascarpone cheese, beating until blended. Add caramel sauce, beating until blended. Add eggs, 1 at a time, beating just until yellow disappears. Stir in flour until just blended. Stir in vanilla. Pour into prepared crust.

4. Bake at 325°F for 1 hour and 25 minutes or until edges are set and center is almost set. Remove cheesecake from oven; gently run a knife around outer edge of cheesecake to loosen from sides of pan. Cool completely on a wire rack, about 2 hours. Cover and chill 8 hours. Remove sides of pan.
5. Microwave candy coating in a microwave-safe bowl at MEDIUM (50% power) 1½ to 2 minutes or until melted.
6. Prepare the Topping: Arrange star cookie cutters on a parchment paper-lined baking sheet. Pour melted candy coating to depth of ¼ inch into cookie cutters, using a wooden pick to spread to corners. Sprinkle lightly with sea salt and sparkling sugar.
7. Freeze 10 minutes or until set. Carefully remove candy coating from cutters. Decorate top of cheesecake with stars.

Chocolate Fudge Cheesecakes

A chewy brownie crust forms the base for these luscious cheesecakes.

ACTIVE 30 MIN. - TOTAL 10 HOURS, 36 MIN.
SERVES 20

CRUST
- ½ cup finely chopped toasted pecans
- 1 (4-oz.) unsweetened chocolate baking bar

FILLING
- 1 cup butter, softened
- 3¾ cups granulated sugar, divided
- 11 large eggs
- 1 cup all-purpose flour
- 1 cup semisweet chocolate chips
- 3 tsp. vanilla extract, divided
- 4 (8-oz.) pkg. cream cheese, softened
- Chocolate Glaze (recipe follows)
- Garnish: chocolate-dipped pecan halves

1. Prepare the Crust: Preheat oven to 325°F. Sprinkle toasted pecans over bottoms of 2 greased and floured 9-inch springform pans.
2. Microwave chocolate baking bar in a microwave-safe bowl at MEDIUM (50% power) 1½ minutes or until melted and

smooth, stirring at 30-second intervals.
3. Prepare the Filling: Beat butter and 2 cups of the sugar with a mixer at medium speed until light and fluffy. Add 4 of the eggs, 1 at a time, beating just until blended after each addition. Add melted chocolate, beating just until blended. Add flour, beating at low speed just until blended. Stir in chocolate chips and 1 teaspoon of the vanilla. Divide batter between pans, spreading to edges of pan over chopped pecans.
4. Beat cream cheese at medium speed until smooth; add remaining 1¾ cups sugar, beating until blended. Add remaining 7 eggs, 1 at a time, beating just until blended after each addition. Stir in remaining 2 teaspoons vanilla. Divide cream cheese mixture between each pan, spreading over chocolate batter.
5. Bake at 325°F for 1 hour or until set. Remove from oven, and gently run a knife around outer edge of cheesecake to loosen from sides of pan. (Do not remove sides of pan.) Cool on wire racks 1 hour or until completely cool.
6. Spread tops of cooled cheesecakes with Chocolate Glaze; cover and chill 8 hours. Remove sides of pans. Garnish, if desired.

Chocolate Glaze

MAKES 2 CUPS

Melt 1 (12-oz.) package **semisweet chocolate chips** and ½ cup **whipping cream** in a 2-qt. microwave-safe bowl at MEDIUM (50% power) 2½ to 3 minutes or until chocolate begins to melt, stirring at 1-minute intervals. Whisk until chocolate is melted and mixture is smooth, stirring at 30-second intervals.

Toffee S'mores Cheesecake

ACTIVE 30 MIN. - TOTAL 9 HOURS
SERVES 16

CRUST
- 2 cups graham cracker crumbs
- 6 Tbsp. butter, melted

FILLING
- 3 (8-oz.) pkg. cream cheese, softened
- 1 cup granulated sugar
- 1 tsp. vanilla extract
- 3 large eggs
- 6 oz. semisweet baking chocolate, melted and cooled
- 1 cup sour cream
- 5 (1.4-oz.) chocolate-covered toffee candy bars, coarsely chopped
- 7 large marshmallows

1. Prepare the Crust: Preheat oven to 325°F. Wrap outside bottom and sides of a 9-inch springform pan with foil. Lightly spray inside bottom and sides of pan with cooking spray. Combine crumbs and melted butter in a medium bowl. Press in bottom and halfway up sides of pan. Bake at 325°F for 10 minutes or until set. Cool crust 10 minutes.
2. Prepare the Filling: Beat cream cheese, sugar, and vanilla with a mixer at medium speed until smooth. Beat in eggs, 1 at a time, just until blended after each addition. Divide batter evenly between 2 bowls. Beat melted chocolate into 1 bowl; stir in ¾ cup of the sour cream. Beat remaining ¼ cup sour cream into second bowl; stir in chopped toffee candy bars. Pour toffee batter over crust. Carefully spread with chocolate batter.
3. Bake at 325°F for 1 hour and 15 minutes or until almost set. Turn off oven. Let cheesecake stand in oven, with oven door open at least 4 inches, for 30 minutes. Remove from oven, and gently run a knife around outer edge of cheesecake to loosen from sides of pan. (Do not remove sides of pan.) Cool on a wire rack 30 minutes. Refrigerate at least 6 hours or overnight.
4. Just before serving, run a small metal spatula around edge of pan; carefully remove foil and sides of pan. Set oven control to broil. Place cheesecake on a baking sheet. Cut marshmallows in half horizontally with dampened kitchen scissors. Place marshmallows, cut side down, on top of cheesecake. Broil about 6 inches from heat 1 to 2 minutes or until golden brown.

Technique Tip: Be sure to chill cheesecake for the full 6 hours before topping with marshmallows and serving. The marshmallows don't keep as well, so add them just before serving.

CARAMEL-APPLE CHEESECAKE

Caramel-Apple Cheesecake

ACTIVE 30 MIN. - TOTAL 12 HOURS, 5 MIN.
SERVES 12

CRUST
- 2 cups cinnamon graham cracker crumbs (about 15 whole crackers)
- ½ cup melted butter
- ½ cup finely chopped pecans

FILLING
- 3 (8-oz.) pkg. cream cheese, softened
- 1 ⅓ cups packed light brown sugar
- 2 tsp. vanilla extract
- 3 large eggs
  Caramel Apples (recipe follows)

GLAZE
- ¼ cup apple jelly
- 1 tsp. water
  Sweetened whipped cream

1. Prepare the Crust: Preheat oven to 350°F. Stir together cinnamon graham cracker crumbs and next 2 ingredients in a medium bowl until well blended. Press mixture on bottom and 1 ½ inches up sides of a 9-inch springform pan. Bake 10 to 12 minutes or until lightly browned. Remove to a wire rack, and cool completely, about 30 minutes.
2. Prepare the Filling: Beat cream cheese, brown sugar, and vanilla with a stand mixer at medium speed until blended and smooth. Add eggs, 1 at a time, beating just until blended after each addition. Pour batter into prepared crust. Arrange Caramel Apples over cream cheese mixture.
3. Bake at 350°F for 55 minutes to 1 hour and 5 minutes or until set. Remove from oven, and gently run a knife around outer edge of cheesecake to loosen from sides of pan. (Do not remove sides of pan.) Cool completely on a wire rack, about 2 hours. Cover and chill 8 to 24 hours.
4. Prepare the Glaze: Cook apple jelly and 1 teaspoon water in a small saucepan over medium, stirring constantly, 2 to 3 minutes or until jelly is melted; brush over apples on top of cheesecake. Serve with whipped cream.

Caramel Apples

Peel 2 ¾ pounds large **Granny Smith apples** (about 6), and cut each one into ½-inch-thick wedges. Toss together apples and ⅓ cup packed **brown sugar.** Melt 1 tablespoon **butter** in a large skillet over medium-high; add apple mixture, and sauté 5 to 6 minutes or until crisp-tender and golden. Cool completely, about 30 minutes.

Mississippi Mud Cheesecake

ACTIVE 20 MIN. - TOTAL 9 HOURS

SERVES 16

CRUST

- 24 thin chocolate wafer cookies (from 9-oz. pkg.), crushed (about 1 ⅔ cups)
- ⅓ cup finely chopped pecans
- 2 Tbsp. granulated sugar
- 6 Tbsp. butter, melted

FILLING

- 4 (8-oz.) pkg. cream cheese, softened
- 1 ¼ cups granulated sugar
- 2 Tbsp. all-purpose flour
- 1 tsp. vanilla extract
- 4 large eggs
- 2 (4-oz.) semisweet chocolate baking bars, melted and cooled
- 2 cups miniature marshmallows
- ½ cup chopped toasted pecans
- ½ cup ready-to-spread chocolate frosting (from 16-oz. container)

1. Prepare the Crust: Preheat oven to 300°F. Wrap outside bottom and sides of 9-inch springform pan with heavy-duty foil. Lightly spray inside bottom and sides of pan with cooking spray. Combine cookie crumbs and next 3 ingredients in a bowl with a pastry blender until crumbly. Press mixture into bottom of pan. Bake 12 minutes or until set. Cool crust on a wire rack 10 minutes.
2. Prepare the Filling: Beat cream cheese, 1 ¼ cups sugar, flour, and vanilla with a mixer at medium speed until light and fluffy. Beat in eggs, 1 at a time, just until blended. Beat in melted chocolate. Pour over crust.
3. Bake at 300°F for 1 hour and 15 minutes or until almost set. Turn off oven. Let cheesecake stand in oven, with oven door open at least 4 inches, for 30 minutes. Remove from oven, and gently run a knife around outer edge of cheesecake to loosen from sides of pan. (Do not remove sides of pan.) Sprinkle with marshmallows. Cool on a wire rack 30 minutes. Sprinkle with pecans.
4. Microwave frosting in a small microwave-safe bowl at HIGH 15 seconds or until pourable. Drizzle frosting over marshmallows and pecans. Refrigerate at least 6 hours or overnight.
5. To serve, run a small metal spatula

around edge of pan; carefully remove foil and sides of pan.

Chocolate-Coffee Cheesecake

ACTIVE 20 MIN. - TOTAL 9 HOURS, 50 MIN.

SERVES 8

CRUST

- 1 (10-oz.) box chocolate-flavored bear-shaped graham crackers, crushed (about 2 ¼ cups)
- 6 Tbsp. butter, melted
- 1 cup plus 2 Tbsp. granulated sugar, divided

FILLING

- 4 (8-oz.) pkg. cream cheese, softened
- ¼ cup plus 1 Tbsp. coffee liqueur, divided
- 1 tsp. instant coffee granules
- 1 tsp. vanilla extract
- 4 large eggs
- 4 (1-oz.) bittersweet baking chocolate squares
- 1 (16-oz.) container sour cream
  Garnishes: blackberries, currants, strawberries

1. Prepare the Crust: Preheat oven to 350°F. Stir together crushed graham crackers, butter, and 1 tablespoon of the sugar. Press mixture on bottom and halfway up sides of a 9-inch springform pan. Bake at 350°F for 10 minutes. Cool crust in pan on a wire rack. Reduce oven temperature to 325°F.
2. Prepare the Filling: Beat cream cheese and 1 cup of the sugar with a mixer at medium speed until blended. Add ¼ cup of the coffee liqueur, coffee granules, and vanilla, beating at low speed until well blended. Add eggs, 1 at a time, beating just until yellow disappears after each addition.
3. Remove and reserve 1 cup cream cheese mixture. Pour remaining batter into prepared crust.
4. Microwave chocolate squares in a medium-size glass bowl at HIGH 1 minute or until melted and smooth, stirring at 30-second intervals; cool slightly. Stir reserved 1 cup cream cheese mixture into melted chocolate, blending well. Spoon chocolate mixture in lines on top of batter in springform pan; gently swirl with a knife.

5. Bake at 325°F for 1 hour or until almost set. Turn off oven. Let cheesecake stand in oven, with door closed, 30 minutes. Remove cheesecake from oven, and gently run a knife around outer edge of cheesecake to loosen from sides of pan. (Do not remove sides of pan.) Stir together sour cream, remaining 1 tablespoon sugar, and remaining 1 tablespoon coffee liqueur. Spread sour cream mixture over cheesecake. Cool on a wire rack. Cover and chill at least 8 hours. Garnish, if desired.

Test Kitchen Tip: Some cracks in cheesecakes are normal and can even make them look prettier. Generally, the more slowly the cheesecake is cooked, the less chance there is for cracking. Use an oven thermometer to make sure your oven stays at the correct temperature. After the cheesecake has cooled in the oven, remove it, and run a knife around the edge. Cool completely on a wire rack; then cover and chill at least 8 hours.

White Chocolate-Raspberry Cheesecake

Raspberry preserves make a luscious layer within this cheesecake.

ACTIVE 22 MIN. - TOTAL 9 HOURS, 20 MIN.

SERVES 12

CRUST

- 2 cups graham cracker crumbs
- 3 Tbsp. granulated sugar
- ½ cup butter, melted

FILLING

- 5 (8-oz.) pkg. cream cheese, softened
- 1 cup granulated sugar
- 2 large eggs
- 1 Tbsp. vanilla extract
- 12 oz. white chocolate, melted and cooled slightly
- ¾ cup raspberry preserves
  Garnish: fresh raspberries

1. Prepare the Crust: Preheat oven to 350°F. Combine first 3 ingredients; press crumb mixture into bottom of a lightly greased 9-inch springform pan. Bake at 350°F for 8 minutes; cool slightly.
2. Prepare the Filling: Beat cream cheese with a mixer at medium speed until creamy; gradually add 1 cup sugar, beating well. Add eggs, 1 at a time, beating after each addition. Stir in

vanilla. Add melted white chocolate, beating well.

3. Microwave raspberry preserves in a small microwave-safe bowl at HIGH 30 seconds to 1 minute or until melted; stir well.

4. Spoon half of cream cheese batter into prepared crust; spread a little more than half of melted preserves over batter, leaving a ¾-inch border. Spoon remaining cream cheese batter around edges of pan, spreading toward the center. Cover remaining raspberry preserves, and chill.

5. Bake at 350°F for 50 minutes or until cheesecake is just set and slightly browned. Remove from oven; cool completely on a wire rack. Cover and chill at least 8 hours.

6. Gently run a knife around outer edge of cheesecake to loosen from sides of pan. Reheat remaining preserves briefly in microwave to melt. Pour preserves over top of cheesecake, leaving a 1-inch border. Remove sides of pan. Store in refrigerator. Garnish, if desired.

Note: To remove seeds from raspberry preserves, press preserves through a fine strainer using the back of a spoon, if desired.

German Chocolate Cheesecake

With a nod to the classic three-layer cake, this luscious cheesecake takeoff comes pretty close to perfection.

ACTIVE 30 MIN. - TOTAL 9 HOURS, 20 MIN.
SERVES 12

> **CRUST**
> 1 cup chocolate wafer crumbs
> 2 Tbsp. granulated sugar
> 3 Tbsp. butter, melted
> **FILLING**
> 3 (8-oz.) pkg. cream cheese, softened
> ¾ cup granulated sugar
> ¼ cup unsweetened cocoa
> 2 tsp. vanilla extract
> 3 large eggs
> **TOPPING**
> ⅓ cup evaporated milk
> ⅓ cup granulated sugar
> ¼ cup butter
> 1 large egg, lightly beaten
> ½ tsp. vanilla extract

> ½ cup coarsely chopped toasted pecans
> ½ cup organic coconut chips or flaked coconut

1. Prepare the Crust: Preheat oven to 325°F. Stir together first 3 ingredients; press into bottom of an ungreased 9-inch springform pan.

2. Bake at 325°F for 10 minutes. Cool crust.

3. Increase oven temperature to 350°F. Prepare the Filling: Beat cream cheese and next 3 ingredients with a mixer at medium speed until blended. Add eggs, 1 at a time, beating just until blended after each addition. Pour into prepared crust.

4. Bake at 350°F for 35 minutes. Remove from oven; gently run a knife around outer edge of cheesecake to loosen from sides of pan. Cool completely in pan on a wire rack. Cover and chill 8 hours.

5. Prepare the Topping: Stir together evaporated milk and next 4 ingredients in a saucepan. Cook over medium, stirring constantly, 7 minutes. Stir in pecans and coconut. Remove sides of pan; spread topping over cheesecake.

Cinderella Cheesecake

This showstopping cheesecake features a creamy peanut butter filling baked in a chocolate brownie crust.

ACTIVE 50 MIN.   TOTAL 13 HOURS, 30 MIN.
SERVES 10 TO 12

> **BROWNIE CRUST**
> 3 (1-oz.) unsweetened chocolate baking squares
> ¼ cup unsalted butter
> ½ cup sifted all-purpose flour
> ⅛ tsp. table salt
> ⅛ tsp. baking powder
> 2 large eggs
> 1 cup packed light brown sugar
> 1½ tsp. vanilla extract
> ½ (1-oz.) bittersweet chocolate baking square, finely chopped
> **CHEESECAKE FILLING**
> 12 oz. cream cheese, softened
> 1 cup packed light brown sugar
> 3 large eggs
> ½ cup sour cream
> 1⅓ cups creamy peanut butter
> **TOPPING**
> ¾ cup sour cream
> 2 tsp. granulated sugar
> Chocolate curls

1. Preheat oven to 350°F. Prepare the Crust: Grease and flour a 9-inch springform pan.

2. Microwave 3 baking squares and butter in a small microwave-safe bowl at MEDIUM (50% power) 1½ minutes or until melted, stirring at 30-second intervals.

3. Stir together flour, salt, and baking powder in a large bowl.

4. Beat eggs and brown sugar in a large bowl with a mixer at medium-high speed 3 to 4 minutes or until batter forms thin ribbons when beaters are lifted.

5. Add vanilla, bittersweet chocolate, and melted chocolate mixture. Beat only until blended.

6. Stir in flour mixture just until combined. Spread 1 cup crust mixture on bottom of prepared pan.

7. Bake at 350°F on center oven rack 13 to 15 minutes or until set. Cool on a wire rack 10 minutes; freeze 15 minutes. Remove from freezer; spread remaining batter up sides of pan to ¼ inch from top, sealing batter to bottom crust.

8. Prepare the Cheesecake Filling: Beat cream cheese and brown sugar with a stand mixer at medium speed until blended. Add eggs, 1 at a time, beating only until yellow yolk disappears after each addition. Beat in sour cream only until blended. Beat in peanut butter until blended.

9. Pour filling into prepared crust. (Mixture will not completely fill crust.)

10. Bake at 350°F for 35 minutes or until center is almost set. A 2-inch circle in center of filling should jiggle slightly when pan is shaken gently. Meanwhile, prepare the Topping. Stir together sour cream and sugar in a small bowl until smooth.

11. Remove cheesecake from oven. Spread Topping over center of cheesecake, leaving a 2-inch border around edge. Bake for 1 more minute.

12. Remove from oven; gently run a knife around outer edge of cheesecake to loosen from sides of pan. Cool completely on a wire rack.

13. Cover and chill 8 to 12 hours. Remove sides of pan. Top with chocolate curls.

Eggnog Cheesecake with Bourbon Caramel

You can also use high-quality prepared caramel sauce. Warm it in a saucepan over low heat, then gradually stir in bourbon to taste.

ACTIVE 15 MIN. - TOTAL 11 HOURS, 36 MIN.

SERVES 10

CRUST
- 2 cups graham cracker crumbs (about 15 whole crackers)
- ½ cup butter, melted
- ½ cup finely chopped pecans
- 2 Tbsp. granulated sugar

FILLING
- 3 (8-oz.) pkg. cream cheese, softened
- 1 ¾ cups granulated sugar, divided
- 2 Tbsp. all-purpose flour
- ½ tsp. freshly grated nutmeg
- 4 large eggs
- 1 cup refrigerated eggnog
- 1 tsp. vanilla extract

CARAMEL TOPPING
- ¼ cup light corn syrup
- ¼ cup water
- ¾ cup heavy whipping cream
- 2 Tbsp. bourbon
- Sweetened whipped cream
- Freshly grated nutmeg

1. Preheat oven to 325°F. Prepare the Crust: Stir together first 4 ingredients in a medium bowl until well blended. Press mixture on bottom and 2 inches up sides of a 9-inch springform pan. Bake for 10 to 12 minutes or until lightly browned. Remove crust to a wire rack, and cool completely, about 30 minutes.

2. Meanwhile, prepare the Filling: Beat cream cheese and 1 cup of the sugar with a stand mixer at medium speed until blended and smooth. Beat in flour and nutmeg. Add eggs, 1 at a time, beating just until blended after each addition. Add eggnog and vanilla, beating until blended. Pour batter into prepared crust.

3. Bake at 325°F for 1 hour and 5 minutes or until almost set. Turn off oven. Let cheesecake stand in oven, with door closed, 15 minutes. Remove cheesecake from oven, and gently run a knife around outer edge of cheesecake to loosen from sides of pan. (Do not remove sides of pan.) Cool completely on a wire rack, about 1 hour. Cover and chill 8 to 24 hours.

4. Prepare the Caramel Topping: Bring corn syrup, ¼ cup water, and remaining ¾ cup sugar to a boil in a medium saucepan over medium-high. (Do not stir.) Boil, swirling occasionally after sugar begins to change color, 7 minutes or until dark amber. (Do not walk away from the pan because sugar will burn quickly once it begins to change color.) Remove from heat. Carefully whisk in cream (mixture will bubble and spatter). Whisk constantly until bubbling stops and caramel dissolves. Whisk in bourbon. Cover and refrigerate until ready to use or up to 2 weeks.

5. Remove sides of pan from cheesecake. Insert a medium-size metal star tip into a large decorating bag; fill with whipped cream. Pipe cream decoratively on cheesecake. Heat caramel until pourable. Drizzle each serving with caramel. Sprinkle with freshly grated nutmeg.

EGGNOG CHEESECAKE WITH BOURBON CARAMEL

Triple Chocolate Cheesecake

ACTIVE 25 MIN. - TOTAL 11 HOURS, 10 MIN.

SERVES 16

CRUST
- ⅔ cup uncooked regular oats
- 4 chocolate graham cracker sheets (16 crackers)
- 2 Tbsp. dark brown sugar
- ⅜ tsp. table salt, divided
- 1 Tbsp. butter, melted
- 1 large egg white

FILLING
- 1 cup granulated sugar
- ¼ cup unsweetened cocoa
- 2 Tbsp. cake flour
- 12 oz. fat-free cream cheese, softened
- 10 oz. ⅓-less-fat cream cheese, softened

4 large eggs, at room temperature
1 oz. bittersweet chocolate, melted and cooled
1 tsp. vanilla extract
2 cups frozen reduced-calorie whipped topping (such as Cool Whip), thawed and divided
1 cup fresh raspberries

1. Prepare the Crust: Preheat oven to 350°F. Spread oats on a baking sheet. Bake at 350°F for 10 minutes, stirring after 5 minutes. Cool oats 10 minutes on pan. Process oats, crackers, brown sugar, and ⅛ teaspoon of the salt in a food processor until finely ground. Add melted butter and egg white; process until moist. Press mixture into bottom and 1 ½ inches up sides of a 9-inch springform pan coated with baking spray.

2. Bake at 350°F for 10 to 12 minutes or until toasted and fragrant. Cool completely on a wire rack.

3. Reduce oven temperature to 325°F.

4. Prepare the Filling: Sift together granulated sugar, cocoa, flour, and remaining ¼ teaspoon salt in a bowl. Beat cream cheeses with a mixer at medium speed until smooth. Add eggs, 1 at a time, beating well after each addition.

5. Add chocolate and vanilla, beating at low speed until just combined. Sprinkle sugar mixture over top of cheese mixture; beat at low speed until combined. Gently fold 1 cup of the whipped topping into mixture. Pour mixture into prepared pan, smoothing top.

6. Bake at 325°F for 1 hour or until cheesecake center barely moves when pan is touched. Remove cheesecake from oven; gently run a knife around outer edge of cheesecake to loosen from sides of pan. Cool to room temperature. Cover and chill at least 8 hours. Serve with remaining 1 cup whipped topping and berries.

Technique Tip: Bringing the cream cheese and eggs to room temperature helps them blend more easily and makes the filling creamier and lump free.

LEMON CHEESECAKE BARS WITH GINGERSNAP CRUST

Lemon Cheesecake Bars with Gingersnap Crust

ACTIVE 25 MIN. - TOTAL 9 HOURS, 25 MIN.
SERVES 16

CRUST
25 gingersnap cookies (such as Nabisco)
2 tsp. cornstarch
2 Tbsp. butter, melted
1 tsp. grated peeled fresh ginger
FILLING
8 oz. ⅓-less-fat cream cheese, softened
4 oz. fat-free cream cheese, softened
½ cup plus 2 Tbsp. granulated sugar
½ tsp. vanilla extract
¼ tsp. baking powder
⅛ tsp. table salt
2 large eggs
¼ cup light sour cream
½ tsp. lemon zest
1 Tbsp. fresh lemon juice
TOPPING
⅓ cup granulated sugar
½ tsp. lemon zest
⅓ cup fresh lemon juice
2 tsp. cornstarch
2 large egg yolks
1 tsp. butter, softened

1. Prepare the Crust: Preheat oven to 350°F. Process cookies and cornstarch in a food processor until finely ground. Add butter and ginger; process until moist crumbs form. Sprinkle mixture into a 9-inch square metal baking pan coated with baking spray. Lightly press into bottom of pan.

2. Bake at 350°F for 14 minutes or until toasted and fragrant. Cool completely on a rack.

3. Reduce oven temperature to 325°F.

4. Prepare the Filling: Place cream cheeses in a bowl; beat with a mixer at medium speed until smooth. Add sugar, vanilla, baking powder, and salt; beat at low speed until well combined. Add eggs, 1 at a time, beating well after each addition.

5. Add sour cream, zest, and juice; beat until combined. Pour mixture on top of cooled crust.

6. Bake at 325°F for 30 minutes or until almost set in the middle. Remove pan from oven; place on a wire rack.

7. Prepare the Topping: Combine sugar, zest, juice, cornstarch, and yolks in a small saucepan, stirring with a whisk until smooth.

8. Place pan over medium-low; cook 5 minutes or until mixture thickens, stirring constantly. Remove pan from heat; add butter, stirring until butter melts. Spread Topping over warm cheesecake. Cool completely on wire rack. Cover and refrigerate overnight. Cut into 16 bars.

Red Velvet–White Chocolate Cheesecake

Whimsy meets elegance in all five layers of this red velvet-white chocolate wonder.

ACTIVE 45 MIN. - TOTAL 13 HOURS, 45 MIN.

SERVES 10 TO 12

> **CHEESECAKE LAYERS**
> 2 (8-inch) round disposable aluminum foil cake pans
> 1 (12-oz.) pkg. white chocolate chips
> 5 (8-oz.) pkg. cream cheese, softened
> 1 cup granulated sugar
> 2 large eggs
> 1 Tbsp. vanilla extract
> **RED VELVET LAYERS**
> 3 (8-inch) round disposable aluminum foil cake pans
> 1 cup butter, softened
> 2 ½ cups granulated sugar
> 6 large eggs
> 3 cups all-purpose flour
> 3 Tbsp. unsweetened cocoa
> ¼ tsp. baking soda
> 1 (8-oz.) container sour cream
> 2 tsp. vanilla extract
> 2 (1-oz.) bottles red liquid food coloring
> **WHITE CHOCOLATE FROSTING**
> 2 (4-oz.) white chocolate baking bars, chopped
> ½ cup boiling water
> 1 cup butter, softened
> 1 (32-oz.) pkg. powdered sugar, sifted
> ⅛ tsp. table salt
> Garnishes: store-bought coconut candies, White Candy Leaves (recipe follows)

1. Preheat oven to 300°F. Prepare the Cheesecake Layers: Line bottom and sides of 2 disposable cake pans with aluminum foil, allowing 2 to 3 inches to extend over sides; lightly grease foil.

2. Microwave white chocolate chips in a microwave-safe bowl according to package directions; cool 10 minutes.

3. Beat cream cheese and melted chocolate with a mixer at medium speed until creamy; gradually add 1 cup sugar, beating well. Add 2 eggs, 1 at a time, beating just until yellow disappears after each addition. Stir in 1 tablespoon vanilla. Pour into prepared pans.

4. Bake at 300°F for 30 to 35 minutes or until almost set. Turn off oven. Let cheesecakes stand in oven, with door closed, 30 minutes. Remove from oven to wire racks; cool completely, about 1 ½ hours.

5. Cover and chill 8 hours, or freeze 24 hours to 2 days.

6. Preheat oven to 350°F. Prepare the Red Velvet Layers: Grease and flour 3 (8-inch) disposable cake pans. Beat 1 cup butter with a stand mixer at medium speed until creamy. Gradually add 2 ½ cups sugar, beating until light and fluffy. Add 6 eggs, 1 at a time, beating just until blended after each addition.

7. Stir together flour and next 2 ingredients; add to butter mixture alternately with sour cream, beginning and ending with flour mixture. Beat at low speed just until blended after each addition. Stir in 2 teaspoons vanilla; stir in food coloring. Spoon batter into prepared pans.

8. Bake at 350°F for 20 to 24 minutes or until a wooden pick inserted in center comes out clean. Cool in pans on wire racks 10 minutes. Remove from pans to wire racks; cool completely, about 1 hour.

9. Prepare the White Chocolate Frosting: Whisk together chocolate and ½ cup boiling water until chocolate melts. Cool 20 minutes; chill 30 minutes.

10. Beat 1 cup butter and chilled chocolate mixture at low speed until blended. Beat at medium speed 1 minute. Increase speed to high; beat 2 to 3 minutes or until fluffy. Gradually add powdered sugar and salt, beating at low speed until blended. Increase speed to high; beat 1 to 2 minutes or until smooth and fluffy.

11. Assemble cake: Place 1 red velvet layer on a serving platter. Top with 1 cheesecake layer. Repeat with remaining layers of red velvet and cheesecake, alternating and ending with red velvet on top. Spread top and sides of cake with White Chocolate Frosting. Store in refrigerator.

White Candy Leaves

ACTIVE 20 MIN. - TOTAL 30 MIN.

MAKES 20 LEAVES

> 2 oz. vanilla candy coating
> Parchment paper

1. Select nontoxic leaves, such as bay leaves. Thoroughly wash leaves, and pat dry. Melt approximately 2 oz. vanilla candy coating in a saucepan over low until melted, about 3 minutes. Stir until smooth. Cool slightly. Working on parchment paper, spoon a ⅛-inch-thick layer of candy coating over backs of leaves, spreading to edges.

2. Transfer leaves gently, by their stems, to a clean sheet of parchment paper, resting them candy-coating sides up; let stand until candy coating is firm, about 10 minutes. Gently grasp each leaf at stem end, and carefully peel leaf away from candy coating. Store candy leaves in a cold, dry place, such as an airtight container in freezer, up to 1 week.

3. Handle leaves gently when garnishing, or they'll break or melt. Arrange candy leaves around base of cake and store-bought coconut candies (such as Confetteria Raffaello Almond Coconut Treats) in center of cake. Accent top of cake with additional candy leaves. For candy pearls, simply roll any remaining candy coating into balls, and let stand until dry.

Cherry Cheesecake Brownies

ACTIVE 34 MIN. - TOTAL 1 HOUR, 24 MIN.

SERVES 18

FILLING

- ½ cup chopped dried tart cherries
- 1 Tbsp. cherry liqueur (such as kirschwasser)
- 1 cup granulated sugar, divided
- 3 oz. ⅓-less-fat cream cheese
- 2 oz. fat-free cream cheese
- 1 Tbsp. all-purpose flour
- ¾ tsp. vanilla extract, divided
- ⅝ tsp. baking powder, divided
  Dash of table salt
- 1 large egg, lightly beaten
- 3 oz. bittersweet chocolate, finely chopped
- 1 oz. unsweetened chocolate, finely chopped
- 3 Tbsp. unsalted butter, diced
- 2 Tbsp. canola oil
- 2 large egg whites
- 1 large egg

CRUST

- 3.4 oz. all-purpose flour (about ¾ cup)
- ⅛ tsp. table salt

1. Prepare the Filling: Preheat oven to 325°F. Place cherries and liqueur in a microwave-safe bowl. Microwave at HIGH 30 seconds or until boiling; let stand 10 minutes.

2. Place ¼ cup of the sugar and cream cheeses in a bowl; beat with a mixer at medium speed 1 minute or until smooth. Add flour, ¼ teaspoon of the vanilla, ⅛ teaspoon of the baking powder, salt, and egg; beat just until blended. Stir in cherry mixture.

3. Coat a 9-inch square metal baking pan with baking spray. Combine chocolate, butter, and oil in a medium microwave-safe bowl; microwave at HIGH 1 minute or until mixture melts, stirring every 20 seconds. Stir until smooth. Let stand 5 minutes. Add remaining ½ teaspoon vanilla, egg whites, and egg, stirring with a whisk until smooth.

4. Prepare the Crust: Weigh or lightly spoon flour into dry measuring cup; level with a knife. Combine flour, remaining ¾ cup sugar, remaining ½ teaspoon baking powder, and salt in a large bowl. Add chocolate mixture, stirring until just combined.

5. Scrape half of the brownie batter into prepared pan. Dot half of cheesecake batter on top. Top with remaining brownie batter. Dot with remaining cheesecake batter; gently swirl with a knife.

6. Bake at 325°F for 40 minutes or until a wooden pick inserted in center comes out with a few moist crumbs. Cool completely in pan on a wire rack. Cut into 18 bars.

Technique Tip: Adding just a bit of flour and baking powder to the cheesecake batter gives it a lighter texture so that it doesn't sink underneath the brownie batter while it bakes. Cherry liqueur amps up the flavor of the cherries, but you can substitute water, if you'd prefer a nonalcoholic version.

METRIC EQUIVALENTS

The recipes that appear in this cookbook use the standard United States method for measuring liquid and dry or solid ingredients (teaspoons, tablespoons, and cups). The information on this chart is provided to help cooks outside the U.S. successfully use these recipes. All equivalents are approximate.

METRIC EQUIVALENTS FOR DIFFERENT TYPES OF INGREDIENTS

A standard cup measure of a dry or solid ingredient will vary in weight depending on the type of ingredient. A standard cup of liquid is the same volume for any type of liquid. Use the following chart when converting standard cup measures to grams (weight) or milliliters (volume).

Standard Cup	Fine Powder (ex. flour)	Grain (ex. rice)	Granular (ex. sugar)	Liquid Solids (ex. butter)	Liquid (ex. milk)
1	140 g	150 g	190 g	200 g	240 ml
¾	105 g	113 g	143 g	150 g	180 ml
⅔	93 g	100 g	125 g	133 g	160 ml
½	70 g	75 g	95 g	100 g	120 ml
⅓	47 g	50 g	63 g	67 g	80 ml
¼	35 g	38 g	48 g	50 g	60 ml
⅛	18 g	19 g	24 g	25 g	30 ml

USEFUL EQUIVALENTS FOR DRY INGREDIENTS BY WEIGHT
(To convert ounces to grams, multiply the number of ounces by 30.)

1 oz	=	¹⁄₁₆ lb	=	30 g
4 oz	=	¼ lb	=	120 g
8 oz	=	½ lb	=	240 g
12 oz	=	¾ lb	=	360 g
16 oz	=	1 lb	=	480 g

USEFUL EQUIVALENTS FOR LENGTH
(To convert inches to centimeters, multiply the number of inches by 2.5.)

1 in				=	2.5 cm			
6 in	=	½ ft		=	15 cm			
12 in	-	1 ft		=	30 cm			
36 in	-	3 ft	-	1 yd	=	90 cm		
40 in				=	100 cm	=	1 m	

USEFUL EQUIVALENTS FOR LIQUID INGREDIENTS BY VOLUME

¼ tsp					=	1 ml		
½ tsp					=	2 ml		
1 tsp					=	5 ml		
3 tsp	=	1 Tbsp		=	½ fl oz	=	15 ml	
		2 Tbsp	=	⅛ cup	=	1 fl oz	=	30 ml
		4 Tbsp	=	¼ cup	=	2 fl oz	=	60 ml
		5⅓ Tbsp	=	⅓ cup	=	3 fl oz	=	80 ml
		8 Tbsp	=	½ cup	=	4 fl oz	=	120 ml
		10⅔ Tbsp	=	⅔ cup	=	5 fl oz	=	160 ml
		12 Tbsp	=	¾ cup	=	6 fl oz	=	180 ml
		16 Tbsp	=	1 cup	=	8 fl oz	=	240 ml
	1 pt	=	2 cups	=	16 fl oz	=	480 ml	
	1 qt	=	4 cups	=	32 fl oz	=	960 ml	
					33 fl oz	=	1000 ml	= 1 l

USEFUL EQUIVALENTS FOR COOKING/OVEN TEMPERATURES

	Fahrenheit	Celsius	Gas Mark
Freeze Water	32° F	0° C	
Room Temperature	68° F	20° C	
Boil Water	212° F	100° C	
Bake	325° F	160° C	3
	350° F	180° C	4
	375° F	190° C	5
	400° F	200° C	6
	425° F	220° C	7
	450° F	230° C	8
Broil			Grill

Month-by-Month Index

This index alphabetically lists every food article and accompanying recipes by month.

General Recipe Index

This index lists every recipe by food category and/or major ingredient.

©2017 Time Inc. Books

Published by Oxmoor House, an imprint of Time Inc. Books
225 Liberty Street, New York, NY 10281

Executive Editor: Katherine Cobbs
Project Editor: Lacie Pinyan
Design Director: Melissa Clark
Photo Director: Paden Reich
Designer: Matt Ryan
Recipe Developers and Testers: Time Inc. Food Studios
Assistant Production Director: Sue Chodakiewicz
Senior Production Manager: Greg A. Amason
Copy Editor: Donna Baldone
Proofreader: Rebecca Brennan
Indexer: Mary Ann Laurens
Fellows: Kaitlyn Pacheco, Holly Ravazzolo, Hanna Yokeley

ISBN-13: 978-0-8487-5183-8
ISSN: 0272-2003

First Edition 2017

Printed in the United States of America

10 9 8 7 6 5 4 3 2 1

We welcome your comments and suggestions about Time Inc. Books.
Time Inc. Books
Attention: Book Editors
P.O. Box 62310
Tampa, Florida 33662-2310
(800) 765-6400

Time Inc. Books products may be purchased for business or promotional
use. For information on bulk purchases, please contact Christi Crowley in
the Special Sales Department at (845) 895-9858.

Cover: Snowy Vanilla Cake with Cake Ball Ornaments, page 358.
Photography by Alison Miksch; Prop Styling by Mindi Shapiro Levine;
Food Styling by Torie Cox
Page 1: Double-Decker Pecan Cheesecake Pie, page 326

Favorite Recipes Journal

Jot down your family's and your favorite recipes for quick and handy reference. And don't forget to include the dishes that drew rave reviews when company came for dinner.

Recipe	Source/Page	Remarks

Recipe	Source/Page	Remarks